Children's Books, Brain Development, and Language Acquisition

Children's books provide supplementary language nutrition for developing brains because their language differs from child-directed speech and adult conversation. Not only are there poetic devices such as rhymes and rhythms, but there are linguistic surprises: funny sound combinations, bizarre morphology, exotic words, and grammatical outliers. Some authors also include ungrammatical forms and constructions. Notably, those exotic creations and violations are masterfully crafted (e.g. not unmotivated caricatures of child talk). Children's authors challenge linguistic expectations to create surprises, which both delight children and trigger their language explorer instincts.

Interactive reading with a child is a bonding experience. Shared attention, laughter, and rhythms synchronize brain activity ('entrainment'). Book reading becomes selfrewarding, thus adding quantity of input to quality. The rewards are measurable. Raised oxytocin levels are associated with phonetic processing and with long-term dividends in empathy and in group affiliation.

Reading a book with a child creates a safe zone for playful exploration. Here, children's books offer something quite unique: three-way cooperation (everyday cooperation tends to be dyadic). Scenarios of alliances and collusion are played out between the child, the reading adult, book characters (sometimes the book itself), and the author. Children act out different personas and attain cognitive control over competing mental faculties that assist language parsing: logical relations that apply across various domains, event models that require tracking of plots and inventories, and predeterminations of outcomes.

It is argued that the enriched linguistic input of children's literature has the potential of accelerating not only language acquisition but also cognitive control. Successful integration of cognitive faculties and language processing facilitates storying – both inner story (for identity and information management) and shared story (for self-validation and participation in distributed cognition).

Ralf Thiede is Associate Professor of English in the Department of English at the University of North Carolina at Charlotte; his teaching and research include Applied Linguistics, Cognitive Science, and Medieval English Language and Literature.

Explorations in Developmental Psychology Series

Developmental Neuropsychology
Janna Glozman

Indigenous Adolescent Development
Psychological, Social and Historical Contexts
Les B. Whitbeck, Kelley J. Sittner Hartshorn and Melissa L. Walls

Learning from Picturebooks
Research from Cognitive Psychology, Early Literacy, and Child Developmental Studies
Edited by Bettina Kümmerling-Meibauer, Jörg Meibauer, Kerstin Nachtigäller and Katharina Rohlfing

Development from Adolescence to Early Adulthood
A Dynamic Systemic Approach to Transitions and Transformations
Marion Kloep, Leo B. Hendry, Rachel Taylor and Ian Stuart-Hamilton

Teachers, Learners, Modes of Practice
Theory and Methodology for Identifying Knowledge Development
David Kirk Dirlam

Children's Books, Brain Development, and Language Acquisition
Ralf Thiede

For a full list of titles in this series, please visit www.routledge.com

Children's Books, Brain Development, and Language Acquisition

Ralf Thiede

Routledge
Taylor & Francis Group
NEW YORK AND LONDON

First published 2019
by Routledge
52 Vanderbilt Avenue, New York, NY 10017, USA

and by Routledge
2 Park Square, Milton Park, Abingdon, Oxon, OX14 4RN

First issued in paperback 2020

Routledge is an imprint of the Taylor & Francis Group, an informa business

Library of Congress Cataloguing-in-Publication Data
A catalog record for this book has been requested

ISBN 13: 978-0-367-58332-3 (pbk)
ISBN 13: 978-0-8153-6189-3 (hbk)

Typeset in Times New Roman
by Apex CoVantage, LLC

For Barbara
(who somehow instinctively knew all this)

Contents

Figures

Tables

Acknowledgments

This book profited substantially from the contributions and enthusiasm of fellow researchers and friends. The seed of the idea for the book germinated in a graduate research project on the linguistics of children's literature with Teofil Husar, Elizabeth Tingley, Elaine C. Hill, Julie Wright, and Brittany A. Stone, the results of which were published in a special issue of the *Southern Journal of Linguistics* (36.3: 2012). Soon after its publication, I was contacted by Jörg Meibauer (University of Mainz), who had co-edited a similar issue on language acquisition and children's literature with Wolfgang Klein (Max Planck Institute for Psycholinguistics, Nijmegen) in *Zeitschrift für Literaturwissenschaft und Linguistik* (41.162: 2011). Jörg subsequently organized a colloquium on the linguistics of children's literature at the University of Mainz in 2015. Thereafter, I was convinced that we are witnessing a new field emerge: Not only are linguists increasingly interested in children's literature, but researchers in children's literature are likewise increasingly engaged in linguistic analysis.

Explicit encouragement for me to write this book came from my department chair Mark West (University of North Carolina at Charlotte), who must have put in a good word on my behalf with Dean Nancy Gutierrez, because I was granted an invaluable reassignment of duty for the Spring semester of 2017. I gratefully acknowledge that opportunity for intensive writing and revising. I also would like to thank two anonymous reviewers (I appreciate your time and wisdom!) and my supportive editor at Routledge, Matthew Friberg.

Thanks abundant are due to Barbara Thiede, my spouse and soulmate. Barbara was infectiously convincing (and convinced) that I was in the right place and in the right time for such a project, working, as I do, in a department with particular strengths in linguistics and in children's literature and (s)addled, as I am, with too many interests to fit one job description. She was my first editor and prime mover—a demanding reader, offering excellent questions and intelligent suggestions for style and substance. I also profited from our shared experience of raising a child to early and joyful literacy. Erik Henning Thiede, now a Ph.D. student at the University of Chicago, alerted me to several relevant scientific publications. And so he closed a circle: A child raised to love books offered insights for a book on the dividends of literacy. What a privilege.

Permissions

Figures and Artwork

Figure 8.1 Book Characters 'Aware' of Reader (Mo Willems), reprinted from *WE ARE IN A BOOK!* ©2010 Mo Willems. Originally published by Hyperion Books for Children, an imprint of Disney Publishing Worldwide. Used with permission. 193

Citations

Special thanks to Sherri Hinchey, Permissions Manager at Penguin Random House LLC; to Sarah Lewis, Contracts Manager at Egmont UK Ltd; and to Bonnie McDonald of the Permissions Department at HarperCollins Ltd in London for going the extra mile to secure copyrights across continents. I would also very much like to acknowledge Katherine Tsamparlis, Editorial Assistant at Education Routledge, for guiding me through the maze of permissions.

Random House Children's Books, a division of Penguin Random House LLC. All rights reserved. **For the UK and Commonwealth (excluding Canada)**: Reprinted by permission of HarperCollins Ltd © Dr. Seuss 1974.

Excerpts from GREEN EGGS AND HAM by Dr. Seuss, TM & copyright © by Dr. Seuss Enterprises, L.P. 1960, renewed 1988. Used by permission of Random House Children's Books, a division of Penguin Random House LLC. All rights reserved. **For the UK and Commonwealth (excluding Canada)**: Reprinted by permission of HarperCollins Ltd © Dr. Seuss 1960.

Excerpt from HAPPY BIRTHDAY TO YOU! by Dr. Seuss, TM & copyright © by Dr. Seuss Enterprises, L.P. 1959, renewed 1987. Used by permission of Random House Children's Books, a division of Penguin Random House LLC. All rights reserved. **For the UK and Commonwealth (excluding Canada)**: Reprinted by permission of HarperCollins Ltd © Dr. Seuss 1959.

Excerpt from HIP CAT by Jonathan London, copyright ©1993 by Jonathan London, used by permission.

Excerpt from HOP ON POP by Dr. Seuss, copyright © by Dr. Seuss Enterprises, L.P., 1963, renewed 1991. Used by permission of Random House Children's Books, a division of Penguin Random House LLC. All rights reserved. **For the UK and Commonwealth (excluding Canada)**: Reprinted by permission of HarperCollins Ltd © Dr. Seuss 1963.

Excerpt from HORTON HEARS A WHO! by Dr. Seuss, Trademark TM & copyright © by Dr. Seuss Enterprises, L.P. 1954, renewed 1982. Used by permission of Random House Children's Books, a division of Penguin Random House LLC. All rights reserved. **For the UK and Commonwealth (excluding Canada)**: Reprinted by permission of HarperCollins Ltd © Dr. Seuss 1954.

Excerpts from THE HOUSE AT POOH CORNER by A. A. Milne, copyright 1928 by Penguin Random House LLC. Copyright © renewed 1956 by A.A. Milne. Used by permission of Dutton Children's Books, an imprint of Penguin Young Readers Group, a division of Penguin Random House LLC. All rights reserved. **For the UK and Commonwealth (excluding Canada)**: Extracts from The House at Pooh Corner by A.A. Milne. Text copyright © The Trustees of the Pooh Properties 1928. Published by Egmont UK Ltd and used with permission.

Excerpt from IF I RAN THE CIRCUS by Dr. Seuss, TM & copyright © by Dr. Seuss Enterprises, L.P. 1956, renewed 1984. Used by permission of Random House Children's Books, a division of Penguin Random House LLC. All rights reserved.

Excerpts from IF I RAN THE ZOO by Dr. Seuss, TM & © 1950, renewed 1977 by Dr. Seuss Enterprises, L.P. Used by permission of Random House Children's Books, a division of Penguin Random House LLC. All rights reserved. **For the UK and Commonwealth (excluding Canada)**: Reprinted by permission of HarperCollins Ltd © Dr. Seuss 1950.

Excerpt from LLAMA LLAMA RED PAJAMA by Anna Dewdney, copyright © 2005 by Anna Dewdney. Used by permission of Viking Children's Books, an imprint of Penguin Young Readers Group, a division of Penguin Random House LLC. All rights reserved.

Excerpts from THE LORAX by Dr. Seuss, ® and copyright © by Dr. Seuss Enterprises, L.P. 1971, renewed 1999. Used by permission of Random House Children's Books, a division of Penguin Random House LLC. All rights reserved. **For the UK and Commonwealth (excluding Canada)**: Reprinted by permission of HarperCollins Ltd © Dr. Seuss 1971.

"The Beaver" is from the book MAMMALABILIA copyright © 2000 by Douglas Florian, used by permission.

Excerpts from MIKE MULLIGAN AND HIS STEAM SHOVEL by Virginia Lee Burton. Copyright © 1939 by Virginia Lee Burton. Copyright © renewed 1967 by Virginia Lee Demetrios. Reprinted by permission of Houghton Mifflin Harcourt Publishing Company. All rights reserved.

Excerpt from MOO BAA LA LA LA by Sandra Boynton, copyright © 1984 by Sandra Boynton, used by permission.

Excerpt from MR. BROWN CAN MOO! CAN YOU? by Dr. Seuss, TM & copyright © by Dr. Seuss Enterprises L.P., 1970, renewed 1998. Used by permission of Random House Children's Books, a division of Penguin Random House LLC. All rights reserved. **For the UK and Commonwealth (excluding Canada)**: Reprinted by permission of HarperCollins Ltd © Dr. Seuss 1970.

"Knight-in-Armour," copyright 1927 by E.P. Dutton, renewed © 1955 by A.A. Milne; from NOW WE ARE SIX by A. A. Milne. Used by permission of Dutton Children's Books, an imprint of Penguin Young Readers Group, a division of Penguin Random House LLC. All rights reserved. **For the UK and Commonwealth (excluding Canada)**: Extract from Now We Are Six by A.A. Milne. Text copyright © The Trustees of the Pooh Properties 1927. Published by Egmont UK Ltd and used with permission.

Excerpts from OH, SAY CAN YOU SAY? by Dr. Seuss, TM and copyright © by Dr. Seuss Enterprises, L.P. 1979. Used by permission of Random House Children's Books, a division of Penguin Random House LLC. All rights reserved. **For the UK and Commonwealth (excluding Canada)**: Reprinted by permission of HarperCollins Ltd © Dr. Seuss 1979.

Excerpts from ON BEYOND ZEBRA! by Dr. Seuss, TM & copyright by Dr. Seuss Enterprises, L.P. 1955. Copyright © renewed 1983. Used by permission of Random House Children's Books, a division of Penguin Random House LLC. All rights reserved. **For the UK and Commonwealth (excluding Canada)**: Reprinted by permission of HarperCollins Ltd © Dr. Seuss 1955.

Excerpt from ONE FISH TWO FISH RED FISH BLUE FISH by Dr. Seuss, ® and copyright © by Dr. Seuss Enterprises, L.P. 1960, renewed 1988. Used by permission of Random House Children's Books, a division of Penguin Random House LLC. All rights reserved. **For the UK and Commonwealth (excluding Canada)**: Reprinted by permission of HarperCollins Ltd © Dr. Seuss 1960.

Poetry selection "I Went to Wyoming One Day in the Spring" from RIDE A PURPLE PELICAN by Jack Prelutsky, text (c) 1986 by Jack Prelutsky. Used by permission of HarperCollins Publishers.

Excerpt from ROALD DAHL'S REVOLTING RHYMES by Roald Dahl, Copyright © 1982 by Roald Dahl, reprinted by permission of David Higham Associates for the UK and by Penguin Random House.

Excerpts from THE RUNAWAY BUNNY text by Margaret Wise Brown. Copyright 1942 by Harper & Row Publishers. Text copyright renewed 1970 by Roberta Brown Rauch. Used by permission of HarperCollins Publishers.

Excerpts from SCRAMBLED EGGS SUPER! by Dr. Seuss, TM and copyright by Dr. Seuss Enterprises, L.P. 1953. Used by permission of Random House Children's Books, a division of Penguin Random House LLC. All rights reserved. **For the UK and Commonwealth (excluding Canada)**: Reprinted by permission of HarperCollins Ltd © Dr. Seuss 1953.

Excerpt from WINNIE-THE-POOH by A. A. Milne, copyright © 1926 by Penguin Random House LLC. Copyright renewed 1954 by A. A. Milne. Used by permission of Dutton Children's Books, an imprint of Penguin Young Readers Group, a division of Penguin Random House LLC. All rights reserved. **For the UK and Commonwealth (excluding Canada)**: Extracts from Winnie the Pooh by A.A. Milne. Text copyright © The Trustees of the Pooh Properties 1926. Published by Egmont UK Ltd and used with permission.

Excerpt from WHO BOP? by Jonathan London, copyright © 2000 by Jonathan London, used by permission.

Excerpt from "Willie Is Willie" [p. 8] from THE WORLD IS ROUND by GERTRUDE STEIN. Book Text Copyright(c) 1939, renewed 1966 by Gertrude Stein. Reprinted by permission of HarperCollins Publishers.

Excerpt from YERTLE THE TURTLE AND OTHER STORIES by Dr. Seuss, TM & copyright © by Dr. Seuss Enterprises, L.P. 1950, 1951, 1958, renewed 1977, 1979, 1986. Used by permission of Random House Children's Books, a division of Penguin Random House LLC. All rights reserved. **For the UK and Commonwealth (excluding Canada)**: Reprinted by permission of HarperCollins Ltd © Dr. Seuss 1950, 1951, 1958.

Excerpt from YOU'RE ONLY OLD ONCE!: A BOOK FOR OBSOLETE CHILDREN: 30TH ANNIVERSARY EDITION by Dr. Seuss, TM & copyright © by Dr. Seuss Enterprises, L.P. 1986. Used by permission of Random House, an imprint and division of Penguin Random House LLC. All rights reserved.

A Book With Too Many Variables

Some Introduction . . .

An author attempted for years
to write poems just like Edward Lears'.
He was sure that his wits
were sufficient for kids,
but his efforts all ended in tears.
(*with apologies to Edward Lears*)

'I finish the rough draft in 20 minutes,' said Margaret Wise Brown, 'and then I spend two years polishing' (Bliven 1946:64). Theodor Seuss Geisel 'used to spend hours standing in his office with his hands in his back pockets, pacing in front of his work, trying to think of ways to make it better,' writes Jessica Contrera (2015): 'He would come up with multiple endings for his sentences, choose one, then change his mind.' Unfortunately for Wise Brown and Seuss Geisel, Caterina Christakos' *How to Write a Children's Book in 30 Days or Less* (2002) was not yet available.

Why is it so notoriously hard to write a children's book? Children's books must reconcile conflicting demands. Publishers want their products to be successful in the marketplace. Parents are looking for books that educate, entertain, or both. Authors may have agendas such as challenging the status quo. Adults make their selections based on their own nostalgic recollections of what a good children's book should be, but the books also need to be captivating and engaging for modern kids. Not a small order.

Maybe in the early days of the children's literature industry there was indeed such a time when writing for children was 'easier' because the communication, as Emer O'Sullivan put it, was asymmetrical (2011:129), imposing adult language and perspectives. However, the lop of that sidedness has shifted over time.

This book asks specifically what children's literature adds to language acquisition that is not already present in speech directed to children, what the linguistic needs of the child are at different stages of maturation, and how children's books align with those needs.

First, however, we must acknowledge how many undefined terms are contained in the previous sentence. To explore the language of children's literature and its impact on development, we need to define the terms that interact. We need to have working definitions of 'children's literature' and of 'language.' There needs to be some operational clarity around the difference between 'language acquisition' and 'language learning.' None of those terms has a generally accepted academic definition (in fact, the publishing industry may have a better consensus about them), so the remainder of this introduction is dedicated to offering stipulative ones.

This is a book about moving targets.

Children's Literature as a Genre

Picturebooks with and without words, story books, cookbooks, how-stuff-works books and how-to books, joke books, whole-word books, phonics books, King Arthur and Captain Underpants . . . so many different kinds of books are 'children's literature' that the term eludes definition. Indeed, some scholars *argue against* doing so. Defining children's literature as a separate genre of literature would seem, to them, to denigrate children. 'Children,' goes John Rowe Townsend's oft-cited polemic, 'are not a separate form of life from people, no more than children's books are a separate form of literature from just books' (1980:196–97). Townsend's remark follows a social paradigm shift that has affected children's literature: Children are no longer considered deficient adults. As children's author Mo Willems (2015) put it: 'Kids are shorter than adults. They're not stupider.' And yet, children are *not* just short people, or else lawyers would try them as adults in courts. They interact with a different canon of literature than adults do. They certainly won't read this book, even if it is written out of love and respect for them.

Children have not always been approached on their terms, and the literature reflects that history. Tempting though it might be to describe changes in the language of children's literature on a linear timeline: From my vantage point as a cognitive linguist, children's literature over the last 400 years has moved back and forth between two cognitive premises (Figure I.1). The extreme points are whether the child's language and social construction is expected to move toward

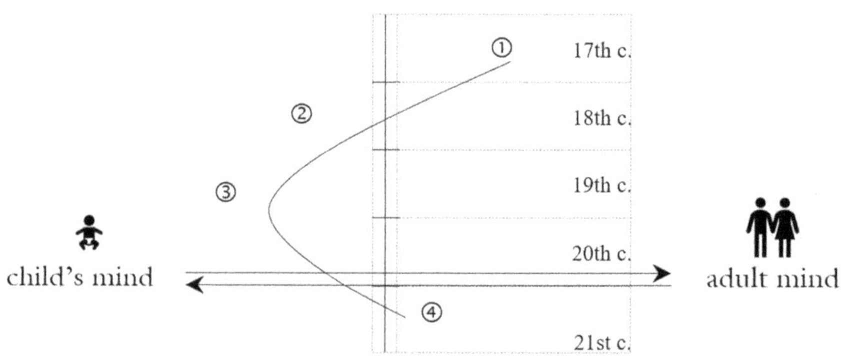

Figure I.1 Trajectories of Approach in Children's Literature

adult norms vs. whether the adult must accommodate to the child's language and identity.

This is how I understand the needs that made the pendulum swing, commenting specifically on four salient developments plotted into Figure I.1:

① ***Bringing the child to the adult: The child as a deficient adult*** • John Locke (1693) argued that children were born completely deficient—a blank slate (*tabula rasa*). He saw the physical and mental development of the child as mutually reinforcing, but could identify only very few available examples of books that would positively support their cognitive development. Books available at the time included Commenius' best-selling *Orbis sensualium pictus*, which appeared in an English translation in 1659, one year after the Latin/German edition. *Orbis pictus* was essentially an encyclopedia of adult life for children, with labels for numbered items in each illustration. Tools, nature, philosophy, professional occupations, arts related to speech (Figure I.2), even torture methods for 'malefactors' portray the adult world to initiate the child.

The language of contemporary American children's books produced by Puritans reflects a similarly accelerated trajectory toward adult life. The likelihood that high child mortality would take children before their time (Meigs et al. 1969:114) made it imperative for that community to begin religious instruction as early and as earnestly as feasible. David H. Watters reviews the older tradition of God as an angry father whose children have disobeyed him: 'all children are guilty of and deserve punishment for desires that run contrary to parental or divine will' (1985/1986:194). Puritan parents felt that they had to replace their children's common speech, which reflects congenital

Figure I.2 Grammar, Rhetoric, Poetry, Music *(Orbis Pictus)*

'depravity' (195), with religious words and language. The child had to commit texts to the heart, where they may be 'read by God' (203)—whether the child understood the import of the words was of secondary concern (210 n. 2). A poem presumed written by Cotton Mather and included in the *New England Primer* illustrates the urgency:

I in the Burying Place may see
  Graves shorter there than I;
From Death's Arrest no Age is free,
  You Children too may die;
My God, may such an awful Sight,
  Awakening be to me!
Oh! that by early Grace I might
  For Death prepared be.

Implanting religious language in children's minds entailed early literacy so that children could read books like *A Token for Children, Being an Exact Account of the Conversion, Holy and Exemplary Lives, and Joyful Deaths of Several Young Children* (Janeway 1671). Children's books for Sunday school, such as the subscription books published and distributed by Daniel Lothrop in Boston, would continue to instill values early, especially again during Prohibition. The final exhortation of Pastor Aaron Pickett at the funeral of Lothrop's mother may well be reflected in his editing policies: 'Oh young man, or young woman, as thou mayest soon die, BE PREPARED TO DIE' (Pickett 1927:20).

② ***Meeting the child half way: Making adult content more palatable*** • The premise that children are born in sin and must be made into good adults by society was turned on its head by Jean-Jacques Rousseau. His novel *Émile, ou de l'éducation* (1762) explicitly rejected 'it-takes-a-village' and described how a personal tutor could help a child's natural goodness and intellect unfold—untouched by the adult evils of society. Émile's tutor invents child-appropriate teaching methods and rewards for achievements (such as being able to decipher an invitation to have cream) and suggests relatable adult literature through which a child could absorb moral lessons, such as *Robinson Crusoe*.

The notion that children are born good ('little angels'), combined with improved life expectancy, removed the urgency behind turning them into adults quickly. Literacy could wait. Rousseau's tutor in *Émile* delays book learning until age 12— as does the narrator of Charlotte Brontë's unpublished 'A Fresh Arrival' (1833).[1] By Brontë's time, brain development theory had provided a new rationale for the delay: 'Physician Extraordinary to the King' Dr. James Johnson explained in 1836 that the child's physical and cognitive development are not mutually reinforcing (as Locke had argued), but mutually exclusive: 'the organ of the mind, in the first stages of our existence, is exclusively occupied with its *animal* functions' (14). In a passage often cited in American publications of the late 1850s and early 1860s, Arthur Helps deduced that in order to guarantee children's vigorous physical growth, 'it is imperative not to omit the importance of keeping their brains fallow, as it were, for several of the first years of their existence' (1857:155). One ought not to compromise a child's physical health with 'bookwork'—unless, ironically, but following a perfectly logical line of reasoning, the child was destined for child labor, in which case there were 'only their early years in which we can teach them book-knowledge' (156). Helps' theory of child development also had its share of detractors. 'Fallacy of Premature Education,' an article in *The New Church Herald*, protested, somewhat exasperatedly: One 'might as well try to dam up the small streams at the source of a river' (rpt. in the *North Carolina Journal of Education* 1859:72).

Sunday schools and public schools aligned children's speech and writing with the normative (i.e. New England) adult language of secondary and higher education. A plethora of 19th-century primers and grammar books contained exercises for correct spelling (orthography) and pronunciation (orthoepy), but for the children the motivation to study those things appears to have been extrinsic. I myself have a collection of these books and have yet to manage to read one of them cover to cover. Those stern and moralizing books gave rise to caricatures of 'grammatomaniacs' and 'schoolmarms who would rather parse than eat' (Mencken [1918] 1956:305), a perception that continues to delegitimize formal grammar in the school room to this day. As early as 1856, one educator questioned the wisdom of assuming that grammar 'can be better understood, at an early age, than any other study' (Jones 1859:233). But attempts were also made to make grammar books more accessible for children. M. L. Nesbitt's *Grammar-Land* (1878, and still in print) summons all parts of speech (all male) to the court of law(s) of Judge Grammar. Mr. Adjective, for example, stands accused of theft (taking nouns like *beauty* and sneakily appropriating them by means of a derivational suffix, *-ful*).

Meeting the child half way did not ease the *pull* on the child to move toward adult language—it merely loosened the *grip*. Parents wanted their boys empowered scholastically, and their girls empowered socially. Children's books were tailored to children's imputed interests, which also meant that children's books of the late 19th century began 'to be written and marketed with gender very much in mind' (Reynolds 1994:30). At the same time, benign linguistic and cognitive neglect prior to school—letting children be children—was licensed as a child's privilege and continued to be a legitimate paradigm of child rearing especially in less-educated communities. Shirley Brice Heath (1983) described life in 'Trackton,' a North Carolina mill town, where caregivers reacted positively to physical communications but ignored or discouraged their youngest children's verbalizations: 'Adults do not consider a young baby either to be able to or need to say words' (75). Perhaps both this verbal neglect and the attitude that children should be kept 'fallow' are residual attitudes from parents whose poverty correlated with high child mortality. For parents whose children might not live to the age of five, investing in their early education may not have made economic sense (Redburn 1998: 253). However, infant mortality came down in late 19th and early 20th century (ibid.).

③ ***Bringing the adult to the child: Understanding the child's mind*** • Educators and child psychologists became convinced that a child's privilege to be a child did not conflict with a child's entitlement to early language and literacy. A better understanding of the child's mind would create a new children's literature that would empower the child to explore, discover, and imagine. The goal was still linguistic and social construction, but the change in approach is dramatized in the Disney version of Mary Poppins: The truce offered by the little angels ('If you won't scold and dominate us, we will never give you cause to hate us') is coopted by an enlightened despot ('Find the fun, and snap! the job's a game.')

For childhood advocates, indoctrination with a spoonful of sugar still smacked of too much adult control. In France, Paul Hazard (1932, 1944) called for 'imaginative, non-didactic books' (O'Sullivan 2011:190). In the U.S., John Dewey denounced traditional children's literature as an 'imposition from above and from outside,' forcing 'adult standards, subject matters and methods upon those who are only growing slowly toward maturity' (1938:18–19). The child's *natural* linguistic and social growth became ever more important.

Jean Piaget explained why children's thinking cannot thrive by imposed imitation of adult thinking: They arrive at their own schemes through assimilation (cf. 1973:70–71), and it is those schemes that structure their language (159)—not repetition after adults. Lev Vygotsky elevated the role of cooperation in that assimilation, especially in interactive play: 'Play creates a zone of proximal development of the child. In play a child always behaves beyond his average age' (1978:102). The paradigm had shifted from 'imposition' to 'transaction' (cf. Rosenblatt 1938), and the language of children's books changed accordingly.

As early as 1921, Lucy Sprague Mitchell, founder of the Bureau of Educational Experiments (BEE, later the Bank Street College of Education), had developed a children's book on the premise that the author needs to meet the child in his or her own world and create scaffolds outward. The child's thinking and language were assumed to be 'embedded' in real-life situations, the space in which they 'recognize and respond to similar purposes and intentions in others' (Donaldson 1978:127). For her pioneering *Here and Now Storybook*, Mitchell wrote 'stories which include the children's first-hand experiences as a starting point' (1921:13).[2] Here-and-now books contained words young children were familiar with, and objects they could experience as appropriate to their cognitive development (cf. Chapter 2 below). Her approach, while inspired by contemporary Soviet Russian pedagogy (Steiner 2015:201), was in line with Jean Piaget's adaptation of Kurt Lewin's concept of 'naïve realism' to children: Children have an egocentric world view and have yet to develop a sense of the expected, hence also cannot process chance. They cotton to the familiar.

Even for the very youngest, of course, a book *itself* also constitutes a 'first-hand' experience. Peter Newell had already excelled at making the book part of the action. His ingenious *Topsies & Turvys* (1893) had two tables of content—one applying when the book was held normally, the other when the book was turned upside down (in which case the elephant on p. 2, for example, turns into an ostrich). *The Rocket Book* (1912) has a hole in each page through which a rocket that was mischievously launched in a basement by Fritz, the Janitor's kid, penetrated 21 flats on its way through the roof. Newell's *The Slant Book* (1910) is cut on an angle so as to provide a slant for each page as we follow a baby carriage's calamitous course down a steep street past perplexed pedestrians. On the premise that the book itself creates a 'here-and-now,' William R. Scott Publishers pioneered a novelty book in 1938, designed for children as young as 18 months. It was, perhaps, the very first American tactile book for babies (Figure I.3). Bliven Jr. gives a description:

> [T]he apple tree had red-glass buttons for apples, the bunny had a tuft of cotton for a tail and there was a bell on the cat's collar that really tinkled. In case the child, tired of playing with the book, tried to eat his literary fare that was quite all right because *Cottontails* was printed on untreated cloth with non-toxic dyes.
>
> (1946:62)

There is a direct link from Lucy Sprague Mitchell's Bureau of Educational Experiments to William Scott's publishing house in the person of

Figure I.3 Cottontails by Ethel McCullough 1938

Margaret Wise Brown, who first studied at the BEE. Wise Brown was responsible for studying the reactions of children to different texts and later became Scott's first children's book editor. Bliven clearly had not seen the book himself (the bell is sewn to a lamb, not to a cat), which explains how he could be unaware that Margaret Wise Brown was not listed as the author of *Cottontails*.[3]

④ ***Meeting the adult half way: Joint attention and cooperation*** • H. L. Mencken still qualified the term *scientific pedagogy* with scare quotes around *scientific* in 1918 (rpt. 156:305). Decades later, it would appear that educators thought they now knew enough to apply their expertise in child development to children's books. It is the age of a new generation of primers such as the Dick-and-Jane series, which both emphasized familiar objects in the here-and-now tradition and moved beginning literacy into whole-word learning. The primers seemed to apply some kind of behaviorist operand conditioning. Their characteristic repetitiveness eventually drove Rudolf Flesch up the wall: The child 'is told what each word means and then they are hammered into his brain' (1955:12). This is not what John Dewey, Lev Vygotsky, and Jean Piaget had intended. If Mencken had scare quotes, so did Flesch:

> "Quack, quack," said the duck.
> He wanted something.
> He did not want to get out.
> He did not want to go to the farm.
> He did not want to eat.
> He sat and sat and sat.

Primers in the Dick-and-Jane tradition also represented a segregated world. Clearly, publications like W. E. B. DuBois' *The Brownies' Book* had not made any transformational impact on the scholastic children's publishing industry. In 1954, John Hersey lamented 'pallid primers' with 'insipid illustrations' of 'abnormally courteous, unnaturally clean boys and girls' (136)—white boys and girls. More than with the whitewashed world of primers, however, Hersey was fed up with their conditioning approach. He questioned why school children should not enjoy more imaginative language and drawings that 'widen rather than narrow the associative richness the children give to the words' (148). Unlike John Dewey, who had voiced some of the same concerns earlier, Hersey was able to produce a provocative counterexample: He mentioned Dr. Seuss (ibid.) in support of his assertion that with a sufficiently engaging book, a child could 'absorb as many as 200 words in the first six months' (144). Clearly, the middle ground had not yet been found between leading the child to adult language/social construction and presenting books that actually engaged children rather than trying to program them.

Hersey's suggestion to let Geisel write a primer was meant as a dare. The industry took it. William Spaulding of Houghton Mifflin actually approached Theodor Geisel with a request to produce a primer with words drawn from a 348-item sight-word list (Nel 2007:4, 19). It was a wildly optimistic attempt to break into the scholastic market; Geisel's work was anathema to the central here-and-there credo since Sprague Mitchell (1921:21):

> Children do not find the unusual piquant until they are firmly acquainted with the usual; they do not find the preposterous humorous until they have intimate knowledge of ordinary behavior; they do not get the point of alien environments until they are securely oriented in their own.

Geisel's approach is probably best characterized by Oscar Wilde's one-liner in 'The Remarkable Rocket' ([1888] 1974:9): 'But I have imagination, for I never think of things as they really are; I always think of them as being quite different.' His barn- and brainstorming *Cat in the Hat* (1957)—using 236 words from Houghton Mifflin's primer list—predictably found 'no acceptance whatsoever in the school system' (Clark 1977:9). It did, however, make quite a splash in the private market (ibid.). Encouraged, Geisel was now on a mission: 'When you try to get rid of Dick and Jane, you're in the middle of a revolution' (ibid.). He carefully calibrated the language of his next 'beginner book' to appeal to *both* the whole-word school endorsed by Hersey *and* the phonics school championed by Flesch. *Green Eggs and Ham* (1960) had an even more restricted vocabulary (50 words), used the very kind of repetition so characteristic of Dick-and-Jane books (to the point of caricature)—and integrated minimal pairs (two words differing in their first sound/letter) in end rhymes that are ideally suited for phonics (cf. p. 49).

The success of 'Dr. Seuss' was a oner-upper to pedagogical experts: They had simply underestimated children. Sprague Mitchell's path-breaking here-and-now books and Jean Piaget's path-breaking application of 'naïve realism' to children turned out to have broken the wrong paths. The industry now delivered linguistic coach work with playful and surprising creativity.

That said, the pendulum is nonetheless swinging back toward increasingly pushing children into aligning their language and social construction with adults, albeit slowed by the drag of still-circulating children's books from earlier times. Margaret Wise Brown's *Goodnight Moon* alone has sold in excess of 48 million copies (Gary 2016:234), and the book dominated a 2016 survey by Carla L. Hudson Kam and Lisa Matthewson of what contemporary parents are reading to their young children. Baby Einstein and Baby Genius, however, promise a fast track for the cognitive and linguistic development of infants and toddlers. Here is a typical blurb of our time, from a web site promoting early reading to young children (earlymoments.com):

> What's the most important trait you'd like to develop in your child? If you're like most parents, intelligence is probably at the top of your list. We all want bright, smart children, which is why we spend so much time choosing the right schools and making sure teachers are exceeding expectations. But remember: as a parent, you have the power to boost your children's learning potential simply by making books an integral part of their lives.

The expectation of excellence has reached toddlers with programs such as Home Instruction for Parents of Preschool Youngsters (HIPPY). Well-educated parents in particular are now spending significantly more 'quality time' such as interactive book reading (as opposed to 'basic care' time) with young children, and they do so with the intention of giving their children an edge over other children in brain development, language acquisition, and early literacy (Dotti Sani & Treas 2016). Indeed, the authors predict that any increase of quality time spent by parents with less schooling will prompt parents with the most education 'to escalate their own involvement in order to maintain a relative advantage for their children' (1094). The emerging paradigm that will drive future children's literature is that 'earlier acquisition propels later learning' (Dickinson et al. 2012:2). Early language acquisition is an indicator for early literacy, and studies on twins show that environmental factors are 'primary determinants' (ibid.) in the development of language, reading, and schooling success. Educated parents are aware of this, and they seek to enhance their children's vocabulary (Rowe 2008). It is only reasonable to assume that publishers of children's books will increasingly supply books that are both engaging for children and based on cognitive and developmental science—fuel for a linguistic and cognitive social arms race intended to "supercharge your baby" (Vance 2018) that has produced *<title>HTML for Babies</title>* (Vanden-Heuvel 2011).

If *defining* literally means 'excluding that which does not belong,' and if what 'belongs' is a moving target, then an *inclusive* approach to children's literature would seem to serve better. Marah Gubar (2011:212) reminds us in this context that Ludwig Wittgenstein modeled such an inclusive approach when he tackled a similarly elusive concept, game. Wittgenstein's common denominator for games was 'family resemblance' ('Familienähnlichkeiten'—*Philosophische Untersuchungen* sec. 67: p. 57). Children build their semantic categories just like that, on family resemblances to archetypes (see Chapter 3): We have a good idea of what a 'typical bird' is (a robin seems to be the gold standard), and then we classify other critters by how closely they resemble that archetype. Our adult ideas of what constitutes children's literature are surely also shaped by what we remember from our own childhood, and even books that run counter to those remembered archetypes align in comparison to them.

The gold standard for a children's book seems intuitive enough. A children's book should be *intended* for children (by parents, educators, authors, or publishers), and it should *benefit* them linguistically and cognitively in an age-appropriate, engaging presentation. Following this line of thinking, MetaMetrix CEO and Common-Core co-author Malbert Smith wants to see children's literature writing, and education altogether, beholden to the Hippocratic Oath ('Above all, do no harm'). For the purposes of this book, I am going to use the following selection criteria when I refer to 'children's literature' hereafter:[4]

(1) **children's literature**: any printed text-based and/or graphic material intended or selected for the benefit or enjoyment of children as specific input for their linguistic, narrative/literary, and cognitive development

This working definition excludes digital children's literature, for reasons that will become apparent in the next chapter.

Language and Its Acquisition

Linguists are faring no better than children's literature researchers when it comes to agreeing on what their terms mean: There is no uncontested definition of 'language acquisition.' There is also no uncontroversial definition of language, nor a consensus on what acquisition is. Since language grows between the ears of a hyper-social species, it is frequently defined in terms of thought and communication. Such an approach immediately brings up the question of what relationship exists between language and cognition: Are the two identical?, unrelated?, or is language a specialized form of cognition? Establishing that relationship is like pondering the relationship between *Gallina gallina domestica* and her *ova*: Which came first? We can make out three major approaches in this chicken-and-egg shell game, each with its own *if-then-so:*

- **If** language development is an *outgrowth* of cognitive development (Piaget), **then** its acquisition is social learning, **so** we study how the child extracts patterns, recognizes analogies, projects schemas and generalizations, and receives reinforcement in interaction.
- **If** language development is *constrained* by cognitive development, **then** the states of cognitive competence provide language with sequential rooms to unfold in (Vygotsky), **so** we study how language unfolds relative to how the stages of cognitive growth enable that process.
- **If** language development is *ahead* of cognitive development, **then** it must be a faculty of the mind that develops on its own terms (Chomsky), **so** we study language acquisition as a biological process of cortical maturation and the triggers of that maturation that are presented in social interaction.

The solution to selecting between these three frameworks is . . . not to. The following chapters will draw from evidence for each one, making careful distinctions as to whether 'language development' refers to acquisition or to learning.

Some language acquisition can indeed be explained as a *consequence* of cognitive development. Chapters 1 and 3, for example, stress that the acquisition of phonemes and words requires an enriched, interactive environment. Joint attention 'gates' the infant's pattern extraction (Kuhl 2010:715); irregularities and surprises trigger her curiosity. (Children's books are very accommodating here.) Without an enriched environment, without meaningful situational interaction with an adult, phonemic perception and lexicon building are suspended. Chapter 2 shows that the child's conscious realization that certain words tend to associate with certain endings (e.g. *-s* for nouns) has an automatic cascading effect on organizing the vocabulary into parts of speech.

Some uses of language are indeed *constrained* by cognitive development, such as the use of templates in English. A template rearranges information within a sentence by saliency. Topicalization, for example, fronts a topic before the subject position and brings into focus whatever constituent now finds itself in clause-final position (e.g. *regrets, I had a few . . .*). English has a number of such templates (see Chapter 8, Table 8.2, p. 186), allowing alternate sentence structures that place just about any part of the sentence anywhere for such information management. However, the selection of the right template is dependent on cooperation—it is driven by what the speaker perceives the listener's needs to be. Therefore, a Theory of Mind (awareness of what another person can/cannot/should know) must be in place before an optimal sentence structure can be selected. Templates are stored in the lexicon, hence are part of the conscious way in which language is put to use. We aim to be cooperative when we select sentence structures so as not to overtax our listeners/readers. For example, embedding relative clauses into each other multiple times, as in Figure I.4 'The rapidity that the motion that the wing that the hummingbird has has has is remarkable' (Pinker 1994:205), causes syntactically well-formed sentences that overwhelm the parser (Chomsky & Miller 1963). Such sentences become particularly confusing when the parser fails so spectacularly that we cannot even cobble together a semantic representation, as is obviously still possible with the hummingbird sentence (cf. Hudson 1996).

Finally, it is not difficult to find examples where language acquisition is *ahead* of the child's comprehension. Around three years of age, an English-speaking child will produce the construction 'Mommy does not / doesn't sleep' instead of opting for the grammatically possible 'Mommy sleeps not' or staying with earlier constructions such as 'no Mommy sleep.'[5] Such linguistic sophistication does not come from explicit instruction or from generalizing from analogy (because by analogy, the progressive aspect for 'Mommy does not sleep' is 'Mommy does not be sleeping'). The brain is ready for those subtle and abstract decisions. Those linguistic processes (explained in Chapter 4, p. 109) can be explained neither

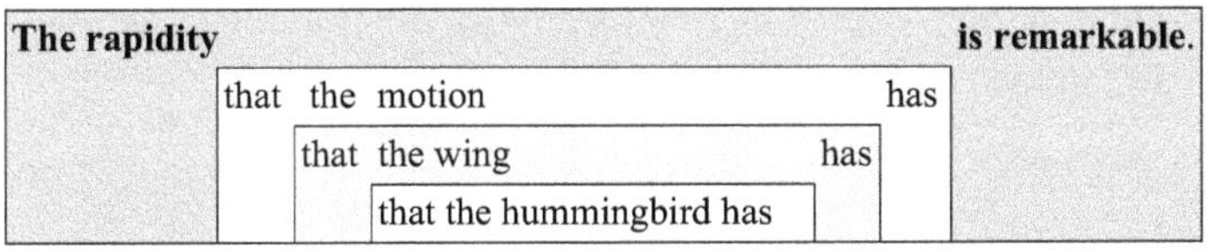

Figure I.4 Center-Embedded Adjective Clauses

to nor *by* a three-year old. In fact, most adult speakers of English cannot explain why *is not sleeping* is better than *does not be sleeping*. A young child is not even capable of following instructions to turn a statement into a question—but can do so spontaneously, as part of a game.

The apparent paradox of adopting all three scenarios (language is triggered by, constrained by, and independent of cognition) becomes manageable when we make some proper distinctions. The interaction between cognition and language is most intimate when it comes to *usage*; autonomy shows up most strongly in *grammar* (the intuitively known universal principles of language). Growing competence in usage is associated with learning. Noam Chomsky (1988) explained that linguistic input has two unrelated properties that should not be confused. First, it provides triggers for language *acquisition*. Once a grammatical property is triggered (such as the settings for weak/strong agreement, cf. Table 4.3, p. 110), the child correctly produces novel forms and avoids pitfalls of ungrammatical structures predicted by analogy. Second, linguistic input provides idiosyncratic information that has to be consciously *learned*—remembered and stored in the lexicon. Acquisition and learning are separate mechanisms, though they may interface.

For the purposes of this book, I shall define each term as follows:

(2) a. **acquisition**: the automatic (unintentional) addition of information, not directly open to introspection or guidance.

b. **learning**: the intentional addition of information that is remembered, as motivated by negotiated salience (interest from inside and outside).

(3) **information**: schemas (stored patterns and relations between them) and scripts (rules and other sequential processes) that are creatively related to one another in order to reconstruct, elaborate, and anticipate.

I added a definition of 'information' so as not to beg any questions. Three assumptions in (3) are worth making explicit. First, information is understood as something dynamic that *happens* in the brain. Second, the definition does not contain any reference to metacognitive thinking (such as reflecting upon reflecting). Third, there is a double entendre in the word 'creative.' Grammar creates in a *technical* sense: It combines finite sets of lawful processes and inventories to generate a theoretically infinite number of sentences. Usage creates with a *purpose*: We put linguistic and cognitive processes to meaningful, often innovative, use—in word games, poetry, jokes, and stories.

(4)

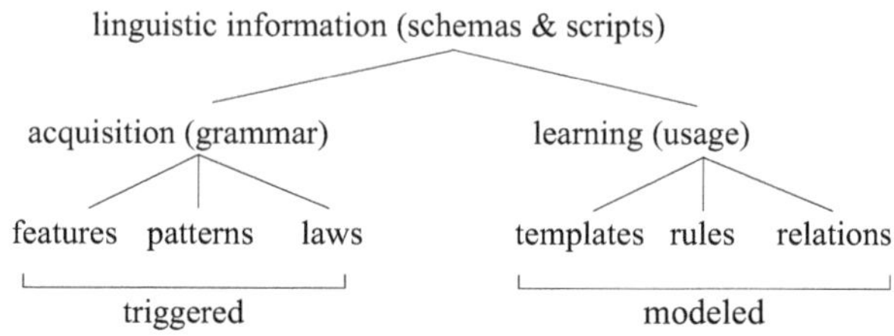

Figure I.5 Linguistic Information (Schemas and Scripts)

Synopsis (4) lays out how the terms stipulatively defined here relate to each other—and how the language of child-directed speech and of children's literature as specific linguistic input assists with language development by triggering or by modeling.

The first part of the book will take a close look at how young children acquire and learn language. Again, as was the case in defining children's needs and how best to meet them, this is not innocent territory. There is a polemical debate in progress about how infants and children come to attain linguistic schemas and scripts. At stake is nothing less than the question whether, as Noam Chomsky claims, human language is a species-specific mental faculty or, as is the working premise of many cognitive scientists today, whether a general ability to extract and model patterns is sufficient. 'Universal Grammar' vs. 'Baby Taking Statistics': The discourse can get a bit heated at times.

Skewering the cognitive-science position, for example, Paula Fikkert ascribes to Maye et al. (2002) the 'extreme position' of 'assuming that all contrasts fall out from statistical learning based on input speech' (Fikkert 2007:540). Yet the authors had stated nothing more than that 'attention to the statistical distribution of speech sounds in the input is *one factor* driving the development of speech perception over the first year of life' (Maye et al. 2002:B108, emphasis mine).

From the other side of the trenches, Ruth Berger (2008: 256) claimed that Chomsky had made a 'sensational retreat' from his tenet that human language relies on innate principles. To the 'horror of his faithful student and prophet Stephen [sic] Pinker,' Chomsky (Hauser, Chomsky, & Fitch 2002) was supposed to have conceded that 'nothing pertaining to the speech faculty of humans is language-specific' (Berger, ibid.; translations mine). Berger's obituary of Universal Grammar was, to borrow a phrase from Samuel Clemens (31 May 1897), 'an exaggeration.' In a follow-up article, Chomsky et al. countered that such wishful thinking rests on ignoring their careful distinction between Language in the broad sense ('all of the capacities that support language independently of whether they are specific to language and uniquely human') and language in the narrow sense, which the authors take to be species-specific (Fitch, Hauser, & Chomsky 2005:181).[6] Among the critics that were specifically singled out for not making the distinction rigorously enough: not-for-prophet Steven Pinker (Pinker & Jackendoff 2005).

Given the conflicting evidence hinted at above (in the three scenarios of how language and cognition might be related), this book uses *both* approaches: Innate Linguistic Endowments and Baby Taking Statistics. I go on the assumption (and will present evidence) that pattern recognition, extraction, and prediction rely on ancient networks in the brain's evolution. They come on line very early in a child's development. Chapter 1 will show that even young infants can laugh out loud at funny words and sounds (and *Mr. Brown Can MOO!* by Dr. Seuss keeps them coming), demonstrating (in sharp contradiction to Piaget and Sprague Mitchell) that they are acutely aware of pattern outliers. The detection of pattern anomalies is near instantaneous (the 'Early Left Anterior Negativity' EEG wave is recorded about a tenth of a second after the *onset* of presentation). However, a second type of brain activity (P600) can come on line later, and it involves rules and relations (and pathways that are likely more recent in evolution and exclusively human). Rules constrain perception, to the point of reworking perception into apperception (perceiving what we think we *should be* perceiving). Chapter 1 will show how motoric rules constrain the perception of speech sounds. Relations are signaled by how the form of one constituent is affected by another—an adjacent speech sound (Chapter 1) or syllable (Chapter 2), or an implied syntactic position that determines whether a pronoun at the beginning of a clause should be *who, whom,* or *whose* (Chapter 4).

Part I of this book asks what the nature of language growth is and how children's books can nurture it by going *beyond* what is typically observed in child-directed speech by adults. Part II asks the reverse: What is the nature of this nurturing? How do books add further enrichment to an environment within which the child acquires language, interfaces language with her own mind's faculties, and taps into the minds of others with language? How does the adults' implied presence in those books serve to engage the child in cooperation beyond the bounds of child-directed speech—thereby leading the child *toward* the conventions of adult speech?

Our species has given itself the nickname *homo narrans*—the narrating human. Books can help children narrate their social place, induce a feeling of entrainment through shared story and language, and even guide children in how to narrate themselves: their memories, assessments, fears, expectations, and identity. Chapter 5 investigates how language forms and interprets predications by interfacing with several unrelated operating systems of the mind that feature prominently in children's books: plotting and populating event models, anticipating outcomes, and making context-independent logical connections—and how language abstracts all of this information into narratives. Chapter 6 explores narrative competence as both empowering and therapeutic. Chapter 7 describes the experience of joint attention and shared reception (entrainment) and how children's books, in providing a safe space for entrainment, become vehicles for linguistic development and social construction. Those two objectives explain the notable and characteristic presence of a dual audience in modern children's books. Chapter 8 extends the observation of a dual audience to a theory of triadic cooperation in children's books—across child, character(s), reading adult, and author. Both kinds of cooperation are identified: inclusive (trusting and altruistic) and exclusive (colluding against the third party).

The conclusion argues that children's books, in a literate society, have become a source of high-quality language nutrition. They empower children, just as lack of quality exposure (e.g. by using television as a babysitter) disadvantages them (Nelson 1973). Books build brains literally.

Notes

1. Christine Alexander, *The Early Writings of Charlotte Brontë* (1983:107). I owe this reference to Elizabeth Gargano (2008:170. n.21).
2. One may presume that the same approach was extended to illiterate adults at that time so they could read to their own children. In 1920, for example, South Carolina superintendent of education John Eldred Swearingen launched segregated literacy 'night schools' with the fraught but apparently effective slogan 'Let South Carolina Secede from Illiteracy' (Janak). Brice Heath (1983:23) describes the common denominator between children's books and the adult materials produced under Swearingen's initiative (such as a simplified daily version of Columbia's main newspaper, *The State*): 'The focus was on teaching "what the pupils desire. Base all examples on everyday life."' The same premise applies today in the use of children's books with adult learners of English as a second language (Smallwood 1989).
3. There is a second connection between the Bureau of Educational Experiments and William R. Scott: Scott had a child enrolled there (Marcus 1992:88). *Cottontails* was apparently conceived by Bill Scott's wife Ethel McCullough (she is listed as the author) and illustrated by Sister Mary Veronica (Bader 1976:236), Ethel's aunt née Ella Sarah McCullough. Margaret Wise Brown and the Scotts reportedly spent hours stitching (Marcus 1992:101). Amy Gary (2016:173) seems to have understood Wise Brown to claim authorship and to give credit for the illustrations to Leonard Weisgard in an article written for *Publisher's Weekly* (Wise Brown 1947), though it is hard to see how she came to that conclusion since the article does not mention *Cottonails* at all.

   The picture in Figure I.3 was kindly taken and provided by Callie Raspuzzi of the Bennington Museum in Vermont.
4. I adopt the notion of children's literature as 'specific input in language acquisition' from Kümmerling-Meibauer and Meibauer (2013:148), who have been forging ahead with establishing the linguistics of children's literature as an academic discipline in Europe.
5. The stages of how negation is acquired have been well studied, starting with the pioneering cross-linguistic study of Henning Wode (1977).
6. Chomsky's 2005 position hardly comes as a surprise and is certainly no turnaround. The idea that the concept of Language 'should be extended to other symbolic processes' (1973:v) comes up in his work as early as in the seventies: 'Given the role of language in human life and probably human evolution, and given its intimate relations to what I have been calling "common-sense understanding," it would not be very surprising to discover that other systems within cognitive capacity have something of the character of the language faculty and its products' (1975:123). I believe that human connectome research is indeed pointing in that direction now.

References

Alexander, Christine. 1983. *The early writings of Charlotte Brontë*. Buffalo, NY: Prometheus Books.

Bader, Barbara. 1976. *American picturebooks: From Noah's Ark to the beast within*. New York: Macmillan.

Berger, Ruth. 2008. *Warum der Mensch spricht: Eine Naturgeschichte der Sprache*. Frankfurt: Eichborn.

Bliven, Jr. Bruce 1946. Child's best seller. *LIFE* 21(23) (2 December).59–66.

Brice Heath, Shirley. 1983. *Ways with words: Language, life, and work in communities and classrooms*. Cambridge: Cambridge University Press.

Chomsky, Noam A. 1973. Introduction. *Language and cognition by Adam Schaff*, ed. by Robert S. Cohen, translated by Olgierd Wojtasiewicz, v–x. New York: McGraw-Hill.

Chomsky, Noam A. 1975. *Reflections on language*. New York: Pantheon, Random House.

Chomsky, Noam A. 1988. *Language and problems of knowledge: The Managua lectures*. Cambridge, MA: MIT Press.

Chomsky, Noam A., and George A. Miller. 1963. Introduction to the formal analysis of natural languages. *Handbook of mathematical psychology*, ed. by R. Duncan Lace, Robert R. Bush, and Eugene Galanter, vol. 2, 269–323. New York: Wiley.

Christakos, Caterina. 2002. *How to write a children's book in 30 days or less*. Bloomington: iUniverse.

Clark, Diane. 1977. Dr. Seuss entices children into a world of words. *The Brownsville Herald*, 23 September, 9.

Clemens, Samuel L. (Mark Twain). 1897. Letter to Frank Marshall White. *New York Journal*, 31 May. Online: twainquotes.com/exaggeration2.jpg.

Contrera, Jessica. 2015. Who was Dr. Seuss? How a rebellious frat boy reinvented children's literature. *The Washington Post*—Arts & Entertainment, 27 July. Online: www.washingtonpost.com/news/arts-and-entertainment/wp/2015/07/27/who-was-dr-seuss-how-a-rebellious-fraternity-guy-reinvented-childrens-literature/.

Dewey, John. 1938. *Experience in education*. New York: Collier.

Dickinson, David K.; Julie A. Griffith; Roberta Michnick Golinkoff; and Kathy Hirsh-Pasek. 2012. How reading books fosters language development around the world. *Child Development Research* 2012, Article ID 602807. Online: www.hindawi.com/journals/cdr/2012/602807/.

Donaldson, Margaret. 1978. *Children's minds*. New York: W.W. Norton.

Dotti Sani, Giulia M., and Judith Treas. 2016. Educational gradients in parents' child-care time across countries, 1965–2012. *Journal of Marriage and Family* 78 (August).1083–96.

earlymoments.com. 10 reasons why you should read to your kids. Online: www.earlymoments.com/promoting-literacy-and-a-love-of-reading/why-reading-to-children-is-important.

"Fallacy of Premature Education, The" 1859. [rpt. from *The New Church Herald*]. *North Carolina Journal of Education* 2(3) (March).72–73.

Fikkert, Paula. 2007. Acquiring phonology. *Handbook of phonological theory*, ed. by Paul de Lacy, 537–54. Cambridge: Cambridge University Press.

Fitch, W. Tecumseh; Marc D. Hauser; and Noam A. Chomsky. 2005. The evolution of the language faculty: Clarifications and implications. *Cognition* 97(2).179–210.

Flesch, Rudolf. 1955. *Why Johnny can't read and what you can do about it*. New York: Perennial Library, Harper & Row.

Gargano, Elizabeth. 2008. *Reading Victorian schoolrooms: Childhood and education in nineteenth-century fiction*. New York: Routledge.

Gary, Amy. 2016. *In the great green room: The brilliant and bold life of Margaret Wise Brown*. New York: Flatiron Books.

Gubar, Marah. 2011. On not defining children's literature. *PMLA* 126(1).209–16.

Hauser, Marc D.; Noam A. Chomsky; and W. Tecumseh Fitch. 2002. The language faculty: What is it, who has it, and how did it evolve? *Science* 298.1569–79.

Hazard, Paul. 1932. *Les livres, les enfants et les hommes*. Paris: Boivin.

Hazard, Paul. 1944. *Books, children, and men*, translated by Marguerite Mitchell. Boston: Horn Book.

Helps, Arthur. 1857. *Friends in council: A series of readings and discourse thereon*, vol. I. London: John W. Parker and Son.

Hersey, John. 1954. Why do students bog down on the first R? A local committee sheds light on a national problem: Reading. *LIFE* 36(21) (24 May).136–50.

Hudson, Richard. 1996. The difficulty of (so-called) self-embedded structures. *UCL Working Papers in Linguistics* 8.1–33. Online: pdfs.semanticscholar.org/d884/44199687496cceaef0ad2c29e85a2003a58c.pdf.

Hudson Kam, Carla L., and Lisa Matthewson. 2016. Introducing the Infant Bookreading Database (IBDb). *Journal of Child Language—First View*, online (2 November). doi:10.1017/S0305000916000490.

Janak, Edward. Swearingen, John Eldred. *South Carolina Encyclopedia*. Online: www.scencyclopedia.org/sce/entries/swearingen-john-eldred/.

Johnson, James. 1836. *The economy of health or the stream of human life from the cradle to the grave with reflections moral physical and philosophical on the septennial phases of human existence*. London: S. Highley.

Jones, Delia W. 1859. Manner of educating females: Essay prepared by Mrs. Delia W. Jones, at the request of the Association, and read at the meeting in Newbern, June, 1859. *The North-Carolina Journal of Education* 2(8) (August).227–37.

Kuhl, Patricia K. 2010. Brain mechanisms in early language acquisition. *Neuron* 67 (9 September).713–27.

Kümmerling-Meibauer, Bettina, and Jörg Meibauer. 2013. Towards a cognitive theory of picturebooks. *International Research in Children's Literature* 6(2).143–60.

Locke, John. 1693 [rpt. 1963]. Some thoughts concerning education. *English philosophers of the seventeenth and eighteenth centuries*, ed. by Charles William Eliot, vol. 37. New York: Collier.

Marcus, Leonard S. 1992. *Margaret Wise Brown: Awakened by the moon*. New York: Quill, William Morrow.

Mary Poppins. 1964. Directed by Robert Stevenson. Produced by Walt Disney and Bill Walsh. Burbank: Buena Vista Pictures Distribution.

Maye, Jessica; Janet F. Werker; and LouAnn Gerken. 2002. Infant sensitivity to distributional information can affect phonetic discrimination. *Cognition* 82.B101–11.

Meigs, Cornelia; Elizabeth Nesbitt; Anne Thaxter Eaton; and Ruth Hill. 1969. *A critical history of children's literature: A survey of children's books in English*. New York: Macmillan.

Mencken, H. L. 1918 [rpt. 1956]. The educational process. *A Mencken chrestomathy: Edited and annotated by the Author*, 301–07. New York: Alfred A. Knopf.

Nel, Philip. 2007. *The annotated cat: Under the hats of Seuss and his cats*. New York: Random House.

Nelson, Katherine. 1973. Structure and strategy in learning to talk. *Monographs of the Society for Research in Child Development* 38(1–2, Serial No. 149) (February–April).1–135.

O'Sullivan, Emer. 2011. Comparative children's literature. *PMLA* 126(1) (January).189–96.

Piaget, Jean. 1973. *The child and reality: Problems of genetic psychology*, translated by Arnold Rosin. New York: Grossman.

Pickett, Aaron. 1827. *Mr. Pickett's Sermon: Occasioned by the death of Mrs. Abigail Lothrop*. Boston: T. R. Marvin.

Pinker, Steven. 1994. *The language instinct: How the mind creates language*. New York: Morrow.

Pinker, Steven, and Ray Jackendoff. 2005. The faculty of language: What's special about it? *Cognition* 95.201–36.

Redburn, David E. 1998. Intergenerational equity: Generational transfers and social justice. Chapter 19 of *Social gerontology*, ed. by David E. Redburn and Robert P. McNamara. Westport, CT: Auburn House.

Reynolds, Kimberly. 1994. *Children's literature in the 1890's and the 1990's*. Plymouth: Northcote House.

Rosenblatt, Louise M. 1938 [5th ed., 1995]. *Literature as exploration*. New York, NY: MLA.

Rousseau, Jean-Jacques. 1762. *Émile, ou de l'éducation*, ed. by Jean-Marie Tremblay. Chicoutimi: Université du Québec à Chicoutimi. Online: classiques.uqac.ca/classiques/Rousseau_jj/emile/emile_de_education_1_3.pdf.

Rowe, Meredith L. 2008. Child-directed speech: Relation to socioeconomic status, knowledge of child development and child vocabulary skill. *Journal of Child Language* 35(1).185–205.

Smallwood, Betty Ansin. 1989. Using multicultural children's literature in adult ESL classes. Center for Applied Linguistics. Online: www.cal.org/caela/esl_resources/digests/childlit.html.

Smith III., Malbert. n.d. (2009?) The hippocratic oath and grade equivalents. *MetaMetrics Position Paper*, 1330L. Durham: MetaMetrics. Online: cdn.lexile.com/m/uploads/positionpapers/TheHippOathandGrdEquiv.pdf.

Steiner, Evgeny. 2015. Mirror images: On Soviet-Western reflections in children's books of the 1920s and 1930s. *Children's literature and the Avant-Garde*, ed. by Elina Druker and Bettina Kümmerling-Meibauer, 189–213. Amsterdam, Philadelphia: John Benjamins Publishing Company.

Townsend, John Rowe. 1980. Standards for criticism for children's literature. *The signals approach to children's books*, ed. by Nancy Chambers, 193–207. Metuchen: Scarecrow.

Vance, Erik. 2018. Can you super-charge your baby? *Scientific American* 318(6) (June).34–39.

Vygotsky, Lev Semenovich. 1978. The role of play in development. *Mind in society: The development of higher psychological processes*, ed. by Michael Cole, Vera John-Steiner, Sylvia Scribner, and Ellen Souberman, 92–104. Cambridge, MA: Harvard University Press.

Watters, David H. 1985/1986. 'I spake as a child': Authority, metaphor, and *The New-England Primer*. *Early American Literature* 20(3).193–213.

Willems, Mo. 2015. I want my books to be played. Transcript of 'Ask Me Another', 12 February. NPR. Online: www.npr.org/2015/02/12/385546965/mo-willems-i-want-my-books-to-be-played.

Wise Brown, Margaret. 1947. Leonard Weisgard wins the Caldecott Medal. *Publisher's Weekly* 52(1) (5 July).40–42.

Wittgenstein, Ludwig. 1977. *Philosophische Untersuchungen. suhrkamp taschenbuch wissenschaft*. Frankfurt am Main: Suhrkamp Taschenbuch Verlag.

Wode, Henning. 1977. Four early stages in the development of L1 negation. *Journal of Child Language* 4(1).87–102.

Part I

The Nurture of Nature

Contributions to Brain Maturation *Beyond* Adult Speech

1 Delightful Sounds

Phonetics to Phonology

BOOM BOOM
SPLATT SPLATT
TICK TICK TOCK
SIZZLE SIZZLE
BLURP BLURP
KNOCK KNOCK KNOCK
A SLURP and a WHISPER
and a FISH KISS, too.
Mr. Brown can do it.
How about YOU?

Mr. Brown Can MOO! Can You?
Dr. Seuss

How could one possibly read a word like SLURP to a baby and expect her to keep a straight face? S-L-U-R-R-P . . . it *is* a funny-sounding word. And then there is Dr. Seuss' visceral groove. The rhythms of language play—*a slúrp and a whísper and a físh kíss tóo—pát-a-cake, pát-a-cake, bá-kér's-mán—áshes, áshes, and áll fáll down*—become body memories, recalled in adult songs and poetry: *when we find oursélves in the pláce júst ríght* ('Simple Gifts,' Elder Joseph).

How we experience the earliest sounds and melodies and rhythms of human speech affects speech processing throughout life. Their perception draws on the left and the right hemispheres, on auditory cortex and premotor cortex all at once (Friederici 2011:1376, 1360). In speech planning, sounds and melodies of speech are primary (cf. Fromkin 1971:49). Rhythms and frequencies guide their acquisition.

As we saw in the introduction, well-meaning parents have sought to accelerate the intellectual development of their babies (p. 10). Baby Einstein, a multimillion-dollar industry (Aigner-Clark 2001), has promoted early learning of vocabulary, colors, and shapes over creative and playful engagement with sounds, making 'Dr. Seuss's Book of Wonderful Noises' look unnecessary. The urge to turn progeny into prodigy marks the return to an adult construction of the child. This chapter will show, however, that books that go *splat!* also develop an infant's brain.

With sound as the central component of speech processing, Baby Einstein needs an iconic linguistic wunderbaby companion—and there are two candidates, depending on what one assumes the relationship between sound and meaning to be. On the one hand, one could argue that infants *discover* meaning through sounds, noticing patterns and making semantic connections. Cognitive scientists are steering their research in this direction, and their scientific vessel's galleon baby should be Baby Aristotle. On the other hand, one could argue that infants *assign* meanings to sounds, using grammar to make the connections. That would be a job for Baby Chomsky. Let us compare the positions.

Meaning From Sound: Aristotle

Aristotle viewed language as σημαντικός τις ψόφος, 'meaning from sound' ('peri psyches'; cf. Long 2011:84). Thus, Baby Aristotle's task is to make chaotic sounds meaningful: first by taking inventory and discovering patterns, then by associating those patterns with contexts. In cognitive science, that is the process referred to as 'baby taking statistics.' Infants note distributions and estimate transitional probabilities. In doing so, they exhibit a talent for patterns. Experiments that expose infants to artificial languages to see how they extract such patterns have shown, as Julie Sedivy put it, just 'how efficient tiny children can be in sucking out information from even quite small amounts of exposure to a language' (2014:225). Babies excel at acquiring the sounds and meanings of languages because of a generic skill: They can gather information and make predictions based on likelihoods. This is the quick and flexible talent for association that we will encounter again for the lexicon, in Chapter 2, in fast mapping (p. 62).

To conceive how an infant extracts information from minimal data, cognitive scientists apply Bayesian statistics, a procedure honed in theoretical chemistry and physics. That approach tests hypotheses from best available data. As better information becomes available, hypotheses and parameters are successively optimized to yield better models. In chemistry and physics, such approximations are necessary if direct measurements are out of reach —usually because the object studied is too small or too large or too complex to experiment on directly. Cognitive scientists face such a constraint: They cannot 'look into the brain' and understand from it *what* it is doing (cf. Chomsky 1988:6) and must hypothesize what the brain *might* be doing at a particular moment. Hence their attraction to Bayesian modeling.

Using Bayesian statistics to develop models of language acquisition also goes well with the premise that language learning is no different from *any* kind of learning. *Cognitive* scientists assume that language acquisition is based on *cognition* (learning from understanding). They do not start with the notion that humans are endowed with language-*specific* faculties. Learning is the same across all domains —it is 'domain general.' Humans are good at extracting patterns, at generalizing, at making predictions based upon those generalizations—and language is no different. No innate 'domain-specific' faculty is needed for language, because language is not separate from cognition. When infants find meaning from sound, they do so with a learning ability that humans have taken to an extraordinary level: 'stochastic' thinking, i.e. extracting patterns from unpredictable data. Babies figure out what the sounds of speech mean.

Meaning With Sound: Chomsky

Noam Chomsky, in contrast, sees language as 'meaning with sound' (2011). Grammar connects the two (Chomsky & Halle 1968:3). To be sure, Chomsky does not disavow statistical modeling: 'The role of statistical reasoning and other cognitive processes in language acquisition, potentially at least, should be a significant area of research' (2011). However, to claim that language can be discovered *solely* with domain-general strategies—taking statistics, extrapolating, pattern finding, associating—amounts, for Chomsky, to saying that there is no such thing as 'language.' But clearly there is. Language is an efficient computational system (ibid.). And that computational system has at least two inherent properties that Bayesian statistics cannot capture, let alone explain.

The first unpredicted property that makes language acquisition efficient is that babies do much more than extract information from *minimal* data: They are able to draw good conclusions even from *insufficient* data. Chomsky dubbed this phenomenon (how something could be acquired without being fully determined by evidence) 'Plato's Problem,' because Plato was similarly puzzled by how humans learn the first thing if learning connects new things to known things (see p. 59).

The second unexplained property follows from the first: Children produce forms that never occurred in the data they encountered ('I am brooming the floor'). They are creative, not just imitative. Their ability transcends 'sucking out information.' Some systemic knowledge is 'triggered' by input, so there must be some linguistic (domain-specific) endowment.

Acquiring the sounds of a language involves an endowment that lets children formulate and apply *accurate* rules, not just statistically optimal ones. Without postulating innate principles from which such accurate rules follow, we have no theory of why they reliably avoid errors that are statistically possible, nor why they proceed in well-defined stages of acquisition. Unlike cognitive scientists, linguists must 'go beyond hand-waiving about analogy and training and pattern formation and so on' (Chomsky 2011).

Chomsky argues that by modeling (associationist, connectionist, Bayesian, etc.), cognitive science has not produced, and will never produce, an *explanatory theory* of why babies make such sure-footed progress and avoid pitfalls. A simple example may serve to illustrate his claim—the planning involved in articulating the phoneme /l/. In English, the sound is different in the words *lip* and *elk*. Its location changes in anticipation of the next phoneme (/i/ is in the front, /k/ in the back), a so-called 'coarticulation' effect. In contrast, a German baby does not experiment with variants of /l/, as the /l/ in *Lippe* ('lip') and *welk* ('wilted') is frontal each time. Coarticulation thus is already rule governed (cf. Whalen 1990) —and so is, as we shall see below, the grouping of different speech sounds into a single abstract phoneme such as /l/.

Exclusive reliance on statistics in the research of language acquisition is essentially a way of avoiding theories that can be verified or falsified. Such an approach may perpetuate grant money, but the 'lack of interest in theory and explanation' (Chomsky 1965:193) draws the same condemnation Noam Chomsky leveled at behaviorist B. F. Skinner (1957) in 1959: 'play acting at science' (1959:39).

A Dual-Track Approach to the Acquisition of Sounds

The contrary approaches of Aristotle and Chomsky divide linguists and cognitive scientists, seemingly preventing Chomsky's envisioned integration of linguistics as a subdiscipline of 'cognitive psychology' (1984:1). Here is the litmus test: Are babies (/are brains) simply good at modeling, i.e. bottom-up processing from sound to meaning? Or are they genetically endowed with faculties to abstract and make rules that follow from inborn principles of language, i.e. top-down processing to connect meaning to sound? My answer is 'yes.' Both. An Aristotle and a Chomsky in every infant.

The brain has it both ways, taking statistics on patterns *and* imposing productive, creative rules. Infants mature into the sound systems of their native languages in stages: patterns followed by rules. Their *perception* proceeds from modeling all sounds they hear based on how they are physically produced (phonetics) to systematizing them with feature-based rules (phonology). Their *production* of sounds follows anatomic growth: lowering of the larynx, growing teeth, developing increasingly fine-motor control. In addition, the emergence of spoken sounds reflects their frequency in the speech of adults. Substitutions along the way, however, also show rules at work. For example, one would have to analyze phonetic features to decide that *sherry* is a reasonable substitute for *cherry*. The brain uses patterns *and* rules, Aristotle's bottom-up approach and Chomsky's top-down approach. Stochastic processing characterizes the initial state, and rule formation comes on line as additional, language-specific pathways mature.

The sounds of language *make sense* only because sense lives in an *enriched* environment of meaningful situational context. Without that added complexity, no association of sound and meaning 'makes sense.' Failure to interact with babies causes their failure to thrive linguistically if not physically; studies of the results of isolation in Romanian orphanages, such as Windsor et al. (2007), have documented the cascading damage resulting from linguistic deprivation: developmental mispronunciations, small vocabulary, minimal syntax. Only if they were placed in foster care did these children's language development improve, though not to the level of that of peers who grew up in an intact family (1377–78).

Children's books that are read aloud and interactively by adults to infants and to young children add to the acquisition of language and speech by providing additional layers of richness in sound, rhythm, stress patterns, pauses, and intonation. Books (not television, not tablets, not computers—books) provide sanctuaries of enriched interaction needed for earliest learning; they supplement child-directed talk with esthetic devices; they trigger the child's explorer mode with playful anomalies and violations; and they entice children to literacy.

Speech Perception: Phonetic Patterns

The division is real: The brain processes both *stored patterns* and *creative combinatorial rules*. Steven Pinker (1999) presented an in-depth study of *Words and Rules* in language production to prove the existence of two kinds of linguistic knowledge in the brain. He argued for listed items and for productive, symbolic, combinatorial rules. Sometimes, we see those two kinds of knowledge compete, such as when a child permits a rule 'MERGE {-ED} to V' to produce the past tense of *hold* as *holded* instead of blocking it to privilege the stored form *held* (16–17).

Literally spectacular advances in imaging cortical pathways have been made since *Words and Rules* was published. We can now visualize the brain's pathways as a functional anatomic 'connectome' and begin to identify which of those pathways respond to specific linguistic tasks (and how quickly). Brain areas (Broca's, Secondary Motor Area, etc.) are understood to provide generic skills (e.g. sequencing); pathways connect to them to requisition those skills for specific tasks (e.g. sequencing sounds or hand motions). Pathways roughly fall into two types: those toward the front and lower portions of the brain, and those that are higher and more toward the center and rear. *Ventral* pathways in the lower portion of the cortex specialize in noticing and storing patterns and abnormalities. *Dorsal* pathways, in the upper portion of the brain, process the kinds of procedural / combinatorial rules that can compete with stored patterns in the way Pinker predicted or can resolve abnormalities flagged ventrally.

In evolutionary terms, the ventral pathways used for language processing are typically older (Friederici, Oberecker, & Brauer 2012:205). Since older brain structures tend to mature earlier in the child than those that appeared later on the evolutionary timeline, some of the baby's pathways are active sooner than others. A four-month old has both early ventral and dorsal pathways that are involved in language perception (Figure 1.1). A major ventral pathway connects the temporal lobe forward to Broca's area and responds to serial speech sounds (but *not* to speech played backwards—this pathway is already biased). Anatomically, the *uncinate fasciculus* connects the temporal cortex to the frontal operculum.

The dorsal pathway maturing at this very early age connects the auditory cortex of the temporal lobe to the motor and premotor cortex, i.e. it maps sound to movement (Friederici, Oberecker, & Brauer 2012:207). We will see below how such mapping of sound to motion makes phonological rules possible, when a second pathway forms at that location and presumably exerts control over the first (Figure 1.2; ibid., 206).

Connecting the auditory cortex with the motor cortex forms a sensori-motor pathway that explains why crying patterns during the first weeks of life—and

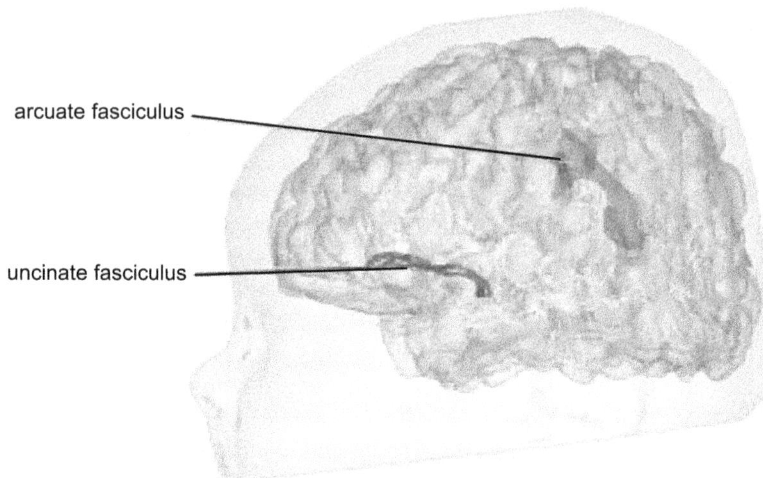

Figure 1.1 Ventral and Dorsal Sound Processing Pathways in Infants; Age: 1–4 months
Friederici et al. 2012: 207

later the intonation contours of baby babbling during the first months of life—are already language specific (Mampe et al. 2009; Boysson-Bardies et al. 1984).

The roles of ventral and dorsal processing in the perception of speech sounds appear to be as follows.

Ventral Processing and Perception: Taking Statistics

Young infants perceive differences between human speech sounds (phonemes), such as the change from /da/ to /ta/, soon after birth (Eimas et al. 1971). The difference between /da/ and /ta/ resides primarily in the 'voice onset time' (VOT), the time it takes before the vowel is heard after the consonant—in the case of [t^ha], there is an 80-ms. silence bridged by unvoiced aspiration / ^{h}/. Infants notice such patterns very early on, which indicates that the pathways capable of detecting those minute differences are ancient. Some corroboration for just *how* ancient those pathways are comes from a study by Kuhl and Miller (1975), who replicated Eimas' experiments with chinchillas.[1] Chinchillas notice the difference between /da/ and /ta/ as reliably as humans do, although their pattern detection skills are not congenitally pressed into linguistic service. Quite unlike chinchillas, human newborns instinctively attend to what is linguistic in their environment, and there is evidence (reviewed and confirmed by Kisilevsky et al. (2009) that their attention to speech and language begins even before birth. In a pioneering experiment by DeCasper and Spence (1986), expectant mothers recorded a prose passage such as *The King, the Mice, and the Cheese* (Gurney & Gurney 1965) or the first 28 paragraphs of *The Cat in the Hat* (Seuss 1957). They then read that text aloud each day for the last six weeks of pregnancy. The newborns unerringly preferred 'their' stories—regardless of whether they were hearing them read in their mother's voice or someone else's.[2]

Young infants have ancient and acute abilities when it comes to picking out phonetic features like VOT (voice onset time). They do so before they learn words (Maye, Werker, & Gerken 2002:B102), which can begin as early as six months (Bergelson & Aslin 2017). The difference between speech sounds is salient for them presumably before they distinguish between word pairs where those same distinctions make a meaningful difference, such as *dummy* vs. *tummy*. Phonetic features are innately salient. They include <±voice> (another feature marking the difference between /d/ and /t/), place and manner of articulation, and <±strident> (/t/ has that feature, /d/ does not).

Janet Werker (Werker & Tees 1984) showed that infants are so good at perceiving those features that they can make out speech sounds from *any* language, even sounds that adults listening to those same recordings will miss. In a lab setting, infants were taught to turn their heads in anticipation of a display of toys to become animated shortly after a syllable changes, say from /ka/ to /qa/—one being a velar *k* pronounced in the back of the mouth (like the English consonant), the second a uvular *k* that is pronounced farther back. The distinction is meaningful ('phonemic') in Nłeʔkepmxcín, an Interior Salish Northwest Indian language spoken in Canada's Thompson River area. Native speakers of that language (alas, there are few) will hear two different words between /kæxm̩/ 'to fry' and /qæxm̩/ 'to secure'; an English speaker fails to hear the difference. In English, the pronunciations /kæp/ and /qæp/ for *cap* would not result in a new word the way *cap* and *gap* do, hence an English-speaking adult will ignore the variation. A healthy six-month-old notices it acutely.

Logically, six-month-old infants *must* notice all the speech sounds in their environment before they can start taking statistics on them. Some of those speech sounds are allophones, i.e. alternate pronunciations of a single phoneme in different environments. Take, for example, the *t*-sound in English. There are six different presentations of that phoneme:

- The *t*-sound in *tea* has a signature 80-ms. aspiration [^{h}] before voice onset of the vowel /i/.
- The voice onset time is much faster when the *t*-sound is in a consonant cluster, as in *step*, for most speakers do not aspirate clusters.
- If the *t*-sound follows a stressed vowel, as in *pótty*, then it is a flap and the voice onset time for the following vowel is as short as the VOT normally associated with /d/—it is identical to the /r/ in Spanish *puro* 'pure, cigar.'
- If the *t*-sound ends a word, such as in *hit*, the tongue just comes to rest on the alveolar ridge (the *t*-sound remains 'unreleased').
- If the *t*-sound precedes a nasal, such as in *oatmeal*, then many speakers pronounce it like the cough-like sound in *uh-oh* (a glottal stop).
- Finally, if the *t*-sound precedes /r/ like in *tree*, then an affricate [č] sounds like the *ch*-phoneme in *chip*.

Will the real *t* please stand up? What would a 'real *t* ' even sound like? These six different allophones (in *tea, step, potty, hit, oatmeal*, and *tree*) are not all pronounced in the same location or manner; they are variants of a single *abstract* phoneme /t/. Before infants can begin chunking them as variants, they must attune to their complementary existence. This kind of intuitive (tacit) phonemic awareness is available to preliterate children, as Jean Berko-Gleason's early experiments with allomorphs showed: Preschoolers and first-graders naturally select the correctly pronounced ending, such as the plural *-s*, depending on the word's last phoneme. A *wug* joined by another is one of two *wugs* (ending /z/); the plural ending for *niz* is /əz/ as in *nizzes;* and *heaf* inflects for number with the ending /s/, *heafs* (Berko 1958).

Infants are aware how sounds distribute and pattern; they laugh heartily at funny sounds and words like S-L-U-R-R-P, and there are sufficient clips on YouTube to prove it. My own son, at 4 months, responded with peals of laughter to the words *Wuppertal* and *Düsseldorf.* Those are funny-sounding city names because they combine sounds in unusual ways. Westbury et al. (2016) looked into why some words sound funnier than others. They generated artificial words and correlated how funny they sounded to people with a measure of how unusual (on a Shannon entropy index) their sound combinations are. Since not only infants but also certain aphasics can laugh out loud at certain words, it seems safe to say that ventral processing detects outliers. The response to pattern anomalies is almost instant; electroencephalography, which can catch even the fastest of reactions, has identified an 'Early Left Anterior Negativity' wave (ELAN), a negative spike in as little as 120 ms, after the onset (!) of the presentation. Westbury et al. speculate that instant detection of anomalies is a survival skill, and that laughter is a release of arousal (and maybe a signal to others) upon the pleasant discovery that the anomaly is harmless (2016:141).

Ventral pathways, including the uncinate fasciculus, thrive on rich data (within context), taking statistics on how they pattern. Dorsal pathways, as we will see, seek to *reduce* that wealth of information by formulating rules that constrain the observed patterns and chunk sounds into abstract phonemes.

Dorsal Processing and Perception: Motoric-Pattern Chunking

Chunking reduces information. Being able to reconcile six different sounds as allophones of a single phoneme /t/ is huge, especially when one considers that other phonemes have their share of allophones as well. Chomsky and Halle reasonably assumed that a child is not already born with an abstract phoneme system in place but has to discover those abstractions from evidence (1968:50). The most logical way there, for an infant, would be through sensori-motor processing such as provided by the immature arcuate fasciculus (Figure 1.1).

Young infants get physical when they hear speech, for the same reason that adults move to the beat of music or to the rhythm of each other's speech (cf. Tierney & Kraus 2013). Infants simulate in their mouths how a sound would have to be formed long before they can actually produce it. An ingenious experiment has put that hypothesis to the test. Janet Werker and colleagues made it impossible for the infants' tongues to explore new positions. They put teething toys in the infants' mouths. Those teethers impeded tongue movement. At six months, when infants have no trouble picking up phonemes from other languages, teether tots score poorly. Restricting tongue movement results in a marked drop in the infants' ability to perceive unfamiliar sound changes such as the /ka/ and /qa/ above (Bruderer, Danielson, Kandhadai, & Werker 2015).

A motoric approach to apperception (controlled perception) explains the sound chunking mentioned above. As mentioned above, the phoneme /l/ in English *lip* sounds quite a bit different from the same phoneme in *elk* (p. 25). Recall that in a word like *elk* or *milk*, the /l/ is pronounced farther back in the mouth because the tongue is moving into position for the next target, velar /k/. Not so in *lip*. Knowledge of how the articulators in the mouth behave, [l] and [ɫ], which sound so very different, can now be analyzed as complementary realizations of a single abstract English phoneme, /l/. Knowing how the sound is produced in different environments guides its perception.

Adults, too, use motoric feedback in speech perception. For one thing, it helps us figure out quickly who in a group of people just started talking to us. Sensorimotor information makes it easier to have a face-to-face conversation in a noisy environment than to have a phone conversation over a noisy connection. The visual contribution to speech perception should not be underestimated. Shown a video of a human face repeating the syllable /ga/ but with the audio of that speaker actually saying /ba/, the viewer will *perceive* /da/. Here is why: 'Mirror neurons' that would normally fire for /ba/ will give no feedback when the speaker's lips are not seen to touch (the video shows her, after all, saying /ga/). Therefore, the closest available stop sound whose features are compatible with the perception of a voiced stop but missing the feedback of lip closure is recovered, and that is /d/. This 'McGurk effect' illustrates the sensori-motoric genesis of feature-based rules: With eyes closed (without the interference of open lips suggesting a different sound), the listener correctly hears /ba/ (McGurk & MacDonald 1976). It is this kind of motoric sub-articulation by the listener (which also tends to limit our reading speed) that appears also to guide the infant's perception of speech sounds.

Dorsal Processing and Perception: Phonological Rules

As the arcuate fasciculus matures, a second pathway is added to that fiber bundle, connecting the temporal cortex to Broca's area. The motoric patterns detected during early infancy can now be paired with processes that can handle 'non-probabilistic hierarchical structures . . . requiring rule learning' (Friederici et al. 2012:206). Stochastic processing now submits to the control of rules.

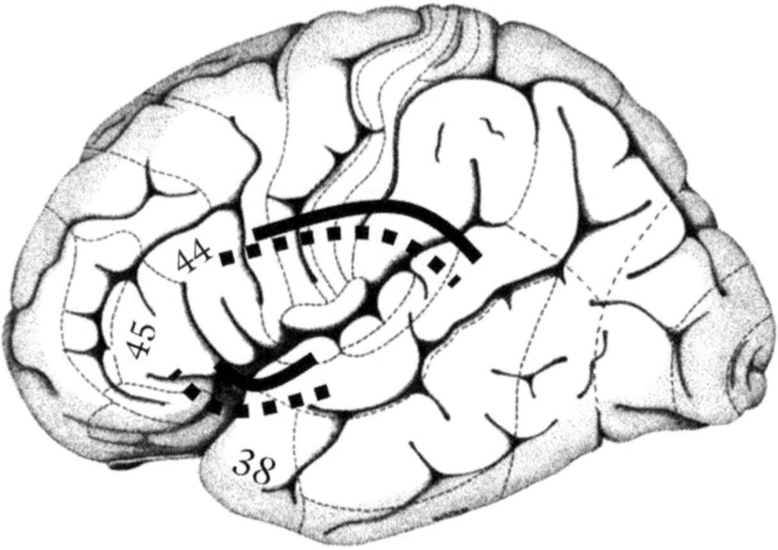

Figure 1.2 Mature Ventral and Dorsal Sound Processing Pathways
—— = same as Figure 1.1 (early pathways)
- - - - = later pathways

The upper two (dorsal) pathways form the mature arcuate fasciculus. Dorsal pathway I (solid) connects the superior temporal gyrus to the premotor cortex; dorsal pathway II (dotted) connects to Broca's area (Brodmann area 44). Ventral pathway I (dotted) connects the superior temporal gyrus to Broca's area (Brodmann area 45) via the uncinate fasciculus; ventral pathway II (solid) connects the anterior superior temporal gyrus to the frontal operculum via the extreme fiber capsule system. For the significance of area 38, see p. 90 below.
adapted from Figure 4.2 (p. 105) and Friederici (2011:1360)

In the course of the infant's second half of the first year, the arcuate pathway of Figure 1.1 is paired with a new pathway that recruits Broca's area to the processing of sound sequences, and it is unique to humans (Friederici, Oberecker, & Brauer 2012:205). With Broca's area involved, sound distribution patterns that have come to make *motoric* sense in speech perception can be abstracted into *rules* of the form

(5) /t/ → [ɾ]/V́__

Read: The abstract phoneme /t/ is realized as a flap [ɾ] in the following environment: after a stressed vowel V́ (as is the case in the word *pótty*). As that process of rule-ordered abstraction unfolds, the child's perception of speech sounds changes. A one-year-old will perceive only the sounds that correspond to language-specific rules of type (5) above. Placed in the same head-turning experiment that a six-month-old infant passes with flying colors relying on pattern extraction, a one-year-old, having shifted from stochastic/sensorimotor *perception* to rule-governed sound *apperception*, reacts directly only to sound changes that are predicted by those rules and ignores other variations (Werker & Tees 1984).

It may seem sad that babies, in their first year of life, essentially train themselves *out of* the ability to perceive sounds that are not part of their native sound system. Once the phonological system is in place, it is all the harder for us adults to hear new sounds when we learn a foreign language. There is even a name for this deficit: 'foreign hearing syndrome.'

Rather than calling the results of phonemic learning a 'deficit' and treating them like a 'syndrome,' however, we should appreciate the benefit of such rule-based specialization: predictability. Our ability to access abstract phonemes from the stream of speech sounds allows us to adjust to different accents, to idiosyncrasies in a speaker's pronunciation, to speech signals masked by noise or cut short by the limited acoustic spectrum of a telephone or of a hearing aid, even to misspeaks. It is fair to say that we hear what we can legitimately expect to hear: Speech sound perception becomes predictive.

A simple experiment demonstrates acoustic apperception at work: If a phoneme such as the /s/ in *legislature* is electronically deleted from a recorded sentence and replaced with a cough sound, the missing /s/ is nevertheless still heard. The brain makes us 'hear' a missing sound where it should be ('phonemic restoration effect').

Phonemic restoration, being predictive, is context sensitive. Out of context, predictive co-creations are less accurate, and what we think we heard could turn out to have been a 'slip of the ear.' The most memorable of such mis-hearings are certainly Mondegreens, which create an alternate reality. Author Sylvia Wright coined the term after she heard the 17th-century ballad 'The Bonnie Earl o' Moray' as saying 'They hae slain the Earl o' Moray/And Lady Mondegreen' (1957:105–12). But there had been but one slaying—the line was 'and laid him on the green.' Mis-hearings have nothing tentative to them—they are committed reality just like visual compensations for the eye's blind spot. I myself have consistently misheard a stanza from John David's 'You are the New Day' as performed by the King Singers.

What I heard was that 'we must pray/for't to occur' that the current night remain yesterday. The actual wording is quite different: We go to bed aware that 'we must pay,' and 'thoughts occur' that that the night may remain so. I read the actual lyrics incredulously on several different web sites before it dawned on me that the original wording makes so much more sense.

Playing both ends against the middle, as predictive listening does, is a hallmark of human thinking in general: The anticipated result of the computation forces itself upon the ongoing computation. Without a sufficiently rich context, perceiving the words *a girl with colitis goes by* in 'Lucy in the Sky with Diamonds' (Pinker 1994:186) probably makes about as much sense as the psychedelic original wording, *a girl with kaleidoscope eyes*. The brain supplies the necessary rearrangements and phonemic substitutions to make that alternate perception happen. Feedforward and feedback loops achieve such deterministic thinking, another ancient design feature of brains: Anticipating outcomes (jumping to conclusions) is clearly a survival skill where taking the time 'to stand back and assess before acting comes with the price of increased risk' (Linden 1999:153). Crucial to applying such predictive processing to speech is the human ability to access abstract representations of sounds, established during the first year of life: We understand and thus predict how sounds *should* combine.

By the same token, we know how sounds typically do *not* combine in our native languages. Babies know it, and they use that knowledge to parse what adults say. Being aware, for example, that the sound sequence /kn/ cannot occur at the beginning of a word in English is useful information in finding word boundaries. To illustrate this awareness with an example from adult speech: The sequence /hihæzækni/ cannot be *he has a knee* because of that constraint (because we say /ni/, not */kni/), so *he has acne* is the predicted parse. Centuries ago, perception would have been the opposite, because /kn/ was fine in word-initial position (which is why we still spell it that way) and nobody had *acne* until the early 1700s. The (sometimes idiosyncratic) rules of what sounds may or may not combine in a language belong into a rule system of phonology called *phonotactics*.

During their first year of life, infants develop two kinds of procedural knowledge: how sounds are pronounced, and how they are combined. Knowledge of such rules helps them to predict what they will hear, to extract words from the adult speech stream independent of who the speaker is, and to develop their very own pronunciation and vocabulary.

Speech Production: Maturation of the Speech Tract

While speech *perception* works toward reduction, speech *production* works toward increase. Over time, the child will become better and better at producing the full phonemic and allophonic inventory of her speech community. There is some predictability in the sequence in which this occurs.

It is said that neonates have inborn cries that caretakers can learn to interpret. Priscilla Dunston (2012) thinks that neonates can indicate hunger (*neh*, based on the sucking reflex), tiredness (*owh*, a vocalized yawn reflex), and wind/need to burp (*eh*). Some weeks later, according to Dunston, the infant will add cries to communicate gassiness (*eairh*) and physical discomfort in general (*eh*), followed, at two and a half months, by cries related to teething (*gen*), loneliness (*lowel*), thirst (*nuh*), and sensory overload (*augh*). Those claims have not been verified independently (cf. Carmichael 2009), and lab measurements have not initially been able to pinpoint such specific detail (Soltis 2004). More recently, however, Saha et al. (2013) developed an Android app that recognizes and 'translates' neonate cries. Dunston has testimony from parents who feel that they have gained a better understanding of what their babies are communicating. Whatever creates that inner reality for them surely deserves further study.

To be sure, physical maturation must be well underway before the child can proceed from sub-articulating phonemes (in order to perceive them correctly) to actually pronouncing them. To articulate vowels, the tongue must be able to move forward and backward. Vowel sounds result from the size of two sound chambers relative to each other: a space in front of the tongue and a space behind it. Moving the tongue backward, however, is not really much of an option for infants. Their larynx is placed so high that the tongue cannot retract to create the large resonating chambers in the front needed for /u/ as in *doom* or to make a space in the back large enough for a good /i/ as in *me*. Note the absence of those two vowels in Dunstan's inventory of neonate cries.

On spectrograms, infant 'vowels' look quite different from adult vowels as a result. That is as it should be, because neonates have priorities here: It would be too dangerous for them to be able to form adult vowels. Their larynx is high so as to allow them to nurse and breathe without mis-swallowing. Over the first year of life, the larynx descends, however, creating space for the two sound chambers in the mouth, and then vowels become increasingly distinct in babbling. Other physiological requirements for speech are teeth; the neural circuitry to coordinate muscles in tongue, lips, velum, glottis, and chest wall; and dorsal feedforward/feedback loops between speech areas, such as the arcuate fasciculus.

Partially as a reflection of physiological maturation, children grow into the sound system of English sequentially. Pediatricians have time charts for speech sounds, or test kits such as Pearson's *Goldman-Fristoe Test of Articulation 3* (GFTA-3, Goldman & Fristoe n.d.). Those charts and tests use classifications like Shriberg's (1993) that go back to early publications such as Templin (1957). According to those charts, the first year of life begins with the emergence of vowels, nasals and stops pronounced in the front of the mouth (/m/, /n/, /b/, /p/, /d/), glides (/y/, /w/), and /h/. They are soon followed (starting about 18 months) by /t/ and by velar sounds (/k/, /g/, /ŋ/), then by labiodentals (/f/, /v/). Later-emerging consonants take especially fine-motor control. The /s/ and /z/ sounds are like /t/ and /d/, except that the tongue leaves a very narrow slit of space to produce turbulence for a fricative at that position. Even adults make substitutions here (cf. *waᴅn't* for *wasn't*, *biᴅness* or *piᴅgin* for *business*, or the alternations *Shabbaᴛ/Shabbos*). The tongue needs to pull back for the fricatives /š/ and /ž/ (as in *shoe* and *treasure*), make pinpoint contact with the alveolar ridge behind the upper teeth for /l/ to allow the airstream to pass laterally, contort backward for /r/, and touch just the right way against the upper incisors for the *th*-sounds /ð/ and /θ/. Those fine-motor control sounds start emerging at 30 months—and some may not be heard until the child is four or five years old. The /ž/ (*treasure*) sound, very

Table 1.1 Typical Sequence of English Consonant Acquisition

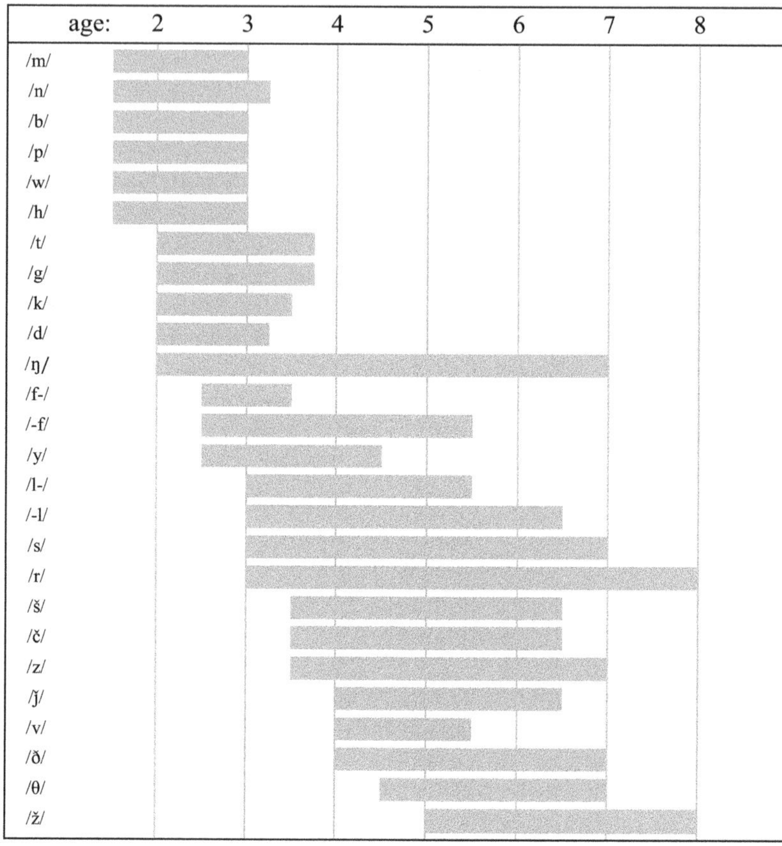

Based on Shriberg (1993) and Williamson (2011)

rare in English, can apparently take six years to emerge. A suggested timeline with ranges for when these consonants are typically heard from healthy, English-acquiring children is given in Table 1.1.

Speech Production: Rule-Based Performance

While early speech production shows not only the effects of physical maturation, frequency/markedness, and the *stochastic* (distribution statistical) signatures of sounds, we also clearly see *rules* of production at work. Neil V. Smith (1973), who documented the language acquisition of his son Amahl, used Chomsky and Halle's (1968) framework to postulate an array of rules that must be in place to explain some of his child's creative output. Smith documented rule ordering and simplification, vowel and consonant harmony, and consonant cluster reduction among those productive mechanisms (Chapter 2). Some rules were temporary as the child moved toward target pronunciations, and Amahl himself was evidently aware of the disparity between his own production and the target (Smith 1973:10):

(6) NVS Say 'jump'
A [ḍʌp]
NVS No, 'jump'
A [ḍʌp]
NVS No, 'jummmp'
A [u:li: ḍɛdi: ġæn ḍe: ḍʌp] ('Only Daddy can say "jump" ')!

Makeshift rules to address disparities are known in second-language learning as 'interlanguage' rules (Selinker 1972), and they are creative. A textbook example of phonological problem solving comes from another child of a linguist, Jessica, the daughter of Bill and Teresa Labov. Jessica found clever workarounds as she adjusted her productive rules toward the target *dad*. After abandoning the reduplication rule with which babies achieve open syllables (*dada* and [dædæ]), she moved to the closed syllable *dad* but apparently became aware of her own child-typical devoicing of syllable-final voiced consonants (*dat*, in this case). To compensate, Jessica nasalized the final consonant to appropriate the feature <+voice>, resulting, at 20 months, in the forms *da-n* [dæn̩], *dadnm* [dædnm], and *da'n* [dæʔn]. Labov and Labov's careful transcriptions show that these are created, not imitated, forms, and that they are not created randomly or desperately, but within a controlled system of phonetic features.

Patterns and Rules in Speech Production: The Either-or Fallacy

On the one hand, there is evidence that infants are sensitive to the stochastic properties of phonetic features. On the other, there is evidence that infants know that features exist and that rules apply to them. Researchers compiling evidence on either side have tended to cluster around either the 'baby taking statistics' or the 'little linguist' approach. Each approach aligns with a tradition of explaining the child's progress in pronouncing speech sounds—unfortunately, as we have seen (p. 14), often in opposition to the other.

The 'little linguist' approach aligns with Roman Jakobson (1941) in focusing on the distinctive features (‹±voice› etc.). Jakobson posited that features universally shared across languages are produced first, and finer, more language-specific distinctions emerge later. His approach, worked out in clinical detail by speech pathologist Stephen Blache (1978), explained the late appearance of such rare sounds as English retroflex /r/ (Elmer Fudd never got the hang of it) and the *th*-sounds, which are both quite exotic among the world's languages. More recent research by Clara Levelt and van Oostendorp (2007) confirmed that distinctive features have explanatory power for the mastery of speech sounds in various languages (focusing especially on Dutch, in their case). One should keep in mind, of course, that comparisons of phonemes across languages are not straightforward

(Beckman & Edwards 339); a sound like the flap [ɾ], as discussed previously (p. 29), can represent a /t/ in English and an /r/ in Spanish (cf. *Betty* and *puro*). Extrapolating from the idea that sounds emerge sequentially, Jakobson also predicted a mirror principle for patients developing dementia: They should first lose the sounds that they learned to produce last. Jakobson's mirror principle has likewise received observational confirmation (Buchwald 2005).

The 'baby taking statistics' approach to why speech sounds emerge sequentially instead of randomly arose in cognitive science. It focuses less on how some features are easier to articulate than others or on how common their features are across languages, and more on frequency of exposure, as illustrated in the lag time until children finally start using the phoneme /ž/ in English. (That sound occurs only in some words borrowed from French. And in *Hoosier*. Hayden (1950:221) found it in a mere 0.03% of the words of her corpus). Frequency effects have been observed in so many areas of language acquisition (Ambridge et al. 2015) that they have no doubt contributed to the temptation of replacing 'baby linguist' with 'baby statistician.' Frequency effects are especially pronounced, however, when one counts types (e.g. a part of speech) rather than tokens (how many times it occurs and in which form, e.g. *bother, bothers, bothering, bothered*) (Edwards et al. 2015:307). This includes types and tokens of morphemes: The non-syllabic plural morphemes /s/ and /z/ (as in *tasks* and *minds*) and {-ED} morphemes /t/ and /d/ (as in *washed* and *cleaned*) are more frequent than the syllabic ones (such as in *kisses* or *wanted*), hence show up earlier in children's speech as well (ibid., 309). Thus, we may also observe a frequency effect in types of speech sounds (rule-produced phonemes) more than in token sounds (observed allophones).

Neither side profits from entrenchment. Phonemes, as we have seen, are rule constructs imposed up on stochastic properties. Infants arrive at those rules before (or just as) the phonemes are needed to distinguish one word from another, so the drive to create them must be innate. Any theory of phonological acquisition must transcend polemics, because it needs to account for *both* the infant's extraordinary 'sensitivity to probabilistic patterns in the input' from adult speech (Maye et al. 2002:B108) *and* the creativity exhibited in the process of rule building, as illustrated by baby Jessica above—from observation alone, infants would not come up with patterns that are 'unattested in typical adult phonology' (Jennifer Smith 2007:539).

Baby Aristotle and Baby Chomsky can't do without each other. Pattern extraction and creative rules must interact (Edwards et al. 2015:310), and *neither is sufficient* to explain the child's progress (cf. Beckman & Edwards 2010:339). Accumulating evidence suggests that rule formation and stochastic perception are codependent and congenitally biased toward language and speech:

- It can be demonstrated *statistically* that children's linguistic output is based on productive grammatical rules—in 'sharp discontinuity' to the imitative profile of Nim Chimpsky, a chimpanzee trained in American Sign Language (Yang 2013:6327).

- The human brain does not (indeed, cannot) treat all incoming information equally, but relies on *biased* pattern perception (cf. p. 27). For example, humans (uniquely, it appears) expect a certain ratio of consonants to vowels in speech, which enables them to identify words and structures (cf. p. 34). An artificial language in which the ratio is reversed renders listeners unable to extract those kinds of rules from the signal (Toro et al. 2008).
- 'Cultural inheritance' can be epigenetically encoded during mid-childhood and passed on to the next generation (Pembrey 2018). For example, a regulatory element within the DCDC2 gene (associated with phonological processing) cleverly called READ1 ('regulatory element associated with dyslexia 1') has a 'repeat unit,' RU1-1, that was found to be significantly associated with the number of consonants across 43 human populations and five continents (DeMille et al. 2018), so an infant might well be biased towards expecting at least a ball-park amount of consonants from birth.
- Human physiology has genetically adapted to speech perception. Newborns show functional lateralization of hearing at the cochlear level (Ari-Even Roth et al. 2016) and at cortical and subcortical levels (cf. survey of literature by Ari-Even Roth et al. (2016:1). Given that signals from the body cross over in the brain, a right-ear advantage in the identification and perception of speech privileges the left hemisphere, which primarily processes speech.
- In turn, a right-ear advantage also reflects phonotactics. As early as 1975, Tadanobu Tsunoda found a right-ear advantage for single vowels among Japanese speakers (a single vowel can have meaning in Japanese) vs. English speakers. Taha Husain (2017), to his own surprise, found a difference in ear advantage when native speakers of Hindi vs. English hear voiced and voiceless aspiration. The bias in sound perception itself becomes physiological reality based on language-specific rules.
- Humans attend to speech in the abundance of sound signals because of its typical 'oscillatory rhythms' of 8 Hz and 4 Hz, which assist in the detection of consonants and vowels: There is a 'robust relation between the time scales associated with speech cues (phonemes, syllables, and intonational phrases) and the time constants underlying neuronal oscillations (low-gamma, theta, and delta oscillations)' (Martins & Boeckx 2014:2). Even facial expressions have this timing profile during speech (ibid., 3), making it instantly possible to connect speech to a specific person in a group of speakers.

The interdependence is mutual, then: Human linguistic profiles bespeak combinatorial rules, and the rules in turn work only on the right kinds of signals. Whether it is the statistics that 'caused the apparently rule-abiding behaviors' or whether the statistics are 'epiphenomena of underlying structures' (Bonatti et al. 2007:924) is not an either-or question. Both are true, and necessary: Perception and rule bias each other.

The place where a child's linguistic growth in pattern extraction and rule formation is stimulated, Beckman and Edwards remind us, is human interaction. Only in joint attention is the infant aware of features and their frequencies:

> . . . human babies differ from infants of other primate species in their capacity to grasp the phonetic intentions of the speakers in their environments and to develop the robust, language-specific articulatory-motor, auditory-visual, and higher-order structural representations that they need to develop in order to be inducted into a particular language community.

Let us look at the importance of interaction both in the infant's perception of speech sounds and in the baby's production of speech. Chapters 7 and 8 will describe the role of joint attention and interaction in language acquisition more generally.

The Role of Interaction in the Acquisition of Speech Sounds

Adults are quite accommodating when they talk to infants. Child-directed talk is hyper-enunciated, with exaggerated ups and downs of pitch (prosody), and focused on context (cf. Table 8.1, p. 184). Decades ago, Jerome S. Bruner had speculated that adults, on some kind of instinct, alter their speech when they talk to infants. He assumed that there must be an interactive 'Language Acquisition Support System' (1983:39; cf. 1978:249). Those were prophetic words. We now know how crucial interaction actually is for the child's perception and production of human speech. The adult's prosody, for example, cues six-month-old infants in to her first association of sound sequences and objects in her environment (Shukla, White, & Aslin 2011). To fast-map communal meaning to sound, infants need a rich and interactive environment.

A six-month-old acquires speech sounds *only* in interactive settings. Patricia Kuhl put American infants with English-speaking parents into three groups and exposed them to Japanese. The experimental group interacted attentively and face to face with a native speaker of Japanese. Control group 1 heard and saw the same speaker on television. Control group 2 only heard the speaker while the screen showed a teddy bear. In the control groups, there was 'no learning whatsoever' (Kuhl 2011). The areas surrounding the auditory cortex were active exclusively in the interactive setting. John Hersey had guessed as much in 1954 when he warned of the 'hypnotic effect' of television and labeled it 'the enemy' of reading (148), anticipating Mary Winn's (1977) seminal rebuke of television as a 'plug-in drug' for children.[3] It is fair to say that infants do not process speech unless they attend to a live human being interacting with them. And that is why we need real children's books.

Children's books can significantly enrich the child's environment and provide a productive setting for adult-child interaction. Not only does interactive book reading set a trajectory toward literacy, but it also maximizes verbal exchanges between child and caretaker. When Anna Sosa (2016) compared interactive play with electronic toys and interactive book reading, the electronics elicited the least amount of words from the adults, the fewest conversational turns, and the fewest parental responses. Traditional toys fared somewhat better in interactive settings. However, the most verbal interaction was over books—a clear winner in all categories. Adults do not just read the book out loud and then put it away: They comment, they ask what will happen next, they answer questions and point out features, they engage in a conversation about the book. Meaning-related talk during book reading, as we will see (p. 70), is predictive of language skills well into the child's school years (Hindman, Skibbe, & Foster 2014).

Children's Books and Phoneme Discrimination

'Noise books,' books that assign phonemes to noises from animals or objects (onomatopoeia), are a subgenre of preliterate children's literature. Eloise Wilkin's *Baby Listens*, published by Esther Wilkin in 1960, still uses 'here-and-now' noises. The illustrations by Eloise Wilkin show a baby listening to a clock (*tick tock*) or to running bath water (*gurgle gurgle glub glub*). But the here-and-now can very well be the interactive book reading session itself, so the scenarios for noises do not need to come from the household. Margaret Wise Brown pioneered a series of noise books with story settings:

> Her "noisy books" (*The City Noisy Book, The Country Noisy Book, The Seashore Noisy Book* and *The Indoor Noisy Book*) are written in sounds and questions that bring the child into the story. They concern a small sightless dog, Muffin, who trots around hearing noises: an automobile's "awuurra awuurra," an airplane's "rrrrr," a frog's "Jugar jugarum," a vacuum cleaner's "mmmzzmmmmmmmmmm" or the hush of a very quiet custard. Nothing could be more fascinating to a four-year-old than listening to his parents' struggles with the vocal demands of the text or more hilarious than the books' surprise questions: "It began to snow. But could Muffin hear that?"
>
> (Bliven 1946:61)

Margaret Wise Brown's attention to speech sounds was not accidental. In her days at the Bureau of Educational Experiments, she also ran experiments on young children's attention to speech sounds. She once read a book in French to three-year-olds. 'They couldn't understand a word,' she said, but: 'They loved every syllable' (Bliven 1946:64).

Never to be outdone, Theodor Geisel's 'Dr. Seuss's Book of Wonderful Noises,' *Mr. Brown Can MOO! Can You?* (1970), invites adult and child on a tour de force on which they have to come up with sounds they could not possibly have observed, anything from a hippo chewing gum to a goldfish kiss. Maybe with a nod to Muffin the blind dog, who focuses entirely on the sounds around him, Geisel drew Mr. Brown with his eyes closed on every page as he rapturously makes those sounds.

Rather than imagining exotic sounds, Leslie Patricelli displaces familiar sounds into surprising scenarios. Her *Toot* (2014) puts an adorably single-haired flatulent baby into various scenarios—tooting. In music class, the noise blends with the percussion instruments (I assume for a toot suite).[4] When running, the baby sounds like a train.

These days, noise books make the sounds themselves, their samplings unencumbered by creativity. Marketed in the language of brain development (Sounds for Baby Education, Baby Genius What Do You Hear, etc.), these books paradoxically coopt the very adult-child interaction that Patricia Kuhl demonstrated to be preconditional for sound processing in the first place. Usborne Baby's Very First Books have buttons to push to match sounds to pictures. Other books provide a sound specific to a single illustration. Lee Wildish and Barry Gibson's *Noisy Zoo*, uses a recurring frame of 'what a noisy ___' ('ah-pooooooooo—What a noisy elephant!'). As one reviewer on Amazon.com remarked dryly, the buttons are too hard to push for a young infant—so some interaction with the adult is, thankfully, required. Thankfully, too, such noise books rarely outlast their battery.

To enrich the environment for sound perception, children's books use rhythm. Anna Dewdney's trochaic *Llama Llama Red Pajama* (2005), for example, focuses more intently on rhythm than on content (see p. 176). Shared rhythm (esp. at the 3–8 Hz rate that is characteristic for speech and facial expressions) joins attention: 'brains really do sync through oscillatory activity' (Martins & Boeckx 2014:3). Some deep bonding occurs between adult and child during such brain-to-brain 'neural coupling.' As in any language play, the rules change to maintain surprise (Bruner 1983:51), and a book does not have to be written in iambic pentameter. Jonathan London's *Who Bop?* is a brilliant example. Its language resembles do-wop scat singing:

Hip De-Dip
and HOP HOP HOP
we like to bo-bip
and do-wop the bop.

There is a long-standing tradition in children's literature that holds on to the importance of rhythm over 'making sense.' It goes back at least as far as Edward Lear's 1862 *Book of Nonsense*:

The Nutcrackers sate by a plate on the table,
  The Sugar-tongs sate by a plate at his side;
And the Nutcrackers said, 'Don't you wish we were able
  'Along the blue hills and green meadows to ride?
'Must we drag on this stupid existence for ever,
  'So idle so weary, so full of remorse,—
'While every one else takes his pleasure, and never
  'Seems happy unless he is riding a horse?'
    ('The Nutcrackers and the Sugar-Tongs')

Jack Prelutsky still wrote rhythmical nonsense verse in 1986, even throwing in some that sounds like vintage Lear:

> I went to Wyoming one day in the spring
> to hear a rhinoceros trying to sing,
> the sound was so strange that it gave me a fright,
> and I ran to Nebraska the very same night.
> (*Ride a Purple Pelican*, 54)

In rhythmic poetry, we experience children's literature at its most playful, and possibly also where the most intense entrainment occurs between adult and child (see Chapter 7).

Rhythmic nonsense verses connect to a yet older tradition, one that we may be in the process of losing. For centuries, some children's rhymes invoked the *motoric* aspect of speech production with choreographed movements for finger-plays (cf. Cullison 1915), rope jumping, and counting-out games. These traditions are not completely extinct: Some parents still know the finger motions to 'This is the church/This is the steeple' and the choreographies of 'I'm a little teapot short and stout' and 'Itsy Bitsy Spider' (a.k.a 'Eensy, Weensy Spider') However, to revisit the trove of rhymes that go with finger games and ritualized movements, one should have a look at Gloria T. Delamar's 1983 collection.[5] It begins with 'Pat-a-Cake' (1):

> Pat-a-cake, pat-a-cake, baker's man,
> Make me a cake as fast as you can;
> Prick it, and pat it, and mark it with a B,
> And put it in the oven for Baby and me.
>
> *Lines 1 & 2*: clap hands. *Line 3*: hold out left hand, palm down; with right had prick it, pat it, and mark it. *Line 4*: extend hands forward as though putting it in oven, then point away from self to indicate Baby, and then towards self. Very young children like to clap their hands throughout.

The adult may guide the infant's hands to synchronize the clapping motion. Clapping can even focus attention on phonemes or letters. In B-I-N-G-O, each letter is replaced in turn with a clap ('[clap] [clap] N-G-O'). Again, children can participate in the clapping even before they can sing the song themselves.

Synchronizing sound and motion is an obvious delight to the infant because it taps into a natural inborn tendency to respond with the entire body to adult speech (Condon & Sander 1974), no doubt owing to the early audio-motoric pathway (Figure 1.1). During the early stages of acquisition, a baby will gleefully participate in performing the ritualized gestures and motions in rhythm with the adult's chanting. The repetition, in turn, enables anticipation: What words come next and what motions come next?

Further assistance for predictive sound processing comes in the form of rhymes. Rhyming focuses on predicting a word that sounds like a previous word. A poem provides the ideal setting; an adult may even expectantly *withhold* a rhyme and wait for the baby to complete it. This could occur with a poem that is very familiar to the child, as in the following 18th-century 'Cradle Hymn' by Isaac Watts, published in the *New England Primer* and frequently reproduced, such as in the American *Lullabies and Ditties* sometime in the early 1870s (n.d.:5):

CRADLE HYMN

Hush, my dear, lie still and slumber;
   Holy angels guard thy bed;
Heavenly blessings without number,
   Gently falling on your head.

One can easily imagine the reader drawing out and raising the pitch of *your* . . ., waiting for the child to complete the verse with the word *head*, especially if the hymn was routinely read or sung at bedtime. Other books ask the child outright to complete a rhyme, and the expected rhyming word (or depicted object) is revealed under a flap or on the next page. Rick Brown's *What Rhymes with Snake?* (1994), for example, is drawn so that a part of a picture depicting an object such as a *pen* becomes part of another object partially obscured by a flap (a *hen*). Here, the delight is in the visual cue competing with the linguistic prediction, because while the rhyme is expected, the hidden object is not. Theodor Geisel ups the ante by violating predictability on both counts, visual and linguistic. Dr. Seuss' 1974 *There's a Wocket in my Pocket!* invents fantastic critters with fantastic names:

Sometimes
    I feel quite CERTAIN
       there's a JERTAIN
         in the CURTAIN.

One of the rhymes even includes a phonotactic violation, *zlock* (to rhyme with *clock*). On the surface, this is 'being silly'—but it is the attunement to sound play that makes this book both endearing and enduring for generations of children.

Dr. Seuss books generally include precisely the kinds of sound combinations whose high entropy (see p. 30) makes words even funnier than *Düsseldorf* and *Wuppertal*. While there is certainly a tradition of funny words in English children's literature (such as Fitzgerald's 1896 *The Zankiwank & the Bletherwitch*), Geisel goes a step further and delights with anomalies such as *illegal* consonant clusters (the *thnead* in *The Lorax* and the *thnadners* in *On Beyond Zebra*) and over-the-top repetitions (such as the *Zizzer-Zazzer-Zuzz*, 'as,' he has the nerve of adding in his *ABC*, 'you can plainly see'). For a detailed inventory of such 'Seuss-isms' see Kathleen Baker (1999) and Richard Lindemann (2005:ch. 3). Another author similarly surprised with a phonotactic violation discussed earlier (p. 34): One of the characters of Mo Willems is the *Knuffel Bunny*, pronounced with the /k/ as it is in the Dutch word for 'cuddle,' *knuffelen* (Willems 2015).

Finally, children's literature scaffolds phonemic perception and production with pauses and prosody. For infants and toddlers, pauses are crucial in detecting boundaries between words and phrases (Männel & Friederici 2009), whereas older children can make do with just the typical pitch change and syllable lengthening prior to the boundary (Steinhauer, Alter, & Friederici 1999). A stanza from another early children's poem, Rosetta B. Hastings' 'The Pretty Fire' (1883), illustrates the point:

> Nice fire, pleas-ant fire,
>   Warm the ba-by's nose;
> Put the foot-ies closer,
>   Warm the lit-tle toes.

Phrase boundaries fall at the end of each line, a natural place to lengthen the last syllable and to make a pause (of which the reader is additionally reminded by the punctuation).

While songbooks for children may nowadays not be quite as popular as recordings by gifted performers and composers such as Raffi or The Wiggles, their role in phonological discrimination should probably not be neglected. The National Institute of Environmental Health Sciences maintains a web page with children's songs under the appropriately named heading 'Kids Health' (kids.niehs.nih.gov/games/songs/childrens/). Here we find stalwarts like 'Ba Ba Black Sheep' and 'Happy and You Know It,' modern additions like Raffi's 'Baby Beluga,' and, truth be told, some entries where the adult words belie the childish melody, like the insalubrious 'Clementine' (whose widower grieves her drowning only 'Til' I kissed her little sister, and forgot my Clementine').

Children's Books and Phoneme Production

If books can provide effective interactive settings for infants to learn how to *pronounce* the sounds of their native languages, then it would seem like a good idea to have books with words composed from age-appropriate phonemes. For infants, all the vowels are fair game, and the consonants from the initial set /m/, /n/, /b/, /p/, /d/, /y/, /w/, and /h/ (see p. 35). Children's books focusing on a restricted set of phonemes do exist, but as far as I can tell they are intended as intervention for children who have a developmental speech problem. A notable author focusing on those initial speech sounds is early childhood specialist Victoria C. McErlean, who has published a 'Toddler Talk' series of books under her pen name Anita Shannon. One of these books, *Consonant-vowel Words*, has just the right set of phonemes, with words like *bee, no, dough, bow*, and *wee* (though it also includes *sea* and *key*).

Some mainstream noise books also highlight words with that initial set of phonemes: *moo, bah, hoo, meow, bow-wow*. They can be interactive in that the adult is expected to set up a frame and the child responds with the noise. Else the book can set up the frame. Eric Carle's *My Very First Book of Animal*

Sounds has the child match each animal with both its hallmark sound and habitat. Noise books can feature mini-narratives, such as *Moo, Baa, La La La* by Sandra Boynton:

A cow says moo.
A sheep says baa.
Three singing pigs say La La La!
"No, no!" you say,
"that isn't right.
The pigs say OINK
all day and night."

Mo Willems' *Who Says That, Cat the Cat?* has a cat ask each animal what its sound is—until it gets to the bunny, who doesn't have any ('Sounds like you need a hug!'). Other books invite toddlers to reproduce 'the sound of' objects from the environment, such as cars (*beep beep*—or, on older models, *awuurra, awuurra*), or sounds that go with emotions or sensations. Kali Stileman's *Snack Time for Confetti* sets up a recurring pattern for what foods Confetti and other animals respectively find *yum* or *yuk*.[6]

Interaction will certainly elicit a child's vocalization when repetition is involved (cf. p. 63). Bill Martin Jr. and John Archambault's repetition of the title phrase *Chicka Chicka Boom Boom* animates the child to chime in with 'boom boom' when it comes around again. The repetitions may be imitative, such as the steam engines' 'I can not. I can not. I can not.' and 'I think I can. I think I can. I think I can' of Watty Piper's *The Little Engine That Could* (1930). Repetitions may cap recurring scripts, as in P.D. Eastman's *Are You My Mother*, or they may be refrains of songs and poems ('If You're Happy and You Know It'). Repetitions were of course the prominent feature of Dick-and-Jane type primers (see p. 8).

For the child who has already mastered the full set of phonemes, a book may still offer some explorational challenges by being devilishly *difficult* to pronounce. Tongue twisters push the child's (and the adult's) motoric ability to produce sound sequences to the limit:

If you like to eat potato chips
and chew pork chops on clipper ships,
I suggest that you chew
a few chips and a chop
at Skipper Zipp's Clipper Ship Chip Chop Shop.
(*Oh Say can you Say?* 1979)

In the same book, Geisel also directly addresses the child's awareness of the differences between juvenile and adult command of pronunciation: 'Are you having trouble in saying this stuff? It's really quite easy for me.' Assuming these lines are read by an adult, this could also be epic tongue-in-cheek: Having outgrown the awareness of disparity ('only daddy can say "jump" '), the child now gleefully discovers that a book can provoke paternal pronunciation pratfalls.

Certainly, authors are aware of children's stages in producing sounds, especially when they alter the spelling to imitate 'baby talk.' In a late-19th-century[7] book entitled *Dolls and Pets* published by Lothrop in Boston, the anonymous author of 'How Ba-by Cleaned the Watch' simulates infant talk to describe how baby watched adults cleaning shiny things in water and resolved to do the same to a watch: 'Go-waw! go-waw-waw!' In *The Daisy Green Stories*, published in 1883 by the same company, author Susie A. Bisbee acknowledges her own daughter as the source of many of the 'childish sayings' in the book. We see consonant cluster reduction ('my mamma's seeping' p. 11) and substitutions for sounds that emerge later ('bruzzer' for *brother* p. 22, 'sink' for *think* p. 26, 'wecipes' for *recipes* p. 50), though not with consistency (e.g. 'truly' p. 49). Modern books will occasionally specifically address such features of child talk, such as *Hooway for Wodney Wat* by Helen Lester and Lynn M. Munsinger (2002), in which Rodney Rat overcomes a class bully notwithstanding his lack of mastery of the voiced retroflex apico-palatal lateral.

Phonics

Opportunities to listen and pronounce sounds in interactive book reading, from *ah-poooooooooo* to *Zizzer-Zazzer-Zuzz*, create a trajectory to literacy. A subgenre that caters to the lucrative scholastic market (cf. Yopp 1995) pays particular attention to phonetics and phonotactics: phonics books. They include

- books about individual phonemes, such as Alice K. Flanagan's *Play Day: The Sound of Long A* ;
- books about consonant 'blends,' such as Brian P. Cleary and Jason Miskimins' *The Frail Snail on the Trail* ;
- books that feature minimal pairs, such as Dr. Seuss's *There's a Wocket in my Pocket* ; and
- books that go through the entire alphabet, such as early primers and *Dr. Seuss' ABC* ('Aunt Annie's alligator . . .')

Others focus on phonemes with alliterations, rhymes, or tongue twisters, such as Lilian Obligado's *Faint Frogs Feeling Feverish and Other Terrifically Tantalizing Tongue Twisters* (1983) with its 'smiling snakes sipping strawberry sodas.'

Like whole-word primers and (if we believe those who bought the t-shirt) the University of Chicago, phonics books can be a place where fun comes to die. Books, once adorable and explorable, can now feel intrusive and directive.

One reason why phonics books feel so different is that the school setting presents a different schema from interactive book reading with a caretaker. Cooperation is now decidedly asymmetric and entails compliance. Unfortunately, phonics can be misleading enough to feel like entrapment to the complying child, undermining the good faith on which compliance is based before it morphs into coercion. In theory, the words presented to novice readers at the cusp of literacy are carefully selected to be phonics compatible. Alas, it is not that easy:

- Many of the high-frequency words in English are (paradoxically) irregular (*does, could, lamb*) and need to be presented as 'sight words' to memorize.
- Many of the 'sight words' on those lists, however, include words that do follow phonics rules (*this, all, but*), blurring the line between regular and irregular.
- Phonics rules can conflict. They license both the presence of the letter *t* in *pitch* /pɪč/ and its absence in *rich* /rɪč/. Any explanation of why it must be present here and absent there must remain arbitrary to the child.
- A teacher may not, in the moment, be able to appreciate what rules or analogies a child brought to the reading pronunciation of a written word. It takes an alert and linguistics-savvy teacher indeed to *appreciate* a child for reading the word *mould* as /mʊd/ (in analogy to *would*) or for spelling *rich* with a *t*.
- The same spelling may mean different things to children in the same classroom, depending on their native speech communities. Here in North Carolina, for example, there are speakers who have preserved the historic distinction between *wet* /wɛt/ and *whet* /ʰʍɛt/, but if they reproduce that distinction reflected in the traditional spellings (*w*- vs. *wh*-), they will likely be "corrected" and told that they succumbed to a 'spelling pronunciation.'

Unless phonics rules and whole-word memorization are carefully and expertly handled, delight in sound can turn into intimidation.

Another reason why phonics books function differently from the familiar children's books at home is that an unfamiliar adult's (the teacher's) speech becomes normative—and may be in face-threatening conflict with the speech that the child acquired at home and from peers. The very existence of a standard phonics literature assumes that all children should pronounce phonemes the 'standard' way. There has never been a 'standard pronunciation' in the U.S., certainly nothing approaching a "Received Pronunciation" of British English. Rendering phonics even more dysfunctional, there are currently three regional shifts in short vowels. For many speakers of American English, the vowels in *cot* and *caught* or in *pin* and *pen* have merged, or the vowels of *pen* and *man* have swapped, etc. (Labov 1996). Phonics books addressing vowels will not be perceived the same in the South, around the Great Lakes, and in California. As is the case with the child who is told that *rich* and *pitch* differ not only in the initial sounds but also in the presence or absence of a *t*, so the child learning that *pin* and *pen* are pronounced differently may be presented with assertions that are simply counter to fact within that speech community, in the name of literacy and with the authority of a self-proclaimed 'standard' speaker who purports to know 'better.'

Finally, phonics books introduce a challenge because kids in the very same classroom will have different sound perceptions and sound pronunciations. In 'Spotlight on Reading,' Bill Labov points out that some children will not perceive or pronounce a difference between *a coal stove* and *a cold stove*. The child with a Hispanic heritage language spoken at home will not fail to read *potato chips* as *potato ships*. Then again, a child who has first learned to write Spanish handily outperforms the child who grew up speaking English when it comes to the soft/hard *c* distinction in *certain* and *curtain*. Phonics books exist to level those differences—essentially, they represent institutionalized linguistic hegemony.

Overall, the phonics approach to literacy is based on the assumption that explicit (as opposed to tacit) phonemic awareness is a prerequisite to spelling. Experimental evidence that conscious phonemic awareness is a prerequisite to literacy is, however, shockingly anemic (Krashen 2003). *Conscious* phonemic awareness may be the *result* of knowing how to spell, not the other way around.

There are some areas in which phonics shines when it comes to developing explicit phonemic awareness. Labov ('Spotlight') points out that word-initial consonants are quite regular in English: 'Even struggling readers who are two years behind in the third grade have mastered the alphabetic principle: they get this first single consonant right 96% of the time!' That high rate may indicate a human perception bias in general, since so many languages, including early child language, only allow consonant-vowel syllables (and many, like Chinese, only monosyllabic consonant-vowel *words*). If that is so, then an abstract phoneme like /t/ may have language-specific prototypes—in English, the aspirated [t^h] preceding a stressed vowel.

As so often, Theodor Geisel's instincts here are right on: Some of his books—*Green Eggs and Ham, Hop on Pop, There's a Wocket in my Pocket*—exploit that regularity systematically.[8] Many of the words rhyme in minimal pairs such that only the first phoneme is different:

> THING
> SING
> That thing can sing!
> SONG
> LONG
> A long, long song
> (*Hop on Pop*)

Note, too, how the repetitive parallelism sets up the focus on those minimal pairs.

Growing to the Sounds of English: What Children's Books Contribute

A young child grows into the sounds of her native language(s) in two complementary processes: bottom-up pattern detection ('taking statistics') and top-down rule

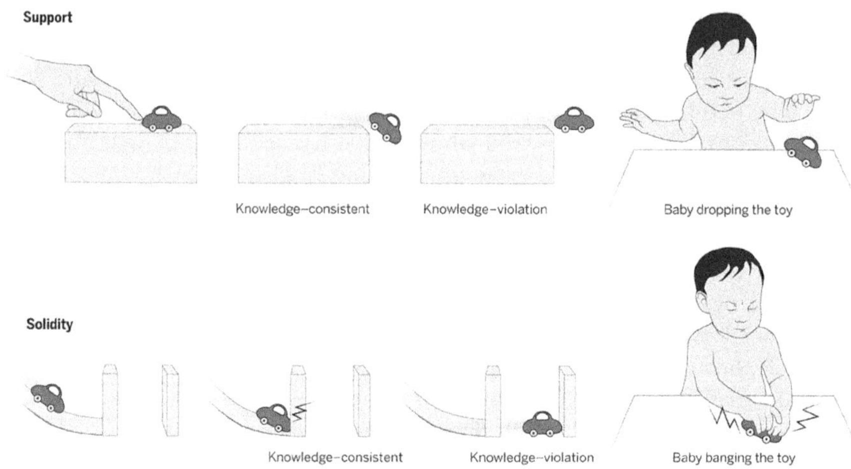

Figure 1.3 Violated Expectations Trigger Exploration

(Schulz 2015:43)

formation, associated with different pathways in the brain. Acquisition proceeds from sensori-motor understanding to feature abstraction—a gain in economy and robustness of processing. The production of sounds, subsequently, increases as the child learns to speak more and more with an adult inventory. The maturation of perception and production follows regular stages and within those stages also reflects frequency effects. We observe both stages of acquisition and frequency effects because the rich data provided in interaction provide the *triggers* for maturation, and they provide *models* of usage.

Children's books provide opportunities for such interaction; indeed, they *add* contributions all their own. They contribute esthetic devices that do not normally occur in child-directed speech: Rhythm, rhyme, alliteration, repetition, sound play, minimal pairs, funny-sounding words, and even phonotactic violations. These departures from child-directed talk surprise the child, meaning that the child has linguistic expectations that these books can violate, arousing linguistic curiosity and exploration.

In Chapter 2, I shall review Chomsky's claim that neonates are endowed with intuitive understanding of such concepts as physical object, intention, goal, etc. that assist in building the initial lexical categories (p. 60). Such expectations can be demonstrated experimentally. In lab setups, infants not yet one year old (11 months), for example, can watch a toy car drive off a block and continue its forward trajectory instead of falling to the ground (Figure 1.3). Other infants observe the car rolling down a ramp and behind a curtain that partially conceals two boards in the way of the car—except that when the curtain is removed, the car appears to have come to rest against the second board, as if it had somehow rolled right through the first. If those infants are presented with a choice of objects (one that was just involved in a physical violation and one novel item), they reach for

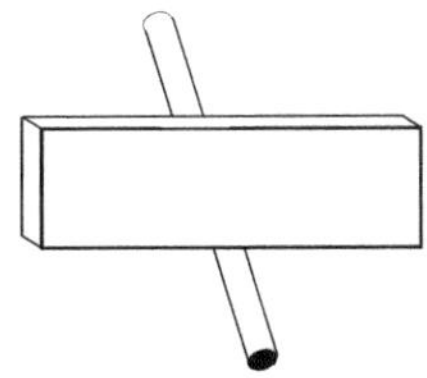

Figure 1.4 Infant Assumptions About a Partly Obscured Object
After Kellman & Spelke 1983

the one that had just surprised them. Then they explore it. The car that just failed to fall down after driving off a block is dropped; if it just appears to have rolled through a solid object, however, the car is banged on the table (Stahl & Feigenson 2015; Schulz 2015). Not only did such experiments document how children snap into explorer mode, they also showed that their exploration results in linguistic learning. If the surprising object is presented with a sound, the infants will associate that object with the sound; they do not as readily associate a sound with an object that has not surprised them (ibid.).

For infants to have expectations violated and to experience surprise, they must have some 'core knowledge' about the world (Stahl & Feigenson 2015:91). That, too, can be tested. Very young infants have been presented with projections of angles on a screen, to find out when they no longer find them novel (i.e. when they habituate to them). The angles change from obtuse to acute (or vice versa), or they change in orientation. Six-week-olds paid attention to both changes in degree and in orientation, while 14-week olds preferably paid attention to changes in degree (Slater et al. 1991). The babies realized when an angle is the same regardless of what direction it points to—a rule-based attenuation just like the abstracted same-ness in allophones of a single phoneme. Slater et al. replicated this test after Cohen and Younger (1984), who found that even newborns can already abstract away from the angle's orientation, which implies that their ability is part of genetic 'core knowledge.' Later experiments indicate that this 'core knowledge' is universal, i.e. independent of culture (Dehaene et al. 2006). It, in effect, explains the results of so many habituation experiments with infants. If four-month-old infants, for instance, become familiar with a setup where a rod partly obscured by a block (Figure 1.4) traverses back and forth, and then are surprised when the block is removed and there are actually *two* rods with a gap where the block used to be (Kellman & Spelke 1983), then they are exploring something that violates their expectation. There is really no other explanation for their behavior.

Thneads, *zlocks*, and *knuffel bunnies* similarly violate the child's linguistic expectations. Phonotactic surprises surely trigger the same explorer instinct as a toy car that appeared to levitate. When children's books add sounds like *mmmzzmmmmmmmmmm* and outlier sound combinations, they arouse interest and trigger exploration. And in turn, surprise and curiosity elicit something that both the reading adult and the intrigued child can share: delight.

Notes

1. Other animals can perceive human speech sounds as well, so those pattern detection pathways must be old indeed. Humans have a long-standing association with animals that understand spoken commands, such as elephants. Chaser, a border collie trained by Wofford College psychology professor John Pilley, has learned to interpret the meaning of some 1,000 human words (mostly for toys and commands) and has reached a level of attainment where he can even associate a new name with a new toy by elimination and fast mapping (NovascienceNow).
2. This author can personally confirm how surely a newborn identifies the rhythms and melodies of a story from other prose, having recited *Die Prinzessin auf der Erbse* ('The Princess on the Pea,' Hans Christian Andersen) to my pregnant wife's belly each night for the last 4 months of her pregnancy. Two days after Erik was born, he grew fussy. He did not want to nurse and could not be comforted. I laid him, chest to chest, against my skin. I talked to him about various topics and after a few minutes began the story, without pause or transition. He instantly stopped fussing, looked up towards me intently, listened with complete calm, and after the story was over fell asleep on my chest.
3. Marie Winn vindicated Hersey's impression of television's 'hypnotic effect' with her observation that children in front of television sets are not interacting but go into an altered state, which makes the TV an insidious babysitter indeed when it comes to language acquisition. Winn went so far so to assume a negative effect of the screen on language *development* and even literacy: Over the years, we may have witnessed a negative correlation between screen time and verbal SAT scores (2002).
4. I meant this to be an allusion to the 'Toot Sweets' in Roald Dahl's movie adaptation of Ian Fleming's *Chitty Chitty Bang Bang*, which is, after all, set in 'Vulgaria.'
5. I was made aware of this resource by Mark West, UNC Charlotte.
6. *Yuk* and *yum* are, of course, known to literate adults as the two mantras of *Still Life with Woodpecker* (Tom Robbins 1980:46).
7. Not dated, but between 1875 and 1887 because the address is given as '32 Franklin Street.'
8. Quite possibly, there is a bit more than just instinct to Geisel's work. A 1965 dissertation by Anna Marie Gruber found that *Hop on Pop* and the *ABC* book are well suited for teaching literacy to kindergartners with a modified spelling-pattern approach developed by linguist Charles C. Fries (1964). Just how much Geisel knew about linguistics is an intriguing question, given the quality of his work, and awaits future exploration.

References

Aigner-Clark, Julie. 2001. Nurturing a 'baby' book: Littleton woman's line of videos, CDs a hit with children. *Denver Post*, 30 May, C-01.

Ambridge, Ben; Evan Kidd; Caroline F. Rowland; and Anna L. Theakston. 2015. The ubiquity of frequency effects in first language acquisition. *Journal of Child Language* 42.239–73.

Ari-Even Roth, Daphne; Minka Hildesheimer; Ilan Roziner; and Yael Henking. 2016. Evidence for a right-ear advantage in newborn hearing screening results. *Trends in Hearing* 20.1–8.

Baker, Kathleen. 1999. Seussisms and violations to universal language constraints. *Working Papers in Linguistics* 6 (Fall). George Mason University. Online: www.gmu.edu/org/lingclub/WP/texts/6_Baker.pdf.

Beckman, Mary E., and Jan Edwards. 2010. Generalizing over lexicons to predict consonant mastery. *Laboratory Phonology* 1(2).319–43.

Bergelson, Elika, and Richard N. Aslin. 2017. Nature and origins of the lexicon in 6-mo-olds. *PNAS—Publications of the National Academy of Sciences* (early edition, September). Online: www.pnas.org/cgi/doi/10.1073/pnas.1712966114.

Berko, Jean. 1958. The child's learning of English morphology. *Word* 14.150–77.

Blache, Stephen E. 1978. *The acquisition of distinctive features*. Baltimore: University Park Press.

Bliven, Jr., Bruce 1946. Child's best seller. *LIFE* 21(23) (2 December).59–66.

Bonatti, Luca L.; Marcela Peña; Marina Nespor; and Jacques Mehler. 2007. On consonants, vowels, chickens, and eggs. *Psychological Science* 18(10) (November).924–25.

Boysson-Bardies, Bénédicte de; Laurent Sagart; and Catherine Durant. 1984. Discernible differences in the babbling of infants according to target-language. *Journal of Child Language* 11(1).1–15.

Bruderer, Alison G.; D. Kyle Danielson; Padmapriya Kandhadai; and Janet F. Werker. 2015. Sensorimotor influences on speech perception in infancy. *PNAS—Proceedings of the National Academy of Science of the United States* 112(44).13531–36.

Bruner, Jerome S. 1978. The role of dialogue in language acquisition. *The child's conception of language*, ed. by A. Sinclair, R. J. Jarvella, and W. J. M. Levelt, 241–56. New York: Springer-Verlag.

Bruner, Jerome S. 1983. *Child's talk: Learning to use language*. New York: Norton.

Buchwald, Adam. 2005. Representing sound structure: Evidence from aphasia. *Proceedings of the 24th West Coast conference on formal linguistics*, ed. by John Alderete et al., 79–87. Somerville, MA: Cascadilla Proceedings Project.

Carmichael, Mary. 2009. Health matters: Making medical decisions for kids. *Newsweek*, 30 January. Online: www.newsweek.com/health-matters-making-medical-decisions-kids-77773.

Chomsky, Noam A. 1959. Review of *Verbal Behavior* by B. F. Skinner. *Language* 35.26–58.

Chomsky, Noam A. 1965. *Aspects of the theory of syntax*. Cambridge, MA: MIT Press

Chomsky, Noam A. 1984. *Modular approaches to the study of the mind: First distinguished graduate research lecture*. San Diego: San Diego State University Press.

Chomsky, Noam A. 1988. *Language and problems of knowledge: The Managua lectures*. Cambridge, MA: MIT Press.

Chomsky, Noam A. 2011. Language and the cognitive science revolution(s): Text of lecture given at the Carleton University, 8 April 2011. Partial transcript courtesy of David P. Wilkins. Online: www.chomsky.info/talks/20110408.htm.

Chomsky, Noam A., and Morris Halle. 1968. *The sound pattern of English*. New York: Harper & Row.

Cohen, Leslie B., and Barbara A. Younger. 1984. Infant perception of angular relations. *Infant Behavior and Development* 7(1).37–47.

Condon, William S., and Lours W. Sander. 1974. Synchrony demonstrated between movements of the neonate and adult speech. *Child Development* 45.456–62.

Cullison, Irene Margaret. 1915. *Mother Goose finger plays*. Philadelphia: George W. Jacobs.

de Boysson-Bardies, Bénédicte; Laurent Sagart; and Catherine Durant. 1984. Discernible differences in the babbling of infants according to target language. *Journal of Child Language* 11(1).1–15.

DeCasper, Anthony J., and Melanie J. Spence. 1986. Prenatal maternal speech influences newborns' perception of speech sound. *Infant Behavior and Development* 9.133–50.

Dehaene, Stanislas; Véronique Izard; Pierre Pica; and Elizabeth Spelke. 2006. Core knowledge of geometry in an Amazonian Indigene group. *Science* 311(5759) (20 January).381–84.

Delamar, Gloria T. 1983. *Children's counting-out rhymes, fingerplays, jump-rope and bounce-ball chants and other rhythms: A comprehensive English-language reference*. Jefferson, NC: McFarland.

DeMille, Mellissa M. C.; Kevin Tang; Chintan M. Mehta; Christopher Geissler; Jeffrey G. Malins; Natalie R. Powers; Beatrice M. Bowen; Andrew K. Adams; Dongnhu T. Truong; Jan C. Frijters; and Jeffrey R. Gruen. 2018. Worldwide distribution of the DCDC2 READ1 regulatory element and its relationship with phoneme variation across languages. *PNAS Latest Articles—Proceedings of the National Academy of Science of the United States*. www.pnas.org/cgi/doi/10.1073/pnas.1710472115.

Dunstan, Priscilla. 2012. *Calm the crying: The secret baby language that reveals the hidden meaning behind an infant's cry*. New York: Avery.

Edwards, Jan; Mary E. Beckman; and Benjamin Munson. 2015. Frequency effects in phonological acquisition. *Journal of Child Language* 42(2) (March).306–11.

Eimas, Peter D.; Einar R. Siqueland; Peter Jusczyk; and James Vigorito. 1971. Speech perception in infants. *Science* 171(3968, New Series) (22 January).303–06.

Friederici, Angela D. 2011. The brain basis of language processing: From structure to function. *Physiological Review* 91(4).1357–92.

Friederici, Angela D.; Regine Oberecker; and Jens Brauer. 2012. Neurophysiological preconditions of syntax acquisition. *Psychological Research* 76(2).204–11.

Fries, Charles C. 1964. Linguistics and the teaching of reading. *The Reading Teacher* 17(8) (May).594–98.

Fromkin, Victoria A. 1971. The non-anomalous nature of anomalous utterances. *Language* 47(1).27–52.

Goldman, Ronald, and Macalyne Fristoe. n.d. Goldman-Fristoe test of articulation 3. PsychCorp—Pearson Clinical. Online: www.pearsonclinical.com/language/products/100001202/goldman-fristoe-test-of-articulation-3-gfta-3.html.

Gruber, Anna Marie. 1965. An investigation of the learning of kindergarten children taught by a modified Fries' linguistic approach in combination with Dr. Seuss' beginner books. Indiana University: Ph.D. dissertation.

Hayden, Rebecca E. 1950. The relative frequency of phonemes in general American English. *Word* 6(3).217–23. doi:10.1080/00437956.1950.11659381.

Hersey, John. 1954. Why do students bog down on the first R? A local committee sheds light on a national problem: Reading. *LIFE* 36(21) (24 May).136–50.

Hindman, Annemarie H.; Lori E. Skibbe; and Tricia D. Foster. 2014. Exploring the variety of parental talk during shared book reading and its contributions to preschool language and literacy: Evidence from the Early Childhood Longitudinal Study-Birth Cohort. *Reading and Writing* 27(2) (February).287–313.

Husain, Taha. 2017. The effect of voice-onset time and aspiration on dichotic listening. Paper presented at the southeastern conference on linguistics LXXXIV, 11 March. Charleston, SC: College of Charleston.

Jakobson, Roman. 1968. *Child language, aphasia, and phonological universals* [*Kindersprache, Aphasie und allgemeine Lautgesetze* (1941)], translated by Allan R. Keiler. The Hague: Mouton.

Kellman, Philip J., and Elizabeth S. Spelke. 1983. Perception of partly-obscured objects in infancy. *Cognitive Psychology* 15.483–524.

Kisilevsky, Barbara S.; S. M. J. Hains; C. A. Brown, C. T. Lee; B. Cowperthwaite; S. S. Stutzman; M. L. Swansburg; K. Lee; X. Xie; H. Huang; H.-H. Ye; K. Zhang; and

Z. Wang. 2009. Fetal sensitivity to properties of maternal speech and language. *Infant Behavior & Development* 32.59–71.

Krashen, Stephen. 2003. False claims about phonemic awareness, phonics, skills vs. whole language, and recreational reading. *NoChildLeft.com* (May) 1(5). Online: www.nochildleft.com/2003/may03reading.html.

Kuhl, Patricia K. 2010. Brain mechanisms in early language acquisition. *Neuron* 67 (9 September).713–27.

Kuhl, Patricia K. 2011. The linguistic genius of babies. *TED Talk*, February. Online: www.ted.com/talks/patricia_kuhl_the_linguistic_genius_of_babies/transcript?language=en.

Kuhl, Patricia K., and James D. Miller. 1975. Speech perception by the chinchilla: Voiced-voiceless distinction on alveolar plosive consonants. *Science* 190(4209) (October).69–72.

Labov, William. 1996. The organization of dialect diversity in North America. *Fourth International Conference on Language Processing*, Philadelphia, 6 October. Online: www.ling.upenn.edu/phono_atlas/ICSLP4.html.

Labov, William. n.d. Spotlight on reading. Presentation handout. Online: www.ling.upenn.edu/~wlabov/Spotlight.pdf.

Labov, William, and Teresa Labov. 1978. The phonetics of *cat* and *mama*. *Language* 54(4).816–52.

Levelt, Clara, and Marc van Oostendorp. 2007. Feature co-occurrence constraints in L1 acquisition. *Linguistics in the Netherlands 2007*, ed. by Bettelou Los and Marjo van Koppen (AVT publications), vol. 24, 162–72. Utrecht: Algemene Vereniging voor Taalwetenschap, John Benjamins.

Lindemann, Richard H. F. 2005. *The Dr. Seuss catalog: An annotated guide to works by Theodor Geisel in all media, writings about him and appearances of characters and places in the books, stories, and films*. Jefferson, NC: McFarland.

Linden, Eugene. 1999. *The Parrot's Lament: And other true tales of animal intrigue, intelligence, and ingenuity*. New York: Plume, Penguin.

Long, Christopher P. 2011. *Aristotle on the nature of truth*. Cambridge: Cambridge University Press.

Mampe, Birgit; Angela D. Friederici; Anne Christophe; and Kathleen Wermke. 2009. Newborns' cry melody is shaped by their native language. *Current Biology* 19(23).1994–97.

Männel, Claudia, and Angela D. Friederici. 2009. Pauses and intonational phrasing: ERP studies in 5-month-old German infants and adults. *Journal of Cognitive Neuroscience* 21.1988–2006.

Martins, Pedro T., and Cedric Boeckx. 2014. Attention mechanisms and the mosaic evolution of speech. *Frontiers in Psychology* 5 (December).1–4.

Maye, Jessica; Janet F. Werker; and LouAnn Gerken. 2002. Infant sensitivity to distributional information can affect phonetic discrimination. *Cognition* 82.B101–11.

McGurk, Harry, and John MacDonald. 1976. Hearing lips and seeing voices. *Nature* 264 (23 December).746–48.

NovascienceNow. 2011. The dog who knows 1,000 words, with Neil Degrasse Tyson. Online: youtu.be/_6479QAJuz8.

Pembrey, Marcus E. 2018. Does cross-generational epigenetic inheritance contribute to cultural continuity? *Environmental Epigenetics* 4(2).1–8. Online: https://doi.org/10.1093/eep/dvy004.

Pinker, Steven. 1994. *The language instinct: How the mind creates language*. New York: Morrow.

Pinker, Steven. 1999. *Words and rules: The ingredients of language*. New York: Basic Books, Perseus.

Robbins, Tom. 1980. *Still life with woodpecker*. New York: Bantam.

Saha, Biswanath; Parimal Kumar Purkait; Jayanta Mukherjee; Arun Kumar Majumdar; Bandana Majumdar; and Arun Kumar Singh. 2013. An embedded system for automatic classification of neonatal cry. *2013 IEEE Point-of-Care Healthcare Technologies (PHT)*, 248–51, Bangalore, India, 16–18 January.

Schulz, Laura. 2015. Infants explore the unexpected. *Science* 348(6230) (3 April).42–43.

Sedivy, Julie. 2014. *Language in mind: An introduction to psycholinguistics*. Sunderland, MA: Sinauer.

Selinker, Larry. 1972. Interlanguage. *IRAL: International Review of Applied Linguistics in Language Teaching* 10(3).209–31.

Shriberg, Lawrence D. 1993. Four new speech and voice-prosody measures for genetics research and other studies in developmental phonological disorders. *Journal of Speech, Language, and Hearing Research* 36(1).105–40.

Shukla, Moninish; Katherine S. White; and Richard N. Aslin. 2011. Prosody guides the rapid mapping of word forms onto visual objects in 6-mo-old infants. *PNAS—Proceedings of the National Academy of Science of the United States* 108(15).6038–43.

Skinner, B[urrhus] F[rederic]. 1957. *Verbal behavior* (The century psychology series). New York: Appleton-Century-Crofts.

Slater, Alan; Anne Mattock; Elizabeth Brown; and J. Gavin Brenner. 1991. Form perception at birth: Cohen and Younger (1984) revisited. *Journal of Experimental Child Psychology* 51(3).395–405.

Smith, Jennifer L. 2010. Review of Paul de Lacy, *The Cambridge handbook of phonology* (Cambridge University Press 2007). *Phonology* 27.527–41.

Smith, Neilson V. 1973. *The acquisition of phonology: A case study*. Cambridge: Cambridge University Press.

Soltis, Joseph. 2004. The signal functions of early infant crying. *Behavioral and Brain Sciences* 27.443–90.

Sosa, Anna V. 2016. Association of the type of toy used during play with the quantity and quality of parent-infant communication. *JAMA Pediatrics* 170(2) (February).132–37.

Stahl, Aimee E., and Lisa Feigenson. 2015. Observing the unexpected enhances infants' learning and exploration. *Science* 348(6230) (3 April).91–4.

Steiner, Violette G., and Roberta Evatt Pond. 1970. *Finger play fun*. Columbus, OH: Charles E. Merrill, Bell & Howell.

Steinhauer, Karsten; Kai Alter; and Angela D. Friederici. 1999. Brain potentials indicate immediate use of prosodic cues in natural speech processing. *Nature Neuroscience* 2(2).191–96.

Templin, Mildred C. 1957. *Certain language skills in children: Their development and interrelationships* (Institute of child welfare monograph series), vol. 26. Minneapolis: University of Minnesota Press.

Tierney, Adam, and Nina Kraus. 2013. The ability to move to a beat is linked to the consistency of neural responses to sound. *The Journal of Neuroscience* 33(38) (18 September).14981–88.

Toro, Juan M.; Marina Nespor; Jacques Mehler; and Luca L. Bonatti. 2008. Finding words and rules in a speech stream. *Psychological Science* 19(2) (March).137–44.

Tsunoda, Tadanobu. 1975. Functional differences between right- and left-cerebral hemispheres detected by the key-tapping method. *Brain and Language* 2.152–70.

Werker, Janet F., and Richard C. Tees. 1984. Cross-language speech perception: Evidence for perceptual reorganization during the first year of life. *Infant Behavior and Development* 7.49–63.

Westbury, Chris; Cyrus Shaoul; Gail Moroschan; and Michael Ramscar. 2016. Telling the world's least funny jokes: On the quantification of humor as entropy. *Journal of Memory and Language* 86 (January).141–56.

Whalen, Douglas H. 1990. Coarticulation is largely planned. *Haskins Laboratories Status Report on Speech Research* SR-101(1102).149–76. Online: www.haskins.yale.edu/sr/SR101/SR101_10.pdf.

Willems, Mo. 2015. I want my books to be played. Transcript of 'Ask Me Another', 12 February. NPR. Online: www.npr.org/templates/transcript/transcript.php?storyId=385546965.

Williamson, Graham. 2011. *Speech sound development chart, from English speech sounds: Phonemes, allophones, and variations in connected speech* (e-book). Online: www.sltinfo.com/wp-content/uploads/2014/01/speech-sound-development-chart.pdf.

Windsor, Jennifer; Leslie E. Glaze; and Sebastian F. Koga. 2007. Language acquisition with limited input: Romanian institution and foster care. *Journal of Speech, Language, and Hearing Research* 50 (October).1365–81.

Winn, Marie. 1977. *The plug-in drug: Television, children, and the family*. New York: Viking.

Winn, Marie. 2002. *The plug-in drug: Television, computers, and family life*. New York: Penguin.

Wright, Sylvia. 1957. *Get Away from me with those Christmas gifts*. New York: McGraw-Hill.

Yang, Charles. 2013. Ontogeny and phylogeny of language, ed. by William Labov. *PNAS: Publications of the National Academy for Science of the United States* 110(16).6324–27. Online: www.pnas.org/cgi/doi/10.1073/pnas.1216803110.

Yopp, Hallie Kay. 1995. Read-aloud books for developing phonemic awareness: An annotated bibliography. *Teaching Reading* 48(6) (March).538–43.

2 Matching World to Mind

The Lexicon

They went together everywhere—
in the  and in the ,
and over to Grandfathers.
Mary's Little Lamb
Edith Francis Foster, 1903

Like Mary's little lamb, our words go with us everywhere. They tell us whether the structure we are in is a house or a barn, and whether the house belongs to someone (grandfather's) or we to it ('home'). How do words get started? Are first words anything like adult words? First words seem to have an altogether different kind of existence in a baby's brain. They emerge at an age that leaves almost no lasting memories: In the earliest stages of a child's development, experiences *build* cortical areas, thus the first words of a human being are not really *entries* in a lexicon—they are lexical prototypes for *categories*. The initial lexicon is seeded with those prototypes, which then attract items whose similarity is determined by set-making rules operating on semantic features, rules that build hierarchical semantic fields and can adjust them dynamically. Children's books as well move from prototypical objects in cardboard picturebooks to feature-based books (things that are yellow, different kinds of trucks, etc.). Before long, books like Edith Francis Foster's start calling attention to the word as a symbol.

Adding Something to . . . Nothing?

Imagine a produce shop in June, the displays laden with fruit. In one bin is something exotic: knobby red balls, golf-ball sized. You ask. Note how many nouns the helpful vendor is using to relate to the item in question:

> Oh, yes. They taste like a **fruit**, but they are actually a **nut**. But you don't eat the nut, you peel off the **skin**, which I guess would be its **shell**, and you eat the white **flesh**. They have a great **taste**, somewhere between a **cherry** and a **plum**. They're called **lychees** (Figure 2.1).

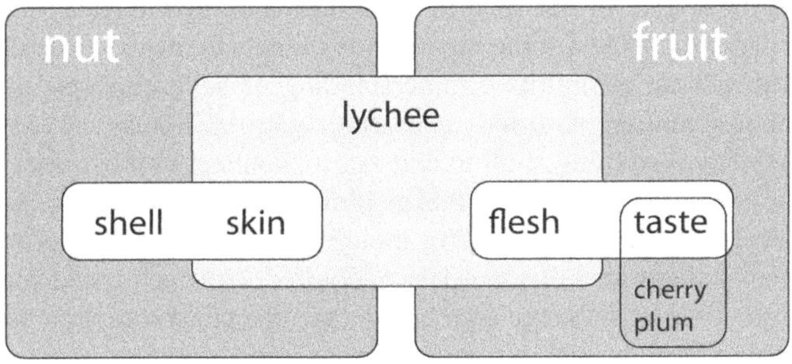

Figure 2.1 Semantic Net: Explaining What a 'Lychee' Is

You just suspended your disbelief and made some cross-categorial connections: A nut can be encased in flesh that tastes like a cherry or plum. A shell does not have to be hard and brittle but can be peeled like an elastic skin. The vendor might not be a trustworthy source: Maybe the outer casing is not exactly the equivalent of a nutshell, since the nut is what's inside the fruit flesh. Not a problem for humans—there are sufficient associations to re-position the entry 'lychee' in our mental lexicon. Large semantic networks are supremely flexible, and they excel at accommodating continuous adjustments, corrections, additions, and deletions (forgetting).

How does a baby *acquire* her first words? There are no other words to relate a new word to, no lexicon within which a word would make 'sense' relative to the semantic features of other words. If humans start out as a blank slate (*tabula rasa*), then solely experience can structure the mind, as John Locke presumed. However, that assertion on its own cannot explain how first experiences *organize* sense in a mental empty space where nothing else is yet anchored. Jerome S. Bruner called it the 'Apostle principle'—'that to learn something about a domain requires that you already know something about the domain and that, perhaps, there is no such thing as *ab initio* learning pure and simple' (1978:243).

The mind comes endowed to 'make sense.' There is a long history to the idea that humans are born with initial-state cognitive endowments. Plato surmised how this could be so: Human life has a prequel. Pre-birth, humans knew the concepts of logic and mathematics and language (Greek, what else), knowledge lost with the trauma of birth (amnesia). Exposure triggers those concepts like forgotten memories. They can be midwived by a good Socratic teacher, and we un-forget (anamnesis): We connect new experiences to concepts that are already within us. Similarly, Talmud *Niddah* 30b conceived that a fetus knows all of Torah (Proverbs 4:4 says 'And he taught me'), but that just before birth, an angel touches the child above the lips, causing amnesia—and also the vertical groove between lip and nose ('Touched by an Angel'). When the growing child encounters a truth thereafter, it will be instantly familiar and attractive.

If for Plato's 'pre-existence' and Talmud's instruction *in utero* we substitute 'genetics' as the source of our species' existence and knowledge, then our brains come equipped with at least some innate endowments to make sense of the world. Those would include an intuitive understanding of such concepts as 'physical object, human intention, volition, causation, goal' (Chomsky 1988:32). First words, if they have anything at all to connect to, connect to those concepts. Wittgenstein, for one, couldn't help but feel as if every word falls 'into a mould of my mind *long* prepared for it' (1958:170), though that mold disappears when filled. Noam Chomsky elaborated that words are acquired with such speed and precision that there is no alternative to the conclusion that 'the child somehow has the concepts available before experience with language and is basically learning labels for concepts that are already part of his or her conceptual apparatus' (1988:28).

The mind in its initial state cannot be a blank slate. There must be some endowment for learning, and some endowment for language. Language acquisition cannot be explained exclusively by learning. Indeed, applying the psychology of learning to language acquisition reminded Bruner of 'C.K. Ogden's parable of the man who wished to find out about Chinese metaphysics and consulted first "China" and then "Metaphysics" in the *Encyclopaedia Britannica* ' (1978:244). More likely, there is a *structural* endowment of pathways, each dedicated to and waiting for specific kinds of experiences in order to mature. Language grows in the 'interplay of initially given structures of mind, maturational processes, and interaction with the environment' (Chomsky 1971:23). The times during which those first specific experiences must trigger such growth are themselves quite specific.

Initial-State Lexicon and the Critical Period

We know about Critical Periods ever since Konrad Lorenz's (1935) pioneering work on imprinting. Lorenz was initially unaware that he was about to pioneer anything; he was relishing the sight of a graylag goose chick hatching in the incubator. He wiped it down with some cotton to free the down feathers from their protective sheaths. What happened next took his research into uncharted territory. The tiny gosling fixed him with one eye, as a bird would when it studies something in detail. She stretched her neck and lowered it, tweeting a perfect graylag goose greeting. The biologist took the chick and slipped her underneath a sitting house-goose who was hatching her own brood. Lorenz heard a questioning *wiwiwiwiwi?* from underneath the hen, to which the matriarch responded with a reassuring *gangangangang*. But the chick was not reassured. She emerged from the warm feathers of mother goose, gave distress calls, and ran toward Lorenz. He returned her, but the chick ran toward him again and to greet him. 'It would have softened a stone,' he recalled. The history-making chick's name was Martina, and Lorenz became her mother. He did not even attempt to insinuate the remainder of the hatchlings in the incubator into the care of other birds. He was now the proud leader of a flock (1949:138–59). The flock led him, in turn, to call for a new fundamental science of *innate forms of thinking* (1941:100).

When birds imprint, they respond (exclusively and irreversibly) to a stimulus during a brief and specific window of time. Once that window closes, there is no more imprinting. Mammals, it turns out, have critical periods for cortical functions as well. The experiments of David Hubel and Torsten Wiesel (1962) demonstrated what happens when one such window closes for domestic kittens. Cells in the cat's visual cortex organize to respond to vertical lines, horizontal lines, angles, etc.—and fail to do so if such visual input is absent during that narrow time period. Stimuli presented *after* the critical period no longer make dedicated neurons develop, and they atrophy. (Hubel and Wiesel also observed cortical 'plasticity': If there is no input from one eye, the cortical space normally dedicated to its retina is claimed by the kitten's other eye.)

Language development toward a full grammar, too, has a genetic timeline, as Steven Pinker pointed out. Pinker called language acquisition a 'one-shot skill': Once the mold is filled, so to speak, 'language-acquisition circuitry is not needed' anymore and should atrophy 'if keeping it around incurs any costs' (1994:294)—the obvious costs being the disproportionate amount of energy that a brain burns through even at rest. The brain, he argued, is *designed* to eliminate those circuits when a stage of maturation would chronologically make them redundant—marking the end of a Critical Period.

Acquisition *is* cortical maturation (p. 13) because it builds cortical structures. That is why we do not consciously remember anything from our first year: We can remember content we have *learned*, not structures we have *acquired*. The order in which those dedicated language areas interface will remain the order in which adults process speech, and that order remains stable for learning foreign languages as well.[1]

Baby's first 100 words reflect how infants understand their environments. From a list of first words compiled from a questionnaire by Leslie Rescorla, Nan Bernstein Ratner extracted 25 words that every two-year-old 'should know' (Evans 2012), mostly nouns:

(7)	Nouns	people:	*Mommy, Daddy, baby*
		food:	*milk, juice, banana, cookie*
		animals:	*dog, cat*
		toys:	*ball*
		body parts:	*nose, eye*
		vehicles:	*car*
		actions:	*bath*
		clothes:	*shoe, hat*
		personal:	*book*
	Adj., modifiers:		*all gone, hot*
	Adv., quantifiers:		*more*
	social words:		*hello, bye-bye, yes, no, thank-you*

Ratner's cherry-picked list came out a bit skewed: Rescorla's inventory also includes verbs such as *hug* and *eat* and *tickle*, as well as some prepositions, *on* and *off*. Either way, all items fall into groups of what is salient: entities, actions, qualities, or directions that matter to the infant. We do not hear words for *ceiling, shelf*, or *gutter*, even if those objects are present in the environment. Baby couldn't care less.

First words are prototypes; they seed semantic categories and attract other words to build lexical fields. Lexical fields such as body parts, foods, living things, proper names, things that can be manipulated by hand, or colors represent the core architecture of the lexicon. Those must be the categories to which the child comes with 'intuitive understanding' (Chomsky 1988:32), i.e. automatically, hence irreversibly. We know that those categories have neuropsychological reality because they can be selectively lesioned. The medical literature describes very specific anomias that correspond to categories established during acquisition. A stroke victim may no longer be able to name body parts, to put names to faces, to identify facial expressions, to correctly identify animals or tools, to recall the names of colors or of fruits and vegetables, for example. A link between aphasia and acquired categories was established by Fernando Cuetosa, Asunción Monsalvea, and Alicia Pérez (2005), and what connects the two is *age of acquisition* (i.e. not frequency of use).

If first words represent prototypes for categories, then some of the semantic 'laws' or 'biases' of early child language follow, notably these two:

- **exclusivity**: There is a one-to-one mapping between word and reference. A bunny cannot simultaneously be a rabbit.
- **whole-object**: A word must refer to the entire concept, not to a subcomponent. If an adult points at a stove and says 'hot,' then the entire object will be labeled as 'hot.'[2]

Before a referent can have more than one label, and before attention can be given to its subcomponents, the basic concepts must be confirmed—the prototypes to which all entries and semantic features in the same category measure up.

When these pioneer lexical fields start attracting *entries*, the young child shifts from acquisition to learning. Unlike acquisition, learning is reversible, and how high up or how far down the lexical tree a word maps is subject to continuous revision and overlearning. During this period of rapid adjustment ('vocabulary spurt'), a word like *doggie* could be underused, referring only to the family's dog like a proper noun (underextension), or overused as a temporary superordinate term, referring generically to domestic, furry, four-legged creatures (overextension). Rematching the features of a word after adding it to a lexical field is the default procedure. This is the very definition of 'fast mapping': the adoption of a word without full knowledge of its semantic features. Adults do that as well, and not just with lychees. For example, *dog* and *bear* will end up as related sisters in the tree of mammals once an adult learns that they are both *canines*. Adjusting entries within a semantic network, even connecting entire lexical fields, is not problematic once the basic architecture of the lexicon is in place. The lexicon is a self-organizing network where entries (so-called 'lemmas') and features are merged hierarchically, much like semantic predications (cf. Figure 4.1).

The fact that early child language directly reflects the child's take on her environments has given rise to the term 'context embeddedness.' Verbal interaction with children tends to be like sports commentary: The words label what is happening *hic et nunc*—here and now. That means, however, that the caregiver can also frame what is to be salient. There are several paths to establishing salience in child-directed talk:

- **negotiating joint focus**: An interlocutor and a trusting child mutually establish which component of the environment shall receive their attention.
- **repetition**: Adults repeat words (their own, or the child's) as a kind of 'focus on form' to assist recognition and memorization. A set of formulaic expressions is used by the adult and soon by the child (e.g. *all gone*).
- **ritual**: An entire script repeats with the same words, as in games (peekaboo), social situations, bath, bedtime, etc.
- **whole-body (sensori-motor) experience**: Words and word sequences are accompanied by physical activities such as waving *bye-bye*, body motions (I'm a little teapot, pat-a-cake), pointing, touching body parts (This Little Piggie, 'where is your nose?'), finger play, and stylized imitations of adult activities (pretend-talking on the phone).

By drawing deliberate attention to words through negotiation, repetition, ritual, and whole-body experience, the adult assists the child in identifying those words and in giving them mental lives. In turn, new words bootstrap the formation of additional conceptual categories (Waxman 2002)—a self-reinforcing win-win for the child.

The Concept of Word

Even (or maybe especially) linguists have a hard time defining what a word is. It is easier to describe what a word does:

(8) **word**: Linguistic unit that can occur freely (i.e. is not obligatorily affixed to another unit), acts as head of a phrase, and has either semantic content or expresses a (lexical or syntactic) function.

Clearly, (8) is a definition for adults. At the one-word stage, words are unlikely to project a phrase—a first noun like *mama* is a noun, not a noun phrase. It may initially not even be a noun; it can be a request ('pick me up'), an expression of relief ('oh, there you are'), etc. Such one-word 'sentoids' are known as 'holophrases.' First words do not combine, nor do they express a lexical function (as the pronoun *he* would—'replace a noun phrase') or a syntactic function (as the determiner *the* would—'mark the content of the following noun phrase as specific and presumed known').

The definition says that an adult word *can* occur freely, but it does not have to. A word can compound with another word and form a single new word. This is where linguists and spell checkers typically part company. Compounds are not always spelled as a single word: *chocolate chip cookie* inflects as a single word (outermost suffix only, not **chocolate chips cookie*), takes a single preceding determiner (not **chocolate chip a cookie*), and is inseparable (not **chocolate chips delicious cookie*) unless by way of further compounding (*chocolate chip sugar cookie*). Computer software, fixated on spaces between 'words,' does not check for compounding. It counts *picture book* as one word, and *picture book* as two.

While adults may not always be sure what a word is, infants appear to have some intuitive concept of it. Initially, infants acquire the intonation contours and stress patterns of adult speech. In perception, this helps five-month-olds identify adult intentions such as praise, prohibition, soothing, and bids for attention—even in some unfamiliar languages (Fernald 1993)—and recurring words reflecting those affects (*peekaboo!*). Stress and intonation also help them identify content words. Infants 7.5 months old assume that a stressed syllable marks the onset of a new word (Jusczyk et al. 1999), which is an effective strategy in English as long as the words actually begin with a stressed syllable. Some do not. In that case, a child might extract the non-word *taris* from the sequence *guiTAR is* (ibid.), or *my ammie* (*my Emmie* ?) from *Miami*. Three months later, infants will have moved on to morphological cues (see Chapter 3). In production, the pitch peaks and primary stresses make their babbling prosody sound more like adult speech ('echolalia'). At that stage, we begin to hear proto-words and pseudo-words like *wiga* that do not have contextual reference ('jargon babbling'). Both in perception and in production, then, an infant has some concept of word-ness.

Imposing shared 'sense' upon the world requires seeding and populating lexical fields. The above discussion seems to imply that infants do this by using sound to connect between a mental concept and a real-world referent. However, a language exists in a community of speakers. Language 'does not "mirror" just a given reality, but draws things into the specific perspective of a given community, shows how they are to be understood, analyzed, and evaluated' (Gipper 1971:758, translation mine; cf. Jones 1990). Doing things with words presumes interaction (Austin 1962). Else 'why talk,' asks Charlie Mangulda, the last living speaker of Amurdag (Harrison 2010). As was the case for speech sounds (Chapter 1), interactive book reading enriches linguistic input *beyond* the vocabulary of typical everyday speech directed to children, triggering the playful exploration of the lexicon *toward* the adult lexicon.

The Very First Books for the Very First Words

The PBS web site PBSparents recommends introducing books to a baby's environment almost immediately: 'By the time she is 4 months old, your baby will show an interest in books and start to explore them by chewing or throwing them.' 'Baby Chunky Board Books' hit the target for that age group; they are made with non-toxic and safe materials to sink their gums into. Board books depict objects from the baby's environment that correspond to earliest semantic/conceptual categories, such as a face, a stuffed animal, a cloth ball (never, curiously, a female breast). And their marketing blurbs or back-cover summaries position them as linguistic input scientifically designed to seed lexical fields. The marketing blurb for Roger Priddy's *First Words (Bright Baby)*, for instance, claims:

> From 'boat' and 'car' to 'apple' and 'banana' this book provides the youngest readers with the fundamental first words that will form the foundation of their vocabulary.
>
> (us.macmillan.com/books/9780312493882)

It is worth noticing the definite article in front of 'fundamental first words'—the implicature is that *it takes a book* to fully structure a child's future vocabulary. In this particular case, Macmillan put a new scientific dressing on an older book, for the vocabulary includes words with consonant clusters (*pants, socks*) that, as Chapter 1 shows, are not age appropriate as truly 'first' words.

Children's picturebooks are not only careful about phonetic features, but also highlight semantic features that are shared by objects. Paul Stickland's *Trucks* is a good example, analyzed in detail by Jörg Meibauer (2015). The book depicts varieties of trucks and describes their different functions. What they have in common is that they are huge in relation to the people depicted, that they have purposes and places to go (indicated by the direction in which the front wheels point), and that they are powerful. Meibauer classifies *Trucks* as non-fiction: The book has 'no introduction, no climax, no complications, no ending—in short, all elements of a narrative are lacking' (2015:65). But of course the narrative is in what the trucks *do*: Each vehicle has a *script* to follow. They deliver pipes and gasoline and trees, load and unload, tow other trucks headed for repair, pick up goods from ships and take them to warehouses.

Typically, pictures in very first baby books satisfy the following criteria:

- whole objects
- scriptability (what does that object do/what can baby do with that object)
- familiarity

There is even a new generation of customized board books that include faces and objects from the baby's *actual* environment.

At this early age, adult and child are negotiating the script of book reading itself, so the long-term goal is to establish shared book reading as a ritual. Part of that script is joining attention (and sound) to pictures. Not only is it easier to explore a new format using familiar objects; recognizing those objects in the pictures on the page also facilitates the realization that they are *representations*. It was not always assumed to be the case that infants treat pictures as representations. For some time, it was assumed that infants were unable to distinguish pictures from three-dimensional objects, because often their reaction to those pictures is to grasp for them (DeLoache, Strauss, & Maynard 1979). Babies, wrote Sprague Mitchell (1948), cannot observe an object 'without making some movement towards it' because their thinking is 'motoric' (13–14). Yonas et al. (2005) studied those grasping motions more carefully. Depictions in books elicited a grasping motion from nine-month-olds in which the hand was approximately horizontal and close to the book surface, quite different from when babies reach for real, three-dimensional objects. The hand comes in obliquely and from above when a baby grasps an actual object. Infants associating depictions with first words act out a script: The object depicted on the page is something they *imagine* grasping. They are not really *attempting* to seize it, but may potentially signal to the adult that they have recognized it.

Representations are processed with an added level of abstraction compared to perceiving three-dimensional objects. A baby does not *have* to act out the script of grasping; a mere mirror-neuron response to a picture is still 'motoric thinking,' only more abstract. Thus, a real-life game of peekaboo can become make-belief with a cardboard book. For example, in Dawn Sirett's *Baby: Peekaboo!*, pictures of stuffed animals and toys wait to be discovered behind flaps. The baby now enjoys the script of peekaboo (cf. Bruner 1983, pt. III). The child can even enjoy hypothetical scripts of what *could* be done with an object: Patricia Hubbell's *Pots and Pans* imagines kitchen implements used as percussion instruments. Among the early here-and-now books with pictures directly from the baby's environment was Edward Steichen's *The First Picture Book: Everyday Things for Babies* (1930). 'Everyday,' however, does not necessarily mean that pictures must refer to the baby's physical environment. Interactive book reading itself already creates an environment, and representations in it can be just as salient as real objects (though pop-up books and touch-and-feel books bridge that distinction). Representations can also enhance reality: An image of a cow jumping over the moon in a child's room, like the tile on the nursery rhyme-themed fireplace in Mary Wise Brown's own childhood home in Long Island (Gary 2016:12), 'takes on meaning' when the child encounters it in 'Hey, diddle diddle' (Brice Heath 1983:255) or recognizes it in *Goodnight Moon*.

There are various ways in which books draw upon interaction between child and reading adult. One approach is to engage the child physically. If an infant can be taught to turn the flaps to reveal hidden pictures, she can become the agent of her own 'surprise'—though there is probably more fun in it when the adult joins in exaggerated amazement (see Chapter 7 for 'entrainment'). Some picturebooks have whole-body experiences scripted in. The 'Playful Discoveries' series of 'Baby Einstein' books, for example, includes a book entitled *Opposites* (Kelman 2007), which addresses spatial concepts such as *over/under* and *on/off*. The book suggests 'tie-in activities':

> To assist your child in understand these concepts, play games that help him use the concepts naturally. For example, help your child bounce on the bed as you recite the children's rhyme "Five little monkeys jumping on the bed," then lift your child off the bed when the rhyme calls for it.[3]

And Eric Carle's *The Very Hungry Caterpillar* features a cardboard page with an apple through which the voracious little critter has supposedly just chomped. There is a hole punched out in the apple for the child to stick a finger through—voilà, instant animated caterpillar.

Books solicit physical activities in a variety of ways:

- **touch**: Some board books feature objects with patches of fur, fabrics, sandpaper, etc. to simulate what they feel like. The most famous of these is certainly Dorothy Kunhardt's *Pat the Bunny*, first published in 1940.
- **movement**: Books instruct children to perform certain movements. Eric Carle's *From Head to Toe*, for example, has children imitate animal motions, such as the elephant's foot stomping—as does *Stomp Like an Elephant* by Anita Shannon [Victoria C. McErlean]. Helen Oxenbury's *Clap Hands* depicts toddlers clapping, waving, and bouncing on the bed.
- **manipulation**: Some early children's books are designed to be manipulated. Besides flaps to reveal hidden or partially obscured pictures, there are pop-up books, car-shaped books with wheels attached, even books that fold into objects. Miles Kelly Publishers offers books that unfold into play mats and re-fold into three-dimensional objects in which a toddler can sit, such as a space ship or a car. Herve Tullet's *Press Here* invites the child to press dots printed on the page to see what 'happens' on the next page—an interactive extension of the 'make-belief grasping' script described above.
- **sound**: Children (or the reading adult) are invited to imitate sounds, such as animal sounds (cf. Chapter 2). Judy Herr and Terri Jo Swim offer such a phonetic activity book with *Making Sounds, Making Music, & Many Other Activities for Infants: 7 to 12 Months*.

The adult reader in shared book reading sessions negotiates meaning with the child. A large-scale study of shared-reading sessions (Hindman, Skibbe, & Foster 2014) found:

> Nearly all mothers referred children to illustrations, making use of one of the unique affordances of books for vocabulary development, and approximately half expanded on or acted out parts of the story or related it to children's own lives.
>
> (305)

Some children's books explicitly script the adults' participation into the text, beyond the 'tie-in activities' mentioned above. For example, a book might have instructions for the adult reader on how to interact with the child. Munro Leaf's *The Story of Ferdinand* has the adult ask which bull was about to enter the bull-fighting arena—and in small font underneath the large, centered text, the book supplies the expected answer, '—FERDINAND.' Or a book might include a word about which the child surely must query the adult. Beatrix Potter opens *The Tale of the Flopsy Bunnies* with a rumination about the "soporific" effect of eating too much lettuce.' The scare quotes acknowledge *soporific* as unfamiliar, so the text prompts a quick Q&A. Authors like Beatrix Potter and Margaret Wise Brown thought of such words as 'juicy words,' sneaky little forays into grown-up talk:

> Miss Brown loves to tuck in words like "sanctimonious" and "ruminating," phrases like "by the incredible velvet that grows on your nose, you are a rapscallion cat."
>
> (Bliven 1946:64)

Modern authors, too, use exotic words in children's books, such as *Constantinople* and *Timbuktu* (*Hop on Pop*, Dr. Seuss). There are more rare words in children's literature than in child-directed or even adult speech (Massaro 2015). A. A. Milne's character Owl makes even Christopher Robin's head spin with his love for big words:

> "The atmospheric conditions have been very unfavorable lately," said Owl.
> "The what?"
> "It has been raining," explained Owl.
> "Yes," said Christopher Robin. "It has."
> "The flood-level has reached an unprecedented height."
> "The who?"
> "There's a lot of water about," explained Owl.
> "Yes," said Christopher Robin, "there is."
> "However, the prospects are rapidly becoming more favorable. At any moment—"
> "Have you seen Pooh?"
>
> (*Winnie-the-Pooh* 140–41)

'Inferential talk' between child and adult reader (evaluating, discovering details, predicting what will happen on the next page) promotes vocabulary acquisition (Hindman, Skibbe, & Foster 2014). Many picturebooks will insert opportunities for adults not just to read the brief texts, but to talk *about* the book with the child. Larry Daste's *Hidden Pictures* brings the principles of whole-object and exclusivity into playful interaction by incorporating hidden objects in pictures that are amusingly out of place there, such as a rocket ship. Some are almost too ingeniously hidden, but the joy of discovery (especially if the child beats the adult to it!) is certainly *shared*. David Wiesner's *Tuesday* relies on co-creative narration by providing no text at all. His Norman-Rockwell-meets-graphic-novel illustrations show frogs on levitating lily pads floating into town at night (to their own surprise), causing hilarious mayhem. It all ends in a police investigation, calling for a plot summary of the narrative just invented for the book. Even a possible sequel is encouraged ("next Tuesday, 7:58 p.m.": flying pigs). A wordless picturebook can be paged through rather quickly, but doing so rather than co-creating it may feel about as empty as being the last speaker of Amurdag. It comes to real life in the narrative created by adult and child for a *make-belief hic and nunc.*

Discovering the Word Through Children's Books

Todd Risley and Betty Hart (1995) found that the amount of words that children hear at home ranges from a mere 600 words (or less) per hour up to 2100 (or more). The range correlates with parental income and educational levels. By the time they reach four years of age, some children will have heard a calculated 30 million words more than others. This notion of a "30-million-word gap" has become somewhat of an academic meme; a search for that exact phrase on Google brings up some 18,000 hits. It has also become a concern for pediatricians who see children from families with low socio-economic status (SES). A 2016 article in a journal of the American Medical Association, *JAMA Pediatrics*, by pediatricians Jenny Radesky, Judith Carta, and Megan Bair-Merritt explains the concern:

> As many as 40% to 50% of the children pediatric clinicians serve are growing up in low-income households. Among the myriad physical and mental health sequelae of early adversity and toxic stress, language development appears to be one area particularly vulnerable to the stressors associated with poverty. The effects of poverty on language development have been documented in children as young as 9 months, becoming more clinically evident by 24 months. The consequences of early adversity-related language delays may be profound, leading to later learning delays, school failure, and lifelong social and economic consequences.
>
> (Radesky et al. 2016:825)

Of course, as Meredith Rowe and Barry Zuckerman point out in the same issue, the quantity of input is not the only indicator. Turn-taking is crucial (Romeo et al. 2018), and so is linguistic quality: In an underprivileged household, young children hear fewer *novel* words, more commands than questions, and receive fewer conversational turns and parental responses (Radesky et al. 2016:827; so also Hoff 2003). In some low-SES communities, adults behave as if a child just ' "comes up" as a talker' by herself (Brice Heath 1983:75; cf. Snow et al. 1979). If quality language input literally acts as 'language nutrition' (Zauche et al. 2017), then those kids are being cortically starved.

Language delay caused by poverty is epidemic in scope. It is intuitively apparent how early interactive book reading could make a difference: With a tradition of shared book reading in the family, books lead to more books, and words to more words, increasing the child's vocabulary. The effect of insufficient linguistic input appears to be exponential and is known as the 'Matthew Effect' ('For unto every one that hath shall be given, and he shall have abundance: but from him that hath not shall be taken even that which he hath' 25:29). The gap is known to persist and grow even with intervention (Penno, Wilkinson, & Moore 2002). This is because a rich lexicon accelerates fast mapping, as a study by Maguire et al. showed (2018:684–85):

> When children have a deeper knowledge of words in context, they can integrate new semantic information into a deeper web of information to better predict what will come next. When encountering an unfamiliar word, this predictive information helps in meaning identification. We suspect that children from low SES homes have difficulties in consolidating information related to known words to build a robust semantic representation that helps them to determine an unknown word's meaning.

If *guessing* the approximate meaning of an unfamiliar word requires more cognitive load to compensate for a low-density lexicon, reading will presumably feel less rewarding. If *learning* and retaining new words takes about three exposures, as Abel and Maguire (2017) found out in EEG tests with 11–14-year-olds (the N400 wave typically recorded when a word does not make sense tends to go away with a third encounter), then the reduced input lessens the chances of fast-mapped words becoming permanent entries in the lexicon.

If, on the other hand, caretakers believe that their babies are potential communication partners, then they 'talk to them in ways which serve both to strengthen that belief and to make it come true' (Snow et al. 1979:287). Child-directed talk from mothers with higher socio-economic and educational status tends to be richer in vocabulary and sentence complexity (Hoff 2003:1373). Interactive book reading additionally enhances a child's vocabulary. The implications are palpable, not just for children's vocabulary but also for their cognitive development (Waxman 2002). The study by Hindman, Skibbe, and Foster found a direct and significant link between the variety of meaning-related talk in shared book sessions and 'stronger language skills among preschoolers.' For children's vocabulary growth to be fueled by children's literature in interactive reading, children's books need to contain different words from those that occur in everyday conversation, which is exactly what Hayes and Ahrens (1988), Sénéchal et al. (2008), and Massaro (2015) found to be the case.

Adults use a traditional subset of words in conversation with children that are unlikely to feature prominently in children's books. As a class project, students and I once compiled a list of 'kindertalk' words that are culturally transmitted over generations, with regional variants. We found words for bodily functions (*booboo, caca, doodoo, dukey* for 'feces,' *make bubbles/teetee, tinkle* for 'urinating'), body parts (*boom boom, bommon, hiney, tushie* for 'buttocks'), genitals (*dingdong, doodle, peenie, wee-wee, weenie* for 'phallus'), familiar items (*binkie, b(l)ankie, binket, diddley, wubble* for 'blanket'; *bibby, bopper, nippy, nuckie, passie* for 'pacifier'), physical states (*booboo, hurt, mimi, ouchie, ouwie* for 'injury'), etc. In contrast, children's books use words that are decidedly low-frequency in child-directed talk: *giant, queen, cupboard*, 'mark it with a B' (*pat-a-cake*), and 'I will become a fish in a trout stream' (*The Runaway Bunny*), to say nothing about *soporific*. Jessica Montag et al. (2015) took the effort to key in 100 children's books and compare their vocabulary with the CHILDES database (which contains natural transcripts) and found them significantly different.

The question of whether vocabulary learning is a matter of quality or of frequency of exposure (600 words vs. 2100 per hour) is answered with a firm 'yes' on both counts. Word frequency very nicely follows Zipf's Law: The highest frequency word occurs about twice as often as the second-most frequent word, diminishing in steps of about 50% each time (Yang 2013). Visually, the frequency curve starts very high, drops precipitously, and flattens out endlessly. Most of the 6000 or so words that we would want a three-year-old to know will occur rarely in everyday speech. Those calculations alone illustrate the essential role of quantity: It gives low-frequency words a higher chance of occurring. A ritual of shared book reading increases the chances for those words to *re*-occur and be retained (Robbins & Ehri 1994). Moreover, the most frequent words in adult English are *function* words (*a, the, be, to*, etc.), the kind which children do not even pay attention to until their syntax calls for them (see Chs. 3, 4). As to quality, Chapter 1 has shown that only child-directed interactive input is processed as language by infants. The mere presence of speech (adults talking to adults, language coming from electronic media) does not constitute linguistic *input* for a baby.

Authors of children's books feel a sense of educational responsibility and advocacy, an awareness that they play an active part in the child's learning of new words. They can literally set out to teach children to identify single words and their associated scripts, as does Pierre Pratt in books like *The Very Busy Life of Olaf and Venus: Home* (2001), in which Olaf the elephant sits alone in his house (the single word reads 'chair'), calls up his little mouse friend Venus ('telephone'), who shows up at the 'door' for shared fun activities like having 'cheese.' They can also recruit the reading adult for assistance (cf. Chapter 8): The author is cast in the role of trainer and the reading adult in the role of coach.[4] Their shared goal is to guide the child toward a rich vocabulary and—the earlier, the better—toward literacy. At the point where children begin to read by themselves (and that could be at the age of 4 in families that enjoy interactive book reading), their books may address the very concept of what a word is and what it does. Kate Banks, for example, wrote a book about word collecting. In *Max's Words*, Max starts a word collection to have something to equal his brother's large stamp collection, and he discovers that words can do something his brother's stamps cannot: They can make a story.

Equally potent catalysts for getting children to reflect upon words are books of word play and joke books. Celebrity actor Fred Gwynne's *A Little Pigeon Toad* and *The King Who Rained* illustrate what happens to standing adult expressions when an extended sense is walked back to the prototypical meaning (there would literally be a 'head' on daddy's beer), or when a homonym or homophone is substituted ('the blue prince for the new room on our house' and a creepy-looking 'coat of arms' hanging in the closet). Similarly, Loreen Leedy and Pat Street (*There's a Frog in my Throat*) list idioms involving animals and illustrate them in ways that sometimes twist the literal meaning (e.g. 'put something in the kitty' with a cat-shaped piggy bank). Tad Hills' *Knock Knock Who's There: My First Book of Knock Knock Jokes* uses peekaboo flaps to uncover punch lines, leaving the salient first word in place. Folding back the 'who?' part of 'Ken who?' completes the joke 'Ken you hear me?' Lewis Carroll even draws attention to the word as an arbitrary sign in *Alice's Adventures in Wonderland.* 'Some words have got altered,' observes Alice after her strange rendition of 'You are old, Father William' (1960:72). The Mock Turtle lists 'uglification and derision' among the parts of arithmetic he took in school (meaning, multiplication and division), and when Alice asserts that there is no such word as 'uglification,' the Gryphon legitimizes it as the antonym of 'beautification' (129). In *Through the Looking Glass*, Carroll includes a looking glass poem (in mirror reverse) that contains words like 'brillig' (from the verb *bryl* or *broil*, 'the time of broiling dinner'), 'slithy' (a blend of *slimy* and *lithe*, i.e. 'smooth and active'), and 'tove' ('a species of badger') ('Jabberwocky,' 191). A subsequent conversation between Humpty Dumpty and Alice reflects upon how much control we have over our words: 'which is to be the master—that's all' (269).[5]

Whole-Word Approaches to Literacy

In his 1955 *Why-Johnny-Can't-Read* attack on the whole-word method of teaching children to read and write (cf. p. 8), Rudolf Flesch reasoned that a child who wants to read material with a 10,000-word vocabulary would first have to memorize the shapes of that many words. He polemically "reminded" the reader of the invention of the alphabet, and he claimed that the whole-word method has 'thrown 3,500 years of civilization out the window' (12), by which he meant that American children are taught to read English 'as if it were Chinese' (ibid.). This blatant stance of cultural arrogance (implying that the Chinese writing system was inferior) was soon to morph into a political narrative when the U.S. woke up to news of a Soviet satellite on 4 October 1957. Literacy was now discussed in terms of national security. In the wake of *sputnik*, books like Arthur S. Trace's *What Ivan Knows that Johnny Doesn't* (1961) asked what the Russians were doing better than the Americans and identified the whole-word method as a major contributing factor in fostering a culture of illiteracy in U.S. schools.

For reasons outlined earlier (Chapter 1), a phonics-only approach to literacy throws Johnny (poor Johnny!) out with the bath water just the same. English spelling is not as phonemic as it was in Anglo-Saxon times, where a single letter or a digraph stood for a phoneme (e.g. *f* for allophones [f] and [v] in *fæder* and *heofon*, *sc* for /š/ in *scip* 'ship'). More importantly, the linguistic house of England never had just one tenant. A word borrowed from a Scandinavian language (Danish being the dominant language of the 'Danelaw' area between 886 and the late 10th century) could be spelled with *sc* but pronounced /sk/, as illustrated by modern doublets like *shirt* and *skirt*. A word borrowed from French (England's de-facto official language between 1066 and 1362) could introduce new phonemes (like the /ž/ in *rouge* or the /oy/ in *royal*) and letter combinations (like the trigraph *eau*, as in *beauty*). Colonialism, war, and trade introduced yet more sounds and spellings, such as *ts-* (as in *tsunami* or *tsetse fly*).

When the printing press increased the pressure toward standardization in the 15th century, dictionaries cemented orthographies that fit Middle English better than they do modern English: The word *knight* was then pronounced /knixt/—but word-initial *kn-* is no longer pronounced today, the Great Vowel Shift changed long /i/ to /aɪ/, and the velar fricative /x/ has survived only in outliers like the word *loch* ('lake'). There is really not much of an alternative to memorizing the entire word if *knight* is to be associated with /naɪt/ (and dissociated from *night*). The *gh* digraph, representing the 'loch'-fricative /x/ that was once pronounced in words like *tough, though, through*, and *daughter*, is a spelling zombie. Erudite lexicographers made words reflect their etymology (French *dette*, for example, was amended to *debt* to reflect Latin *debit*). Patriotic lexicographers like Noah Webster introduced national spellings (such as *-ize* for *-ise*). While the spelling of many English words is still phonemic, the pronunciation of many other words (*indict, niche, pizza, quinoa, victuals, plumber*) is unpredicted from their spelling.

The whole-language approach assumed that reading draws upon more cues than just spelling and therefore forged an interdisciplinary approach (Yetta Goodman 1989). Reading draws from 'minimal language cues selected from perceptual input'; it is, essentially, a 'psycholinguistic guessing game' (Ken Goodman 1967:126) combining semantics, syntax, pragmatics, and 'graphophonemics.' That premise still put the focus on the whole-word. Frank Smith emphasized the ancillary contribution of 'sounding out' to reading: 'Phonics will in fact prove of use—provided you have a rough idea what a word is' (2005:31).

In interactive book reading, children look at the illustrations 95% more than at the picture text (Evans & Saint-Aubin 2005). The idea that the child's attention must be drawn to the word before attempting to read it has tradition in the U.S. There were two approaches. In picture-guessing books such as Edith Francis Foster's *Mary's Little Lamb* (1903), words (mainly nouns) are replaced, in line with the text, with little iconic illustrations in red ink so that the adult can read the sentences and pause at the picture to have the child supply the appropriate word (Figure 2.2). Ms. Foster had earlier published the monochrome word-guessing book about (the bird) *Jimmy Crow* (1899), of which one story appeared in the December 1899 issue of *Little Folks*. Other books use the icon as a rebus, such as the 1849 *Mother Goose in Hieroglyphics* by George S. Appleton, where an icon of a can, for example, stands in for the modal *can*.

The second approach to drawing children's attention to words was to associate a single written word with a single picture illustration. There is an even older tradition for books of that type, such as the 1820 *Infant's Cabinet of Birds & Beasts* (anonymous). Recent books such as the *Bob Books Sight Words* series by Bobby Lynn Maslen typically boldface a word illustrated by an accompanying drawing and maybe repeat the word in large letters by itself on a dedicated page. Those illustrations can set up clever schemas, as in Christoph Niemann's *Words* (2016), where a drawing of a pizza box with a single slice left in it represents 'only.' That format can, for literate children, be expanded into a vocabulary builder, where a page would depict a complex setting with subcomponents (things that belong to a house, railroad, garden, etc.), as is the case in a book from the 1880s entitled *The Children's Object Book* (anonymous)—actually not unlike *Orbis pictus* in its design.

MARY'S LITTLE LAMB.

II

"MOTHER! Mother!" cried little Mary, running into the . "Mr. Clover says he doesn't need this — it's extra — and I may have it for my very own!" Yes, now it was Mary's little lamb — and how they loved each other! They went together everywhere — in the and the , and over to Grandfathers, to play with little Aunt Hannah. Mary's Aunt Hannah was only three years older than herself, and they played together all the time. The two little thought the was beautiful, but it was not very clean. "I don't want a dirty, dusty little lamb," said Mary; "I want a nice, clean, white lamb." "Then we must wash it." said little . "Father washes all his in the , every spring." Out by the stood the with the big wooden

Figure 2.2 Mary's Little Lamb (Edith Francis Foster 1903)

In 1953, Joseph and Ruth Low took another gander at Mother Goose, using rebuses in which the depicted object could form part of a word, such as *uni* preceding an ear of *corn* (for 'unicorn') or a picture of a garden *hoe* followed by the word *me* (for 'home'). Their book is more of an advanced orthographic puzzle than a first taste of literacy, since one would already have to know the spelling of *home* in order to backtrack from the pronunciation of *me* as /mi/. In the 1960s, the rebus invited itself into the school room for show and tell. Richard W. Woodcock created the Peabody rebus reading program to teach literacy skills to mentally impaired children. He also tested the books in kindergarten (Woodcock 1968). He found that learning to read with rebuses was "markedly easier" than learning with traditional orthography and recommended the use of rebus books in schools (ibid., 1). If the whole-word method was too slow, maybe the rebus approach would work better.

More recently, A. J. Funn [Dale Vandenborre] revived the tradition of rebus puzzles for use in schools with 'Glyffix,' a system of annotated hieroglyphics. Drawing from a game he played with his own children to exchange 'secret messages' ('New Language' 2014), he is publishing books that presuppose spelling skills to solve the visual puzzles. The words 'Once upon a time' in *Freeda Fireflight's Fantastic Flight* (2015), a sequel to *Penelope's Imagination Runs Wild* (2013), are encrypted as 1S ⇪ 💡 Ⓐ 𝕋 🍋(-l).

It turned out that both whole-word and rebus approaches are too late when introduced in the school room. Holistic approaches work much better for preschool children (Degkwitz 1966); by the time they come to elementary school, they have outgrown their holistic bias, with the surprising exception of highly gifted children (Müller 1964). The efficacy of whole-word approaches in U.S. schools is, at any rate, obscured by the fact that a *Gestalt* teaching approach to reading was likely never really fully implemented in the first place. Rudolf Degkwitz (ibid.) describes that American parents, worried that their children were making slow process in reading, received brochures from their schools with pictures of Chinese-like characters. They were asked to memorize them—in an attempt to make them experience that learning how to read is not easy. Parents apparently coopted the schools by teaching their children the alphabet (alphabet song, etc) and sounding out words with them at home.

Ideally, then, children are introduced to reading and writing with a combination of sounding out and recognizing sight words (that resist sounding out). Again, it is a testimony to the linguistic genius of Theodor Geisel to have recognized this so clearly (cf. p. 49). In *Green Eggs and Ham*, Geisel actually juxtaposed sight words such as *could* and *would* that differ in their initial letters and phonemes. Cathryn Falwell found a similarly ingenious way to focus a child's attention on spelling. Her protagonist of *Word Wizard*, Anna, discovers that with her spoon she can make quite a stir by arranging alphabet cereal into words and rearranging them into Anna-grams. Anna uses her spelling spoon to help a lost little boy, Zack, across the ocean by changing *ocean* into *canoe*; then she turns *shore* into *horse* to carry them both home.

The whole-language approach was likely correct in its working premise. In reading a word, several things conspire: There are (mind reading or plot-driven) expectations of what the word will be within context, a point of recognition (*const* . . . can go several ways, but *constip* . . . leaves only the options *constipation, constipate(d), constipating*), and predeterminations of what the part of speech is going to be given its upcoming syntactic position and current context. To fast-forward to the point of recognition, our eyes even seem to take in the ends and beginnings of words simultaneously, which explains a) why proofreading is notoriously difficult, and b) why we can read a (carefully contrived, of course) text with easy-to-predict words such as this, widely circulated on the Internet:

> Aoccdrnig to a rseearch sduty at Cmabridge Uinervtisy, it deosn't mttaer in waht oredr the ltteers in a wrod are, the olny iprmoetnt tihng is taht the frist and lsat ltteer be in the rghit pclae. The rset can be a toatl mses and you can sitll raed it wouthit porbelm. Tihs is bcuseae the huamn mnid deos not raed ervey lteter by istlef, but the wrod as a wlhoe.

Matching Two Worlds to Mind: Bilingual Word Books

Orbis pictus was conceived as a bilingual book, matching native vocabulary with Latin words. In 1659, a bilingual book would naturally have aimed to further the child's knowledge of Latin. But there are other reasons for having bilingual books, even before school.

Immigrants have heritage languages. They may not intend to make sure that the children are truly bilingual, but that they should still embrace their heritage. Thus, these bilingual children's books may be mostly in English. Eva Klapp's *Zauberlinda, the Wise Witch* (1901) is set in the U.S. but has a character, Pete Pumpernickel (from Ilsenburg near Goslar) who uses words like the exclamation *potstauzend* (p. 55), of which the original German spelling is *Potztausend*, of course. Other bilingual books go so far as to present the foreign language and add an English translation, on the assumption that there is someone available who can mother both tongues. Since there is usually no grammatical rhyme or reason to such a book, it must be directed at a young audience who is English dominant but exposed to a foreign language spoken at home. An early example, also for German immigrants, is *My very first little German Book* (early 1900s, anonymous); note the small-print Germlisch translations in the following (admittedly cherry-picked) examples:

> Der Mond und die Sterne leuchten uns.
> (The moon and the stars light us.)
>
> Mein Luftballon fliegt fort und bleibt in einem Baum stecken.
> (My balloon flies away and sticks in a tree.)
>
> Heute morgen hat mich das Kindermädchen auf die Strasse geführt.
> (My nurse took me this morning into the streets.)
>
> "Alle Leute werden sagen," meint sie, "Ei, wie schön sie sind!"
> ("Everybody," said she, "will cry, 'Oh! how beautiful they are!'")

The book's archaic spelling of *Brod* for *Brot* ('bread') and the atavistic presence of the old dative ending *-e* on the noun (*unter dem Tische* 'under the table') are features indicative of a 'colonialization effect' (which include holding on to and emphasizing archaic forms), and the division of the book into exercises (*Uebungen*) confirms that German was no longer a first language for these young children. At an age where exercises begin, a 'first' little German book would have been too little, too late, to pass on the language and was likely intended to pass on a heritage identity.

Children's books can also be bilingual or multilingual to instill an appreciation of linguistic diversity. Ginger Foglesong Guy's 2006 *¡Perros! ¡Perros! Dogs! Dogs!* uses canine vignettes to teach nouns, adjectives, prepositions and standing expressions in Spanish and English. The two languages are presented equivalently in the same font size this time. Wording and content are simple enough to engage a younger child. Again, having an occasional bilingual children's books read to them does not make children bilingual, so the intent of such books is probably not so much the preservation of a heritage language or culture but sensitization to the co-existence of another language, potentially also to broaden the child's in-group affiliations.

Maybe, however, those books are also doing some parental convincing. Particularly in the United States, there has been a long-standing irrational prejudice against raising children bilingually. Dieter E. Zimmer (1988:50) sums up how the cards were stacked against bilingualism in the 1960s (translation mine):

> Up until the sixties, linguists looked down on bilingualism. Over and over, empirical studies of bilingual kids had shown: Their scholastic performance is lower than that of their monolingual peers, they test lower for intelligence, and their linguistic uprootedness makes them unstable. Since the sixties, that perception has changed. New studies conclude almost uniformly that not only do once-asserted disadvantages of bilingualism fail to manifest themselves, but that bilingual children actually have a bit of an edge over monolinguals. Their reasoning is more flexible, they can think outside the box, they are wittier.

Zimmer recommends, however, that the languages spoken have separate domains (spoken in different environments or with different persons) to guarantee native attainment and consistent separation (ibid.). Following that logic, maybe it would be better to have a bilingual book separated into two parts, or halves of the page, one for each language, and maybe read in two different environments.

Such books do exist. The most ambitious among them are intended to preserve endangered languages, and I will pick just one example. Sabrina Wong (2013) describes a children's book created by the community of Pangnirtung, Baffin Island, in response to a competition initiated by Inhabit Media and supported by Canada's 'Healthy Children's Initiative Fund' through the Dept. of Education of the Government of Nunavut and by the Canada Council for the Arts. The winning entry, by Vera Evic, is written in the original Inuktitut on the bottom half of each page; an English translation, using the Roman alphabet, occupies the top of the page. The Pangnirtung-Uqqurmiut Inuit Artist Organization then produced vibrant artwork. ᑕᖅᑭᓕᐊᖅᑐᑦ *Trip to the Moon* is intended for children age 4–6 and dedicated to the children at Mianiqsivik Pairivik daycare in Pangnirtung. It clearly reflects commitment to Inuktitut language, oral tradition, and art. If indeed, as Wong's review suggests, children can choose to 'read the story in either English or Inuktikut,' they would seem to be able to switch between those languages and writing systems, which bodes well for the power of children's books to create a viable space for two first languages.

Multilingualism is the default globally (cf. p. 146 below), but the world's linguistic landscape is unstable. English is doing so well that the majority of its speakers has learned it as a second language (which will eventually affect the native language itself). At the same time, hundreds of languages are disappearing. If there is a local future for youths preventing their exodus to urban areas, and an infrastructure for the education of the children with a sufficient presence of native speakers, children's books could be instrumental. They could make the difference whether the child will grow up to speak the language or to reminisce nostalgically about knowing who its last speaker was.

Notes

1. The idea that second/foreign languages are 'acquired' because their progress also follows a 'natural order' (Krashen & Terrell 1983) rests on a redefinition of metalinguistic awareness as 'language learning,' using the term 'acquisition' to refer to automatic and intentional progress alike. Learning and acquisition are defined differently in this book (see Introduction).
2. This example comes anecdotally from M. Hoffman (1968) via John Macnamara (1972:4).
3. www.earlymoments.com/baby-einstein/List-of-Baby-Einstein-Books/Opposites
4. For the differences between the two, see Michael Heah, 'Coaches vs. Trainers,' The Nation, 15 April 2013, www.nationmultimedia.com/business/Coaches-VS-Trainers-30203957.html. Part II of this book will investigate the complex relationship between child, reading adult, and author.
5. The consequences of being in linguistic receivership are explored in George Orwell's *1984* and 'Politics and the English Language.'

References

Abel, Alyson D.; Julie Schneider; and Mandy J. Maguire. 2017. N400 response indexes word learning from linguistic context in children. *Language Learning and Development* (27 November). doi:10.1080/15475441.2017.1362347.

Austin, J. L. 1962. *How to do things with words*, ed. by J. O. Urmson and Marina Sbisà, 2nd ed., 1975. Cambridge, MA: Harvard University Press.

Bliven, Jr., Bruce 1946. Child's best seller. *LIFE* 21(23) (2 December).59–66.

Brice Heath, Shirley. 1983. *Ways with words: Language, life, and work in communities and classrooms*. Cambridge: Cambridge University Press.

Bruner, Jerome S. 1978. The role of dialogue in language acquisition. *The child's conception of language*, ed. by Anne Sinclair, Robert J. Jarvella, and Willem J. M. Levelt, 241–56. New York: Springer.

Bruner, Jerome S. 1983. *Child's talk: Learning to use language*. New York: Norton.

Chomsky, Noam A. 1971. *Problems of knowledge and freedom: The Russell lectures*. New York: Vintage Books.

Chomsky, Noam A. 1988. *Language and problems of knowledge: The Managua lectures* (Current studies in linguistics series), vol. 16. Cambridge, MA: MIT Press.

Cuetosa, Fernando; Asunción Monsalvea; and Alicia Pérez. 2005. Determinants of lexical access in pure anomia. *Journal of Neurolinguistics* 18.383–99.

Degkwitz, Rudolf. 1966. Es ist nicht egal, wie man lesen lernt. *Die Zeit*, 29 April. Online: www.zeit.de/1966/18/es-ist-nicht-egal-wie-man-lesen-lernt.

DeLoache, Judy S.; Mark S. Strauss; and Jane Maynard. 1979. Picture perception in infancy. *Infant Behavior and Development* 2(1).77–89.

Evans, Heidi. 2012. Every 2-year-old should know at least these 25 words: Researchers: A checklist for toddler language development. *New York Daily News*, Monday, 20 February. Online: www.nydailynews.com/life-style/2-year-old-25-words-researchers-article-1.1025968.

Evans, Mary Ann, and Jean Saint Aubin. 2005. What children are looking at during shared book reading: Evidence from eye movement monitoring. *Psychonomic Science* 16(11) (November).913–20.

Fernald, Anne. 1993. Approval and disapproval: Infant responsiveness to vocal affect in familiar and unfamiliar languages. *Child Development* 64(3) (June).657–67.

Flesch, Rudolf. 1955. *Why Johnny can't Read and what you can do about it*. New York: Perennial Library, Harper & Row.

Gary, Amy. 2016. *In the great green room: The brilliant and bold life of Margaret Wise Brown*. New York: Flatiron Books.

Gipper, Helmut. 1971. Bedeutung. *Historisches Wörterbuch der Philosophie*, ed. by Joachim Ritter, vol. 1, 758–59. Darmstadt: Wissenschaftliche Buchgesellschaft.

Goodman, Ken. 1967. Reading: A psycholinguistic guessing game. *Journal of the Reading Specialist* 6(4).126–35.

Goodman, Yetta M. 1989. Roots of the whole-language movement. *The Elementary School Journal* 90(2).113–27.

Harrison, K. David. 2010. The last speaker. *National Geographic*. youtube/O89PkSNTtbg.

Hart, Betty, and Todd R. Risley. 1995. *Meaningful differences in the everyday experience of young American children*. Baltimore: Paul H. Brookes.

Hayes, Donald P., and Margaret G. Ahrens. 1988. Vocabulary simplification for children: A special case of motherese? *Journal of Child Language* 15.395–410.

Hindman, Annemarie H.; Lori E. Skibbe; and Tricia D. Foster. 2014. Exploring the variety of parental talk during shared book reading and its contributions to preschool language and literacy: Evidence from the Early Childhood Longitudinal Study-Birth Cohort. *Reading and Writing* 27(2).287–313.

Hoff, Erika. 2003. The specificity of environment influence: Socioeconomic status affects early language development via maternal speech. *Child Development* 74(5).1368–78.

Hoffman, M. 1968. Child language. McGill University, Department of Psychology: Unpublished master's thesis.

Hubel, David H., and Torsten N. Wiesel. 1962. Receptive fields, binocular interaction and functional architecture in the cat's visual cortex. *Journal of Physiology* 160.106–54.

Jones, Edward Ellsworth. 1990. *Interpersonal perception*. San Francisco: W. H. Freeman.

Jusczyk, Peter W.; Derek M. Houston; and Mary Newsome. 1999. The beginnings of word segmentation in English-learning infants. *Cognitive Psychology* 39(3–4) (November).159–207.

Krashen, Stephen D., and Tracy D. Terrell. 1983. *The natural approach: Language acquisition in the classroom*. Hayward, CA: Alchemy Press, Pergamon.

Lorenz, Konrad. 1935. Der Kumpan in der Umwelt des Vogels: Der Artgenosse als auslösendes Moment sozialer Verhaltensweisen. *Journal für Ornithologie* 83.137–213, 289–413.

Lorenz, Konrad. 1941. Kant's Lehre vom Apriorischen im Lichte gegenwärtiger Biologie. *Blätter für Deutsche Philosophie* 15.94–125.

Lorenz, Konrad. 1949. *Tiergeschichten: Er redete mit dem Vieh, den Vögeln und den Fischen*. Vienna: Borotha-Schoeler.

Macnamara, John. 1972. Cognitive basis of language learning in infants. *Psychological Review* 79(1).1–13.

Maguire, Mandy J.; Julie M. Schneider; Anna E. Middleton; Yvonne Ralph; Michael Lopez; Robert A. Ackerman; and Alyson D. Abel. 2018. Vocabulary knowledge mediates the link between socioeconomic status and word learning in grade school. *Journal of Experimental Child Psychology* 166.679–95. doi:10.1 Ol 6/j.jecp.2017.10.003.

Mandel, Denise R.; Deborah G. Kemler Nelson; and Peter W. Jusczyck. 1996. Infants remember the order of words in a spoken sentence. *Cognitive Development* 11.181–96.

Massaro, Dominic W. 2015. Two different communication genres and implications for vocabulary development and learning to read. *Journal of Literacy Research* 47(4).505–27.

Meibauer, Jörg. 2015. What the child can learn from simple descriptive picturebooks: An inquiry into Lastwagen/Trucks by Paul Stickland. *Learning from picturebooks: Perspectives from child development and literacy studies*, ed. by Bettina Kümmerling-Meibauer, Jörg Meibauer, Kerstin Nachtigäller, and Katharina J. Rohlfing, 51–70. London and New York: Routledge.

Mitchell, Lucy Sprague. 1921 [rpt. 1948]. *Here and now storybook*, illustrated by Hendrik Willem van Loon and Christine Price. Mineola, NY: Dover.

Montag, Jessica L.; Michael N. Jones; and Linda B. Smith. 2015. The words children hear: Picture books and the statistics for language learning. *Psychological Science* 26(9). 1489–96.

Müller, Heinrich. 1964. *Methoden des Erstleseunterrichts und ihre Ergebnisse*. Meisenheim am Glan: A. Hain.

PBSparents. n.d. Baby reading milestones. Online: www.pbs.org/parents/education/reading-language/reading-milestones/baby-language-development-milestones/baby-reading/.

Penno, Julie F.; Ian A. G. Wilkinson; and Dennis W. Moore. 2002. Vocabulary acquisition from teacher explanation and repeated listening to stories: Do they overcome the Matthew effect? *Journal of Educational Psychology* 94(1).23–33.

Radesky, Jenny S.; Judith Carta; and Megan Bair-Merritt. 2016. The 30 million-word gap: Relevance for pediatrics. *JAMA Pediatrics* 170(9) (November).825–26.

Rescorla, Leslie. 2012. Vocabulary checklist. Handout, American Association for the Advancement of Science annual meeting, panel Late talkers in any language: Finding children at risk worldwide, organized by Nan Bernstein Ratner. Online: www.medicalhomeportal.org/link/1747.

Robbins, Claudia, and Linnea C. Ehri. 1994. Reading storybooks to kindergartners helps them learn new vocabulary words. *Journal of Educational Psychology* 86(1).54–64.

Romeo, Rachel R; Julia A. Leonard; Sydney T. Robinson; Martin R. West; Allyson P. Mackey; Meredith L. Rowe; and John D. E. Gabrieli. 2018. Beyond the 300-million-word gap: Children's conversational exposure is associated with language-related brain function. *Psychological Science* 29(5).700–10. DOI: 10.1177/0956797617742725.

Rowe, Meredith L., and Barry Zuckerman. 2016. Word gap redux: Developmental sequence and quality. *JAMA Pediatrics* 170(9) (September).827–28.

Sénéchal, Monique; Stephanie Pagan; Rosemary Lever; and Gene P. Ouellette. 2008. Relations among the frequency of shared reading and 4-year-old children's vocabulary, morphological and syntax comprehension, and narrative skills. *Early Education and Development* 19(1).27–44.

Smith, Frank. 2005. *Reading without nonsense*, 4th ed. New York, London: Teachers College, Columbia University.

Snow, Catherine; Akke de Blauw; and Ghislaine van Roosmalen. 1979. Talking and playing with babies: The role of ideologies of child-rearing. *Before speech: The beginning of interpersonal communication*, ed. by Margaret Bullowa, 269–88. Cambridge: Cambridge University Press.

Touched by an Angel. 2010. National Jewish Outreach Program, 5 August. Online: www.jewishtreats.org/2010/08/touched-by-angel.html.

Trace, Arthur C. 1961. *What Ivan knows that Johnny doesn't*. New York: Random House.

Waxman, Sandra R. 2002. Early word-learning and conceptual development: Everything had a name, and each name gave birth to a new thought. *Blackwell handbook of childhood cognitive development*, ed. by Usha Goswami, 102–26. Malden, MA: Blackwell.

Wittgenstein, Ludwig. 1958. *Preliminary studies for the 'Philosophical Investigations': Generally known as The Blue and Brown Books*. New York: Harper Colophon.

Woodcock, Richard W. 1968. Rebus as a medium in beginning reading instruction. *IMRID Papers and Reports* 5(4), 35pp. ERIC 046 631. Online: files.eric.ed.gov/fulltext/ED046631.pdf.

Wong, Sabrina. 2013. Review of *Trip to the moon* by Vera Evic. *CM* 20(8) (25 October), University of Manitoba. Online: umanitoba.ca/outreach/cm/vol20/no8/triptothemoon.html.

Yang, Charles. 2013. Ontogeny and phylogeny of language, ed. by William Labov. *PNAS: Publications of the National Academy for Science of the United States* 110(16).6324–27. Online: www.pnas.org/cgi/doi/10.1073/pnas.1216803110.

Yonas, Albert; Carl E. Granrud; Mey H. Chov; and Amelia J. Alexander. 2005. Picture perception in infants: Do 9-month-olds attempt to grasp objects depicted in photographs? *Infancy* 8(2).147–66.

Zauche, Lauren Head; Ashley E. Darcy Mahoney; Taylor A. Thul; Michael S. Zauche; Arianne B. Weldon; and Jennifer L. Stapel-Wax. 2017. The power of language nutrition for children's brain development, health, and future academic achievement. *Journal of Pediatric Health Care* 31(4) (July/August).493–503.

Zimmer, Dieter E. 1988. *So kommt der Mensch zur Sprache: Über Spracherwerb, Sprachentstehung, Sprache & Denken* (Haffmans TaschenBuch), vol. 16. Zurich: Haffmans Verlag.

3 Morphemes A-Morphing

Moses supposes his toeses are roses;
Moses supposes erroneously,
For nobody's toeses are roses or posies,
As Moses supposes his toeses to be.

Morphemes are a lot of work—certainly for adults learning a foreign language. Mark Twain tried his hand at German, with its intimidating array of endings that must agree for number and case: 'When a German gets his hands on an adjective, he declines it, and keeps on declining it until the common sense is all declined out of it. It is as bad as Latin' (Clemens 181). Twain felt no more enlightened by being taught German morphology than a child might feel who is taught phonics (see p. 48): As soon as he was taught a rule, he saw 'that there are more exceptions to the rule than instances of it' (ibid., 177). His sentiments echo the mock exasperation of Cambridge classical scholar and linguist Richard Porson (1759–1808), who, while famously accomplished in classical Greek, felt that he had met his match in Germanic morphology and insisted that 'life is too short to learn German' (Carlyle 1860:455). One can only imagine what choice words either of these gentlemen would have had to offer on Charles Yang's 'Tolerance Principle' of adopting morphological rules in the face of exceptions (Yang 2016).

Children who grow into English have to seize and tame their share of little morpho-beasties. Why is there a *to* (sign of infinitive) in *I want him to go away* and not in *I made him go away*? Is it *heavenlier* or *more heavenly* (or either)? Can a *quicker picker upper* really be grammatical? What is the difference between *Why don't you be a man about it and set me free* ('You Leave me Hanging on,' The Supremes) and *Why aren't you a man about it*? And how do children master morphology such as tense and agreement by the time they are three years old when it eludes many an adult learning English at the local community college? Is there a Porson Syndrome for morphology in the sense that there is a 'foreign hearing syndrome' for sound perception (see p. 33)?

Though not typically discussed together in the literature, morphology and phonology share some characteristics. We shall see that children are sensitive to distributional properties of morphemes, including allomorphs, and that their rapid acquisition in the third year of life indicates, if not a Critical Period, then at least a Sensitive Period. There is also some speculation that both in phonetics and in morphology, children have access to a universal set of features and commit to a subset that operates in their first languages (Chomsky 2000:100–01, so also Fries 1957:v).[1] Certainly, we see that children form morphological rules for proper inflection even of made-up words like *wug, niz*, and *heaf* (cf. p. 30) and for the creative derivation of new parts of speech (e.g. *the buzzer is buzzering*).

Brother, Can You Paradigm? Interfaces With Phonology and Syntax

Before getting in too deep (deeply?), a brief overview of what morphemes are is in order. In English, morphemes do things to words (like the regular plural morpheme), they do things to phrases (like indicating with a determiner whether the noun phrase is newly introduced to the discourse), and they do things to clauses (like the agreement *-s*, which harmonizes the singular number feature between subject and predicate). Some morphemes do things to entire sentences. Welsh has a morpheme, *a*—QST in (9) below—that turns a statement into a question:

(9)

A	glyweisti	a	gant y Pysc
QST	you have heard	QST REL	sang the Fish
Wrth	ymdraffull	ymplith	y gurysc?
when	he floundered	among	the reeds
Trech	anyan nac	adysc.	
nature	wiser than	learning	

'Did you hear what the fish sang as he floundered among the reed stalks? Nature is wiser than education.'

(Jones et al. 1870:126)

Children first need to discover that morphemes are not the same as syllables. The word *shoe* has one syllable; so does the word *shoes*—but *shoes* has two morphemes: The meaningful noun *shoe* and the number inflection *-s*, indicating 'more than one' (plural). But not everything is so regular in English: The plural of *foot* is not **foots*. English has its own fair share of the exceptions Mark Twain was ascribing to German, so a child needs to be constantly aware of potential idiosyncrasies. Progress may entail the morphological reanalysis of existing entries in the child's lexicon, just as it may require updating and revising semantic features (cf. p. 62). The baby-talk adjective *allgone* (as in *allgone juice*) is a point in case: *all* turns out to be a free morpheme (degree/intensifier "adverb"), and *gone* is a form of *go* (looking quite like a verb with verbal perfective aspect *-en*, but here the participial ending turns out to be derivational, not inflectional, which entails that the correct auxiliary to use is *be*, not *have: The juice is all gone.*).

Children also need to discover the degree to which, in their native languages, syntax and morphology divide their labors in the construction of sentences. Some languages let morphology do most of the work, some put mainly syntax in charge. Languages can be plotted on a line between those two extremes. One extreme is to let syntax do virtually *all* the work. Chinese is such an 'isolating' (Gabelentz 1883:3) language: Every syllable is a word, making it an interesting matter to decide whether typically co-occurring words like 大學 (*dà xué* 'major school' = university) should be called a compound (like *chocolate chip cookie* in English—cf. p. 64). Chinese has no prefixes or suffixes and relies on a number of function words that indicate adjectival function, perfective aspect, question, classification of a noun, etc. At the other end of the scale are 'polysynthetic' languages such as the Inuit language Kalaallisut (a.k.a. West Greenlandic), where morphology leaves very little work to do for syntax and forms some very long words on the fly (and large white spaces in between them if the text has a justified right margin). Kalaallisut morphology is capable of expressing the equivalent of an entire English sentence with a single word (after Olsen 2004:117):

(10) Silagissiartuaarusaarnialerunarpoq.

sila-	*-gi-*	*-ssi-*	*-artu-*	*-aa-*	*-rusaar-*	*-nia-*	*-ler-*	*-unar-*	*-poq*
weather	good	becomes	go	slowly	gradually	again	begin	probably	3sg

'It looks like the weather is eventually going to improve.'

Children acquiring a polysynthetic language 'make very few mistakes in the ordering of the affixes' (Miller 1993:27), suggesting morphology mirrors syntax in the way it arranges morphemes (Baker 1988, cf. Miller 1993:38–42). It is reasonable to speculate, as did Jan Marius Hoogvliet (1885:83.XXVIII),[2] that morphology and overt syntax may be a single module of language and to refer to it as 'morphosyntax.' At the very least, morphology and syntax interface.

The interaction between morphology and syntax is especially intricate in an inflecting language like English (which is located somewhere between the two extremes of language typology). To be sure, English has been all but stripped of the rich array of inflections that once existed in Old English, a Germanic language. That loss of inflections was the result of some kind of creolization effect during the intimate language contact with Danish (esp. during the Danelaw period of 886 to the late 10th century). Very few English inflections remain productive today (Table 3.1), though the grammatical machinery necessary for an inflecting language remains largely intact, just more streamlined. For example, only one inflection can attach to a word; the system no longer generates dual inflections such as tense *and* agreement, as in *thou establishedst the earth above the waters* (Ps. 136.6 as cited in "Scriptural Views" 1840:364). Taking stock of the remaining inventory of inflectional morphemes, English has one number, two aspects, two degrees, one tense, and one agreement (*-st* for second person singular, as in *thou mayest soon die* (p. 4) having been the latest victim of attrition).

The distinction between 'lexical' and 'functional' inflection in Table 3.1 indicates whether the suffix is added in the lexicon directly or requires some syntax to be added. This being the sparse remnant of a rich Germanic inflection system, there is an exception to every type above—listed forms that do not inflect productively and have to be memorized, like the sight words in Chapter 2. Some nouns and verbs change vowels instead of taking a suffix (*goose/geese*), some

Table 3.1 Modern Edited English Inflections

	type	*values*	*suffixation*	*example*
lexical	number	plural	N + *-s*	*shoes*
	aspect	progressive	V + *-ing*	*I am just saying.*
	. . .	perfective	V + *-en*	*He has taken them.*
			V + *-ed*	*He has polished it.*
	degree	comparative	A + *-er*	*She was/talked faster.*
	. . .	superlative	A + *-est*	*She is/talks the fastest!*
functional	tense	past	V + *-ed*	*You snored.*
	agreement	3rd sg.	V + *-s*	*She agrees.*

N = noun, **V** = verb, **A** = adjective or adverb; not listed are possessive *-'s*, which can no longer be considered an inflection today (see Table 3.4), and ordinal *-th* (as in *seventh*), which could be argued to be derivational (deriving a new part of speech) rather than inflectional.

adjectives would rather send a substitute than be inflected themselves (*good/better*, not **gooder*), modals don't agree at all (*he must*, not *he *musts*), and a verb should not take progressive aspect in Standard American English if it is stative (*!I am knowing the answer*) or refers to an instantaneous action (e.g. *!That bomb is exploding* vs. *There were bombs exploding all night*).

Inflections are always the last (outermost) suffix on a word (*friend-ship-s*, not **friend-s-ship*). Derivational affixes arrange in hierarchical order (*hell-ish-ness*, not **hell-ness-ish*). Compounds exhibit the mirroring of syntax suggested by Baker: When all the other reindeer *called* Rudolf *names*, they engaged in *name calling* (again, the inflection can only be outermost, hence not **names calling*).

Overall, English morphemes stand on their own ('free morphemes') or must attach. 'Bound morphemes' like *-ize* can turn a noun like *weapon* into a verb ('derivational morpheme'); the suffix *-s* can add agreement to a verb or number to a noun ('inflectional morpheme'). English has recycled some morphemes by pressing them into multiple service. The suffix *-ed* can be disambiguated only with auxiliaries: without an auxiliary, *hugged* is past tense; *has/had hugged* is perfective aspect (with present or past tense); *was hugged* is passive voice. Similarly, *is/was swimming* is progressive aspect, but without auxiliary the *-ing* is a derivational suffix (*Swimming is fun*). The additional structure needed for those auxiliaries attests to the chummy symbiosis between English morphology and syntax.

Infants are known to fixate on particular sounds when they adopt a morpheme such as the plural *-s*. Perceptually, a suffix that adds another syllable (*dishes*) should be easier to make out than a suffix that does not (*wants*). One might also assume that a voiced ending (*berries*) is easier to hear than a voiceless one (*bits*). A frequency effect may additionally influence the child's perception of suffixes. Roger Brown looked at samples of three parents' speech and found that the voiced plural /z/ was the most frequent, with a surprisingly low occurrence of the voiceless /s/. The syllabic allomorph /əz/ (*dishes*) was rather the exception (Table 3.2).

A large-scale analysis of child-directed talk to babies up to 25 months old, culled from the CHILDES database, confirmed Brown's observation: /z/ was

Table 3.2 Plural Allomorphs in the Speech of Three Sets of Parents

	allomorph	*Adam's*	*Sarah's*	*Eve's*
plural	/z/	48	32	23
	/s/	7	17	8
	/əz/	2	8	2

(Brown 1973:360)

most frequent (51.8% by type), followed by /s/ (30.1%) and finally by /əz/ and by zero inflection (Davies, Rattanasone, & Demuth 2017:48). I presume that /z/ dominates because of the higher frequency of open syllables (ending in vowels) in words used with children (cf. the 'kindertalk' words, p. 70).

Based on frequency of exposure, one would surely expect that children adopt the /z/ plural allomorph first, but no. Infants as young as 18 months pay preferential attention to /s/ in their perception of the plural morpheme. They also demonstrate, in cleverly designed tests involving made-up words and pictures, that even at that tender age they understand the morpheme's number function, so this is also a morphological, not just a phonotactic, rule. They do not score well on /z/ and /əz/ (Davies, Rattanasone, & Demuth 2017). If there is any frequency effect, it might hold for the outlier morpheme /əz/, which is used only as a last resort in English to dissociate the suffix from a preceding phoneme if it is likewise a sibilant (i.e. after words ending in /s/ *kiss*, /z/ *rose*, /č/ *match*, /ǰ/ *judge*, /š/ *dish*, or the occasional final /ž/ *garage*). Davies et al. hypothesize that the time signature of /s/ gives it preferential recognition by babies: /s/ has a longer duration than /z/. But I suspect there is a larger picture.

Recall that Labov and Labov's daughter Jessica had a final /t/ in the word *dad* (p. 37). In the morphology of early childhood, there appears to be a prohibition in general against producing syllable-final voiced consonants. Devoicing a final consonant is, interestingly, also a morpho-phonetic hallmark of German, so a generic rule 'syllable-final consonants are voiceless' may not be all that far-fetched. Arguing along the lines of Chapter 1, I assume that a bias against producing final voiced consonants causes a bias against perceiving them as well. And arguing along the lines of Chapter 2, I assume that /s/ is the *prototypical* number ending. If so, then early functional morphemes behave like early lexical morphemes (words): They are subject to a mutual exclusivity principle. Any new morph encountered must have a new function/meaning. Only in the course of maturation will that principle be relaxed, allowing synonyms (*bunny, cottontail, rabbit*, and *knuffel bunny*) and allomorphs (/s/, /z/, and /əz/).

Syllable-final devoicing is but one morpho-phonological regularity that can be observed both in baby talk and in natural languages. Another one is harmony across adjacent syllables: the bias toward using the same consonants or vowels. In the word *binkie* 'blanket,' the vowels harmonize; in the word *gigak* 'belly button' (observed by the author), the consonants harmonize (all velar stops). Harmonizing both vowels and consonants results in reduplication, e.g. *mimim* 'milk' (another personal observation). Harmony maximizes economy in processing. It is

Table 3.3 Hebrew Vowel Patterns

paradigm	*voice*	*form*	*meaning*
Qal	active	קָטַל *katal*	'He killed.'
Niph'al	passive	נִקְטַל *niktal*	'He was killed.'
Pi'ēl	intensive active	קִטֵּל *kitel*	'He destroyed.'
Pu'al	intensive passive	קֻטַּל *kutal*	'He was destroyed.'
Hiph'îl	causative active	הִקְטִיל *hiktil*	'He caused a death.'
Hoph'al	causative passive	הָקְטַל *hoktal*	'His death was caused.'
Hithpa'ēl	intensive reflexive	הִתְקַטֵּל *hitkatel*	'He destroyed himself.'

(after Gesenius 2006:510–11)

a real morpho-phonetic process and operates in a language such as Turkish. For example, the suffix equivalent for the English preposition 'on' harmonizes with low /a/ for a word like *adam* 'man'—*adamda* 'on the man'—and with high /i/ for the word *kedi* 'cat': *kedide* 'on the cat.'

Babies pay attention to vowels because of their potential morphological significance. Stem vowels can change even in English verbs to signal tense and aspect, and words with an irregular past tense form are acquired and listed even before the {-ED} rule comes on line. The verbs *drink, ring, sing,* and *sink* all have /ɪ/ for the base form, /æ/ for past tense (*drank*), and /ɑ/ or /ʌ/ for perfective aspect (*drunk*). Those verbs used to belong to class III of Germanic 'strong verbs' (class III being the one in which an *n, m,* or *l* is followed by a consonant; cf. Lehnert 1973:98–99), so the change of stem vowels was once part of the regular grammar and survives in what is now called 'irregular' verbs. (Some verbs, like *bind*, have since dropped out of the pattern). Such vowel sequences are significant not only in verbal 'ablauts,' but across word sequences in general, such as reduplications (*ding -dang -dong, chit-chat*, etc.; cf. Forsyth 2016). Semitic languages make systematic use of vowel patterns in grammar. In Hebrew, the consonants ק *kuf*, ט *tet*, and ל *lamed* form the root ('shoresh') for the word קטל 'kill.' (Right to left!) Of course, 'ktl' is not a word. Hebrew is not usually written with diacritics to indicate vowels, which presents the occasional challenge in translations and at bar mitzvahs. Which vowels are inserted into the consonantal lattice is, as in English strong verbs and nouns, a morphological decision. The sequence /a/—/ɑ/ is a simple past: *katal*. Other vowel patterns (partly achieved with prefixes) signal passives, causatives, and reflexives (Table 3.3).

Not just vowels undergo regular morphological changes. Welsh has an intricate system of changing a word-initial consonant within specific syntactic environments. The word *cath* 'cat,' for instance, mutates after the numeral 'one' to *un gath* but nasalizes after the possessive article 'my' to *fy nghath*. After the preposition *yn* 'in,' the city of Bangor mutates to *ym Mangor*, after *o* 'from' it is *o Fangor* ('Y Treigladau,' BBC Cymru). And who does not know the city of *Llanfair Pwllgwyngyll*, whose outrageous full name (Figure 3.1) is used as a password by the rebel army in the cult film 'Barbarella'? The first two words are *llan* 'church,' and *Mair* 'Mary' mutated for the possessive case (*Fair*).

Figure 3.1 Platform Ticket, Llanfair Pwllgwyngyll Station
Purchased by the author during his studies at Bangor University/Prifysgol Bangor in 1978/79. The full name means 'Church of Mary at the white-hazel pool near a rapid whirlpool [and the] Church of St. Tysilio of the red cave.'

Consonants and vowels can have implications far beyond just distinguishing one word from another. They can carry signals that are important for morphology and syntax. To be able to figure this out, infants are biased toward to expecting a particular ratio of vowels to consonants (Toro et al. 2008; see p. 39). In English, they also pay close attention to the word-initial and word-final phonemes. In a large-scale study of young children acquiring English, Andrew Radford concluded that infants use hallmark lexical inflections (Table 3.1) before they are two years old (1990:35) to sort the lexicon into parts of speech. They do *not*, as is popularly assumed, soley rely on semantic criteria. A noun is not always, as is still taught in schools, a name for a thing or person or place or idea: It can be an action (like a *bath* or a *baby massage*). A verb does not always say what someone does or what something is: In *he underwent surgery*, the agent (a surgeon, hopefully) is implied and the action is done to the subject, and yet the sentence is in the active voice. Nouns, for young children, are the words that pluralize with a final /s/. Verbs can have aspect endings, adjectives/adverbs can take degree endings. In this earliest morphology, **mommy talks* is ungrammatical—an /s/ has no business appearing on a verb. It associates with nouns only.

Radford found a progression from the emergence of lexical inflections to functional free morphemes. Those include articles, of which the indefinite article is particularly tricky in English. Originally the numeral *ān* 'one' in Old English, it still goes only with count nouns (hence *an apple*, but not **a water*), and since there is no plural of 'one,' there is no plural indefinite article (*a spoon—spoons*). Not only do these semantic constraints apply to the use of articles, they also require syntactic structure. The article has scope over the entire noun phrase: In 'the cat in the hat,' it is *cat in the hat* that is presumed known and specific, not just *cat*. The entire noun phrase, thus, becomes the complement of a determiner, which projects a 'determiner phrase' (Figure 3.2).

Radford's argument throughout is that these new layers of syntax come on line in chronological stages. Until they do, toddlerese cannot generate *a spoon* any

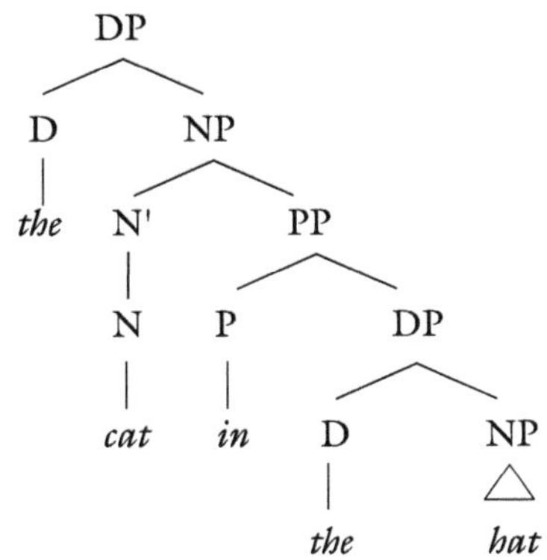

Figure 3.2 The Determiner Phrase

more than *mommy talks*. Parents know this instinctively and rarely call out young children on what may look, from their perspective, like a grammar mistake. If they do, they will run into the same mental barrier observed by psychologist Martin Braine (1971), whose famous passage is here reproduced in full because it is so frequently cited only as a sound bite in the literature:

> For experimental purposes, I have occasionally made an extensive effort to change the syntax of my two children through correction. One case was the use by my two-and-a-half-year-old daughter of *other one* as a noun modifier. Over a period of a few weeks I repeatedly but fruitlessly tried to persuade her to substitute *other* + N for *other one* + N. With different nouns on different occasions, the interchanges went somewhat as follows: "Want other one spoon, Daddy"—"You mean, you want THE OTHER SPOON"—"Yes, I want other one spoon, please, Daddy"—"Can you say 'the other spoon'?"—"Other . . . one . . . spoon"—"Say . . . 'other'"—"Other"—"Spoon"—"Spoon"—"Other . . . spoon"—"Other . . . spoon. Now give me other one spoon?" Further tuition is ruled out by her protest, vigorously supported by my wife. Examples indicating a similar difficulty in using negative information will probably be available to any reader who has tried to correct the grammar of a two- or three-year-old child.
>
> (160–61)

The reason why the entire paragraph is reproduced here is because it includes the family's reaction, which is rarely quoted. Both the girl and her mother torpedo 'further tuition' in (too) advanced morphology. Their vigorous protests were entirely justified, in my opinion, because children are not deficient adults. At any given stage, they have a working grammar. Successive grammars periscope from older ones the way Russian dolls stack upon each other: Each one looks finished and beautiful until the bigger one is added on top. Braine's point, in his paper, actually was that children do not seem to make use of 'negative evidence.' The immediate question that arises, of course, is why children should ever feel any need to adjust their grammars if they look finished and beautiful—can they somehow incorporate 'positive evidence'? This is known as 'the logical problem of language acquisition,' or, in honor of Carl Lee Baker (1981), 'Baker's Paradox.'

If Radford is correct and morpheme systems come on line in the course of maturation, we have a possible solution to that paradox: At some point, the child's brain is ready to process morphology that attaches to words lexically, then morphology that associates with a local phrase, followed by morphology with syntactic hierarchical scope over a clause. A recent publication by Goucha, Zaccarella, and Friederici (2017) seems to point toward that kind of maturation and neural reality in the brain. A pathway from what is labeled area 38 in Figure 1.2, meeting up with the black line at the frontal operculum, seems responsible for 'local combinations,' whereas the dotted line leading to area 44 of Broca's area takes on 'hierarchical syntax processing.' Given the discussion above, it seems logical that the imposition of rules upon speech sounds leads the child's attention to morphemes with syntactic functions.

A maturational schedule also may help solve a second problem: the impression that children acquiring English seem to plateau and then make a sudden jump in their language abilities. This 'discontinuity' effect can be explained as well. The determiner system contains more than just articles; it is, in fact, a rather sizeable system in English. Table 3.4 shows the parts of speech that can occupy the place of the article (i.e. that cannot occur next to an article).

The demonstratives and quantifiers can also function like / as pronouns (e.g. 'I want some.'/'Those are mine.'). Radford therefore subsumes the entire pronominal system of English under the 'D-system' (determiner system), which includes personal pronouns (*I/me, you, . . .*), interrogative pronouns (*who/whom, whose*), indefinite pronouns (*someone, . . .*), possessive pronouns (*mine, yours, . . .*),

Table 3.4 The Determiner System of English

part of speech	*α*	*form*	*NP*
definite article		*the*	*spoon(s)*
indef. article, sg.		*a*	*spoon*
indef. article, pl.		*Ø*	*spoons*
def. possessive determiner clitic	*John*	*'s*	*spoon(s)*
def. proximal demonstrative det., sg.		*this*	*spoon*
def. proximal demonstrative det., pl.		*these*	*spoons*
def. distal demonstrative det., sg.		*that*	*spoon*
def. distal demonstrative det., pl.		*those*	*spoons*
quantifier		*some, several, . . .*	*spoons*
def. personal possessive pronominal det.		*my, your, his, her, its, our, your, their*	*spoon(s)*

'relative' pronouns, etc. When all these forms start emerging in the child's speech, it looks like there is a dramatic jump in development, but mainly we are witnessing the acquisition of a functional local category that merges with a noun phrase. Until that happens, a child will use a formulaic place holder such as 'other one.'

Morphemes affecting the structure of an entire clause will be discussed in Chapter 4. Here are the points to carry over into the survey of children's books below:

- Consonants and vowels do more than distinguish one word from another. In order to figure out the morphology of their native languages, infants must pay close attention to their patterning. Infants' stochastic perception of how consonants and vowel distribute is biased from birth.
- Lexical morphemes (words) and functional lexical morphemes (e.g. the plural ending) appear to obey a mutual exclusivity principle, which must be relaxed to allow synonyms and allomorphs.
- Phonotactic rules apply to adjacent sounds (e.g. coarticulation), to specific positions (e.g. word-final devoicing of consonants), or across syllables (e.g. harmony). They are the precursors to allomorphic rules (e.g. the choice of how to pronounce the endings *-s* and *-ed* depending on the preceding phoneme).
- Infants use lexical morphemes to categorize their lexicon into nouns (*-s*), verbs (*-en/-ed, -ing*), adjectives/adjectives (*-er, -est*), and prepositions (*-Ø*).
- Three types of English morphemes emerge sequentially based on brain maturation. Lexical inflections of the kind that identify parts of speech attach in the productive lexicon. Free lexical-functional morphemes such as D (determiner) take a lexical phrase—such as NP—as complement and affect that entire phrase. These local concatenations are ventral in the brain and involve pathways to the frontal operculum of Broca's area. At the final stage of syntactic acquisition, a pathway in the arcuate fasciculus connects to Broca's Area 44 to process morphemes that require hierarchical syntactic processes because they apply to entire clauses.
- Insofar as these three types of morphemes emerge sequentially within a defined maturational time frame (between age 1.5 and 3 years old), there appears to be a Critical Period (or at least a Sensitive Period) for morphology.
- At each stage, the child has a fully operational grammar with rule-based output and biased perception. It is not possible to coax a child into processing morphemes without the prerequisite grammar in place. Any attempt to encourage linguistic growth must rely on positive evidence, the saliency of which arises, in its own time, in playful negotiation and surprise.

Morphology in Children's Books

Since production and perception are processed differently, children can be aware of the disparity between their own output and how adults talk ('Only daddy can say *jump*,' p. 37). For adult language learners, Robert Lado predicted that the greatest discrepancies should cause the greatest difficulties (1957:59–60). Wolfgang Klein turned this 'Contrastive Hypothesis' on its head: The greatest differences to the target language stick out like sore thumbs and are easy to address. It is with increasing expertise that the disparities become more and more subtle and the learner starts having a 'matching problem' (1986:62). Adults learning a second language typically cease and desist at some premature and convenient 'end point.' Children growing into their first languages do not have that luxury because their acquisition structures their brains, as becomes starkly apparent when one compares the brain scans of a healthy and of a neglected three-year-old (Perry & Pollard 1997).

Children's books, we have seen, can provide salient input for children discovering sounds and words, supplementing parental child-directed talk. Since there is so much to learn and understand when it comes to morphology, one would think that morphological errors ('I holded the bunny') provide teachable moments. But adults do not, as we saw, react with formal corrections ('No, it's *held*, not **holded*'). Rather, they sometimes model correct form with recasts ('You held the bunny!? That must have been nice.'), paraphrases, questions, etc. However, even those reactions are so unsystematic, inconsistent, and infrequent that they do not rise to the level of 'noisy feedback' (Marcus 1993:78), let alone complete or just partial feedback (59). Children's books have different tricks between their sleeves. In the following, we investigate how children's books go beyond adult child-directed speech in providing provocative positive evidence and making morphemes, including functional morphemes, salient for the child. They use literary devices like repetition and rhyme, language play, and morphological violations to capture the child's attention.

One way in which children's books' authors draw attention to a particular morpheme is by the use of repetition. A song by Raffi uses repetition to play with vowel harmony ('I like to eat, eat, eat eepples eend beeneenees'). A passage in *The Story of Ferdinand* (Leaf 1936) repeats verbs inflected with *-ing* for progressive aspect. The peaceful, flower-loving bull had just had the misfortune of sitting down on a bumble bee:

> He ran around puffing and snorting, butting and pawing the ground as if he were crazy.

Similarly, here is a sentence from Robert Kraus' *Another Mouse to Feed*, in which the many children of a mouse family decide to give their hard-working parents a break and take on small jobs for pay:

> Edgar, modeling himself after his father got two after-school jobs: delivering newspapers and sweeping up in a grocery store.

Douglas Florian's *mammalabilia* contains a poem entitled 'The Beaver' that consists simply of compounds that end in the derivational morpheme *-er* :

> Wood-chopper
> Tree-dropper
> Tail-flopper
> Stream-stopper

Just as effectively, an author can also choose to cap off the repetition of suffixed words with their bare form. In his poem 'I am waiting waiting waiting,' Jack Prelutsky repeats *waiting* six times in the first stanza, followed by 'I can't wait' in the third (*The Dragons Are Singing Tonight* 1995:9):

> I am waiting waiting waiting for my dragon egg to hatch,
> I've been waiting waiting waiting for a year,
> Ever since I found it hidden in my mother's garden patch—
> Now I think my baby dragon's almost here.
> . . .
> I am counting off the seconds till my dragon first appears,
> Poking through the shell to freedom with a horn,
> I can't wait to see its winglets, tiny muzzle, tail and ears,
> When my brand new baby dragon's finally born.

Similarly a poem by Margaret Wise Brown, 'Three White Rabbits Running' (*Under the Sun and the Moon* 1993:28) repeats (ingeniously, I think) three single line three times almost verbatim, alternating the form 'running' in the first lines with 'ran' in the refrain. The juxtapositions of a verb with and without the suffix call attention to the productivity and regularity of the morpheme.

An author can also choose a single stem and present different derivations of it, which calls attention to morphemes by way of contrast rather than repetition. Evelyn Schroth pointed out that Theodor Geisel likes to use such 'polyptotons': '*cooked by my cooks in my Cookermobile, turned on her Un-thinker and unthinks the thing away, the smog you smogged up, the wubble wubbled in a wubble-some way*—shades of Jabberwocky, but also a return to classical rhetoric' (1978:749). Polyptotons also run through *Runaway Bunny* by Margaret Wise Brown:

> "If you become a fish in a trout stream," said his mother,
> "I will become a fisherman and I will fish for you."

Likewise, we find polyptotons in the writing of A. A. Milne, *fauthor* of *Winnie the Pooh* :

> "I think the bees suspect something!"
> "What sort of thing?"
> "I don't know. But something tells me that they're *suspicious* !"
> (1961:15)

Some of the derivations do not involve added morphemes, as in *a fish/I will fish*. In these special cases, the word undergoes what is known as a 'function shift,' and Winnie-the-Pooh has noticed the inconsistent applications of this process in English:

> Cottleston, Cottleston, Cottleston Pie,
> A fly can't bird, but a bird can fly.
> (ibid., 74)

Of course, children's authors will also deliberately use morphology to derive anomalous forms. Parents may adore those forms in children because they are cute. When they occur in children's books, adults tend to perceive them as off-putting. One author who has drawn the ire of parents and librarians in particular is Barbara Park, whose heroine 'Junie B. Jones,' the Amelia Bedelia of grammar, writes replete with such anomalous forms such as *bestest* (*Junie B. Jones and the Stupid Smelly Bus*, 1992:2), *rided* (ibid., 5), *hanged out my tongue* (*Mrs. Jones has a Monster under her Bed*, 1997:11), and *runned* (ibid., 14).

In an interview, the author quotes an irate grandmother from Minnesota about not using the 'Queen's English': 'People act as if I'm teaching children how to blow up cats' (Grossman 2007). The author has a share of enthusiastic followers, but the irritation she is capable of exciting shows that parents expect children's books to elevate their loved ones out of their kindertalk rather than indulge them in it. Junie B. Jones is sassy enough as a character and should not additionally be a bad role model in morphology.

There appears to be a solid line that authors should not cross, between engaging the child in language play and caricaturizing child language. Dan Slobin found out what happens when an adult mirrors a child's morphology, by repeating *readed* after his daughter Heida, then four years and seven months old (1978:53):

DAN: Oh, that's right; yeah, I readed the beginning of it.
HEIDA: *Readed ?!* [annoyed surprise] *Read !* [insisting on the obvious].
DAN: Oh, yeah—read.
HEIDA: Will you stop that, papa?
DAN: Sure.

Not every surprise, then, is delightful; Heida's was 'annoyed surprise.' Surprises of that kind are unlikely to trigger exploration because the annoyance is the result of lost rapport and trust, compromising the safe zone within which playful exploration is fun. The child, aware of the disparity between own and adult grammar, feels put on the spot. It appears that Barbara Park has crossed that line for at least some of her audience—presumably younger children and protective adults.

In contrast, some authors brilliantly get away with anomalous morphology because they present it playfully instead of caricaturizing child language. Milne makes a game out of polyptotons by deriving non-existing forms:

> He squeezed and he squoze, and with one last sqooze he was out. (*House at Pooh Corner* 144–45).

Lewis Carroll directly comments on whether anomalous morphology is childish or just non-standard:

> "Curiouser and curiouser!" cried Alice (she was so surprised, that for the moment she quite forgot how to speak good English). (*Alice in Wonderland* 35).

Authors can make morphology into a game, as Pippa Goodhart did with her over-generation of diminutive plurals ('Three little ghosties/sat on their posties,/eating burnt toasties,/telling big boasties'). Henrik Drescher's 'When you cross a beastie, then he'll feastie' (*Pat the Beastie, 1993*) adds an anomaly in that diminutives are not added to verbs. These violations are designed to surprise both the child and the adult reader alike because they are creative, not imitative.

A. A. Milne, purveyor of fine heffalumps and woozles, plays with morphology in such a way as to delight a dual audience. In the following passages from *Winnie the Pooh*, he draws attention to functional morphemes and productive morphology with interesting violations:

- Determiners—gender-marked article: When the narrator queries Christopher Robin why he named his bear Winnie when he was a boy, Christopher Robin responds: "He's Winnie-ther-Pooh. Don't you know what 'ther' means?" (3). It is probably safe to assume that Milne modeled *ther* on the German gender-marked article *der*.
- Determiners—pronouns without any reference at all: Winnie the Pooh ruminates in a poem whether there is some truth to the fact "That what is which and which is what?" (100). Piglet, in turn, "discovered that it would be never, and was trying to remember what 'it' was, and hoping it wasn't anything nice . . ." (115)
- Unattached auxiliaries:

> 'We can't all, and some of us don't. That's all there is to it.' (74)
> 'Why does a chicken, I don't know why.' (75)

- Outlier irregular (strong) plural/reanalysis of subjunctive *were* as plural:

> Look at their tracks! Three, as it were, Woozles, and one, as it was, Wizzle." (40–41)

- Perfective-aspect suffix paired with passive-voice auxiliary:

> [Owl, having been misunderstood by Pooh to have sneezed when pronouncing the word *issue*] "You can't sneeze without knowing it."
> "Well, you can't know it without having been sneezed." (ibid., 51)

- Morpho-scrambles (there is possibly a better term for this):

> "Help, help!" cried Piglet, "a Heffalump, a Horrible Heffalump!" and he scampered off as hard as he could, still crying out, "Help, help, a Herrible Hoffalump! Hoff, Hoff, a Hellible Horralump! Holl, Holl, a Hoffable Hellerump!" (ibid., 69)
> "Well," said Owl, "the customary procedure in such cases is as follows."
> "What does Crustimoney Proseedcake mean?" said Pooh. (50)

Roald Dahl, by the way, elevates Milne's morpho-scrambles to a native way of speaking in *The BFG*:

> 'Just because we happen not to have actually seen something with our own two little winkles, we think it is not existing. What about for instance the great squizzly scotch-hopper?'
> 'I beg your pardon?' Sophie said.
> 'And the humplecrimp?'
> 'What's that?' Sophie said.
> 'And the wraprascal?'
> 'The what?' Sophie said.
> 'And the crumpscoddle?'
> 'Are they animals?' Sophie asked.
> 'They is common animals,' said the BFG contemptuously. 'I is not a very know-all giant myself, but it seems to me that you is an absolutely know-nothing human bean. Your brain is full of rotten-wool.'

- Reanalysis of morpheme boundaries by analogy: Upon hearing the word *ambush*, Winnie the Pooh launches into an anecdote of falling into a *gorse-bush* (120).
- Plural inflection within derivations and on non-count nouns:

> And then I look about for things,
> Like Rushings-Out, and Rescuings
> And Savings from the Dragon's Lair . . . (Milne, *We Are Six*, 57)

Theodor Geisel extended his funny sound combinations to stoo-roarus morphology, including a type of morpheme that has yet to receive an official name in English grammar. I call it a 'compounding morpheme' that links roots together, a bit like the *-o-* in Wallace and Gromit's *Thrill-o-matic* (a theme ride in Blackpool) or the *-a-* in *workaholic, hunkalicious*, and *meatasaurus*.[3] Geisel's *-ma-* appears to have two allomorphs that seem sensitive to consonant harmony, *-fa-* and *-ba-*:

- Compounding morphemes

-ma-	sala-ma-goo (*The Butter Battle Book*)
	dil-ma-dilts (*Great Day for Up!*)
	zomba-ma-tant (*If I Ran the Zoo*)
	whisper-ma-phone (*The Lorax*)
	yuzz-a-ma-tuzz (*On Beyond Zebra*)
	sala-ma-sond (*Yertle the Turtle*)
-fa-	motta-fa-potta-fa-pell (*If I Ran the Zoo*)
	fotta-fa-zee (*You're Only Old Once!*)
-ba-	brigger-ba-root (*If I Ran the Circus*)
	bar-ba-loots (*The Lorax*)

- Two inflections on a single stem (degree plus tense/aspect)

  I biggered my factory. I biggered my roads.
  . . .
  I went right on biggering (*The Lorax*)

- Derivation conflicting with compounding order: "a quicker quacker-backer" (*Oh Say can you Say?*) [should be *a quicker back-quacker*]
- "Polysynthesis": Ham-ikka-Schnim-ikka-Schnam-ikka Schnopp (*Scrambled Eggs Super!*)
- Hyper-suffixation (*On Beyond Zebra!*)

  He *only* comes out of his hole, I'm afraid,
  When the right kind of softish nice music is played
  On a kind of a hunting horn called the o'Grunth.
  And to learn how to play it takes month after month
  Of practicing, practicing. Isn't much fun-th.
  And, besides, it's quite heavy. Weighs almost a tun-th.
  That's why few people bother to play the o'Grunth
  So the Flunnel's been out of his tunnel just one-th.

- Degree inflection on a pronoun: "There is no one alive who is you-er than you!" (*Happy Birthday to You!*)

The fact that these violations occur in children's books is a testament to the linguistic expertise of their authors. It is very easy after all, as Eeyore finds out when he is trying to compose an ode to Christopher Robin (see p. 117), for things to keep going wrong. *Supercalifragilisticexpialidocious*, for instance, cannot be a single word, as the song by the Sherman brothers claims, because *ex-* is word-initial, thus *-ic* must be word final. Richard Lederer has ferreted out the parts of this 'conglammeration' (Herman 1931): *super* 'above,' *cali* 'beauty,' *fragilistic* 'delicate,' *expiali-* 'to atone,' *docious* 'educable'—i.e. 'atoning for extreme and delicate beauty [while being] highly educable' (Lederer 1998:40–41). There is a clear word boundary between *fragilistic* and *expiali-*, and violating it for the sake of a compound is, to quote Mary Poppins again, 'Not at all attractive to my way of thinking.'

Among the literary devices used to highlight morphology we have seen repetition, repetition ending with a counterexample, polyptotons, mismatches, and all kinds of masterfully creative violations. Authors of children's books can create a morphological exploratorium. Their language can go considerably beyond what we find in the spontaneous speech that adults direct at children—and it seems to add to their works' endurance when they do so. Some authors repeatedly test out their material on children (sometimes their own) to find out what delights and surprises them, and in the course of doing so they amass a level of expertise on par with applied linguists. It is hard to see how a child's interest in word formation could be stimulated as keenly by any other device than children's literature.

Notes

1. I am quoting the complete passage from Fries (1957:v) here because it is difficult to find, yet important: 'A child in learning his native language has learned not only to attend to (receptively and productively) the particular contrasts that function as signals in that language; he has learned to *ignore* all those features that do not so function. He has developed a special set of "blind spots" that prevent him from responding to features that do not constitute the contrastive signals of his native language. Learning a second language, therefore, constitutes a very different task from learning the first language. The basic problems arise not out of any essential difficulty in the features of the new language themselves but primarily out of the special "set" created by the first language habits.'
2. 'Tusschen analytische en synthetische talen bestaat geen wezenlijk in de natuur liggend verschil'—There is no fundamental design difference between analytical and synthetic languages. I came across this reference in Jan Noordegraaf (2006:144).
3. My comparison does not do Geisel justice, because his infixes have integrity on their own, whereas *-aholic, -alicious*, etc. in English are endings spliced from existing words and grafted, with minor changes to the first vowel, onto other roots. Harold Wentworth (1942) discussed *-eroo* as such an example of 'neo-pseudo-suffixes'; Arnold Zwicky has popularized the term 'libfixes' because he sees them as 'liberated' parts of words (arnoldzwicky.org/linguistics-notes/libfix-postings). I owe the reference to Wentworth to Zwicky, who has it from Ben Zimmer.

References

Baker, Mark C. 1988. *Incorporation: A theory of grammatical function changing*. Chicago: University of Chicago Press.

Baker, Carl L., and John J. McCarthy (eds.) 1981. *The logical problem of language acquisition*. Cambridge, MA: MIT Press.

Braine, Martin D. S. 1971. On two types of models of the internalization of grammars. *The ontogenesis of grammar: A theoretical symposium*, ed. by Dan J. Slobin, 153–86. New York: Academic Press.

Brown, Robert. 1973. *A first language: The early stages*. Cambridge, MA: Harvard University Press.

Carlyle, Thomas. 1860. Gryll Grange: By the author of 'Headlong Hall.' *Frazer's Magazine* 61 (April).447–62.

Chomsky, Noam. 2000. Minimalist inquiries: The framework. *Step by step: Essays on minimalist syntax in honor of Howard Lasnik*, ed. by Roger Martin, David Michaels, Juan Uriagereka, and Samuel Jay Keyser, 89–156. Cambridge, MA: MIT Press.

Clemens, Samuel. 1880. The awful German language. *Selected shorter writings of Mark Twain*, ed. by Walter Blair, 177–94. Boston: Houghton Mifflin, 1962. Originally published in *A tramp abroad.*

Davies, Benjamin; Nan Xu Rattanasone; and Katherine Demuth. 2017. Two-year olds' sensitivity to inflectional plural morphology: Allomorphic effects. *Language Learning and Development* 13(1).38–53.

Forsyth, Mark. 2016. The language rules we know—but don't know we know. BBC (8 September). Online: www.bbc.com/culture/story/20160908-the-language-rules-we-know-butdont-know-we-know.

Fries, Charles C. 1957. Foreword. *Linguistics across cultures: Applied linguistics for language teachers*, by Robert Lado, v. Ann Arbor: University of Michigan Press.

Gabelentz, Georg von der. 1883. *Anfangsgründe der chinesischen Grammatik: Mit Übungsstücken*. Leipzig: Weigel.

Gesenius, Wilhelm. 2006. *Gesenius' Hebrew grammar*, edited and enlarged by E. Kautzsch, translated by A. E. Cowley. Mineola, NY: Dover.

Goucha, Tomás; Emiliano Zaccarella; and Angela D. Friederici. 2017. A revival of the *Homo loquens* as a builder of labeled structures: Neurocognitive considerations. *Neuroscience and Biobehavioral Reviews*, in press. doi:10.1016/j.neubiorev.2017.01.036.

Grossman, Anna Jane. 2007. Is Junie B. Jones talking trash? *The New York Times*, 26 July, G1. Online: www.nytimes.com/2007/07/26/fashion/26junie.html.

Herman, Helen. 1931. A-muse-ings. *Syracuse Daily Orange*, 10 March. Syracuse, NY: Syracuse University. Online: www.visualthesaurus.com/cm/wordroutes/tracking-down-the-roots-of-a-super-word/supercal31.jpg.

Hoogvliet, Jan Marius. 1885. *Studia Homerica: Specimen literarium inaugurale*. University of Leiden: Ph.D. dissertation, Leiden: van Doesburgh.

Jones, Owen; Edward Williams; and William Owen Pughe. 1870. Amryw ganuau, nis gwyddis pwy a'u cant: Englynyon y klyweit. *The Myvyrian archaiology of Wales: Collected out of ancient manuscripts*, 127–30. Denbigh: Thomas Gee.

Klein, Wolfgang. 1986. *Second language acquisition*, translated by Bohuslaw Jankowski (Cambridge textbooks in linguistics). Cambridge, New York: Cambridge University Press.

Lado, Robert. 1957. *Linguistics across cultures: Applied linguistics for language teachers*. Ann Arbor: University of Michigan Press.

Lederer, Richard. 1998. *Crazy English: The ultimate joy ride through our language*, revised edition. New York: Gallery Books, Simon & Schuster.

Lehnert, Martin. 1973. *Altenglisches Elementarbuch: Einführung, Grammatik, Texte mit Übersetzung und Wörterbuch* (Sammlung Göschen), Band 5125. Berlin: Walter de Gruyter.

Marcus, Gary F. 1993. Negative evidence in language acquisition. *Cognition* 46.53–85.

Miller, D. Gary. 1993. *Complex verb formation* (Current issues in linguistic theory), vol. 95. Amsterdam: John Benjamins.

Noordegraaf, Jan. 2006. Hoogvliet, Gabelentz, en het Sjineesch: Uit de geschiedenis van het taaltypologie. *Amicitia in academia: Composities voor Els Elffers*, ed. by Jan Noordegraaf, Frank Vonk, and Marijke van der Wal, 143–53. Amsterdam: Stichting Neerlandistiek VU; Münster: Nodus.

Olsen, Carl Christian. 2004. Kalaallisut—grænlenska. *Norðurlandamálin með rótum og fótum*, ed. by Iben Stampe Sletten, 113–27. København: Nordisk ministerråd, Norden. Online: norden.diva-portal.org/smash/get/diva2:702376/FULLTEXT01.pdf.

Perry, Bruce D., and Ronnie Pollard. 1997. Altered brain development following global neglect in early childhood. *Society for Neuroscience: Proceedings from the 27th Annual Meeting*, New Orleans, 25–30 October. Washington, DC: Society for Neuroscience. Online: childtrauma.org/wp-content/uploads/2013/12/PerryPollard_SocNeuro.pdf.

Radford, Andrew. 1990. *Syntactic theory and the acquisition of English syntax: The nature of early child grammars of English*. Oxford, Cambridge, MA: Basil Blackwell.

Schroth, Evelyn. 1978. Dr. Seuss and language use. *The Reading Teacher* 31(7) (April).748–50.

Scriptural views of Holy Baptism, as established by the consent of the ancient church, and contrasted with the systems of modern schools, by Members of the University of Oxford. 1840. *Scripts for the Times* 2(67). London: Rivington.

Sherman, Richard M., and Robert Sherman. 1964. Supercalifragilisticexpialidocious. *Mary Poppins*. Orlando: Disney.

Slobin, Dan. 1978. A case study of early language awareness. *The child's conception of language*, ed. by Anne Sinclair, Robert J. Jarvella, and Willem J. M. Levelt, 45–54. New York: Springer.

Toro, Juan M.; Marina Nespor; Jacques Mehler; and Luca L. Bonatti. 2008. Finding words and rules in a speech stream. *Psychological Science* 19(2) (March).137–44.

Wentworth, Harold. 1942. The neo-pseudo-suffix '-eroo.' *American Speech* 17(1) (February). 10–15.

Y treigladau—The mutations. 2014. *Learn Welsh—Grammar*. BBC Cymru Wales. Online: www.bbc.co.uk/wales/learnwelsh/pdf/welshgrammar_mutations.pdf.

Yang, Charles. 2016. *The price of linguistic productivity: How children learn to break rules of language*. Cambridge, MA: MIT Press.

Zwicky, Arnold. Libfix postings. *Arnold Zwicky's Blog*. Online: arnoldzwicky.org/linguistics-notes/libfix-postings.

4 Morphosyntax and Semantics

Bootstrapping Maturation

This is the dog that worried the cat
That killed the rat that ate the malt
That lay in the house that Jack built.

A dog bothers the cat responsible for the demise of a rat that had helped itself to malt from a house built by Jack. . . . Unsurprisingly, it gets successively more convoluted after that. 'This is the dog' plays with structure the same way one would play with 'Russian dolls': The house that Jack built is the location of the malt, which becomes the rat's meal, which in turn becomes the cat's meal, which may likely become the dog's meal. Unless something happens to the dog.

The syntactic term for such nesting (structures inside structures) is 'recursion.' Minimal rules can produce infinite output simply by being applied repeatedly or by calling on each other. For an example of the latter, imagine a noun-phrase rule NP → (ART) N (PP) that contains an optional article, the noun projecting the noun phrase NP, and an optional prepositional phrase, and another rule PP → P NP which says that a prepositional phrase PP must contain an object noun phrase. Just those two rules can generate a nested structure like *cat Z in the hat of cat Y in the hat of cat X in the hat of* . . . all the way down to *cat A*, who resides in the hat of *the Cat in the Hat*. Phrase structures can plug into each other like subroutines in a computer program, though running such a program can lead to undesired results, as I found out in 1978 when I learned how to program at the University of Bangor, Wales, and earned my first raised eyebrow. My code had two subroutines pointing to each other without a counter to stop them from doing so infinitely, thus forcing a shutdown of an entire DEC-10 mainframe just to terminate my program. At that time, mainframes, unlike little *cat Z*, had no VOOM to abort individual programs. When it comes to language, humans (with the possible exceptions of Immanuel Kant and William Faulkner) know when it is time to stop embedding.

In the first part of this chapter, I will describe three hallmarks of the interface of semantics and English syntax: MERGE, phoricity, and syntactic movement. Merging is what a human combinatorial grammar is all about: pairing words and phrases into hierarchical structures. Phoricity comes into play when words in different parts of the resulting structure share a reference, such as a pronoun and a noun phrase (e.g. 'Donald*i* never blames himself*i* '). Moving involves raising a constituent (e.g. fronting the *wh-* proform from the object position in '*Whom* did you meet ~~*whom*~~ in the store?'). Of these three operations, MERGE is probably the only one that is part of Universal Grammar. The discussion of literature below will show that children's books, nursery rhymes, and songs can focus the child's attention on both semantic and syntactic structure. Their arsenal again includes outliers, mismatches, and playful violations.

MERGE: Building Structure From the Bottom Up

When an infant points to a ball and utters a single word meaning 'ball,' we presume that that speech act reflects labeling. When an infant points to a fur coat and says 'kitty,' there is no mistake. A single word can be a holophrase (see p. 63): This object is a ball, that fur coat is kitty-like in one or more of its properties. Both utterances look like predications at the one-word level.

Predications capture some kind of 'aboutness' relation—B says something about A. Usually, that implies the presence of at least two words (cf. McNeill 1970), such as 'pillow dirty' (Brown 1973:125). What B says about A could be anything from membership in a class ('is a baby'), a quality ('is hot'), a location ('is in the refrigerator'), an action ('is sleeping'), a state ('is dead'), etc. Christopher Robin and Pooh decide on a predication when Pooh is holding a long pole in his hands and calling it the North Pole (*Winnie-the-Pooh* 127).

Milne's playful *mis*-identification urges us to look at what the meaning of *is* is. Spanish, for instance, has two kinds of *is* and makes a distinction between an inalienable predication (*ser*) and a situational one (*estar*). A child could make a *ser*-type statement by pointing to an object A and labeling it B, 'ball.' Following the logic of Franz Clemens Brentano (1874:276–90), labeling is already an act of predication: 'A exists' (276; so also Grace De Laguna 1927, discussed in Brown 1973:127). From there it is only a small step to saying 'AB exists,' as in 'pillow dirty': Predication asserts a *pairing* of A and B.

We observe predicating pairings naturally in English, even without the use of a linking morpheme (such as *is* or *as*). An adjective in a noun phrase like 'good father,' for example, predicates a quality onto a noun: 'the father is good' (Steinthal 1860:101, cf. Jespersen 1924 [1963]:149). Pairings occur in many syntactic places, and they do not even have to be adjacent:

(11) a. He is a *good father*. ‖ 'the father is good'
b. They elected *him president*. ‖ 'he is president'
c. They think of *him* as *president*. ‖ 'he is president' (maybe)
e. Mark drank the *wine cold*. ‖ 'the wine is cold'
e. *Mark* drank the wine *cold*. ‖ 'Mark is cold'
f. I want *you gone*. ‖ 'you are gone' (ideally)

The examples of (11) illustrate a technical problem Edwin Williams struggled with in his famous article 'Predication': 'The environments of predication are quite diverse' (1980:206). The bottom line for Williams was that predication amounts to associating ('coindexing') a noun phrase with another constituent, within certain structural limits:

(12) If NP and X are coindexed, NP must c-command X or a variable bound to X. (Williams 1980:206)

The constituent-command (c-command) constraint essentially means that the NP and X (or a substitute for X) must be dominated by the same node in a tree. If they are sisters (same level), like DP and I' in Figure 4.1, then they c-command each other, which is fine. Mostly, X is found farther down the tree (like V' in the same figure).

I have two issues with (12). First, it defines one term (predication) with another (coindexing), which just kicks the can down the road. Second, predication does not by definition always involve a noun phrase, as Williams presumes in (12). This is obvious from the following examples:

(13) a. *To err* is *human*. (infinitive)
b. *Whatever you can do* is *fine*. (clause)
c. *More expensive* isn't always *better*. (adjective phrase)
d. *All that glitters* isn't *gold*. (pronominal quantifier)

What is more, a noun-noun compound like *tramp lady* can be some kind of predication ('the lady is a tramp'). Even a compound adjective with an adverb, as in *tough talking lady*, predicates something ('the talking is tough'). Clearly, predication is a pairing procedure.

Georg von der Gabelentz formalized Brentano's notion of predication as pairing. He captured the essence of syntax (Chinese syntax, in this case) with the following function (1883:iv):

(14) $f(A, B) = x$

Formula (14) means that a constituent x is created by pairing A and B. Semantically, (14) says AB exists. Structurally, (14) looks like a minimal tree, with x as the dominating node and A, B c-commanding each other. The only thing this formula misses is that if the terms A and B reflect a predication, we do not know which of the two is the "subject." Noam Chomsky's operation MERGE addresses that difficulty of interpretation by saying that A and B form an unordered set in which one term is *head* and the other a *complement* that was merged to it—an interface that is 'ambiguity free' (Fodor 1998).

What is special about MERGE is that a set {A,B} can itself be merged into another set, {C,{A,B}}, yielding properties that Chomsky has claimed for decades to be hallmarks of human language: hierarchical and recursive binary structures (Chomsky 2017). The sentence 'The cat in the hat comes back,' expressed as an unordered set, is {*back*,{*come*,{{*in*,{*hat*,*the*}},{*cat*,*the*}}}}. Goucha, Zaccarella, and Friederici (2017) propose that each set should be labeled for its head, which makes it, in their view, that much easier to turn into a tree structure. As an unordered, hierarchical semantic structure, it would presumably plot as in Figure 4.1, where s is a set (here, headed by a determiner D, a preposition P, a verb V, or an adverb A), and would then map to syntax.[1]

The semantic structure on the left side of Figure 4.1 may be simpler still if it initially contains just the content words and if the function words are added during mapping to surface.[2]

How a semantic structure is mapped into linear word order is very much language specific. There is a binary choice to be made of how to order each set, and languages can indeed place determiners after nouns, have postpositions instead of prepositions, have the subject follow the verb, etc. English is quite consistent in placing heads first, followed by complements: A determiner phrase is *the cat*. In contrast, in Haitian Creole the determiner follows the complement in the same noun phrase, *chat la* (except that we also see the occasional head-last determiner phrase in English, as when Mycroft addresses Sherlock as *brother mine*). Chapter 8 will address how such binary choices are realized in part as a function of cooperation in discourse.

The interface between local concatenations and hierarchical structure building appears to have cortical reality. Region 44 of Broca's area is 'linked in' whenever hierarchical syntactic structures need to be processed (even for an 'artificial language,' though that term is an oxymoron to begin with). The pathways in Figure 4.2 connecting Brodmann areas 45, 38, and 22 map 'local' combinations (like single MERGE pairs) to hierarchical ones, as indicated in Figure 4.1.

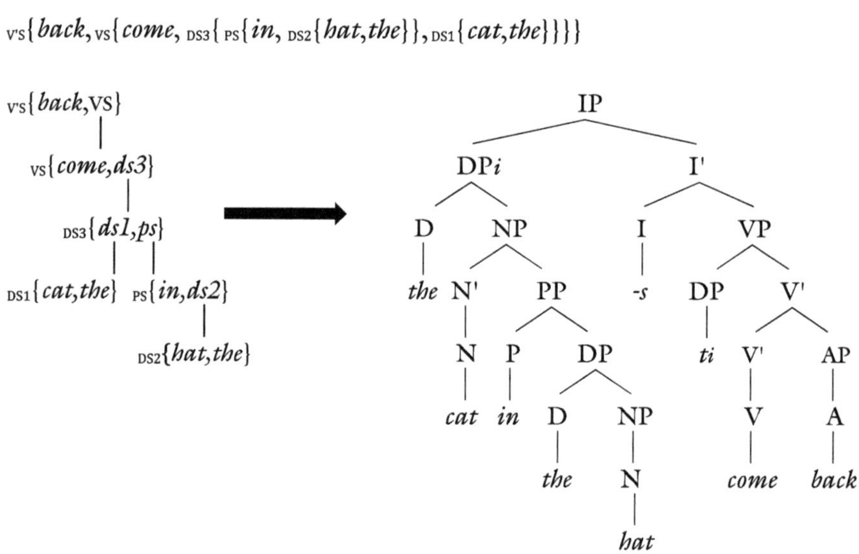

Figure 4.1 Mapping a Merge Set to Syntactic Structure

Note that Figure 4.2 depicts an adult brain. In children, Broca's areas 44 and 45 appear to compete rather than cooperate (Figure 4.3), which presumably means that children's syntax is more autonomous than adults', i.e. less context sensitive. Certainly, young children tend to interpret sentences literally—oblivious to irony, metaphor, sarcasm, figurative speech.

The discussion of predication here dovetails with the discussion of first words in Chapter 2. If objects depicted in a cardboard picture book are salient for their scripts (this is what the object can do/this is what I can do with that object), then it is easy to see how nouns naturally merge with verbs. Verbs *contain* scripts. The verb *eat*, for example, specifies something being consumed. That verb-complement set can then be merged again to a suitable agent (who is animate and masticates with volition). The verb *put* specifies an object and a location, *give* an object and a beneficiary, etc. We even categorize our verbs by their scripts, calling them intransitive, transitive, ditransitive, complex transitive, etc. (Levin 1993). It was, incidentally, this realization (that verbs come with structural blueprints to accommodate their scripts) that led to the elimination of much of the phrase structure machinery of early generative-transformational grammar, because the verb's structural requirements were specified redundantly (once in the lexicon for each verb, and once in matching syntactic phrase structure rules).

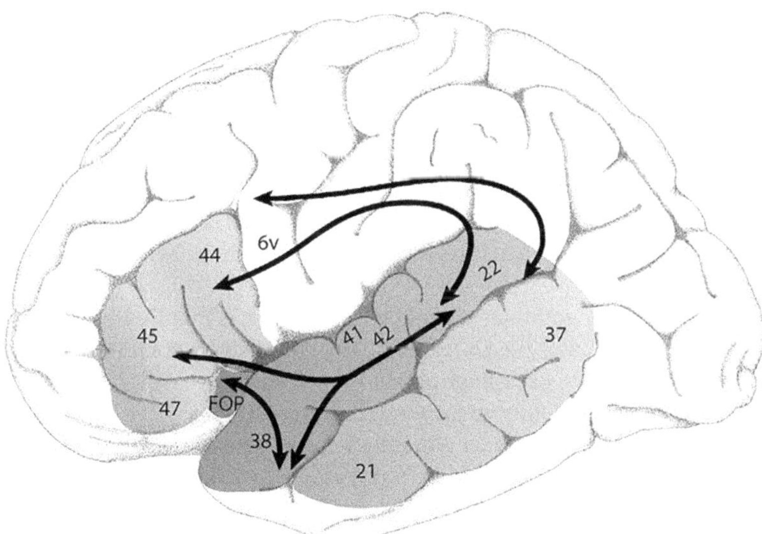

Figure 4.2 Language Processing Pathways (Goucha et al. 2017)

Ventral pathways:	FOP/38 = local combinatorial processing
	45/38/22 = semantic processing
Dorsal pathways:	44/22 = syntactic/hierarchical processing
	6v/22 = phonological/articulatory processing

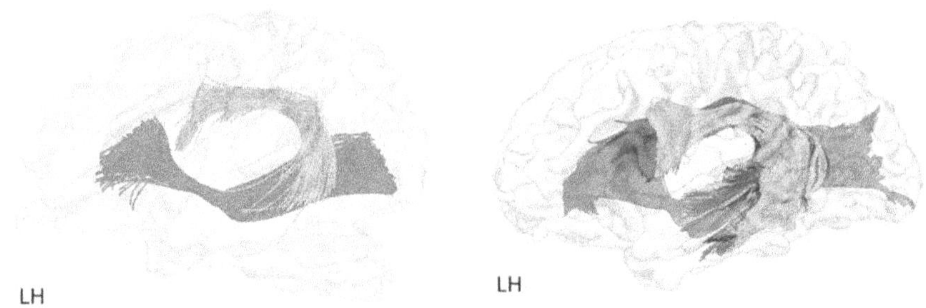

Figure 4.3 Neonate and Adult Pathways to Broca's Areas 44 and 45
(Perani et al. 2011:16058)

The current literature refers to the bundle of criteria for what is a suitable object etc. with the term *thematic role* (or θ-role for short).

Phoricity: Words Pointing to Other Words

Every grammar book mentions pronouns, but not always why we use them: economy. Research by Gordon, Grosz, and Gilliom (1993) showed that *not* using pronouns (as in 'Susan gave Betsy a hamster. She asked Betsy whether she liked the gift,' 313) actually makes sentences harder to process. Using a computational model with the ability to look ahead and backward, the authors postulated the existence of a 'repeated-name penalty' (322). In discourse, a pronoun signals sustained reference (i.e. that no new item or agent is being introduced, which would normally be signaled by a slight pause or slower speech preceding the noun: cf. Seifart et al. 2018). The relationship between the pronoun and its antecedent (referred to as a 'binding' relation) thus serves as a cohesion device.

The other thing that grammar books fail to mention is that English has not just 'pronouns,' but a *system of proforms*. Since the grammar books mostly ignore this system (with the notable exception of Mary M. Clark 2010), there is actually no established set of names for those proforms, and the existing terms are inadequate. For example, the term *pronoun* is typically a misnomer, like so much else in our grammatical terminology: A word like *it* does not stand 'in place of' (*pro*) a *noun* but of an entire noun phrase, such as *Eeyore's missing tail*. In rare occasions, the proform *one* is indeed a pronoun. Table 4.1 is a representative sampling of proforms from *Winnie-the-Pooh*.

Proforms can also be phonetically silent, in which case the literature speaks of ellipsis (e.g. ' "Oh!" said Pooh. "I know." But he didn't really [~~*know*~~].'). Similarly, infinitives have phonetically silent subjects. In the sentence *few people bother to play the o'Grunth* (*On Beyond Zebra!*) 'few people' would be doing

Table 4.1 A Sampling of English Proforms in *Winnie-the-Pooh*

proforms	*type*	*examples*
one	pro-N	'You had a big green *balloon*; and one of Rabbit's relations had had a big blue *one* . . .' (12–13)
that, it, he	pro-NP	'*That* was *the first verse*. When ***he*** had finished *it*, ***Eeyore*** didn't actually say that ***he*** didn't like *it*.' (75)
there	pro-PP	'. . . but the nicest people go straight *to the animal they love the most*, and stay *there*.' (ix)
so	pro-VP	'I *saw one once*,' said Piglet. . . . '*So* did I,' said Pooh. (56)
which	pro-IP	'If *it is a good morning*,' he said. '*Which* I doubt.' (84)

both the bothering and the playing. The theory is that a phonetically unrealized pronoun PRO is in the second subject position ('[few people] bother [PRO] to play the o'Grunth'), and the first subject 'controls' the second.

Interpreting proforms takes expertise in knowing how far to look backward (or anticipate forward) to find the binding constituent. Sometimes an antecedent is remote, with too many words intervening. At other times, there is more than one possible antecedent within the permissible range. In such cases, the proform may have to be interpreted pragmatically. An example of ambiguous reference comes from *Alice in Wonderland*. The White Rabbit has entered an incomprehensible poem to enter as evidence into an incomprehensible court proceeding; Alice demurs that the jury won't find an atom of meaning in it:

> 'If there's no meaning in it,' said the King, 'that saves the world of trouble, you know, as we needn't try to find any.'
>
> (159)

Syntactically, the pro-NP *any* could refer to 'trouble' or to 'meaning.' Suppose that our linguistic working memory is just large enough to retain the content words that make up a 'complete functional complex' (CFC), i.e. all grammatical functions (subject, complements) associated with a head (Chomsky 1986a:15, 1986b:169). Working memory should thus be able to hold about four lexical items. We can visualize this as a push-down stack where items enter from the top and decayed items drop out of the bottom. All syntactic interpretation must occur within the stack, including finding an antecedent (in which case the antecedent moves back to the top). I have found by experimentation that disambiguation is greatly helped if that stack is joined by a second, two-entry stack for topics (items at the left periphery of a sentence or with contrastive primary stress). Table 4.2 shows why the syntax from Carroll above is ambiguous:

When the word *any* is added to the stack (pushing out *we*), it can relate to two available binders in the topic stack, and the intended antecedent must be chosen

Table 4.2 Pronoun Resolution in a Pushdown Stack

Stack		Topics	
find	lexical items	*trouble*	topics
try		*meaning*	
not-need		~~*poem*~~	
we			
~~*trouble*~~			
~~*world*~~			
~~*save*~~			
~~*that*~~(={~~*no-meaning,poem*~~})			
~~*say*~~			
~~*king*~~			

(The entry *poem/it* is carried over from preceding text.)

based on context. Such interpretation benefits from cooperation between writer and recipient, to which I will return in Chapter 8, as well from the ability to interface to a running event model (Chapter 5).

If linguistic working memory is as limited as I think it is, then presumably we have strategies to keep it from being overloaded. Noam Chomsky's research suggests that each CFC is processed in a phase (2001), after which each fully interpreted element is presumably deleted from the processing space (Richards 2008). Flushing the workspace increases economy of processing. Other strategies of economy are to assume that the structure to be processed has the simplest tree structure possible ('minimal attachment') and that the words ahead belong into the constituent currently being processed unless some signal word clearly announces otherwise ('late closure'):

> Alice could see . . . *that* all the jurors were writing down "Stupid things!" on their slates . . .
>
> (145)

Without the complementizer *that* in the above quote from *Alice in Wonderland*, the reader could misconstruct *all the jurors* as the object of the verb *see* ('Alice could see all the jurors'). The complementizer signals instead the beginning of a clause, clarifying that *all the jurors* is not the object of *see* but the subject of *were writing down*. Using a complementizer instead of omitting it (which is often possible) is partially an act of cooperation by the author to prevent the reader/listener from going down the 'garden path' and having to recommit while parsing the sentence. What was once crossed out by English teachers with a gloss of 'wordiness' turns out to increase processing speed by precluding garden paths.

Complementizers belong to a class of function words in English that point to the SYNTACTIC FUNCTION of another constituent rather than to its SEMANTIC CONTENT.

A complementizer announces that the object of a verb is going to be a clause. Auxiliaries have been seen to specify the function of a suffix like *-ed* (see p. 85). So-called 'expletives' are place-holders for subjects that are located farther to the right of a sentence, and they announce whether the subject to expect is a noun phrase ('In the great green room, *there* was *a telephone*'—the opening line of *Goodnight Moon!*) or a finite clause ('"*It* is my opinion *that you never think at all*," the Rose said, in a rather severe tone,' *Through the Looking Glass* 203) or a non-finite clause ('"*It*'s a little Anxious," he said to himself, "*to be a Very Small Animal Entirely Surrounded by Water*,"' *Winnie-the-Pooh* 131).

There are also words identifying the SEMANTIC FUNCTION of a constituent: Passive *by* identifies its complement as a semantic subject prior to passivization ('North Pole discovered *by* Pooh'/'Pooh found it'; *Winnie-the-Pooh* 129). 'Dative-movement' *to* and *for* mark a former semantic indirect object demoted to the right periphery ('I gave *him* a box of paints to paint with'/'Why didn't I give it *to him* in the morning?', *Winnie-the-Pooh* 89). These little function words (complementizers, auxiliaries, expletives, functional markers *by, to, for*) make parsing easier for the listener/reader. They are sign posts announcing the syntactic or semantic function of the constituent to follow.

The phoric (word-pointing) system of English proforms provides a sophisticated device for cohesion, and the connections being made are in reference to other constituents' semantic content, syntactic function, or semantic function. For the child, understanding that system of backwards-pointing ('anaphoric') and forward-pointing ('cataphoric') words unlocks the art and enjoyment of narrative. They signal whether a constituent has been around before or is about to be newly introduced, what its function would have been in the default word order, and what the boundaries are to the next constituent.

Syntactic Movement and Its Triggers

One of the surprising characteristics of an inflecting language like English, in which morphology and syntax interact so intimately, is the existence of bound morphemes with their own syntactic position. It sounds like a contradiction in terms. Subject-verb agreement is such a morpheme. Once populated by several endings, English agreement now has one remaining overt member, third-person singular *-s*. There is a syntactic position for that ending; in Figure 4.1, it is the head of the inflection phrase (IP). The existence of IP forces the subject of the verb phrase to rise. Once determiners are added to the noun phrases in *the cat in the hat*, the resulting determiner phrase (DP) needs a case—and a subject case is available in IP above, hence the mandatory syntactic movement. There are still some details to discuss, because the structure, read from left to right (i.e. linearized), reads *the cat in the hat -s come back*. Either the *-s* feature is assigned downward, or the verb *come* is raised to I, to derive *comes*.

Things get really interesting at this point, because agreement in an inflected language can be either weak or strong. Table 4.3 gives some examples. The inflection node contains morphology for either tense or agreement (mostly zero). English agreement is

Table 4.3 Strong and Weak Inflection

subject	*I*		*VP*
	TNS	*AGR*	
They	*Ø*	***have***	*~~they have~~ no imagination.*
I	*Ø*	***am***	*~~I be~~ very tired after that last sentence.*
You	*did*	*Ø*	*not ~~you~~ exactly **miss**.*
I	*can*	*Ø*	*~~I can~~ **see** Russia from my house.*
It	*Ø*	*does*	*~~it do~~ **remind** me of something.*
A Heffalump	*Ø*	*has*	*~~a Heffalump has~~ been **eating** it.*
We	*Ø*	*Ø*	*~~we~~ **say** good-bye.*

(Main verbs are shaded—strongly inflected if raised to AGR)

weak, strong enough merely to attract function verbs (modals, auxiliaries), but not main verbs. In German, strong agreement attracts even main verbs, which explains the difference in word order. Note, however, that the first two verbs in Table 4.3 are indeed main verbs, the last holdover of once-strong agreement in Anglo-Saxon. Milne always uses *have* as a strongly inflected main verb ('"Pooh," said Rabbit kindly, "you haven't any brain,"' *Winnie-the-Pooh*, 93), and it shows most conspicuously when the content of 'I' is fronted for questions ('"Have you an umbrella in your house?,"' ibid., 15).

In modern English, most of the agreement endings have fallen silent and there is only one tense ending (past), and none for present tense or future. Nevertheless, the inflection machinery still operates on the assumption that the morphology is in place. We have, essentially, an atavistic grammar here working with mostly zero morphemes, which must be particularly challenging for children to discover (and is most certainly difficult for adult learners of English to master). In *you did not exactly miss*, the intervening *not* seems to introduce some kind of barrier (Chomsky 1986a) between the past tense ending *-ed* and the verb *miss*, resulting in the suffix being stranded (*You -ed* ⊢ *not* ⊣ *exactly miss*). Since *-ed* is a bound morpheme, it needs some host body, and English has adopted a semantically empty dummy auxiliary, *do*, whose only purpose is to rescue stranded suffixes ('*do*-support'). Possibly, the language pressed emphatic *do* into that service (as in *it does remind me of something*).

The aforementioned fronting for questions requires an additional functional morpheme, the complementizer C. The entire IP merges to it to form CP, the complementizer phrase. In questions, whatever is in I moves to C. English *wh-* words move into the top position directly dominated by CP (its 'specifier' position), left empty in Figure 4.4. Nowadays, we do not expect to find main verbs other than *be* and the occasional *have* in C, though Shakespeare still raises them in formal speech or for lines with special import, such as 'Why call you for a sword?' (Thiede 2009). If the only occupant of I is *-s* and *-s* rises from I to C (Figure 4.4), then *do*-support must again rescue the stranded morpheme ('Does the cat in the hat come back?'). Even

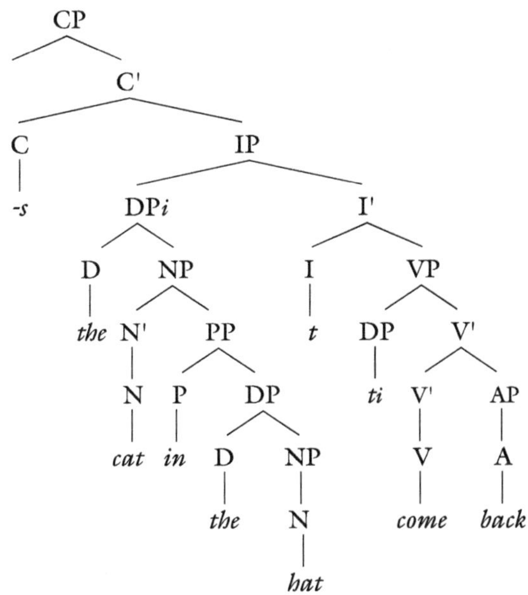

Figure 4.4 Question Formation in English

if I contains Ø, *do*-support still applies (presumably also to mark the position and make the sentence interpretable as a question: 'Do cats in hats come back?').

Besides moving into and out of I and *wh*-fronting, generative-transformational grammar used to have a number of transformations involving movement, such as passivization, clefting, or extraposition (cf. Baker 1978). I have argued elsewhere that such stylistic rearrangements do not involve movement but templates stored in the lexicon (Thiede 2007) and will come back to these rearrangements in a discussion of information management in Chapter 8 (see p. 187).

Funny Grammar: Inventive Language in Children's Literature

Earliest children's books can present single-word labels for depicted objects that imply scripts (see Chapter 2). A one-word script, however, can be enough to drive a story line: In Carin Berger's *Ok Go* (2009)—possibly with a nod to P. D. Eastman's *Go Dog. Go!*—the pages populate with more and more fantastic critters in automobiles, with an increasing occurrence of the word 'go' on each page. At the point where the page is crammed full and chaotic with cars and with 'Go! Go! Go! Go! . . . ,' a new page reads 'uh-oh!,' and the next reads 'Stop!,' after which all the cars come to a halt with 's-c-r-e-e-c-h!' Only after that do we see short phrases in which the critters explore environmentally friendly behaviors and modes of transportation ('Use your feet, Pete'). Other books present successive episodic scenes with similarly minimalist vocabulary, such as Emily Gravett's *Orange Pear Apple Bear* (2006), which has all the words it needs listed in the book title (plus *there*).

Books for young children can use simple MERGE pairs. Speech pathologist Philip Eichten wrote a book with illustrations to go entirely with two-word combinations, as part of a series called 'Baby Talk Help.' Giles Andreae invites children to come up with their own two-word combinations in *Pants* (2003): Different animals can be seen goofing around with underpants. They let none go to waist: Camels wear them on their humps, zebras on their heads, and so on. The expectation is that the child comments on the amusing drawings by Nick Sharratt with two-word brief combinations like 'camel pants!' *The Foot Book* by Theodor Geisel contains adjective-noun pairs ('slow feet,' 'quick feet,' 'sick feet,' etc.) and noun-noun pairs ('trick feet').

However, *The Foot Book* also features two-level hierarchical sets where a prepositional phrase is merged to a noun, and with alternate linearizations ('feet in the morning,' 'feet at night'/'up in the air feet,' 'over a chair feet'). Prepositional phrases with adjectival function usually follow the noun because of a preference of English to place 'heavy' modifiers postnominally. To preserve or break up a pattern, children's books can place a 'heavy' modifier prenominally. Denise Fleming's book *Beetle Bop* (2007) similarly has 'striped beetles' and also constructions like 'hide-in-the-crack beetles.'

Are some authors aware of how much parsing prowess they can expect at particular age levels? It appears so, not only for syntactic complexity but also for pronoun resolution. It is likely that a child's working memory is yet smaller than an adult's. The consequence for children would be that their syntactic range for resolving proforms is narrower. This is how I interpret the observation that four-year-old children perform at chance level in eye-tracking tasks with personal pronouns *he*, *she*, . . . but are much better at resolving reflexive pronouns *himself*, *herself* (Bergmann et al. 2012): Reflexive pronouns refer to the subject of the same clause (*Mama Bear hurt herself*), hence have their antecedents very close by. If a child cannot reach as far back as an adult to find a binder for a proform, then an author could accommodate by reducing the amount of words between the two. That could ultimately mean using fewer proforms, meaning in turn that the tolerance for a 'repeated name penalty' (cf. Almor et al. 2017) might be higher for children: a young child might find repetition more helpful where an adult experiences it as costly. Narratives for young children tend to keep their subplots and inventories limited anyway, so a repeated name is not automatically suspect for introducing something new. One can find examples where authors repeat noun phrases rather than referring back to them with proforms. This is a rhetorical device (diaphora), of course (children's literature being literature), but one that may be particularly effective with children (boldfacing mine):

> **Amelia Bedelia** read,
> *Change the towels in the green bathroom.*

> **Amelia Bedelia** found the green bathroom.
> "Those towels are very nice.
> Why change them?" she thought.
> Then **Amelia Bedelia** remembered
> What Mrs. Rogers had said.
> She must do just what the list told her.
> "Well, all right," said **Amelia Bedelia**.
> **Amelia Bedelia** got some scissors.
> (Peggy Parish, *Amelia Bedelia*)

Repeating noun phrases rather than replacing them with pro-NPs could also be how an author makes the linguistic persona of a character more child-like, as A. A. Milne does with Winnie the Pooh:

> That buzzing-noise means something. You don't get a buzzing-noise like that, just buzzing and buzzing, without it meaning something. If there's a buzzing-noise, somebody's making a buzzing-noise, and the only reason for making a buzzing-noise that *I* know of is because you're a bee.
> (*Winnie-the-Pooh* 6)

> He could see the honey, he could smell the honey, but he couldn't quite reach the honey.
> (*Winnie-the-Pooh* 14)

Knowledge of how constituents are ordered allows children to point to the correct illustration when the text presents alternatives such 'a red dog on a blue tree' vs. 'a blue dog on a red tree' (Eastman, *Go Dog. Go!*). But the benefits of the child's growing syntactic expertise are much larger than that. The ability to process increasingly complex MERGES has a cascading effect on fast-mapping new words into the child's vocabulary (the 'vocabulary spurt/ explosion'). The child can adduce a wealth of information about a word from its syntactic environment without prior knowledge of its exact meaning—or even its approximate meaning. Lewis Carroll demonstrates how exactly that works, in 'Jabberwocky' (191):

> 'Twas brillig, and the slithy toves
> Did gyre and gimble in the wabe:
> All mimsy were the borogroves,
> And the mome raths outgrabe.

Morphosyntax tells us a surprising lot about those strange words. Some of them (*brillig, slithy, mimsy*) must be adjectives—*mimsy* a scalar adjective because it can take the degree adverb *all*, describing the (mental?) state the *borogroves* were in. The word *mome* looks like either another adjective or part of a compound *mome raths*, either way answering the question 'what kind of *raths*?' The definite articles and plural suffixes clearly identify *tove, wabe, borogrove*, and *rath* as nouns, and *outgrabe* must be the past tense of a strong irregular verb *outgribe* (as if things were not irregular enough). *Gyre* and *gimble* feel like regular verbs. We know that *toves* are <+animate>, because they are the agents of whatever actions *gyre* and *gimble* refer to. Since those actions take place in a location ('in the wabe'), we presume that they might denote movements. Maybe their activities cease when the mome raths have finally outgribben.

Not being able to use morphosyntactic cues efficiently to make sense out of unfamiliar words is, of course, distracting and frustrating; this is precisely the deficit identified in Maguire et al. (2018; cf. p. 69). Children's book authors therefore can make syntactic structure salient or ancillary for the child in a variety of ways:

- **Ambiguity**: Deliberate or not, an author can produce ambiguous syntactic structures. In the phrase 'green eggs and ham,' the color adjective could have scope over just 'eggs' (as the Spanish translation has it—*Huevos verdes con jamón*) or over the entire NP, meaning that both the eggs and the ham are green. The illustrations disambiguate the wording: The Spanish interpretation is wrong—both the egg yolk and the ham are drawn in rich emerald (but the Spanish breakfast is certainly more trochaic that way). The following reply by Winnie-the-Pooh is also ambiguous:

  > "Oh, Bear!" said Christopher Robin. "How I do love you!"
  > "So do I," said Pooh. (*Winnie-the-Pooh* 71)

  To decide what the proform *so* refers back to, one must resolve the 'camera angle' (Kuno 1987:29) of the reply: Does Pooh apply *love you* reciprocally (Pooh loves Christopher Robin back), or does he apply it as from Christopher Robin's perspective (Pooh loves Pooh just as Christopher Robin loves Pooh)? Quite possibly, Pooh meant to express the former but ended up saying the latter, a consequence of having very little brain.
- **Minimalism**: Jack Prelutsky's *If Not for the Cat* uses Haiku to keep sentence structure very narrowly confined, and the simple syntax gives him the opportunity to introduce rare words. In a single haiku on jellyfish, he uses the words *translucent, undulate, and gelatinous*.

  It has long been an axiom in second-language pedagogy that new content should be introduced using familiar forms (and pictures), and new forms with familiar content. The same would seem to apply to first-language acquisition. Using minimalist syntax frees up processing space for fast-mapping new content.
- **Overtaxing the parser**: Lewis Carroll cut the facets of the following gem of a sentence in *Alice in Wonderland* (122):

  > "Never imagine yourself not to be otherwise than what it might appear to others that what you were or might have been was not otherwise than what you had been would have appeared to them to be otherwise."

The sentence structure is mischievously impervious to parsing, signaling to the young audience both that a) there still is quite a discrepancy between their syntactic performance and the adults' and b) that pretentiously over-quoiffed adults (the Duchess, in this case) can produce pompous gobbledygook with supreme self-importance just so long as they hold positions of power.

- **Anomalous syntactic merges**: Unsurprisingly when it comes to linguistic impossibilities, it is Theodor Geisel who pulled off a startlingly anomalous structure (at least for children and linguists) by merging a clause to a demonstrative determiner and repurposing it as a proper noun—'that Sam-I-am!' (*Green Eggs and Ham*).
- **Anomalous function shifts**: A favorite device of A. A. Milne's is to use a function word as if it were a content word, i.e. an unbound proform. In *Winnie-the-Pooh* for example, Eeyore answers Pooh's how-are-you with "Not very how," adding: "I don't seem to have felt at all how for a long time" (45). Geisel uses the same technique, e.g. in *Horton Hears a Who!* He also uses an interjection as a noun in *The Cat in the Hat Comes Back* ('Then the Voom—It went VOOM!'), as does Milne in *The House at Pooh Corner*:

  > "You mean it isn't ho-*ho*-ish any more?" said Piglet hopefully. (46)
  >
  > "I'm waiting for the ho-ho to come-come." (53)
  >
  > "*Hooshing* me?" said Eeyore in surprise. "Hooshing *me*? You didn't think I was *hooshed*, did you? I dived." (102)

  Authors can also indicate function shift by inflecting one part of speech as another, essentially using inflectional morphology as derivational morphology—even if the result is semantically somewhat odd:

  > And the turtle-doves are cooing,
  > And the woods are up and doing,
  > For the violets are blue-ing
  >   In the green. ('Noise by Pooh,' *House at Pooh Corner* 82)

- **Confounding binding relations**: Rabbit, in a passage in *Winnie-the-Pooh*, becomes uncooperative with Pooh by changing pronouns, thus forcing the child into a double take when resolving binding relations:

  > "Hallo, Rabbit," he said, "is that you?"
  > "Let's pretend it isn't," said Rabbit, "and see what happens."
  > "I've got a message for you."
  > "I'll give it to him." (114)

- **Thematic mismatches**: Merging heads and complements that violate thematic roles is a favorite technique of nonsense poetry, but can be found as well in nursery rhymes:

Hi diddle diddle, the cat and the fiddle,
The cow jumped over the moon.
The little dog laughed to see such fine sport,
And the dish ran away with the spoon.

The pairings and actions are outside of the usual thematic selections. Children's books can systematically reverse the expected AGENT and AFFECTED roles of an action. This is explored systematically in *The World Turned Upside Down* (anonymous, 1820:9):

The bear runs away, the
Lamb is pursuing;
If he catches the bear,
There'll be terrible doing.

Reversing AGENT and AFFECTED arguments of the verb to produce comical results has long tradition. A recently rediscovered and restored medieval ballroom in the basement of a house in Pirna, Germany, has murals on which thematic roles are reversed: After one mural in which hunters are going to the forest, another depicts animals hunting the humans, a bear and a stag carrying a captive hunter on a pole, a seasoned game warden roasting on a spit, and another dressed and consumed by animals gathered at a table (Böhme 2015:8).

Nonsense poems became a staple of children's literature with Edward Lear (see p. 42). While in 'Hi diddle diddle,' inanimate objects aspire to locomotion, in 'The Table and the Chair' (1871) they are actually having a discussion about it:

I
Said the Table to the Chair,
'You can hardly be aware,
'How I suffer from the heat,
'And from chilblains on my feet!
'If we took a little walk,
'We might have a little talk!
'Pray let us take the air!'
Said the Table to the Chair.

II
Said the Chair to the table,
'Now you know we are not able!
'How foolishly you talk,
'When you know we cannot walk!'
Said the Table with a sigh,
'It can do no harm to try,
'I've as many legs as you,
'Why can't we walk on two?'

Jack Prelutsky still wrote rhythmical nonsense verse in 1986, even throwing in some that sounds like vintage Lear:

> I went to Wyoming one day in the spring
> to hear a rhinoceros trying to sing,
> the sound was so strange that it gave me a fright,
> and I ran to Nebraska the very same night.
> (*Ride a Purple Pelican,* 54)

Finally, children's authors draw attention to morphemes with syntactic consequences, i.e. C (complementizer), I (inflection) and its heads TNS (tense) and AGR (agreement), even if those heads are zero. There are several ways of drawing attention to those positions:

- **Absence and presence of *do*-support**: In *Green Eggs and Ham*, Theodor Geisel illustrates what happens to the zero-agreement features of first-person singular inflection when a barrier (negation) is present or absent and additionally identifies the position by alternately filling it with a modal. He even throws in emphatic *do*:

  > I do not like them in a box.
  > I do not like them with a fox.
  > . . .
  > I do so like
  > green eggs and ham!

- **Anomalous and Hyper-inflection**: The previous chapter quoted the use of *biggered* and *biggering* in *The Lorax* (p. 97). Similarly, given that we can only have one inflection on a word at a time in English (p. 84), the following double inflection *lightnings* is quite unexpected (anonymous, cited in Delamar 1983:15):

  > It drizzles, it rains,
  > It pours, it hails.
  > It lightnings, it thunders,
  > All the children run home.

  A similarly hyper-inflected weather report occurs in Dr. Seuss's *Horton Hatches the Egg* ('It poured and it lightninged!'). Eeyore's 'POEM' in honor of Christopher Robin includes self-referential comments that become part of the rhyme scheme (*House at Pooh Corner* 165–66). Toward the end, the pedantic donkey gets tangled up in number agreement:

  > I
  > And all your friends
  > Sends—

I mean all your friend
Send—
(*Very awkward this, it keeps*
going wrong)
Well, anyhow, we send
Our love.
END.

- **Highlightning modals**: Theodor Geisel underlines modals in *Oh Say Can You Say?*, drawing attention to the position I:

  A simple thimble <u>could</u> cost less
  Than a single shingle would, I guess.

  Additionally raising a modal from I to C marks both positions, and Milne occasionally highlights the modal with italics to express urgency:

  "*Could* you ask your friend to do his exercises somewhere else?" (*House at Pooh Corner* 31)

  "*Could* you stop turning round for a moment, because it muddles me rather?" (ibid., 100)

In drawing attention to scripts, to MERGE pairs, and to alternative linearizations; by manipulating proforms (changing them, using them as content words, making their reference harder to resolve) or by reducing the space between proform and binder at the cost of repeating content words; by making the child concentrate on syntactic knowledge to impute meaning to nonsense words; by presenting minimalist, obfuscatorily complex, or outlier syntactic structures; by highlighting *do*-support, inflection, modals, and I-to-C movement; even by misusing inflections—authors challenge children with a creative firework of atypical linguistic data. Few of these are likely to occur in child-directed speech (or even in speech between adults).

In all four chapters of part I of this book, we have seen children's literature go dramatically *beyond* caretaker speech, presenting them with outlandish sounds, exotic words and neologisms, bizarre morphology, and strange syntactic constructions. These authors play with language to amuse and surprise; they are utterly disinterested in modeling everyday speech. They step outside of it. They are in on a secret: Children are *not* deficient adults, they do *not* learn just by rote imitation and repetitive drills, and they brim with creativity. There is more to children than just being shorter than adults (p. 2)—they are genuinely different, and they need a literature genuinely their own. The author's challenge is to embrace that difference, even if it demands years' worth of revision and editing for a single book.

To the adult, what these authors are doing may look like so much whimsical 'merriment and what-not,' to quote Eeyore. For the child, these linguistic extravaganzas are brain food—triggers, *literally*, of neural growth. They may very well accelerate the connectivity of pathways in Broca's areas 44 and 45 (Figure 4.3). And just as a baby delights in being tossed in the air and caught by a parent's safe hands, so a child delights in escaping the gravity of everyday language and returning to it with a sense of security and belonging.

Notes

1. The formatting of merge sets in Figure 4.1 corresponds to my earlier formulation of idea density (Davis & Thiede 2000:111).
2. A study of slips of the tongue (Fromkin 1973) showed that Spoonerisms etc. affect content words only, never articles or auxiliaries etc. In a mis-speak like 'I broke the whistle on my crotch' (instead of 'I broke the crystal on my watch,' ibid. p. 232), the words *crystal* and *watch* might have been closer together originally and then separated by function words as they were added later. Note also that a typical patient suffering from Broca's aphasia will omit function words and functional morphemes. The exact nature of the interface between semantic MERGE sets and syntactic surface structures is still very much in need of investigation.

References

Almor, Amit; Veena A. Nair; Timothy W. Boiteau; and Jennifer M. C. Vendemia. 2017. "The N400 in processing repeated name and pronoun anaphors in sentences and discourse." *Brain & Language* 173.52–66.

Baker, Carl Lee. 1978. *Introduction to generative-transformational syntax*. Englewood Cliffs, NJ: Prentice-Hall.

Bergmann, Christina; Markus Paulus; and Paula Fikkert. 2012. Preschooler's comprehension of pronouns and reflexives: The impact of the task. *Journal of Child Language* 39(4).777–803.

Böhme, Dirk. 2015. 'Verkehrte Welt' in Pirna. *Pirnaer Anzeiger* 20(15) (21 October).8. Online: www.pirna.de/downloads/PA_20-15.pdf.

Brentano, Franz C. 1874. *Psychologie vom empirischen Standpunkte*, vol. 1. Leipzig: Duncker & Humblot. Online: archive.org/stream/psychologievome02brenoog.

Brown, Roger. 1973. *A first language: The early stages*. Cambridge, MA: Harvard University Press.

Chomsky, Noam A. 1986a. *Barriers* (Linguistic inquiry monograph), vol. 13. Cambridge, MA: MIT Press.

Chomsky, Noam A. 1986b. *Knowledge of language: Its nature, origin, and use* (Convergence). New York: Praeger.

Chomsky, Noam A. 2001. Derivation by phase. *Ken Hale: A life in language*, ed. by Michael Kenstowicz (Current studies in linguistics), vol. 36, 1–52. Cambridge, MA: MIT Press.

Chomsky, Noam A. 2017. Language architecture and its import for evolution. *Neuroscience and Biobehavioral Reviews*, in press. doi:10.1016/j.neubiorev.2017.01.053.

Clark, Mary M. 2010. *The structure of English for readers, writers, and teachers*, 2nd ed. Glen Allen, VA: College Publishing.

Davis, Boyd, and Ralf Thiede. 2000. Writing into change: Style shifting in asynchronous electronic discourse. Chapter 5 of *Network-based language teaching: Concepts and practice*, ed. by Mark Warschauer and Richard Kern, 92–120. Cambridge: Cambridge University Press.

de Laguna, Grace. 1927. *Speech: Its function and development*. Yale University: Ph.D. dissertation.

Delamar, Gloria T. 1983. *Children's counting-out rhymes, fingerplays, jump-rope and bounce-ball chants and other rhythms: A comprehensive English-language reference*. Jefferson, NC: McFarland.

Fodor, Jerry A. 1998. Do we think in mentalese? Remarks on some arguments of Peter Carruthers. *In critical condition: Polemical essays on cognitive science and philosophy of mind*, ed. by Jerry A. Fodor, 63–74. Cambridge, MA: MIT Press.

Fromkin, Victoria A. 1973. The non-anomalous nature of anomalous utterances. *Speech errors as linguistic evidence*, ed. by Victoria A. Fromkin, 215–42. The Hague: Mouton.

Gordon, Peter C.; Barbara J. Grosz; and Laura A. Gilliom. 1993. Pronouns, names, and the centering of attention in discourse. *Cognitive Science* 17(3).311–47.

Goucha, Tomás; Emiliano Zaccarella; and Angela D. Friederici. 2017. A revival of the *Homo loquens* as a builder of labeled structures: Neurocognitive considerations. *Neuroscience and Biobehavioral Reviews*, in press. doi:10.1016/j.neubiorev.2017.01.036.

Jespersen, Otto. 1924 (rpt. 1965). *The philosophy of grammar: A study of the living language, emphasizing the ideas that must underlie the science of grammar*. New York: Norton.

Kuno, Susumu. 1987. *Functional syntax: Anaphora, discourse and empathy*. Chicago: University of Chicago Press.

Levin, Beth. 1993. *English verb classes and alternations: A preliminary investigation*. Chicago: University of Chicago Press.

Maguire, Mandy J.; Julie M. Schneider; Anna E. Middleton; Yvonne Ralph; Michael Lopez; Robert A. Ackerman; and Alyson D. Abel. 2018. Vocabulary knowledge mediates the link between socioeconomic status and word learning in grade school. *Journal of Experimental Child Psychology* 166.679–95. doi:10.1 Ol 6/j.jecp.2017.10.003.

McNeill, David. 1970. The development of language. *Carmichael's manual of child psychology*, ed. by Paul Mussen, vol. 1, 1061–61. New York: Wiley.

Perani, Daniela; Maria C. Saccuman; Paola Scifo; Alfred Anwander; Danilo Spada; Cristina Baldoli; Antonella Poloniato; Gabriele Lohmann; and Angela D. Friederici. 2011. Neural language networks at birth. *Proceedings of the National Academy of Science PNAS* 108(45) (20 September).16056–61. Online: www.pnas.org/cgi/doi/10.1073/pnas.1102991108.

Richards, Marc. 2008. Two kinds of variation in a Minimalist system. *Varieties of competition*, ed. by Fabian Heck, Gereon Müller, and Jochen Trommer (Linguistische Arbeits Berichte), vol. 87, 133–62. Leipzig: Universität Leipzig.

Seifart, Frank; Jan Strunk; Swintha Danielsen; Iren Hartmann; Brigitte Pakendorf; Søren Wichmann; Alena Witzlack-Makarevich; Nivja H. de Jong; and Balthasar Bickel. 2018. Nouns slow down speech across structurally and culturally diverse languages. *PNAS – Proceedings of the National Academy of Science of the United States* (14 May). doi: 10.1073/pnas.1800708115.

Steinthal, Heymann. 1860. *Charakteristik der hauptsächlichsten Typen des Sprachbaues*. Berlin: Ferdinand Dümmler's Verlagsbuchhandlung.

Thiede, Ralf. 2007. MERGE and information management. *Human Sciences* 55.57–70. Online: www.sid.ir/fa/VEWSSID/J_pdf/64413865510.pdf.

Thiede, Ralf. 2009. Stylistics and syntax: Exploitation of mixed systems in English. *Southern Journal of Linguistics* 33(2).72–91. Online: libres.uncg.edu/ir/uncc/listing.aspx?styp=ti&id=15301.

von der Gabelentz, Georg. 1883. *Anfangsgründe der chinesischen Grammatik: Mit Übungsstücken.* Leipzig: Weigel.

Williams, Edwin. 1980. Predication. *Linguistic Inquiry* 11(1).203–38.

Part II

The Nature of Nurture

Concerted Cultivation *Toward* Adult Speech

5 Interfacing Language and Cognition

Why, sometimes I've believed as many
as six impossible things before breakfast!
Lewis Carroll
Through the Looking Glass

Strange things occur in children's books. On Tuesday, 1 November 1981, a tabby cat is observed reading a map, and later a street sign (J. K. Rowling, *Harry Potter and the Philosopher's Stone*). A huge snort (a steam shovel) manages to pick up a baby chick and place it gently back into its nest (P. D. Eastman, *Are You my Mother?*). Kitty O'Sullivan Krauss takes a dive into an airborne inflatable swimming pool floating over her house (Dr. Seuss, *Oh, the Thinks you can Think!*). Thinks become things when language interfaces with cognition, just as they do in biblical Hebrew (the word דָּבָר *davar* means both 'word/idea' and 'thing'). In children's literature as well, anything can be spoken into existence—and kept in existence, like Tinkerbell in J. M. Barrie's *Peter Pan*. This is cognitive control pure, one of the many moving targets in cognitive science. As explored in Part I of this book, cognition involves both dorsal and ventral pathways, pattern-associative and rule-controlled thinking. The sections below explore with examples from children's books how the linguistic system enhances its narrow bandwidth and compensates for its lossiness and limited workspace by interfacing with ancient cognitive faculties: event modeling, predetermination, and cross-domain generalization (logic).

Event Models: Plots

When a script populates with agents, we have an event. When events succeed each other, they become episodes. Their setting may be consistent, and the plots may or may not develop toward a resolution or consequence. Episodes can be thusly telic, but they do not have to be in order to cohere. Sarah Catherine Martin's *The Comic Adventures of Old Mother Hubbard and Her Dog* (1805) is such a series of coherent but non-developing episodes. All episodes share the same schema: Old Mother Hubbard goes away on an errand, returns to her house, and finds her dog doing something one would expect only a gentleman to do, down to smoking a pipe:

> She went to the cobbler's
> To buy him some shoes;
> When she came back
> He was reading the news.
> (26)

The episodes do seem to make the newshound increasingly anthropomorphic with each doggerel, but they do not contribute to a main plot: The book ends with the dog's passing and a monument in his honor.

Sequences of non-telic episodes within a setting are not unique to Mother Hubbard. Several books give their episodes an 'if-then' structure. *The Runaway Bunny* (1942) applied the idea of chaining 'if-then' scenarios from a French love song, 'Les Métamorphoses' (included in Tiersot 1915:87-90). A young lady counters each pursuit scenario with a countermeasure: 'Si tu te fais chasseur/Pour m'y chasser, / je me ferai la carp / Dans un vivier' (If you turn yourself into a hunter to chase me there, I will turn myself into a carp in a fishpond). Margaret Wise Brown was evidently taken with the lover's pursuit of his koi mistress and drew marvel from it, enough to compose an English counterpart (Amy Gary 2016:116). The sequences here are set in motion by the little bunny's startling announcement to his mother that he is running away. On every page after that cheeky declaration of emancipation, the bunny hatches a new getaway plan and his mother counters it with a recovery plan for each contingency. The if-then scheme even links one episode to the next:

> "If you become a mountain climber,"
> said the little bunny,
> "I will become a crocus in a hidden garden."
> "If you become a crocus in a hidden garden,"
> said his mother, "I will be a gardener. And I will find you."
> "If you are a gardener and find me,"
> Said the little bunny, "I will be a bird
> And fly away from you."

Unlike Mother Hubbard, *The Runaway Bunny* has a simple ring structure: The final page refers back to the first ("Shucks," said the bunny, "I might just as well stay where I am and be your little bunny") – a surprising, but not unanticipated denouement quite similar to the surprising final two lines of the French song ('Ah! tiens, voilà mon coer/Mon cher amant!' – Oh, wait, here is my heart, my dear lover). Similarly, Laura Joffe Numeroff's 'If you . . .' series of books sets up one episode leading to another. In *If you Give a Moose a Muffin* (1991), the generous act of giving a moose a muffin inevitably leads to a request for jam, after which the moose munches his way through the entire supply of muffins, which in turn necessitates a trip to the store for more muffin mix. And again, the final page points back to the first: The moose requests another muffin.

Episodes can also be subplots. In *The Little Engine that Could* by 'Watty Piper' [Arnold Munk] ([1930] 1976), the recurring scene is that of a clown and a group of toys asking various locomotives to take their train cars over the mountain so the children on the other side have toys to play with and wholesome food to eat. The predictable ending is that they eventually do find an engine that can. The 'Little Blue Engine' is initially unsure whether she is strong enough to perform the haul, but with determination ('I think I can') she lives up to the predetermined outcome ('I thought I could').

If episodes form subplots, then a child needs to keep a running inventory of its elements and characters. The plot may even be about the inventory itself. In Phoebe Gilman's *Something from Nothing* (1992), a baby blanket made by a grandfather becomes worn down. Rather than having his unsentimental mother throw it out, little Joseph asserts that 'Grandpa can fix it'—a refrain to which Joseph will return again and again as the cloth is transformed into a jacket, then a vest, then a tie, a handkerchief, and finally a button. When that is lost, the sequence appears to have come to its conclusion, because even Grandpa cannot make something from nothing. Yet there is one more way to honor the memory of the beautiful night-sky cloth: Joseph joins the episodes into a story.

Silesian-German author Janosch [Horst Eckert] explores what happens when the characters of his story do *not* pay sufficient attention to what is around them in *The Trip to Panama* (1979). Inspired by the alluring sweet smell of bananas on a discarded crate that says 'Panama' on it, little bear and little tiger turn the crate into a road sign and follow it to Panama. They end up where they started (I'll explain why on p. 133), but thinking that they are now in Panama, they do not pay enough attention to recognize objects they had originally left behind. When they repair a foot bridge, a bottle with a map inside floats by. The narrator tries to get the tiger and the bear to notice it, but it floats by undetected, a lost opportunity to find pirate treasure: 'Too late!'

Another German author who likes to make inventory (literally 'inventory') part of the resolution of a story is Walter Moers, whose Münchhausen-inspired Käpt'n Blaubär is best known to English readers from *The 13½ Lives of Captain Bluebear*. One of the author's go-to popular narrative setups is to have the old sea bear spin tall tales for his three grandchildren, which usually begin by describing what his current cargo and destination are, or rather were, before his mission becomes impossible because of some outlandish occurrence, which the crafty bear solves by making creative use of his freight. One such story is occasioned by the little bears' request for spending money; Captain Bluebear produces a lucky penny and is instantly "reminded" of a sailor's yarn. The destination of the voyage in question is Essen, where he is to deliver a cargo of bullfrogs to a branch office of the German Meteorological Service (presumably by taking his iconic two-masted cutter up the Rhine-Herne Canal . . .). On route, he chances upon the wreck of a golden ship (which had sunk because of its major design flaw—being made of gold).[1] To raise it, he sends his frogs through a tube into the hull of the sunken vessel, where the amphibians pump themselves full of air and the wreck rises to the surface, ready to be towed to a dry dock. Asked by his grandchildren how come he is not a rich bear, their grandfather reminds them of the inventory: He had to share the profits with all those frogs, which left little for himself, except for that penny ('Ein echtes Goldschiff').

Event models interface with and augment syntactic processing in the resolution of proforms. Chapter 4 introduced a linguistic workspace within which the resolution of proforms can take place: a four-argument pushdown stack and a two-item pushdown stack for topics. Once an intended antecedent has dropped out of both stacks, a proform can no longer refer to it syntactically (be 'bound'). Nonetheless, we can *reconstruct* the antecedent of a proform that is no longer linguistically accessible by referring to the inventory of an event model. The following passage from *Through the Looking Glass* is a good illustration:

> "There's **one other flower** in the garden that can move about like you," said the Rose. "I wonder how you do it—" ("You're always wondering," said the Tiger-lily), "but she's more bushy than you are."
>
> "Is she like me?" Alice asked eagerly, for the thought crossed her mind, "There's another little girl in the garden, somewhere!"
>
> "Well, she has the same awkward shape as you," the Rose said: "but she's redder—and her petals are shorter, I think."
>
> "They're done up close, like a dahlia," said Tiger-lily: "not tumbled about, like yours."
>
> "But that's not *your* fault," the Rose added kindly. "You're beginning to fade, you know—and then one can't help one's petals getting a little untidy."
>
> Alice didn't like this idea at all: so, to change the subject, she asked "Does **she** ever come out here?"
>
> (204)

There is no syntactic way for *she* in the last line to be bound by *one other flower* in the first line of this quote. The presence of a flower/girl other than Alice is, however, part of a subplot inventory. The linguistic system makes reference to a *cognitive* module to resolve a *linguistic* problem—the remote antecedent of *she*.

The existence of such an interface was shown to exist experimentally by Glenberg et al. (1987). Subjects found it quite impossible to find the antecedent of the boldfaced proform in the following passage:

> Warren spent the afternoon shopping at the store. He set down his bag and went to look at some scarves. He had been shopping all day. He thought **it** was getting too heavy to carry.

Their difficulty was as I would expect, because the intended binder, *his bag*, is not present in either stack, as shown in Table 5.1.

Table 5.1 Failed Pronoun Resolution in a Pushdown Stack

Stack		Topics	
{heavy,carry}	**lexical items**	*Warren*	**topics**
get			
it (?)			
thought			
~~*Warren*~~			
~~*all day*~~			
~~*shop*~~			

But Glenberg et al. also presented another version of the same narrative:

> Warren spent the afternoon shopping at the store. He picked up his bag and went to look at some scarves. He had been shopping all day. He thought **it** was getting too heavy to carry.

The subjects now readily construed the antecedent of *it* as *his bag*. What the linguistic workspace did not allow, a reference to the running event model permitted. In the first version, Warren set the bag down; it is no longer part of the inventory. In the second version, he picked it up, and it is now available to interpret the pro-form *it*. Good authors will keep track of what the reader's mental inventory of an event model is—the same way a video game author will be careful to keep stock of what an avatar has (or should have) collected during a quest. Some of what the avatar is carrying might be useful for solving a puzzle or vanquishing an enemy. Sherlock Holmes and Hercule Poirot demand the same attention to detail: A detail could be a clue.

Children's authors like Janosch and Moers direct their young readers' attention to subplots and their inventories. Paying attention to details not only ensures that children can follow the story; they can also make discoveries. A character may turn out to be mistaken, or even untruthful. Little tiger and little bear, at one point, ask a fox for directions. The fox was about to celebrate his birthday in the company of a goose. The picture shows him seated, the goose draped over the fox's leg and left arm, eyes closed. Without much reflection, the fox tells tiger and bear to turn left—because he does not wish to be disturbed. It would appear as if the fox and the goose were just about to get *very* friendly with each other. Attention to the illustration, however, also reveals a knife and a fork, and a goose-sized cauldron in the background. Paying attention to details of possible plots makes it possible to know whether a character is a trickster, an author trustworthy, a story line consistent. Having one's attention distracted creates gaps between settings and outcomes. Those gaps can be exasperating in a school book, challenging in 'Hills Like White Elephants,' and delightful in magic shows.

A second interface between language and cognition involves a yet different operating system, one that can interact with both event models and syntactic processing: predetermination.

Predetermination

According to a distinction by developmental psychologist Gina C. Mireault (2017), the *un* expected is magical—the *mis* expected, especially in social settings, is funny. Both magic and humor have tradition in children's literature.

Fairy tales full of magical occurrences and creatures crossed into children's literature in the early 19th century around the time of Jakob and Wilhelm Grimm's *Kinder- und Hausmärchen* (1812). They have a long history in Indo-European culture (Graça da Silva & Tehrani 2016), but originally they were shared among adults. Grimm's fairy tales, sanitized in successive editions (Luu 2018), offered up the world of magic to children. Funny books for children, too, make their appearance in early 19th-century Europe and America. Works like *The Comic Adventures of Old Mother Hubbard and Her Dog* (1805; see p. 125) and *The World Turned Upside Down* (1820, q.v. p. 116) have no pedagogical ambitions and are offered with the sole purpose of entertaining with funny mis-expectations and anticipations. Magical and humorous books ushered in what is now, in hindsight, called the 'golden age' of children's books in English literature, giving us authors like Lewis Carroll.

In magic and humor, the child's interest focuses on what to expect. Having expectations, however, requires that the child make predictions. That ability has been noted several times in passing: when an infant witnesses a car seeming to float or a ball seeming to roll through a solid board (p. 50), and also when an infant laughs at words with unexpected sound combinations (p. 30). From the very beginning, an infant makes predictions about both linguistic input and unfolding event models.

As children become accustomed to poetry, for example, they become experts at anticipating words that rhyme. Authors know this and can invite the child to call out a word that 'sounds like.' They can also invite the child just to *think* of a likely match without necessarily saying it out loud, as in the 'Duloc' song from the movie *Shrek*, which offers either *place* or *grass* to set up the rhyme after 'wipe your . . . ' (it is *face*, of course).

Books are particularly suitable for generating expectations: They have pages to turn. Something unpredicted or mispredicted can await on the next page. In interactive book reading, adults often ask the child what will happen next. When the little bunny wants to turn himself into a fish, what do you think his mommy is going to do? If Joseph's little vest is no longer wearable, what will his clever grandfather turn it into next? Entire books are conceived around the game of predicting the outcome of an event on the next page. Sue Porter's *Moose Music* (1994) sets the scene with Moose finding a fateful fiddle and playing it—with a 'dreadful ear-splitting screech that rattled all the leaves on all the trees for miles around.' The moose is understandably delighted. The author then sets up various scenes upon which the antlered aficionado intrudes: A group of beavers putting the final tree trunk upon a dam, a bear edging toward the end of a branch to reach for a bees' nest . . . the turn of the page delivers dire disaster when the moose starts playing. There is even unpredicted magic at the end: A voice from the forest says, 'What lovely music.' It's a lady moose. The final illustration looks like pink nuclear explosions of love.

Authors expect the child to make use of two unique properties of the printed page: 1) You must read all of it before turning the page to maintain an accurate event model, and 2) you should co-create the narrative by predicting what lurks on the other side of that sheet of paper.[2] Children's books make deliberate decisions about which words go on which page. Adults call it 'suspense.'

In evolutionary terms, the ability to anticipate the outcome of an event is crucial for any predator or flight animal—and humans are both top predators and at the same time, as Temple Grandin points out, tasty (2005:276). It is a gift to be able to think methodically, but in a split-second survival situation such linear reasoning would have fatal consequences (see Linden, p. 34). Predetermination is equally important for learning, if learning involves successive optimization by checking a hypothesized result against actual results (Gopnik 2017:62)—a procedure nicely illustrated with the Suppose-a-Tron in Mrs. Frizzle's magic school bus (Cole 1997). Predetermination relies on ancient pathways, certainly older than language itself, and we have seen below that those pathways mature early (p. 51).

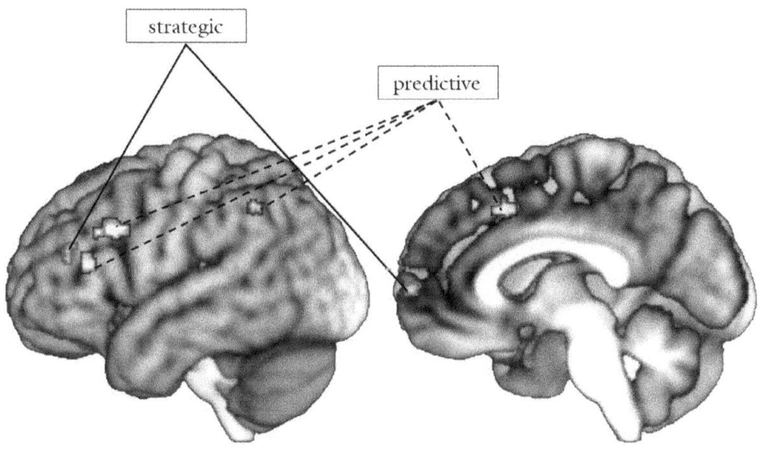

Figure 5.1 Strategic and Predictive Processing in Knapping

(Stout et al. 2015:11)

Evolutionary neuroscientist Dietrich Stout explores those ancient predictive pathways as the origin of 'action syntax.'[3] At Emory University, Stout is exploring how the brain makes predictions and forms strategies as volunteers learn how to knap stone tools the paleolithic way. Subjects being trained in the art of stone tool knapping viewed screens with projects in progress on which the researchers indicated strike points and displayed flakes (Stout et al. 2015:5; cf. Stout & Khreisheh 2015). The subjects were asked to make predictions ("If the core were struck in the place indicated, is what you see a correct prediction of the flake that would result?") or to think about appropriate strategies ("Is the indicated place to hit the core a correct one given the objective of the technology?"). Figure 5.1

shows where brains typically process how to plan a strike strategically and where predictive processing takes place.

It is easy to see how predictive processing interacts with event models, anticipating outcomes. Phonetic processing, too, is predictive, as we saw in the discussion of slips of the ear and phonemic restoration above (p. 33). Even syntactic parsing makes use of predictive strategies such as expecting minimal attachment and late closure (p. 108). In fact, predetermination may be so powerful as to override the need for syntactic well-formedness. Recall the hummingbird sentence (Figure I.4): 'The rapidity that the motion that the wing that the hummingbird has has has is remarkable' (Pinker 1994:205). Mysteriously, that sentence becomes easier to process with just one overt occurrence of *has*: 'The rapidity that the motion that the wing that the hummingbird has is remarkable.' The reason for this would appear to be predictive processing. The predicted verb *has* is utilized for full interpretation before it is even presented: 'The rapidity that the motion *has*.' The anticipated complete functional complex (see p. 107) is deleted from the workspace, except for the verb *has* (which is awaiting confirmation). The other two cycles proceed likewise; the verb *has* is effectively held over from one cycle to the next, meaning that just *one* confirmation validates all three predictions (Figure 5.2). Hence, the sentence 'The rapidity that the motion that the wing that the hummingbird has is remarkable,' while syntactically ungrammatical, is preferable to the syntactically well-formed version with its three tokens of *has* crowding out the workspace.[4]

Predeterminations (anticipated results) and plots (event models with inventories) can complement each other, bringing significant details into focus. They can also interfere with each other, and we 'jump to conclusions' prematurely. Children's stories can exploit the consequences of jumping to conclusions as a trope: An acorn drops on the head of Chicken Little (a.k.a. Henny Penny), and the erroneous conclusion that the sky must be falling creates mass hysteria. Likewise, predeterminations and *language* can complement each other (facilitating real-time parsing) and compete (resulting in slips of the ear and garden-path parses).

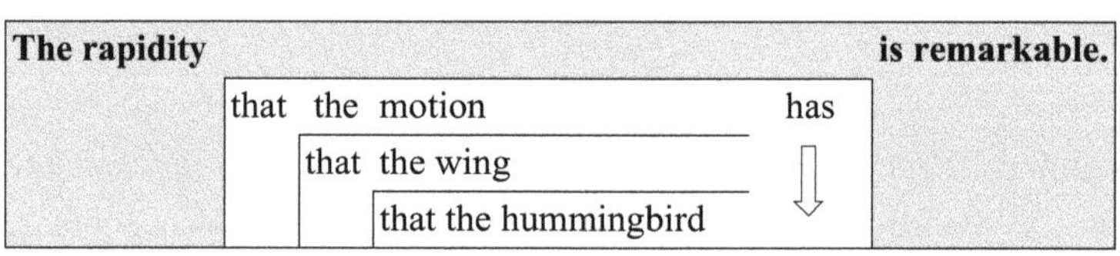

Figure 5.2 Forward-Passing in Embedded Cycles

Logic

With logic, the child's development has advanced to 'the extreme end of disembeddedness' (Lindfors 1987:280). Logic generalizes context-independent, generalizable relations across schemas and scripts. That quality makes it a unique cognitive ability, because ordinarily we do not see principles and procedures learned in one domain transfer to other domains (Bruner 2003:42).[5] As Thomas Wilson understood it in 1567, logic pertains to 'thynges generally spoken without all circumstaunces' (2). Speaking of things without circumstances is a nicety of domestication that freed our species from living from one split-second survival situation to the next. From cardboard picturebooks onwards (cf. p. 65), children's books demand that the child be able to process *representations*, the earliest form of abstracting relations and transferring them across domains. The most advanced demands on logic are probably placed by children's books with riddles:

> Without a bridle or a saddle,
> Across a ridge I ride and straddle;
> And ev'ry one, by help of me,
> Tho' almost blind, are made to see.
> Then tell me every pretty dame,
> And witty master, what's my name? ()
>
> (anonymous, *The Puzzling Cap* 1805:21)

Riddles are closely associated with logic in *Alice in Wonderland*—and Lewis Carroll's logic is often decidedly at the extreme end of disembeddedness. Asked by the Hatter if she can solve a riddle, Alice replies 'I believe I can guess that' (95):

> "Do you mean that you think you can find out the answer to it?" said the March Hare.
> "Exactly so," said Alice.
> "Then you should say what you mean," the March Hare went on.
> "I do," Alice hastily replied; "at least—at least I mean what I say—that's the same thing, you know."
> "Not the same thing a bit!" said the Hatter. "Why, you might just as well say that 'I see what I eat' is the same thing as 'I eat what I see'!"

Carroll seems to want to make a point of demonstrating that logic is not the same as common sense, and hence best not applied to language. Roald Dahl's *BFG* understood that point: 'What I mean and what I say is two different things.'

Other authors, in contrast, invite their young audience to check the common-sense logic of a story line. In *The Trip to Panama*, Janosch has the little bear and the little tiger ask for directions on their way to their dream destination. Each time, they are told to turn left. The author interrupts the narrative to address the child: If they are being turned repeatedly to the left, where will their journey end? And indeed, the two friends do end up where they started, yet unlike the alert(ed) reader, they remain unaware of it. In this story, logic resides at the reader's level, whereas the characters let themselves be guided by predetermination.

How language—specifically syntax—interacts with logic has always been a contentious question. The so-called Port Royal Grammar (Arnauld & Lancelot 1660) assumed that logic maps into the world's natural languages through a shared universal-grammar interface. The idea that there is a universal grammar, that therefore there is fundamentally only one human language, was taken up by Noam Chomsky, who credited the 'rationalist thought' of the Port Royal Grammar to Renée Descartes (1966). Heymann Steinthal (1860), on the other hand, assumed just the opposite: that the linguistic faculty allowed humans to create representations and relations, using parts of speech and grammatical functions. He argued that it was the linguistic faculty that gave rise to human consciousness (89, 93), which in turn *created* logic. Hence language is, 'on closer examination, not even a poor logic system, but no logic at all' (94). Certainly, logicians have pointed out for a long time that a single word does not mean the same thing to two people or at two different points in time (e.g. Sigwart 1904 vol. I.:48–9).

Yet there surely must be *some* logic in language if it is an economic computational system, and there is ongoing research, particularly in the field of pragmatics (Ariel 2008), to capture that logic formally. It is possible to do this along the lines entertained, for argument's sake, by Bertrand Russell, who described logical relations in sentences with formal propositions:

(15) 'The father of Charles II (F) was executed (E)'
$\exists x\ ((F(x) \wedge \forall y\ (F(y) \rightarrow x = y)) \wedge E(x))$[6]
'there is one and only one thing x such that x is the father of Charles II and x was executed'

Proposition (15) just as accurately describes 'pillow dirty' (there is one and only one thing x such that x is my pillow and x is dirty), which has a completely different syntax. Logical relations are semantic, then—but they are informationally quite lossy for ignoring the 'circumstaunces.' The father of Charles II, for example, is marked 'given' within the discourse for being placed at the left periphery in the subject position via passivization. Proposition (15) also does not reflect the decision to omit the agent (absence of a *by*-phrase), that the event is not currently occurring (I = TNS), nor that the existence is implied of a Charles I—all of which is instantly clear to a language user. The logical structure shows only the type of relation between two variables, F and E; the content comes from language.

Relations in propositions capture basic semantic relations, not syntactic structures. Not even the relations expressed by functions words (*is, and, or* . . .) have any resemblance to those expressed by logical symbols ($\Leftrightarrow$, $\wedge$, $\vee$ . . .). We already had to ask what the definition of *is* is (p. 103). It turns out that not even the definition of a word like *and* is consistent. It can coordinate constituents with equal syntactic function (*Jack and Jill went up the hill*), in which case the names can be reversed (*Jill and Jack*). It can also be a superordinating conjunction (another grammatical term that does not officially exist yet), as in *Give a moose a muffin and he'll want some jam to go with it*, where the first constituent (*give a moose a muffin*) is clearly a subordinate adverbial clause and cannot swap places with the main clause. In other words, *and* can sometimes mean *plus* (∧) and sometimes *if—then* (→). Note also that *and* can add information in iteration. whereas ∧ cannot: *He talks and talks and talks* has implicatures that cannot be captured in A ∧ A ∧ A (where A = 'he talks'). It is the same with *is*, as Gertrude Stein's poem 'Sacred Emily' taught us so well: 'Rose is a rose is a rose is a rose./Loveliness extreme.' R ≡ R ≡ R ≡ R: redundancy extreme.

The incompatibility of syntactic function words with logical signs was one of the critique points in Jim McCawley's famous 1981 takedown *Everything that Linguists have Always Wanted to Know about Logic (but were ashamed to ask).* As was sometimes the case with McCawley's work, his penetrating wit was liberally applied to a strawman, here in the person of Noam Chomsky, who, yes, referred to the output of linguistic processing as 'logical form' (LF), but, no, never intended to equate the word 'formal' as applying alike to the workings of syntax and logic. From the very beginning, Chomsky had objected to the notion that 'the study of formal (or semantic) properties of natural language should model itself on the study of formal (or semantic) properties of logic and artificial languages' (1955.I:17–18).

The desire to apply formal logic to syntax is, however, deeply engrained. I suspect that the culprit is prescriptive grammar, which thrives in older children's books. Enlightenment philosophers in Europe attempted to render natural language more suitable for logic, hoping to turn its speakers into better thinkers. Their efforts thus filtered down to grammar books and primers. Authors like Bishop Robert Lowth successfully edited out perfectly grammatical constructions such as negative concord. Two negatives logically 'destroy one another,' he tells his young son Thomas for whom the book was originally intended and whose name occurs in several of the illustrative sample sentences.[7] If that logic could truly be applied to language, then the Rolling Stones' *I can't get no satisfaction* would mean that the speaker is incapable of getting no satisfaction, i.e. gets some satisfaction no matter how hard he or she may try not to. But that is a Lewis-Carroll type of argument.

Negative concord was never not grammatical in English. Chaucer's description of the Knight (*Canterbury Tales* General Prologue ll. 70–01) contains a *quadruple* negative to emphasize how steadfast he was in not offering offense:

> He **never** yet **no** vileinye **ne** sayde
> In al his lyf, unto **no** maner wight.

Double negatives in children's books can emphasize otherness with non-standard speech, as when Topsy says 'nobody never made me' in Stowe's *Uncle*

Tom's Cabin (Rahn 227). Then again—and this is why adults adore children for their ability to 'wonder' before they drive all inquisitiveness out of them (Sagan 1996:122)—otherness and non-standard mean something different in children's literature than they might in adult literature: They are triggers for surprise and exploration. In transcending the vanilla standards of everyday speech, authors can entice child and adult with their mastery of language. Brander Matthews remembered a passage where Huck Finn described a storm on Jackson Island with language 'which will not parse, which bristles with double negatives, but which none the less is one of the finest passages of descriptive prose in all American literature' (1899:xxxi).[8]

Interfacing Linguistic Processing and Cognitive Faculties

Linguistic processing interfaces with generalization / logic, predetermination, and inventory tracking / event modeling. Those are separate cognitive faculties—and thus they can compete with each other. Their interfaces with language are distinct. They are, as neural pathways generally are, bidirectional: Language both avails itself of the services of logic, predetermination, and event modeling and controls those cognitive modules (e.g. selects between them). In the following, I would like to demonstrate how this interplay works in a single poem, 'Said a Bug' by Margaret Wise Brown (*Under the Sun and the Moon* 1993:16).

The single event is a philosophical discussion between bugs. The inventory of this event, besides bugs, are grass blades and sky. The plot appears to be simply a discussion, but one of the turns introduces a subplot that divides bugs into flying and crawling insects. That subplot gives rise to an idea that anticipates a turn: We discover that one participant in the discourse is capable of flight and is prompted to 'buzz up.' The predicted ending is that this will now occur and that the flying bug will find out the answer to the question of perspective. However, the author is toying with that anticipation and flouts it. Instead, we are surprised with a mis-anticipated ending: We learn that there are butterflies overhead (in fairness, they are also depicted in the illustration), and that 'buzzing up' could result in bumping into one of them. The surprise is prepared by suspense: Each word of the last sentence has its own line, drawing out the reading time until the last word. From the given inventory, a listener/reader should expect that the thing not to bump into is a grass blade, but no. The last word, *butterfly*, turns the last sentence into a joke—the child recognizes and resolves a surprising incongruity.

The child resolves a surprise ending that does not conform to expectation. In addition, the child needs to confront a logical problem. It concerns the word *high*, which is a scalar adjective (i.e. it can be associated with a degree adverb such as *very* or, as in line 7, 'how'). The logical problem is in the projection of that scale relative to other things. In the first stanza, the 'great' grass blades seem so tall that a bug has to look 'away up.' They are 'piercing the sky.' That scale changes with a change of perspective in the second stanza: The blades are no longer piercing the sky, but the sky is high above them. We now have *two* scales to measure the grass blades against: The sky is high above the 'blades so high.' The third stanza uses logic to offer a resolution to the ambiguity: The selection of scale depends on the observer's 'eye' or 'camera angle' (cf. p. 114 above).

Logic is one of the faculties with which humans *impose* control over their perception, changing perception to apperception. The adoption of one scale vs. another changes the meaning of 'high' for the child. We have here, in a poem for children, the equivalent of an 'observer effect' in quantum physics, where the presence or absence of observation determines the definition of a current of electrons: Observed (by a detector), it behaves like particles, unobserved it behaves like waves (Weizmann Institute 1998). The poem appears to head for a logical conclusion by sending a bug from one perspective (the ground) to another ('above those grass blades'). However, that is not really a logical solution, because changing from one dimension to another does nothing to unify the two. We never get to settle on a unified definition of 'high' for bugs contemplating blades of grass. The poem instead changes the *topic* and cautions against bumping into a butterfly.

In contrast to the busy event model (the illustration as well is visually busy, crowded with grass blades, bugs, flowers, and butterflies), the surprise ending, and the logic, the language of the poem is tranquil and contemplative. Margaret Wise Brown achieves her signature soothing, hypnotic effect with simple words, musical rhythm, repeated words and lines, and persistent rhymes. 'Said a Bug' sheds light on what distinguishes literary art for children from child-directed talk (and from inferior authors): It arouses the child's cognitive and linguistic interest and activity and provides a release from that arousal. A sudden drop from arousal is closely associated with satisfaction and triggers reward responses in the brain (Nell 1988:38). The repeated experience of such rewards from literature leads a child to associate reading with reward and satisfaction, enhanced only by the pleasure of sharing that experience with a loved one.

Notes

1. I would be remiss in not mentioning the other famous vessel to sink because of the same design flaw, the Ruby Yacht of Omar Khayyam. It is recovered by Rocky and Bullwinkle in season 5 (1963–1964), episode 1. Unbelievably, there is a Wikipedia entry for it at en.wikipedia.org/wiki/The_Ruby_Yacht.
2. Some children's authors, of course, have also sought to alter those basic properties of the printed page. Claude Delafosse and Philippe Biard's *Pyramids*, for example, alternates pages made of paper and of transparent plastic. Turning the transparent page, which is strategically illustrated on both sides, advances each construction phase of the Great Pyramid or reveals cutouts.
3. Along those same lines of thought, William Calvin (1998) had earlier proposed that ballistic motions in general (e.g. throwing a projectile at a moving animal) was a catalyst in the evolution of human intelligence and language.

4. In addition to greater ease of processing, the sentence with the single occurrence of *has* also avoids repetition. English prefers not to duplicate even when the grammar calls for it. For example, the adjective *friendly* is generally not turned into an adverb by adding a second *-ly* (!*she smiled friendlily*) and most native speakers resort to haplology, the omission of the unit to be repeated. Note, of course, that the word *has* must be identical as it is passed on because the verb ultimately agrees with the nearest subject—hence **The rapidity that the motion that the wing that the hummingbirds has is remarkable*.
5. Recent evidence suggests that budgerigars can achieve some logical domain transfer underlying grammatical/logical thinking, recognizing shared patterns underlying strings with different content (Spierings & ten Cate 2016).
6. The logical notation follows http://en.wikipedia.org/wiki/On_Denoting.
7. I owe this information to "Bishop Lowth was not a fool!", a web site featuring Ingrid Tieken's research on the bishop's work and correspondence.
8. The good professor may have improvised his lines here: To the best of my knowledge, Huck's descriptions of storms on Jackson Island do not contain double negatives; they might have in the original manuscript. Still, his point is well taken: We experience language as 'fine' because of its author's mastery, which includes transcending usage rules the way we see it done in good children's literature. He is wrong in one respect: It is not 'none the less' fine prose, but *because* of its non-conformance to common taste. The theory that art thrives in the offense against taste is explored in detail in Mainusch & Mertner (1973).

References

Ariel, Mira. 2008. *Pragmatics and grammar* (Cambridge textbooks in linguistics). Cambridge, New York: Cambridge University Press.

Arnauld, Antoine, and Claude Lancelot. 1660. *Grammaire générale et raisonnée contenant les fondements de l'art de parler, expliqués d'une manière claire et naturelle*. Paris: Bossange & Masson. Online: 2nd ed. 1810: archive.org/details/grammairegnr00arnauoft

Bishop Lowth was not a fool! 2010. Universiteit Leiden. Online: research.leiden.edu/news/bishop-lowth-was-not-a-fool.html.

Bruner, Jerome S. 2003. The narrative construction of reality. *Narrative intelligence*, ed. by Michael Mateas and Phoebe Sengers, 41–62. Reprinted from *Critical Inquiry* (1991) 1.1–21.

Calvin, William H. 1998. The emergence of intelligence. *Scientific American Presents* 9(4).44–51. Online: www.williamcalvin.com/1990s/1998SciAmer.htm.

Chomsky, Noam A. 1955. *The logical structure of linguistic theory*. MIT dissertation. Online: alpha-leonis.lids.mit.edu/chomsky/chomsky_thesis.pdf.

Chomsky, Noam A. 1966. *Cartesian linguistics: A chapter in the history of rationalist thought*. New York: Harper & Row.

Gary, Amy. 2016. *In the Great Green Room: The brilliant and bold life of Margaret Wise Brown*. New York: Flatiron Books.

Glenberg, A. M.; M. Meyer; and K. Lindem. 1987. Mental models contribute to foregrounding during text comprehension. *Journal of Memory and Language* 26.69–83.

Gopnik, Alison. 2017. Making AI more human. *Scientific American* 316(6) (June).60–65.

Graça da Silva, Sara, and Jamshid J. Tehrani. 2016. Comparative phylogenetic analyses uncover the ancient roots of Indo-European folktales. *Royal Society Open Science* 3 (20 January).150645. doi:10.1098/rsos.150645.

Grandin, Temple, and Catherine Johnson. 2005. *Animals in translation: Using the mysteries of autism to decode animal behavior*. New York: Simon & Schuster.

Lindfors, Judith Wells. 1987. *Children's language and learning*, 2nd ed. Englewood Cliffs, NJ: Prentice-Hall.

Lowth, Robert. 1967 [1762]. *A short introduction to English grammar*, Scolar Press facsimile. Ann Arbor: University of Michigan. Online: 1799 edition: archive.org/details/shortintroductio00lowtrich.

Luu, Chi. 2018. "The fairytale language of the Brothers Grimm." JSTOR Daily (2 May), daily.jstor.org/the-fairytale-language-of-the-brothers-grimm.

Marcus, Gary. 2008. *Kluge: The haphazard construction of the human mind*. Boston: Houghton Mifflin.

Mainusch, Herbert, and Edgar Mertner. 1973. *Genius and taste I: Englische Literaturtheorie im 18. Jahrhundert*. Munich: Goldmann Wilhelm.

Matthews, Brander. 1899. Biographical criticism. *The writings of Mark Twain*, ed. by Charles Dudley Warner, v–xxxiii. Hartford, CT: American Publishing Company.

McCawley, James D. 1981. *Everything that linguists have always wanted to know about logic (but were ashamed to ask)*. Chicago: University of Chicago Press.

Mireault, Gina C. 2017. Laughing matters. *Scientific American Mind* 28(3) (May/June).44–49.

Nell, Victor. 1988. The psychology of reading for pleasure: Needs and gratifications. *Reading Research Quarterly* 23(1) (November).6–50.

Rahn, Suzanne. The changing language of black child characters in American children's books. *Infant tongues: The voice of the child in literature*, ed. by Elizabeth Goodenough, Mark A. Heberle, and Naomi Solokoff, 225–58. Detroit: Wayne State University Press.

Russell, Bertrand. 1905. On denoting. *Mind*, New Series, 14.479–93. Online: masi.cscs.lsa.umich.edu/~crshalizi/Russell/denoting/.

Sagan, Carl. 1996. *The Demon-haunted world: Science as a candle in the dark*. New York: Random House.

Sigwart, Christoph. 1904. *Logik. Erster Band: Die Lehre vom Urteil, vom Begriff und vom Schluss*, 3rd ed., vol. 1. Tübingen: Mohr.

Spierings, Michelle J., and Carel ten Cate. 2016. "Budgerigars and zebra finches differ in how they generalize in an artificial grammar learning experiment." *PNAS – Proceedings of the National Academy of Science of the United States* (20 June).E3977–84. doi: 10.1073/pnas.1600483113.

Steinthal, Heymann. 1860. *Charakteristik der hauptsächlichsten Typen des Sprachbaues*. Berlin: Ferdinand Dümmler's Verlagsbuchhandlung.

Stout, Dietrich. 2010. The evolution of cognitive control. *Topics in Cognitive Science* 2(4).614–30. doi:10.1111/j.1756–8765.2009.01078.x.

Stout, Dietrich; Erin Hecht; Nada Khreisheh; Bruce Bradley; and Thierry Chaminade. 2015. Cognitive demands of lower paleolithic toolmaking. *PLoS ONE* 10(4) (15 April).1–18. doi:10.1371/journal.pone.0121804.

Stout, Dietrich, and Nada Khreisheh. 2015. Skill learning and human brain evolution: An experimental approach. *Cambridge Archaeological Journal* 25(4).867–75. doi:10.1017/S0959774315000359.

Tiersot, Julien, ed. 1915. *Sixty folksongs of France*. Boston: Oliver Ditson Co.; New York: Chas. H. Ditson & Co.; Chicago: Lyon & Healy.

Weizmann Institute of Science. 1998. Quantum theory demonstrated: Observation affects reality. *ScienceDaily*, 27 February. Online: www.sciencedaily.com/releases/1998/02/980227055013.htm.

Wilson, Thomas. 1567. *The Arte of Rhetorike, for the use of all Suche as are Studious of Eloquence, Sette Foorthe in Englishe*. London: Jhon Kinston, 1584 [Early English Books Online].

6 Becoming *homo narrans*

> '. . . I know who I was when I got up this morning, but I think
> I must have changed several times since then.'
> Lewis Carroll, *Alice in Wonderland*

In Wonderland, things / words just do not make sense as they did when Alice first woke up in her bed that morning. Here, out of the blue, 'multiplication' turns into 'uglification,' and the substitution is portrayed as perfectly reasonable (as the antonym to 'beautification')—except that being an antonym of *some* word is no rationale for replacing another (cf. p. 72). The inhabitants of Wonderland seem to have abandoned common sense, if they ever had any. Indeed, even Alice's own story is beginning to fall apart. She seems to have been different persons in the course of the day, each of a different size. Alice is surely beginning to ask herself, as Lewis Carroll appears to be asking his young audience: How is sense "made," and how common is it? If we are not to set our identities adrift at the mercy of circum- and happenstance, then it must be incumbent upon us to *impose* sense upon the world around us. What we call 'the world' is a set of narratives, down to all of the declarations that make up civilization (cf. Searle 2010). We are *homo narrans*, the narrating human. For *homo narrans*, something is *sensible* only if we can narrate it as implied in the very etymology of the word *sense* (from Latin *sensus* 'faculty of feeling, thought, meaning'). 'Which is to be the master—that's all.' Indeed.

How is sense made at the sentence level? The traditional answer has been that a sentence must be syntactically correct and that its logic must be provable in truth values (e.g. Ayer 1936). I took a different approach above and argued for a modular system: a messy, hence ingenious interplay between language (a computational array in its own right) and competing (maybe cooperating) mental faculties. I propose the same interfacing at the so-called 'macrolinguistic' level of narrative/pragmatics here, though on different terms and for different purposes.

The ability to see relations across domains independent of context (logic), the ability to anticipate outcomes intuitively, and the ability to keep track of plots/subplots and the inventories implicated (event modeling) may have evolved independently and may thus come 'on line' in the child's brain at different stages of maturation. Predetermination appears to be a very ancient ability. It was needed in the prehistoric manufacture of stone tools (p. 131) and can be observed in experimental setups with infants as young as 11 months old (p. 50f). Event tracking may a be similarly old ability; language and logic likely are later additions to the human brain. With ancient and modern components wired together, the resulting patchwork resembles what Gary Marcus (2008) called a "Kluge"—a modular jumble in which the components may have different agendas and modes of processing, sometimes reinforcing and at other times inhibiting each other. But it is precisely in that patchwork of faculties that narrative thrives —if the child learns to control its components.

Enter children's literature. Authors of children's books can act like trainers in teaching children how to coordinate their faculties. Children's books can address language, predetermination, and logic quite specifically and intentionally. Some distribute the child's cognitive processing loads evenly across all abilities at once, as does Mark Twain in *Adventures of Huckleberry Finn* (see p. 151). Others may play to a particular faculty. The afforded benefit for children is to learn to use narrative to exercise and perfect their control over all of them, both in their own brains and in communicating their stories to adults.

Narrating is the process by which we create or share a story. In other words, I understand 'story' both as the result and as the starting point of narration:

- *Internal narration reduces information.* Creating an inner story means selecting memorable details and mapping them into a bare-minimum representation (gist) of how they relate to one another.
- *External narration (storytelling) adduces information.* Sharing a story elaborates that skeletal representation into an experience again, to be imagined by others.

Distilling (internally) and elaborating (externalizing) a story sounds a bit like compressing a picture to save storage space on a computer and later decompressing it for viewing. It is a nice metaphor, as long as we respect the differences between minds and computers. Reducing the file size of a picture on a computer works by *taking advantage* of redundancies: Instead of storing each of 3000 individual pixels of white space in a row, a format like JPG notes that the next 3000 pixels are going to be white space, thereby reducing thousands of bits of information into just a handful without losing any information. When the picture is extracted again to be displayed, those 3000 pixels are restored as per instruction, and the original picture is visible again. The reduction and recreation of information stored by humans, on the other hand, is not algorithmic. Humans *ignore* redundancies. We do not prioritize 'exact detail'—in fact, we may be biologically incapable of handling large amounts of raw data for more than a split second. Human reduction is ruthlessly selective, and our elaborations subsequently highly imaginative: We both create and recall when we narrate.

I will proceed in three steps. First, I will explore the creation of 'inner story' as efficient information management (reducing information). Then, I will describe how a child learns to *tell* a story by elaborating and structuring it in alignment with the audience's anticipated needs (adducing information). Finally, I will return to the interfaces explored on the sentence-level processing of language in the previous chapter—event models, anticipation, logic—and show how children's literature spreads cognitive loads across those cognitive faculties (distributing information)—with empowering consequences for the child.

The Mnemonic Efficacy of Inner Story: Reducing Information

In the acquisition of the sound system, phonological rules were seen to reduce phonetic perception by interpreting all speech sounds into a limited set of phonemes, thus decreasing information; output, on the other hand, aimed at increase (p. 33). A similar bottleneck is overcome in syntactic processing: Purging the syntactic workspace as soon as its content is fully interpreted is a crucial workaround for limited memory resources (p. 109). And yet we are able to convey rich information with such limited resources. Narrative likewise overcomes processing constraints. A story *stores* only 'full interpretations,' if you will, retaining the substance and eliminating the accidentals. Neuroscience is beginning to focus on the fact that we think in abstractions; in fact, one visitor of the 2017 joint conference of the Society for the Neurobiology of Language and the Society for Neuroscience came away from the event with the impression that 'it seems that abstraction is the thing the brain cares *most* about, doing so rapidly and robustly in sensory cortex' (Matchin 2017). Stories drastically reduce the amount of the information retained (Daniel Kahneman estimates by 95%). There are at least three priorities that influence what ends up in the 5% we retain:

- Stories require *selection*. Even witnessing an event is already a selective process. For a noteworthy occurrence that we will likely tell someone about later, we would want to pay attention to the 5 W's[1] that will be needed for the 'orientation' part of storytelling (Labov 2001). Children likely learn to strategize their selective attention as they grow into storytellers.
- Other details are retained for their role in *outcomes*. Daniel Kahneman's research (Redelmeier, Katz, & Kahneman 2003) suggests that the 'narrating self' routinely overrides the 'experiencing self' based primarily on good or bad outcomes (win or loss, pain-free vs. painful endings, etc.). Alcino Silva (2017) explains how this happens. The amygdala, which handles strong emotions, uses CREB (CAMP-responsive element-binding) proteins to reach out to neurons in the neocortex. Any neurons that likewise contain CREB respond by stabilizing their synaptic connections, optimizing retention.
- We retain information on how one story connects to others. Story parts need to be *linked*, and stories are linked to each other, such that 'one recollection summons the next, establishing intricate sequences of memories that help us to better predict and comprehend the world around us' (Silva 2017:32).

> Discontinuities, such as Alice's in Wonderland, are experienced as disorienting and deeply disturbing.

When stories are shared, any missing information is recreated (just as in phonemic restoration, cf. p. 33, or for the visual 'blind spot') or even updated with feedback from others. The reduction/elaboration account of storied memories is well attested in forensic psychology: Selective retention and elaborative unpacking compromise the reliability even of well-intentioned eyewitnesses (cf. Cutler & Penrod 1995).

We have 'a mind for' stories, and an exceptional memory for them. A given list of items (table, pond, water, alligator, trap, hunter, somersault, nose) can more easily be recalled (especially after reading this chapter) when they are arranged to make sense as a story. Competitors in modern memory championships are really storying champions.

The mnemonic efficacy of stories has been long known and exploited. For example, information can be visually arranged as a navigational story. The Greek poet and orator Simonides (556–468 BCE) imagined walking through a building in which each room contained items iconic for the next topic to address in a speech (Wittrock 1977:155). It is an easily mastered technique, and Thomas Wilson still recommended it in his 1551 *The Rule of Reason* (Bizzell & Herzberg 2001:699).

The effectiveness of visualized inner narration (walking through an imagined building with imaginary inventory) tells us that an inner story does not have to be exclusively verbal. David Wiesner's *Tuesday* is a series of wordless drawings and makes sense as that. Some people prefer visual stories to verbal ones altogether, notably Dr. Temple Grandin, a professor of animal science at Colorado State University and a beneficiary, as she sees it, of autism. She characterized her memories as decidedly *visual*, and language as extraneous to her inner stories:

> I think in pictures. Words are like a second language to me. I translate both spoken and written words into full-color movies, complete with sound, which run like a VCR tape in my mind. When somebody speaks to me, his words are instantly translated into pictures.
>
> (2006:19)

Brain scans and diagnostic tests performed on Temple Grandin by Cooperider et al. (2011) suggest a reason for her preference for visual inner stories: Her brain is massively connected to the visual cortex, but 'compromised' in the areas indicated in the perception and parsing of speech sounds in Figure 1.2, left superior temporal gyrus and left inferior frontal gyrus.

Distilling a story from experiences is thus not a prerogative of the language faculty; rather, there appears to a domain-general 'Universal Generative Faculty' (Hauser & Watumull 2017). Indeed, studies with patients of traumatic brain injuries have shown a dissociation; storytelling can be impaired when all other linguistic abilities are spared. The conclusion is that losing the ability to form normal narratives 'may reflect a deficit at the interface between cognitive and linguistic processing rather than a specific linguistic disturbance' (Marini et al. 2011:2904).

Hauser and Watumull speculate that being able to generate narratives *across* domains (notice that even Temple Grandin's 'movies' are 'complete with sound') may be a particularly human skill—maybe it is the essence of what Steven Pinker intuitively referred to as 'mentalese' (1994:ch. 3). Not being tied to a specific domain makes our narratives abstract to the point of synesthesia. Illustrated children's books can evoke visual and physical sensations simultaneously. Ed Young's *Moon Mother* (1993), for example, stimulates various senses at once. The opening page describes primordial earth as perpetually warm and beautiful, with lakes, rivers, grass, and full of flowers and trees. The ethereal pastel painting on that page shows neither lakes nor rivers. It is a hazy composition of vivid, light colors—blues, white, yellows, and greens—*evoking* a flowered meadow, of trees with dots of red fruit or maybe blossoms, and of bright sky. While the picture omits details mentioned in the words, it invites sensations not mentioned in the text: The feeling of sun on bare skin, the sounds of birds, peace, quiet, rest. The very haziness of the picture disallows focusing on any particular detail; the viewer is *looking at* rather than *looking for*, which also engenders a feeling of unfamiliarity as in a first arrival.

Shared Story: Adducing Information

It happens to married couples eventually: A mere reference will bring up an entire shared experience. 'Just like Thanksgiving last year!' means something to those two—one would have had to be there to make sense of the allusion. Spouses eventually develop something like a 'private code' based on their shared history, often unintelligible to eavesdroppers (Leisi 1978:35–45).

In modern culture, so-called 'memes' can likewise make allusions to shared stories, except that they are seasonal and fade with the stories. For example, 'hiking the Appalachian trail' was once a well-understood reference to marital infidelity: A South Carolina governor had covered his six-day disappearance in 2009 with such a purported hike (Cope 2015). Theoretically, a culture could communicate in memes altogether, an idea that was dramatized in episode 2 of *Star Trek—The Next Generation* season 5, 'Darmok.' The Tamarians, a first contact for the starship Enterprise, communicate via allusions to their shared myths and stories ('Mirab, his sails unfurled'). Since their civilization is described as peaceful, ancient and isolated, it presumably has a stable, shared story tradition, and there would have been little need to elaborate on the stories' well-known plots until the Enterprise persisted in establishing contact. For the crew of Captain Picard, however, communication breaks down in the same way it does for outsiders overhearing a couple's insider language: There is no shared reference. The crew of the Enterprise has no idea what happened when Mirab's sails were unfurled, hence is (initially) unable to guess what the first officer of the Tamarian space ship seems to be recommending to his captain about how to proceed in establishing communication. The Tamarians, having turned their memes into lemmas (vocabulary entries), are unable to elaborate. (How their children learn those stories so that they can refer to them later is beyond this author's ability to fathom; maybe Captain Picard would have had fewer problems conversing with the children of that species).

Humans are not like Tamarians in one respect: They did not evolve to live in stable harmony and isolation; in fact, few of us are even monolingual. Being bilingual (or multilingual) is, as Vivian Cook observed, 'a normal part of human existence'; he concluded that 'it may well be unusual to know only one language' (Cook 2001:159). Why? If multilingualism is in our genes, then it may have some survival value, and our history provides evidence. We cooperate across linguistic boundaries for constructive reasons (e.g. trade and treaties across tribes and nations) and for violent reasons (e.g. slavery, alliances with outsiders to deprive a third party of their resources). The ability to elaborate, to communicate our stories to someone who does not share our background, is our anti-isolation insurance. We are a hyper-cooperative species—one reason why Chapter 8 will explore how cooperation (to include and to exclude) plays out in children's literature.

Narration is instant and automatic, indicative of a very ancient information processor of the brain (just like predetermination and event modeling)—potentially so ancient that we may ask whether it exists in great apes. There are some intriguing indications that it does. For example, the YouTube channel 'Kokoflix' features what the Gorilla Foundation calls a 'story' by Michael (a long-time companion of the world-famous Koko) in response to the question 'What can you tell me about your mother?' The gorilla is seen to respond using hand signs he was taught: 'squash meat gorilla mouth tooth cry sharp-noise loud bad think-trouble look-face cut neck girl's-lip hole.' Judging by the footage, his response has focused sincerity and communicative intent. The authors point out that Michael was a bushmeat orphan, so this could be Michael's narration of his memory of seeing his mother killed and butchered by poachers (Gorilla Foundation 2008). The hand signs are iconic and not connected by syntax, hence do not necessarily indicate the existence of a 'language' in the sense that American Sign Language (from which Michael's signs were borrowed) is an actual language. However, the web site does add that this was a 'memory that he conveyed several times,' so the signed sequence is also not random.[2] The web site does not say whether at those occasions Michael told his story by using the exact same signs in the same sequence. If not, we can conclude that he possessed an inner visual story complete with sound (sharp-noise loud), and a way to externalize that story using whatever signs he had at his command at that time.

Turning a story into an experience for others is a learned skill. We can observe how those skills of elaborating and structuring develop in children. Lucy Sprague Mitchell, for example, recorded the following narration by a four-year-old:

> Once there was a table and he was taking a walk and he fell into a pond of water and an alligator bit him and then he came up out of the pond of water and he stepped into a trap that some hunters had set for him, and turned a somersault on his nose.
>
> (1921:24)

The author offered the transcript as support for her here-and-now approach to children's literature, an example of the 'disjointed' thinking and 'confusion' that occurs when a child's narrative is not context-embedded (ibid.). But even confabulated, it *is* a story, and it shows a maturing narrative grammar at work. Conjoined by *and*, and linked by the protagonist *table*, are a traditional opening and six episodes, one with a subplot (an explanation for the presence of a trap). Each of the episodes is based on a single verb's script (cf. the discussion of scripts implied in card-board picturebooks on p. 65):

take (table, walk)
fall into (table, pond)
bite (alligator, table)
come out of (table, pond)
step into (table, trap)/*set* (hunters, trap, for table)
turn (table, somersault, on nose)

To Sprague Mitchell, the episodes looked "abandoned" in unrealities (ibid.), and they are fantastic slapstick indeed, but there is no reason to impute disorientation.

If there is any sense of feeling 'abandoned' in narration, it is typically created by the ease with which those stories arise within us. They seem to tell themselves, so autonomously that we appear to 'witness' our inner narrations. Among the authors who experienced this receivership was J. M. Barrie, who claimed that in the writing of *Peter Pan*, his protagonist 'was beginning to develop an independent personality and dictate to his creator' (Green 1954:65). Such experiences have given rise to the 'bicameral mind' theory (Jaynes 1976), according to which the linguistic left hemisphere receives and edits 'Old Brain' narratives. So independent from content is the creative process that actions can feel more important than their agents, or who is affected (see Crago 2014:24). Crago notes that the table is a human being (ibid.) when it turns a somersault *on his nose*.

That said, this four-year-old narrator is already an expert at externalizing his narrative with SENTENCE GRAMMAR. There is the narrative past, which projects the fiction into unverifiable time and space (*once there was*). There is the use of the perfective aspect (q.v. Table 3.1) in the subplot of a trap *that some hunters* ***had set*** *for him*. By definition, 'aspect' reflects the speaker's assessment of the completion of the action denoted in the main verb (about to begin, about to end, ongoing, etc.). The perfective aspect in Edited "Standard" English encodes *two* linguistic features: First, it indicates completed action with a 'currently relevant state.' It also has a resultative sense, being the same inflection as is used in English passive constructions. The young narrator has mastered both features: As a result of the hunters' action, the trap is there when the table comes out of the pond, and constitutes a new danger to it. The perfective aspect also indicates that the episode of the hunters setting a trap for the table is a 'flashback,' action that was completed prior to the narrated actions of the table. In other words, the narrator had an 'origo' in mind, a narrative fixpoint to which other episodes relate as prior, concurrent, or subsequent (the 'make-belief *hic-et-nunc*' of p. 69). The linguistic tools of narration are operating with some maturity here.

Narrative grammar—guiding the externalization/elaboration of a story—is honed in performance. Initially, the child advances a story line by arranging single-verb scripts into dyads of threat and reversal, an organizing principle that can also be observed in dreams and in fairy tales (Crago 2014:21). Such early "dialectic" narration presumably still takes its marching orders from sentence-level processing, which is binary, we recall: Early lexical reference is binary—the either-or Mutual Exclusivity Bias of labeling (p. 62)—and so is mapping into merge sets and syntactic structures (cf. Figure 4.1). To participate fully in adult story space, a child needs to align with adult expectations of how a narrative should be structured. An adult would share a recalled experience, for example, in components identified by William Labov (2001):

- **Abstract**: *An optional setup for the story*—'I remember when my family went on vacation to the beach.'
- **Orientation**: *The who, when, where, and/or why of the story*—'My sister and I were walking along the shore and collecting shells.'
- **Complicating Action**: *The plot of the story*—'We saw a swimmer waving his hands in the air and calling out for help. A rip current was pulling him out to sea. We ran down the beach and alerted a lifeguard.'
- **Resolution**: *What happened, in which the problem posed by the complicating action comes to a conclusion*—'The lifeguard paddled out on his surfboard and rescued the swimmer.'
- **Evaluation**: *Optional comments, made at any point in the story, that explain why the story is being told or why the events are notable*—'It's a good thing we were there or who knows what might have happened!'
- **Coda**: *Returns the listener back to the present. This is the storyteller saying that the story is over*—'And we all lived happily ever after!'

At four years, our young author above already shows elements of such an adult narrative grammar. There is a formulaic orientation (*Once there was a table . . .*), a protagonist (a walking table—just as in Edward Lear, p. 116), there are complicating actions and resolutions, and the last resolution seems to act as a coda: The table somersaults in celebration of its survival of three perils (falling into a pond, being bitten by an alligator, and stepping into the hunters' trap). What is missing is a sense of purpose: There is no setup of the topic's significance for the audience, and no evaluation. Nor does the child yield the floor with a coda.

Authors can train children in the art of narrative grammar, especially the parts with which the four-year-old narrator of the table story previously had some difficulty: abstract, final resolution, evaluation, and coda. Samuel Clemens, himself by inclination an episodic writer (Blair 1962:viii), famously presented Dorothy Quick of his 'angelfish club' of young girls with an unfinished manuscript and asked her to invent a resolution (Cooley 1991:38). Virginia Lee Burton actually used the ending suggested by 12-year-old Richard 'Dickie' Berkenbush for *Mike Mulligan and his Steam Shovel* (Silvey 2004:17–18). Janosch invites his young audience to supply the evaluation in *Schuddelbuddel baut ein Haus* ('The House of 1000 Rooms,' 1980). Shnoodles (as he is called in English) and his diminutive pony friend Schnuddelpferdchen build a house and add more and more rooms on top of each until it looks like a surreal construction out of a Dr. Seuss book. The book asks the child to make a prediction of what is likely going to happen (the towering infirmity comes crashing down, of course). The author withholds the final words of the story: The big forest bear is about to add the evaluation and addresses the two: 'You two goofballs! This is what happens when . . . '—and a note instructs the child to complete the bear's moral.

The narrative competence that develops interactively with adult scaffolding appears to decline in mirror reverse. Boyd H. Davis and Margaret Maclagan (2018) chronicle a patient's declining narrative competence from a full Labov-type 'canonical' structure as above (freely generated or scaffolded by the interrogator) to small stories (such as 'shadow stories' interjected into a larger narrative), narrative 'chunks,' or simple 'chronicles' (repetitive and formulaic narration without plot, as in the 'table story' above). As the patient's dementia progressed, her ability to spontaneously tell a story that 'her audiences thought was a full story that made a point, one with a beginning, a middle and an end' declined. The neural correlate may be a loss in interconnectivity between narrative and cognitive domains.

Narrative and Cognition: Distributing Information

As a domain-general information management system, narrative connects event models (plots and their inventories), predetermination, and logic. Those are the same faculties whose contributions to language were explored in Chapter 5, but with a difference in scope here. When *language* interacts with those faculties, the objectives are local: to parse/disambiguate, to verify syntactic functions and semantic truth values. When *narrative* interacts with them, the objectives are strategic: to control plots, to create suspense, and to make compositional sense.

- **Event models demand critical control**: We saw how event models help resolve pronouns with remote antecedents in Chapter 5. Here, event models enable children not only to follow plots, but also to interrogate them. David Wiesner's *The Three Pigs* (2001) presupposes exactly such a critical ability. As the pneumatically hyper-endowed wolf puffs down the first pig's straw house, he blows his intended victim through the illustration's panel frame. The pig realizes right away what that implies: He was just blown out of the story. The next panel has the traditional wording 'and ate the pig up.'—but the illustration shows a nonplused wolf surveying the barren wreckage. The pig, meanwhile, is now outside the scripted plot and walks *between* the panels of his story. He invites the other two pigs to join him in the third dimension: 'Now we have room to move.' They fold the strewn pages of their evacuated story into paper airplanes. Exploring panel-free white space—and now looking photorealistic rather than like their former fairy-tale illustration selves—the pigs discover pages of *other* familiar plots. One shows a dragon fated to be slain by a knight. The pigs convince the dragon that he too can leave his story. Together, they eventually decide to 'go home' into the stone house. They re-enter their story not on the deadly terms of the original plot, but on theirs: The blow-hard wolf gets his final come-uppance when he shows up and a dragon answers the door. Wiesner's pigs model the empowerment of interrogating 'given' scripts and taking control of the storyline—critical thinking (see 'cognitive appraisal,' p. 156 below).

- **Predetermination creates suspense**: Predetermination assists 'depth-first' sentence parsing, anticipating what structure is going to be processed (cf. Figure 5.2). It also engages the child interactively in following a story, predicting what happens next. Children's books are designed to invite anticipation, down to the placement of the words on the page, planned strategically to make gratification dependent on page turning. When children are literate, the architecture of the book changes to accommodate macro levels of narration, and the suspense is created with narrative delays across several pages (subplots, drawn-out descriptions, red herrings, etc.). Those techniques are strategically employed in *Adventures of Huckleberry Finn*, for instance (discussed below). Predetermination and expectations —even those that turn out to be false because the author had a surprise in store —make reading a playful activity in which the reader is allowed to slow down for the good parts and skim ahead expectantly (Nell 1988:16–20 s.l. 'Study 2').
- **Logic relates parts to overall sense**: In sentences, logic relates meaningful parts into propositions; in story and literary discourse, logic negotiates coherence on a macro level. 'Sense' in a story is not proven in propositional truth values (à la A. J. Ayer 1936); children (and adults) make sense of a story based on how its components relate, a quality Jerome S. Bruner called 'hermeneutic composability' (2003:47). The hermeneutics of shared story require cooperation. Classical logic has little to say about compositional/cooperative rules, but Jean-Yves Girard has taken up the challenge of creating an interactive logic suitable for analyzing how we share stories. 'Ludics' (Girard 2002) formalizes the hermeneutic composition of sense in dialogue —a Socratic game theory, so to speak, in which two 'players' interactively advance step by step. A game-theory logic explains how we exchange information, co-construct knowledge, and resolve cognitive tension (Fleury Quatrini, & Tronçon 2011:139). Success comes in a so-called *daïmon*, a move that terminates a 'felicitous exchange that satisfies both parties' designs' (Winterstein 2011:103). It is immediately clear how Girard's logic of rules plays out in children's literature. For example, we see how the rules of the story are continuously negotiated and advanced between author and child in Thatcher Hurd's *Art Dog* (1996). Art dog creates imaginative graffiti at night and is taken into custody because the police mistake him for an art thief. The author's next move advances the story only if the child agrees that a character inside an illustration can affect the very illustration: Art dog paints a ladder to the barred window and paints an open window over the bars to escape

> from prison.[3] The ramification of accepting that move is that the game can advance to the next move: Art Dog can go ahead and confront the real culprits to capture them—in a painting. The child must now accept the rules of that move: The thieves can be captured in the painting only if they are unable to do what Art Dog did just a few pages ago—change the picture they are in to escape it. The story ends by Art Dog painting the sky in Vincent-van-Gogh like designs. It must now be accepted that the protagonist can fly, whereas previously he needed his brush mobile to get around. The story of Art Dog is essentially a game between author and child, whose logic relies on 'resolving cognitive tensions' (here: by renegotiating rules).

Authors get to decide to which domains their readers' attention goes (if they are game): building and updating their event models, predetermining outcomes, seeing the logical connections between parts and whole—or the language itself. Mark Twain achieves a perfectly even distribution in *Adventures of Huckleberry Finn*. The book is full of suspenseful anticipation and opportunities to jump to conclusions (e.g. when Tom finds the remains of a recent camp fire on Jackson Island, on which he thought himself alone); there are logical problems to be solved at every turn of events (how to get Tom out of the abusive clutches of Pap, how to thwart the con men 'Duke' and 'Dauphin,' how to free Jim); and there are events to keep in mind because they become part of the main plot (e.g. the corpse in the house floating down the Mississippi, whose face Jim does not want Tom to see, which turns out in the end to have been Pap's body). Just as much attention goes to language, which is used to profile the characters: Tom can change registers depending on whom he talks to, and the con men can affect enough of a British accent to pass as the English heirs to Peter Wilks' fortune.

The hallmark of Theodor Geisel's fiendishly unpronounceable book *Oh Say Can You Say?* is its dismissal of predictability, narrative coherence, or logic. The attention is entirely on the language: It is clear from the start that there is not going to be an overall plot. It is fruitless to anticipate outcomes because the language drives everything, and the child is explicitly admonished —twice!—not to ask 'why,' because it does 'not matter.' The language is there to be played with; cracks and stacks and sacks are introduced just to pile them up into a lingual tour de force.

Munro Leaf's *The Story of Ferdinand* invites predetermination. The premium is on connecting subplots to predict how they might advance and resolve the main plot. After a few episodes illustrating how peacefully absorbed the young bull is in his appreciation of nature and the lovely smell of flowers, plots suddenly intersect: Five men arrive to scout for fierce bulls for the arena. Ferdinand inadvertently sits on a bumble bee. The expression on his face hints at what will happen on the next page—he bounds over the meadow in pain. That subplot now interacts with the previous one, because the five men mistake his agony for fierceness and load him into a cart. On the day of the bull fight, the narrative takes time to mention that 'all the lovely ladies had flowers in their hair.' It then proceeds to announce what the banderilleros, picadores, and the matador are there for. Their job is to make the bulls mad and madder. When Ferdinand enters the arena, the child can make two predictions: Either the bull fighters are going to make Ferdinand mad, or Ferdinand's peaceful nature will prevail. The seemingly serendipitous detail of the flowers in the ladies' hair becomes the game changer: Ferdinand sees all the flowers in the crowd and sits down to smell them. He is then returned to his pasture. The story does not *develop* as a 'sequence of events that unfolds with a sense of inevitability,' as Crago defines story (2014:190). It is not inevitable story logic that foreseeably drives this narrative: The bumble bee and the flowers in the ladies' hair are surprises whose potential import for the plot the child must size up.

A book that relies very heavily on thinking things through step by step, on the other hand, is Edwin A. Abbott's *Flatland: A Romance of Many Dimensions* (1884). It is not a very popular book, perhaps because of the intellectual demands it places on its young readers; I became aware of it many years ago only because our son received it as a gift from his eclectic and brilliant chess teacher at the time, Bruce Pandolfini. Abbott explores in precise detail what the limitations would be for beings inhabiting a two-dimensional world trying to comprehend a three-dimensional one ('Spaceland'):

> Dimension implies direction, implies measurement, implies the more and the less. Now, all our lines are *equally* and *infinitesimally* thick (or high, whichever you like); consequently, there is nothing in them to lead our minds to the conception of that Dimension. No 'delicate micrometer'—as has been suggested by one too hasty Spaceland critic—would in the least avail us; for we should not know *what to measure, nor in what direction.* When we see a Line, we see something that is long and *bright; brightness*, as well as length, is necessary to the existence of a Line; if the brightness vanishes, the Line is extinguished. Hence, all my Flatland friends—when I talk to them about the unrecognized Dimension which is somehow visible in a Line—say, 'Ah, you mean *brightness*': and when I reply, 'No, I mean a real Dimension,' they at once retort 'Then measure it, or tell us in what direction it extends'; and this silences me, for I can do neither.
>
> (viiii)

The young reader is challenged to imagine how similarly difficult it is for human beings to comprehend a four-dimensional world (just as it was difficult for the crawling bugs in Margaret Wise Brown's poem 'Said a Bug' to imagine sizing up the tall grass blades in flight—see p. 136). After Einstein's publication of his Theory of Relativity, Abbott's book gained brief popularity, and a letter to *Nature* makes a direct reference to *Flatland* when discussing how we might erroneously ascribe to time the physical effects of a fourth dimension that we can not perceive (Garnett 1920:629).[4] The relations in Flatland are logically consistent and apply across domains. Here, they are also the vehicle for social satire (higher-order shapes are treated differently from simpler shapes, women are mere lines, talk of a higher-order dimension is suppressed and punished, etc.).

How an author distributes and assigns cognitive load could be the subject of an entire aesthetics of literature based on cognitive science. One could easily establish profiles like the ones in Figure 6.1, which summarizes my intuitive judgments of the four examples above. Having some kind of profile of cognitive demands

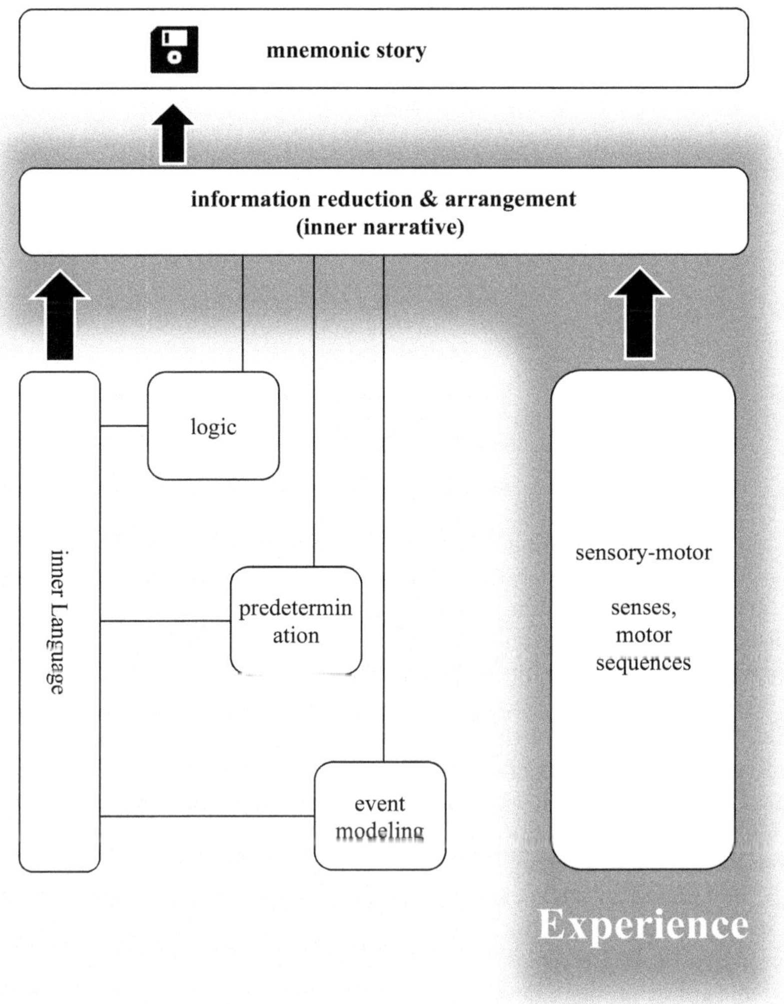

Figure 6.1 Inner Narrative and Cognition

Inner narration is domain general, extracting salient information from the five senses, from motoric sequences such as stone tool knapping (cf. p. 131 above) or ballistic motion (Chapter 5, n. 3) and from inner language (cf. Figure 4.1/Figure 4.2). The filtering/ordering process (inner narration) interfaces with the same cognitive faculties that also assist linguistic processing (Chapter 5), but on a macro level, to create a story that 'makes sense' compositionally and relationally.

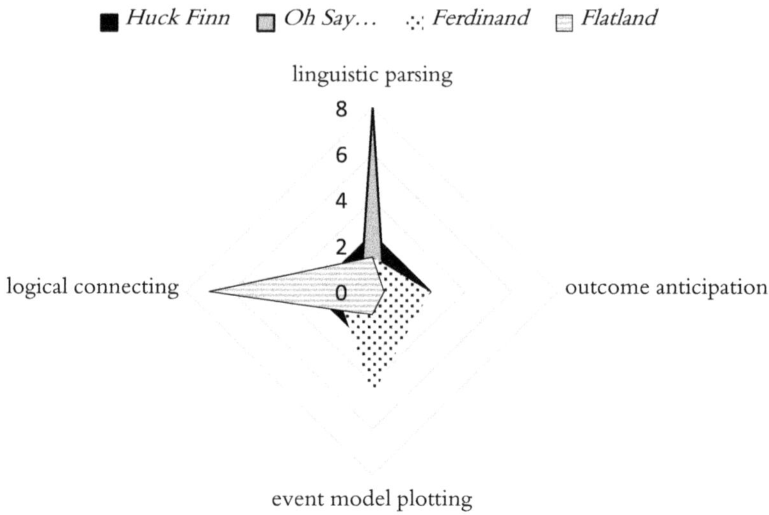

Figure 6.2 Cognitive-Demands Profile of Four Children's Books

would, in turn, allow specific marketing to children according to age or current interest. Certainly, matching readers' preferences to cognitive-load profiles is easier when the books are delivered on electronic devices that provide feedback on reading behavior (scrolling speed, length of sessions, highlighting, etc.) to the publisher. Consumer profiling of adults is already very specific for adults' preferences in viewing, listening, shopping, news selection, and financial decision making (Alter 2012; Rhomberg 2015). We should expect such increasing sophistication in the marketing of children's literature.

If linguistic and cognitive faculties interface in the manner hypothesized above, then we have yet another reason why children should be exposed to diverse kinds of children's books (Figure 6.2). In addition to training the infant's ear for the sounds of her native languages, in addition to building vocabulary and semantic fields, in addition to advancing syntax and early literacy, children's books can specifically stimulate integrative control of cognitive faculties. And they can do so in such rewarding and playful ways that children can hardly wait until the next trip to the public library.

Inner Monologue: Narrative as Central Controller

Uncritically allowing any one cognitive faculty to lionize and bias inner narrative can have self-defeating consequences, even for adults. Novelist Karen Thompson Walker illustrated this in a TED Talk on the whaleship Essex, which was rammed and sunk by an enraged sperm whale (the original 'Moby Dick') on 20

November 1820. The crew, transferred to their small whaleboats, plotted their escape route to South America, which was thousands of miles away, rather than sailing to the Marquesas Islands, which they thought was populated by cannibals. The predetermined bad outcome of sailing to the closer islands loomed so prominently in their mental narratives that it produced an actual horror story—their decision turned out fatal for most of the crew.

Logical generalizations, just like imagined plots and outcomes, can result in biases, for example when relations abstracted from specific events are projected as stereotypes to entire domains. Such stereotypes can prejudice children at an early age, as is well documented in children's literature research. Jerri Kropp and Charles Halverson (1983), for example, demonstrated that children preferentially remembered books that catered to their social construction of gender. Girls and boys showed different retention of Pat Hutchins' *The Best Train Set Ever* [a.k.a. *Peter's Train Set*], Norma Klein's *A Train for Jane*, Lois Lenski's *Debbie and her Dolls*, and Charlotte Zolotow's *William's Doll*. Their bias may very well be reinforced by elevated oxytocin levels that accompany interactive book reading: An experiment by De Dreu et al. (2011) indicated that oxytocin-enhanced social bonding extends perceived in-groups. Book authors thus sometimes surprise their young audience by deliberately setting up a stereotype that turns out *not* to apply, especially in addressing ethnic diversity, gender roles, and disabilities. Author Cece Bell, for example, narrates her own childhood experience in *El Deafo* (2014), and the very 'disability' that *others* her (having to rely on a bulky 'phonic ear' contraption that receives sound from a microphone around the teacher's neck) becomes her cool 'superpower' (when the teacher forgets to take off the microphone and the protagonist gets to overhear her conversations with fellow teachers—and a trip to the bathroom).

A child who develops (self-)critical narrative control over competing cognitive faculties is an empowered child. Children's literature can aim to assist with encouraging the child's narrative control over them. Authors sometimes deliberately setup unintended consequences to demonstrate what happens when the narrative is biased toward one faculty, at the neglect of the others. Rather than going through all possible permutations of faculties inhibiting each other, I will name three representative examples where adults act as trainers (authors) or coaches (adults reading with a child) to engage the child's narrative control of cognitive faculties by setting up biased scenarios:

- **Reliance on inventory at the expense of logical relations**: In Janosch's 'Wandertag nach Paderborn' (1980), Shnoodles' pony sidekick Schnuddelpferdchen talks his reluctant friend into a daytrip to Paderborn (and beyond), offering as incentive to carry not only him but also his baggage. The author establishes a routine of keeping track of the luggage items, even asking the child to fill in the blanks in an inventory list: two suitcases, another suitcase, and an empty bottle. When the big-hearted itsyhippus tires of the burden, he asks Shnoodles to please carry two of the suitcases, to which Shnoodles readily agrees. The author reviews: now Shnoodles is carrying two suitcases, and his pony is carrying one suitcase and a bottle. It is not until the illustration on the next page that the reader realizes the error of assuming that Shnoodles just relieved his friend. The pony is still carrying Shnoodles.

- **Reliance on logic at the expense of predetermination**: John Newbery's *A Little Pretty Picture Book* (1787) sternly sabotages playful reading by enforcing reading for sentence-based logic. In his preface, the author enlists the parent as logic coach with the following instruction:

  > Would you have a *Wise* Son, teach him to reason early. Let him read, and make him understand what he reads. No Sentence should be passed over without a strict Examination of the Truth of it; and though this may be thought hard at first, and seem to retard the Boy in his Progress, yet, a little Practice will make it familiar, and a Method of Reasoning will be acquired, which will be of Use to him all his Life after. (10)

  If wisdom comes from reasoning, then safety lies in parsing. No skipping to the good parts.
- **Reliance on predetermination at the expense of logic**: Overreliance on predetermination is known as 'jumping to conclusions,' and tricksters like Broer Rabbit outsmart others time and again by setting them on a narrative garden path that some prudent application of logic should certainly have precluded them from following. But not just literary characters can be made to jump to conclusions: The reader, too, can be tempted to go astray. Janosch sets up a scenario in which Kasper leaves home stealthily ('schleicht auf leisen Sohlen') to bring home a rabbit for lunch. He gathers salad in the field, a staple rabbit food. Meanwhile, Rabbit chills in his den slurping a glass of strawberry milk. On the wall are pictures of a hunter and a dog, and a note saying 'all is well (almost).' The reader who surmises that the rabbit is about to end up as lunch will stand corrected for not having considered the equally plausible possibility that Rabbit might be invited *to* lunch. Kasper and Rabbit enjoy a civilized vegan meal in each other's company (*Kasper Mütze holt einen Hasen*, 1987).

Narrative control puts children in charge of their inner monologues, making them critical instead of reactive. This is achieved in two ways:

- **Cognitive appraisal**: We can monitor our inner monologues and interrogate them critically. A number of authors such as Lewis Carroll, Mo Willems, Theodor Geisel, and Walter Moers repeatedly nudge children to question both the characters in the book and (concomitantly) their own assumptions as co-creators of the story. Failure to appraise permits self-defeating and self-inflicting narratives that can be summed up in the words of Marshall Rosenberg (2005:132): 'I myself am not behaving in harmony with my own needs.'

- **Narrative authorship**: We are also the creators of our inner stories and can choose not only to appraise them, but to rewrite them, as do the three pigs in David Wiesner's book and Art Dog in Thatcher Hurd's.

Among the *observable indicators* of narrative control over cognition is the ability to deferred gratification. Certainly, it was a top pedagogical priority for John Newbery. Among the 163 (!) rules for children in chapter 2 of *A Little Pretty Pocket-Book*, for example, is an etiquette for delaying gratification at the table (1787:102):

> 4 Offer not to carve for thyself, or to take any Thing, though it be that which thou dost greatly desire.
> 5 Ask not for any Thing, but tarry until it be offered thee.
> 7 When thou hast Meat given thee, be not the first that begins to eat.

From Aesop's Fables to *Charlie and the Chocolate Factory*, children's literature brims with examples of why it is better to defer gratification than to indulge 'selfishly.' Children can learn to exert such self-control by means of inner narrative. Walter Mischel and Nancy Baker proved this experimentally in 1975. They placed two marshmallows in front of children and made it clear that eating one of them (while the experimenters temporarily left the room) meant that they could not eat the second (when they returned). Knowing from an earlier study that children who resisted instant gratification used auto-suggestive Jedi mind tricks to distract their own attention, they supplied two narratives: One was to describe the abstract qualities of marshmallows and to transfer them to the domain of clouds; the other was to rehearse an *imagined* gratification (thinking about a tasty pretzel that was actually not available). Both narratives helped the children defer gratification—the pretzels even more than the clouds.

Follow-up studies documented the long-term *efficacy* of such cognitive self-empowerment: Children who mastered the narrative art of delaying gratification by choosing a different inner story did better in school (scoring an average of 210 points higher on the SAT) and had fewer behavioral problems; as adults, they had a higher graduation rate at college and higher incomes as well as fewer problems with addiction (Lickerman 2012). No wonder that self-control has such a central place in children's literature through the ages.

Works like *The Three Pigs* neither enforce nor offer alternative narratives (as Walter Mischel did in his marshmallow experiments)—they *model* playfully that it is possible to appraise a story critically and to choose to change it. Wiesner illustrates, literally, thinking out of the box. The questioning child is no longer expected to emulate enlightened despots like John Newbery, but to think critically by being able to ask *cui bono*—who is the beneficiary in / of this story? Am I acting in harmony with my own needs? Surely, like the Grimms' *Bremen Town Musicians*, children are entitled to choose a story that ends with something 'better than death,' better than being devoured by wild beasts for being 'naughty'

(Bewick, *The History of Little King Pippin*),[5] better than having one's thumbs cut off for sucking them (Hoffman, *Der Struwwelpeter*, 1845).[6] Ludic reading—reading as play—presupposes freedom.

The following two chapters focus on how children's literature, particularly in interactive reading, can create a safe space through entrainment (Chapter 7) and cooperation (Chapter 8). Such a safe space—Maryanne Wolf (2016:62) calls literacy 'the one safe haven a child can have in any culture'—is important because children construct their social selves through story, both for themselves and in dialogue:

Inner Story as autobiography: Children's author Katherine Paterson maintained: 'My life is based on a true story' (1989).[7] The words are Jonah's as he emerges from the mouth of a whale ("Incredible as it seems, . . ."), but Paterson adopted them as her own motto. She rightfully understood constructed contiguity as the privilege of a lifetime. In contrast, when Alice is asked by the Caterpillar to explain her inability to explain who she is, she is flustered: ' "I can't explain *myself*, I am afraid Sir," said Alice, "because I'm not myself, you see" ' (67). 'Myself ' is a *history* (the word from which we derive the shortened word *story*), so Alice's disconnectedness is understandable: Her recent experiences and selves in Wonderland have been anything but contiguous. A disjointed history can unhinge even a confident person such as Alice; being detached from one's story altogether amounts to an erasure of the self. A victim of severe head trauma once described to me what amnesia feels like: 'I looked into the mirror and saw absolute emptiness, just a void.' To explain himself to himself, he had to recreate his story/history. Tellingly, recovery from amnesia can be supported by narrative therapy (Madigan 2011:26). Narrative (re-)constructs the self, and children's books can provide playful safe zones within which the child can try on different personas to narrate their own story: sassy as in Mark Twain's *Advice to Little Girls*, independent-minded like Margaret Wise Brown's *Runaway Bunny*, stalwart to the end like Dr. Seuss's elephant in *Horton Hatches the Egg*, or supportive like the little mice in Robert Kraus' *Another Mouse to Feed*.

Shared Story as validator: Spiritual directors, therapists, social workers, and even academic advisors are trained in 'attentive listening.' This is because through narrating, as Wilhelm von Humboldt explained some 30 years before Alice fell down the rabbit hole, we not only explain ourselves to ourselves but also validate that understanding in dialogue with others (1836:53).[8] In the case of children, validation comes typically from approval—from parents (Dr. Seuss, *The Cat in the Hat*) or from a higher power (like Santa Claus in Chris van Allsburg's *The Polar Express*). Even Oompa-Loompas can be powerful validators (Roald Dahl, *Charlie and the Chocolate Factory*). On the notion that 'we are what we tell' (Bers 2003), children's books can put a premium on how children present themselves for self-validation: 'Whether I shall turn out to be the hero of my own life, or whether that station will be held by anybody else, these pages must show' (Charles Dickens, *David*

> *Copperfield*). Social validation of the self occurs as the story positions the teller within distributed cognition. That can be a struggle because the child has to negotiate multiple voices (own and adult). Christopher, in Mark Haddon's *The Curious Incident of the Dog in the Night-Time*, professes difficulty with processing multiple voices, presumably because he is on the Asperger's side of the spectrum. Even a pun like 'his face was drawn but the curtains were real' with its triple meaning of *drawn* makes him feel as if three voices were coming at him talking about different things (2003:10; cf. Meibauer 2017:379). Learning to negotiate, share, and validate stories promotes the child's inner stories from untellable to intelligible, and children's books are a safe playground for exploration.

Children's literature can help children to mature as *homo narrans* in two ways: by empowering them to become critically aware narrators of their own inner stories, and by showing them how to position their maturing selves eloquently within adult space.

Raising empowered narrators through children's books requires exposure to wide-ranging and diverse literature. The prevalent perception, however, is that too many children and students do not enjoy reading, hence avoid it and are not proficient readers, and thus cut themselves off from printed information with all the resulting consequences for lifelong learning and informed citizenship. Consequently, parents seek to instill a natural desire for reading, with a routine of book reading from infancy. Dorothy Butler suggested that books be given at the baby shower: 'Ideally, a small pile of good books awaits the new baby's arrival' (1998:11). 'The love of books,' wrote Astrid Lindgren, 'must be established early, preferably as early as mother's milk' (2017:189). When children grow up with books, they will naturally take to reading as a 'paratelic' activity (Nell 1988:7), i.e. an activity pursued because it is a *reward in itself*. The adults' ultimate agenda in encouraging the enjoyment of playful reading, of course, is to accelerate the child's literacy, with the *cognitive dividends* that the child have a larger vocabulary, become an eager and proficient reader who retains information easily, and gain a cognitive edge over children who are not steeped in a reading culture at home. That line of reasoning is meant to set the child up for success in such a way that the child enjoys every moment of it.

Notes

1. The '5 W's' are *who, what, when, where,* and *why*—and they could be, in these political times, supplemented by a few new choice letters such as the two A's ('are you [. . .] kidding me?' and 'am I dreaming?'), as added by Luke Burns for the *New Yorker* (2017). Anticipated future needs for narrating focuses selective attention to details, much more so than the design of language itself (as assumed by Benjamin Lee Whorf 2012 [1957]).
2. It is of course necessary to resist interpretation and anthropomorphizing. Then again, the great apes are anthropomorphous and interpretable. Michael even anthropomorphized himself: The sign for 'cry' traces an imaginary tear from an eye down the cheek, but only human eyes secrete tears in response to powerful emotions. His companion

Koko, I would like to add, seems to have used Michael's final sign *hole* as a metaphor for 'death' (Patterson & Linden 1981:191):

MAUREEN: *Where* do *gorillas go when* they *die?*
KOKO: *Comfortable hole bye.*
MAUREEN: *When* do *gorillas die?*
KOKO: *Trouble old.*

3. A child is entirely capable of negotiating/accepting the rules of a story's *narrative* reality. Author Crockett Johnson forwarded a review from the North Carolina *Winston-Salem Journal and Sentinel* of his *Harold and the Purple Crayon* (1955) entitled 'Draws Anything' to his editor. He himself had received it from a clipping service. The author, 'Dave Marion Age 4,' wrote: 'Harold can draw whatever he wants with his purple crayon, and then it really is' (Nel 2012:153). Surely young Dave knew the difference between everyday *really* and storybook *really*. David N. Marion, the young author of this review, was a particularly bright child according to his brother Rich Marion, but was hit by an automobile soon after his letter and sustained extensive damage to his right frontal lobe. Even so, he managed to earn a bachelor's degree in Sociology from Salem College before he passed away in 2011 (Rich Marion, personal communication 08 August 2017).
4. I owe this reference to a Wikipedia article on 'Flatland.'
5. The publication date is given at around 1810 on archive.org; however, the book is already advertised on p. 124 of a 1787 edition of Newbery's *A Little Pretty Pocket Book* under 'Books Sold by I. Thomas.'
6. It should not go without mention that Dr. Heinrich Hoffman identified himself as 'Arzt der Irrenanstalt,' a doctor in the local 'lunatic asylum.' Likewise, it should not surprise that the book was lovingly translated into English by Samuel Clemens [Mark Twain], who also invented a cure for stammering (removing the under-jaw), with testimony for its efficacy by 'Zeb. Leavenworth, St. Louis' ('Those Blasted Children,' 1864 [1963:32]).
7. I owe this reference to Hugh Crago (2014:171).
8. The original quote from von Humboldt is: '. . . der Mensch versteht sich selbst nur, indem er die Verstehbarkeit seiner Worte an Andren versuchend geprüft hat' (man understands himself only by verifying the intelligibility of his words, testing them against others). Cf. Michael Bamberg (2005:223): 'By offering and telling a narrative, the speaker lodges a claim for him-/herself in terms of who he/she is.'

References

Alter, Alexandra. 2012. Your e-book is reading you. *The Wall Street Journal*, 19 July. Online: www.wsj.com/articles/SB10001424052702304870304577490950051438304.

Ayer, Alfred Jules. 1936. *Language, truth, and logic*. London: V. Gollancz.

Bamberg, Michael. 2005. Narrative discourse and identities. *Narratology beyond literary criticism: Mediality, disciplinarity*, ed. by Jan Christoph Meister, 213–38. Berlin: Walter de Gruyter.

Bers, Marina Umaschi. 2003. We are what we tell: Designing narrative environments for children. *Narrative intelligence*, ed. by Michael Mateas and Phoebe Sengers (Advances in conscious research), vol. 46, 113–28. Amsterdam, Philadelphia: John Benjamins.

Bizzell, Patricia, and Bruce Herzog. 2001. *The rhetorical tradition: Readings from classical times to the present*, 2nd ed. Boston, New York: Bedford, St. Martin's.

Blair, Walter. 1962. Introduction. *Selected shorter writings of Mark Twain*, ed. by Walter Blair, vii–xxvi. Boston: Houghton Mifflin.

Bruner, Jerome S. 2003. The narrative construction of reality. *Narrative intelligence*, ed. by Michael Mateas and Phoebe Sengers (Advances in conscious research), vol. 46, 41–62. Amsterdam, Philadelphia: John Benjamins. Reprinted from *Critical Inquiry* (1991) 1.1–21.

Burns, Luke. 2017. Additions to the five journalistic 'W's. Daily shouts. *The New Yorker*, 31 January. Online: www.newyorker.com/humor/daily-shouts/additions-to-the-five-journalistic-ws.

Butler, Dorothy. 1998. *Babies need books: Sharing the joy of books with children from birth to six*, revised edition. Portsmouth: Heinemann.

Cook, Vivian James. 2001. *Second language learning and language teaching*, 3rd ed. New York: Oxford University Press, Arnold.

Cooley, John. (ed.) 1991. *Mark Twain's aquarium: The Samuel Clemens Angelfish correspondence 1905–1910*. Athens, London: University of Georgia Press.

Cooperider, Jason R.; Temple Grandin; E. D. Bigler; J. S. Anderson; A. L. Alexander; S. Doran; C. Ennis; M. B. D. Prigge; A. L. Froehlich; B. A. Zielinski; N. T. Lange; N. Adluru; and J. E. Lainhart. 2011. Dr. Temple Grandin: A multimodal neuroimaging case study of a savant with autism. Paper presented at the International Meeting for Autism Research, October. PowerPoint Online: www.researchgate.net/publication/277816213_Dr_Temple_Grandin_A_neuropsychological_and_multimodal_neuroimaging_case_study_of_a_savant_ with_autism.

Cope, Cassie. 2015. How hiking the Appalachian trail became code for an affair. *The State* (Columbia, SC), 01 December. Online: www.thestate.com/news/special-reports/state-125/article47320885.html.

Crago, Hugh. 2014. *Entranced by story: Brain, tale and teller, from infancy to old age*. New York: Routledge.

Cutler, Brian L., and Steven D. Penrod. 1995. *Mistaken identification: The eyewitness, psychology, and the law*. Cambridge, New York: Cambridge University Press.

Davis, Boyd H., and Margaret Maclagan. 2018. "Narrative and ageing: Exploring the range of narrative types in dementia conversation." *European Journal of English Studies* 22(1).76–90.

de Dreu, K. W.; Lindred L. Greer; Gerben A. Van Kleef; Shaul Shalvi; and Michel J. J. Handgraaf. 2011. Oxytocin promotes human ethnocentrism. *PNAS—Proceedings of the National Academy of Science of the United States* 108(4).1262–66.

Fleury, Marie-Renée; Myriam Quatrini; and Samuel Tronçon. 2011. Dialogues in ludics. *Logic and grammar: Essays dedicated to Alain Lecomte on the occasion of his 60th birthday*, ed. by Sylvain Pogodalla, Myriam Quatrini, and Christian Retoré, 138–57. Berlin, Heidelberg: Springer Verlag.

Garnett, William. 1920. Letter to the editor. *Nature* (12 February) 104.629. Extract available at www.math.brown.edu/~banchoff/abbott/Flatland/Reviews/1920nature.shtml.

Girard, Jean-Yves. 2002. Locus solum: From the rules of logic to the logic of rules. *Mathematical Structures in Computer Science* 11(3).301–506.

Gorilla Foundation. 2008. Michael's story, filmed by Ron Cohn. youtu.be/DXKsPqQ0Ycc.

Grandin, Temple. 2006. *Thinking in pictures: My life with autism*, revised edition. New York: Knopf Doubleday, Random House.

Green, Roger Lancelyn. 1954. *Fifty years of Peter Pan*. London: Peter Davies.

Hauser, Marc D., and Jeffrey Watumull. 2017. The universal generative faculty: The source of our expressive power in language, mathematics, morality, and music. *Journal of Neurolinguistics* 43(B).78–94.

Humboldt, Wilhelm von. 1836. *Über die Verschiedenheit des menschlichen Sprachbaues und ihren Einfluss auf die geistige Entwickelung des Menschengeschlechts*. Berlin: Königliche Akademie der Wissenschaften, Dämmler.

Jaynes, Julian. 1976. *The origin of consciousness in the breakdown of the bicameral mind*. Boston: Mariner, Houghton Mifflin.

Kropp, Jerri Jaudon, and Charles F. Halversion. 1983. Preschool children's preferences and recall for stereotyped versus nonstereotyped stories. *Sex Roles* 9(9) (February).261–72.

Labov, William. 2001. Uncovering the event structure of narrative. *Linguistics, language, and the real world: Discourse and beyond*, ed. by Deborah Tannen and James E. Atlantis (Georgetown university round table on language and linguistics), 63–83. Washington, DC: Georgetown University Press.

Leisi, Ernst. 1978. *Paar und Sprache: Linguistische Aspekte der Zweierbeziehung* (Uni-Taschenbücher), vol. 824. Heidelberg: Quelle & Meyer.

Lickerman, Alex. 2012. The power of delaying gratification: How to develop impulse control. *Psychology Today*, 29 July. Online: www.psychologytoday.com/blog/happiness-in-world/201207/the-power-delaying-gratification.

Lindgren, Astrid. 2017. Why do we write children's books?, translated by Elizabeth Sofia Powell. *Children's literature: Annual of the Children's Literature Association and the Modern Language Association division on children's literature* 45.188–95. Baltimore: Johns Hopkins University Press.

Madigan, Stephen. 2011. *Narrative therapy*. Washington, DC: APA.

Marcus, Leonard S. 1992. *Margaret Wise Brown: Awakened by the moon*. Boston: Beacon Press.

Marini, Andrea; Valentina Galetto; Elisa Zampieri; Lorenza Vorano; Marina Zettin; and Sergio Carlomagno. 2011. Narrative language in traumatic brain injury. *Neuropsychologia* 49.2904–10.

Matchin, William. 2017. Abstractness, innateness, and modality-independence of language: reflections on SNL & SfN 2017. *Talking brains: News and views on the neural organization of language*, moderated by Greg Hickok and David Poeppel, 20 November. Online: www.talkingbrains.org.

Meibauer, Jörg. 2017. Pragmatics and children's literature. *Doing pragmatics interculturally: Cognitive, philosophical and sociopragmatic perspectives on language use*, ed. by Rachel Giora and Michael Haugh, 371–87. Berlin, Munich, Boston: De Gruyter Mouton.

Mischel, Walter, and Nancy Baker. 1975. Cognitive appraisals and transformations in delay behavior. *Journal of Personality and Social Psychology* 31(2) (February).254–61.

Mitchell, Lucy Sprague. 1921 [rpt. 1948]. *Here and now storybook*, illustrated by Hendrik Willem van Loon and Christine Price. Mineola, NY: Dover.

Nel, Philip. 2012. *Crockett Johnson and Ruth Krauss: How an unlikely couple found love, dodged the FBI, and transformed children's literature*. Jackson, MS: University Press of Mississippi.

Nell, Victor. 1988. The psychology of reading for pleasure: Needs and gratifications. *Reading Research Quarterly* 23(1) (November).6–50.

Paterson, Katharine. 1989. My life is based on a true story. *Magpies* 2 (May).5–10.

Patterson, Francine, and Eugene Linden. 1981. *The education of Koko*. New York: Holt, Rinehart and Winston.

Pinker, Steven. 1994. *The language instinct: How the mind creates language*. New York: Morrow.

Redelmeier, Donald A.; Joel Katz; and Daniel Kahneman. 2003. Memories of colonoscopy: A randomized trial. *Pain* 104.187–94.

Rhomberg, Andrew. 2015. Should authors and publishers spy on readers? *Digital Book World*, 09 January. Online: www.digitalbookworld.com/2015/should-authors-and-publishers-spy-on-readers/.

Rosenberg, Marshall B. 2005. *Nonviolent communication: A language of life*, 3rd ed., foreword by Deepak Chopra (Nonviolent communication guides). Encinitas, CA: Puddledancer Press.

Searle, John. 2010. *Making the social world: The structure of human civilization.* New York: Oxford University Press.

Silva, Alcino J. 2017. Memory's intricate web: A technical revolution provides insight into how the brain links memories, a process critical for understanding and organizing the world around us. *Scientific American* (July).22–29.

Silvey, Anita. 2004. *100 Best books for children.* Boston, New York: Frances Tenenbaum, Houghton Mifflin.

Twain, Mark. [Samuel Clemens]. 1864. Those blasted children: Lick House, San Francisco, Wednesday, 1964. *Mark Twain's San Francisco: Being a generous and uninhibited cornucopia of reports, speculations, satires, brickbats, musings, topical verse, and other observations by Mark Twain*, ed. by Bernard Taper, 27–33. Berkeley, CA: Heyday Books.

Walker, Karen Thompson. 2012. What fear can teach us. *TED Talk*, June. Online: www.ted.com/talks/karen_thompson_walker_what_fear_can_teach_us.

Whorf, Benjamin Lee. 2012 [1957]. *Language, thought, and reality*, ed. by John B. Carroll, Stephen C. Levinson and Penny Lee, 2nd ed. Cambridge, MA: MIT Press.

Winterstein, Grégoire. 2011. Ludics and presupposition projection. *Proceedings of the Eighth International Workshop of Logic and Engineering of Natural Language Semantics (LENLS 8)*, Takamatsu, Japan, ed. by Alastair Butler, 94–105. Online: www.linguist.univ-paris-diderot.fr/~gwinterstein/docs/Pub/Winterstein-LENLS8.pdf.

Wittrock, Merlin C. 1977. The generative processes of memory. *The human brain*, ed. by Merlin C. Wittrock, 153–84. Englewood Cliffs, NJ: Prentice-Hall.

Wolf, Maryanne, with Stephanie Gottwald. 2016. *Tales of literacy for the 21st century.* Oxford: Oxford University Press.

7 Entrainment Through Story

> And what terrible critics these babies are! What a perverse preference they have for the soft jingle of nonsensical melody; blank verse with its five accents and want of rhythm does not soothe: they must have the –
>
> "Lalla, lalla, lalla,
> Aut dormi, aut lacta"
>
> of their prototype of Roman days.
>
> How they revel and delight in the mother's measured song of –
>
> "Dance, little baby, dance up high,
> Never mind, baby, mother is nigh;
> Crow and caper, caper and crow,
> There, little baby, there you go."
>
> Percy B. Green (1899:15)

Philosopher John Locke, knowing children's desire for approval, observed that they adopt what they esteem in / from others. This being so, he reasoned, then why not present books to children as a reward? If we simply gave children books as a reward for good behavior, then 'what those about them make to be a reward to them will really be so' (1692:§129). But just calling something a reward does not make it so. Children, wrote Rousseau, usually read their teacher's mind better than the teacher can read in the child's heart (1762.2:83).[1]

Author Valerie Tripp described how a child comes to think of book reading as a rewarding activity ('Bibliography')—not through dispensing, but through sharing:

> Even before I could read, my parents showed me what a pleasure reading could be. My father read aloud to my sisters and my brother and me at night, before we went to sleep. He'd stretch out on the bed, and we'd surround him as he read Charlotte's Web, Madeline, Beezus and Ramona, The Secret Garden, Cinderella, and hundreds of other wonderful stories. Sometimes he would get so caught up in the language and humor of the

> story, he'd read chapter after chapter, forgetting to stop. We'd all keep still so he'd keep reading.

Tripp recreated her memory in *Again, Josephina!*, one of her many books for the 'American Girls' series. In the scene, the source of pleasure is the piano playing of Tía Dolores (2000:2–3):

> Josefina thought it sounded like a lullaby that a mother might sing to her baby. She couldn't help swaying back and forth in time to the music. Papá and all her sisters had dreamy, faraway looks on their faces, as if they were remembering something happy. The music seemed to have cast a spell over them.

Josefina decides to learn from her aunt how to play the piano, but finds the learning difficult—the title refers to the refrain of 'again, Josephina!' during the lessons. She gets to the point of giving up when she sees her one-year-old brother Antonio react to her playing the way she once had to Tía Dolores':

> Antonio gave Josefina a happy, drooly, baby grin as she gently put him on the floor. He stood next to the piano bench and slapped the top with his hand, as if he were saying, "Begin!"
>
> When Josefina began to play, Antonio crowed with delight. He bounced himself up and down on his chubby legs in time to the music. He bounced with so much enthusiasm that he fell, *plop*, on his bottom.

Antonio's rhythmic rapture is so reinforcing that Josephina gets caught up in it and feels 'happier at the piano than she ever had before' (ibid., 24–27). Love of books, like love of music, arises from sharing, not from a transaction.

The previous chapter established how deeply such sharing defines us as a species. In shared story, teller and audience can mirror each other's brain processes. Biologists call the phenomenon where an organism aligns its neurophysiological processes with something outside its body *entrainment*.

The realization that bodies synchronize under certain conditions did not originally come from observing living organisms, but, of all things, clocks. Dutch physicist and inventor Christiaan Huygens (1673) observed two of his pendulum clocks ticking in 'harmony' (the term *entrainment* was grandfathered in later; it is not original with Huygens). The two clocks were traveling on board the Duke of Belfort's ship in a French expedition against the Turks on Crete, to calculate the vessel's position more accurately. They clocks were paired for redundancy (if one should stop, it could be reset to the other) and attached to a single wooden beam mounted on a central pedestal. Huygens noticed that they synchronized so precisely that only a single tick could be heard between them. Transmitting their energy through the beam to which they were affixed, they aligned their swings (in opposite direction), and would do so again when disturbed.[2] The experiment can be easily duplicated: Placed on a piece of cardboard across two empty soda cans lying on their sides, mechanical metronomes set to the same tempo will synchronize as well (Pantaleone 2002; see Bahraminasab 2007).

Much research has since gone into 'coupled oscillations.' Some applications are mechanical, such as cancelling vibrations between two rocket engines. Others also involve human behavior. Pedestrians on the London Millennium Footbridge over the river Thames, for example, caused the bridge to sway, then unconsciously reacted to that sway by beginning to synchronize their steps. That synchronization set in motion a self-reinforcing feedback that made the bridge unsafe to cross, requiring structural modifications (Strogatz et al. 2005).

This chapter takes a closer look at entrainment involving human brains, in particular well-understood oscillatory entrainment (brains measurably synchronizing to frequencies and rhythms). Since language has frequencies and rhythms, I propose that interactive book reading can bring about oscillatory entrainment between adult and child to the rhythms of the book's language. I will discuss some works that seem particularly capable of synchronizing the brains of an adult and a child to their (performed) rhythms (meter, tempo, syncopation). Just like the sound of an adult heartbeat or the frequency of comforting 'hush-pats' on the back, the unison of entrainment experienced to the rhythms of children's books can be therapeutic, signaling safety and confirmation.

Rhythmic entrainment across a group is natural and can be observed among bioluminescent algae and bugs and even across cells (such as pacemaker cells in the heart). Schools of fish and flocks of birds synchronize their movements, behaving like a single, large organism. Bodies align to circadian rhythms in nature, e.g. synchronizing light-dark cycles seasonally. Such rhythmic entrainment is not only natural, it is vital. A misalignment of rhythms can potentially be fatal. A subtle lesion in an infant's brain stem, for example, may be the cause for failing to harmonize the rhythms of light-dark cycles and breathing, causing infants to die in their sleep from prolonged sleep apnea, a condition known as Sudden Infant Death Syndrome, or SIDS (Franciosi 1987).

The oscillations of the human brain (our 'brain waves') are divided into bands, each associated with brain activities (See Table 7.1 for a summary of early research into cortical oscillations)—although the division was originally about as arbitrary as 'the straight-line country borders between the African nations drawn the the colonialists' (Buzsáki 2006:112). Oscillations can be reinforced or suppressed with medication or biofeedback. The brain responds to rhythms from outside presented visually, e.g. with strobe goggles that have embedded LED lights. The brain also responds to acoustic rhythms (clicks, drumming), and to rhythmic activities such as dancing. Put all three together, as in a discotheque or 'rave' house with pounding rhythms and synchronized strobe lights, and an entire group of people can tribally experience synchronized brain wave bands.

Entrainment can be therapeutic. With the right frequency of light pulses, for instance, it is possible to render someone who is depressed (whose dominant brain frequencies may be in the theta band) or highly agitated (high-beta band) into a calm and peaceful state of alertness (alpha). French psychologist Pierre Janet discovered in the late 1800s that he could ameliorate the condition of agitated

Table 7.1 Human Brain Wave Bands

frequencies	*band*	*associated brain states*
> 39 Hz	gamma	? subjective awareness, epilepsy
20–38 Hz	high-beta	intensity, new experiences, excitement, anxiety
12–21 Hz	beta	focused thinking, problem solving, decision making
8–12 Hz	alpha	'resting state': calm and peaceful alertness
3–8 Hz	theta	dreaming sleep, meditation, creativity, intuition
.5–3 Hz	delta	deep, dreamless sleep, deep meditation
<.5 Hz	infra-low	? regulating brain timing, network functions

(composite of Huang 2008:39; Hughes 2008)

or depressed patients at the Salpêtrière Hospital in Paris by having them watch a simple strobe light that he created by placing a spinning wheel in front of a kerosene lamp (Piéron 1982). David Siever confirmed that when 'audio-visual entrainment' synchronizes brain waves to just the right rhythm of light flashes, the level of norepinephrine, a 'stress hormone,' comes down. Not only that, carefully selected pulses of light/sound also elevate the levels of beta endorphin, serotonin, and melatonin, hormones that are associated with satisfaction (2006:9). Tina Huang (2008) presents a comprehensive survey of such 'brainwave entrainment' research, and the list of therapeutic applications is quite impressive. Current research at MIT investigates the use of gamma-range oscillations to counteract the effect of Alzheimer's disease, which impairs gamma oscillations (Trafton 2016).

Entrainment with light pulses can be potent enough to be weaponized. An individual from Maryland once sent a strobe animation via Twitter to Kurt Eichenwald, a journalist with epilepsy, with the intent of triggering a seizure. Mr. Eichenwald had the presence of mind to drop his phone to the floor. The assault was apparently motivated in part by antisemitism and quickly drew imitators, with comments such as 'let's see if he dies' (Ellis & Park 2017).

Humans experience entrainment both involuntarily and voluntarily.

Involuntary entrainment is a reflexive response to *physical* sensations, so primal that we are nearly incapable of suppressing it. In an article on infant laughter, Gina C. Mireault related how at a funeral, her three-month-old laughed after someone sneezed. It was his first laughter, and it was 'so powerful as to provoke his audience to go from sadness to joy—together and almost instantaneously' (2017:46). 'Together and almost instantly' is a tell-tale sign for involuntary behavior, usually an indicator of ancient, autonomic pathways. Yawning is just as infectious. So is seeing someone eat: Watch how in 'The Great British Baking Show' (PBS; 'The Great British Bake Off' on BBC), contestants sometimes involuntarily perform chewing motions when they watch their tasty entry being sampled by the judges. How do we get a baby to open her mouth for a spoonful of food? Open your own mouth. Neuroscientist Vilayanur S. Ramachandran invented the term 'Gandhi neurons' (his collective term for sensory and motoric mirror neurons) to drive home his point of how profoundly interconnected we are at the level of the autonomous nervous system: Even phantom pain (pain perceived from a limb that has been amputated) can be relieved by watching someone else's intact limb being massaged (Ramachandran 2009).

Voluntary entrainment includes the sought-out experience of *narrated* sensations and actions (displaced in space/time or imagined). That is why the term *narration* is applied in the previous chapter both to reducing information (to retain an inner story) *and* to elaborating (to propagate the experience to someone else). Narration (storytelling, including interactive book reading) can cause brains to synchronize their processing, simulating a direct feed between them with a bandwidth exceeding the informational content of speech alone. This kind of entrainment has implications for what makes a children's book enjoyable, especially in interactive reading.

Entrainment and Language: Rhythmic Biases Toward Speech

Human speech has rhythmic profiles, and infants synchronize with them, possibly already prior to birth. Infants' rhythmic sensitivities bias their very perception of speech. They respond physically to talk directed to them by synchronizing both their tongue movements (cf. p. 31f.) and their body movements in time to the syllables (p. 43). Vowels and consonants alternate in the theta-band range. Facial movements match those frequencies and allow an infant to pick out who among several people is talking to them (cf. p. 39). If an infant's 'sampling rate' does not match the 'speech envelope,' then the actual rhythms of syllables do not match the expected ones. The infant misses out on some of the (faster) signals; such inadequate entrainment may cause developmental dyslexia (Power et al. 2013). Specifically, these children have difficulties in the lower frequencies (2 Hz and below) that characterize the beat of stressed syllables in English (Power et al. 2016).

Successful entrainment to the rhythms of speech is crucial because individual languages have different timing signatures (Kösem & van Wassenhove 2016:537). Some, like English, distribute their primary stress peaks evenly across phrases in the low delta range (below 4 Hz), speeding up or slowing down intervening unstressed syllables in between those peaks as needed ("In the GREAT g r e e n ROOM there was a TELephone and a RED b a l LOON"). Other languages, like Spanish, assign even time slots to all syllables regardless of stress ("En la gran ha·bi·ta·ción ver·de, hay un te·lé·fo·no, un glo·bo ro"). Infants can make out those differences in timing after birth, and even before birth (Nazzi Bertoncini, & Mehler 1998).[3]

The previous chapters have identified how rhythmic motoric behavior can emphasize and enhance the rhythms of speech, which broadens the bandwidth of entrainment. Adults and children synchronize texts with choreographed motions (finger games, clapping, stomping), with melodies (children's songs), and with the exaggerated sing-song and presentational tempo of child-directed talk. Jointly tuning into the same frequencies makes infants and adults feel that they are already 'on the same wavelength' even at an early stage. They need to be: Speech production and listening are not 'independent processes within the boundaries of individual brains' (Stephens et al. 2010:14425) but operate across those boundaries.

Current research is revealing intricate correlations between oscillations and linguistic entrainment. For example, increasing the load on working memory triggers an alpha-band reponse associated with the inhibition of irrelevant details to reduce that load; when that happens, it negatively affects the subject's ability to entrain to the delta and theta frequencies of the speech envelope (Hjortkjær et al. 2018). In contrast, de-synchronization of this type of alpha-band response was shown to have a 'disinhibition' effect on syntactic processing pathways, allowing them to process 'syntactically more difficult sentential content' (Vassileiou, Meyer, Beese, & Friederici 2018:293). Oscillations entraining to the speech envelope do not stop abruptly when the speech signals end but continue for a few cycles, indicating a predictive quality of entrainment (Kösem & van Wassenhove 2016:540, Riecke et al. 2018). On my understanding of apperception in understanding, there would have to be a substantial overlap between anticipation and recognition at any rate (cf. Heuer et al. 2017 on anticipatory "attentional bias"). Delta-range entrainment is crucially important, in English, for the prediction of rhymes, since rhymes fall on stressed syllables (Leong & Goswami 2017). Rhyming words correctly predicted in an interactive reading session, in turn, are retained at a high rate (Read, Macauley, & Furay 2014).

Entrainment, an ancient survival mechanism, has been pressed into service for human communication. Specifically, linguistic interaction profits from two qualities of entrainment: Entrainment *enhances* the linguistic data stream in interaction, and it is *rewarding*.

Data Enhancement

If human communication were as simple as encoding and decoding linguistic information, then there would be no need for entrainment. We would be able to encode all the information we wish to convey in language. Encoding and decoding are necessary *but not sufficient* for successful communication. This shortcoming was already apparent in the so-called 'Shannon-Weaver' model of communication (Shannon 1948; Schramm 1961), which made allowances for 'noise,' interference degrading the signal. Somehow, recipients can compensate for such lossiness in transmission. Philosopher H. Paul Grice sought to explain how they do it: After decoding 'what is said,' the listener must 'evaluate' the meaning (Grice 1989:25). Unfortunately, Grice's model begs the same question as the old one—what is that evaluation based on? And is ascertaining 'what is said' not itself an evaluation? Stephen Levinson (2000) recognized this circularity and dubbed it the 'Gricean Circle.' Mira Ariel (2008:266) explains:

> On the one hand, we need 'what is said' in order to determine the pragmatic inferences, but on the other hand, we need pragmatic inferences in order to determine 'what is said'. . . . So, which of these comes first?

Ariel's solution is that both levels (decoding and evaluation) are simultaneous and parallel. That solution agrees with my assumption about how our brains work: that the predetermined result of a computation imposes itself upon the very computation (cf. p. 33). Deirdre Wilson and Dan Sperber assumed that our evaluation is guided by what we assume is relevant to the discourse (Wilson & Sperber 2004). Essentially, this is mind reading. Greg Stephens et al. (2010:14425) have demonstrated how such 'mind reading' works: Successful understanding involves 'neural coupling'—brains duplicating each other's processing to such a degree that information *not* encoded in the speech stream by the sender is nonetheless also activated by the recipient. A central portion in this kind of entrainment is surely triggered by acoustic cues. A speaker's voice tells us much about that speaker's intention, confidence or hesitance, attitude, etc. We are so sensitive to those acoustic cues that we can tell *just by listening* whether a speaker is smiling—not only that, but whether it is a full smile or not (Drahota, Costall, & Reddy 2008).

But why did humans never develop natural languages in which each signal unambiguously has one meaning, the way English Enlightenment philosopher John Wilkins (1668) thought we should? The answer is that our evolution went the opposite way. Animal communication by and large relies on a ratio of one-signal-to-one-meaning. In a split second, an animal's trusted call for 'danger from the air' can save lives even if the members receiving that call cannot see the predator approaching. Unambiguity comes at a price, however. Simple, straightforward signals can be imitated by outsiders (vocal mimicry). For example, a Margay cat can imitate the distress call of a pied tamarin monkey pup in the Amazon jungle, luring concerned adult tamarins to their deaths (Calleia et al. 2009). Human speech, in contrast, is impossible to coopt by predators because the speech signals on their own are meaningless (even to other humans who speak a different language such as Nłeʔkepmxcín—see p. 29). Meaning is created through combining signals (=grammar). That setup (creating meaning by combining meaningless signals), however, dramatically decreases the amount of information relative to the number of signals needed. Human speech is high in informational *entropy* (decrease in information = increase in entropy).

Being the beneficiaries of a lossy communication system with high entropy, humans compensate for the lossiness by synchronizing their brains. 'Understanding,' as Wilhelm von Humboldt pointed out almost two centuries ago, is not the result of 'passing on' material ('Übergeben eines Stoffes,' 1836:54)—as if pouring information into someone's head with a 'funnel,' the way Nuremberg philologist Georg Philipp Harsdörffer shamelessly advertised his little book on poetics (1650). Von Humboldt (1836:54) defined a 'message' as a 'harmonizing stimulant' ('harmonisch stimmende Anregung'). As with Huygens, we may grandfather in the term *entrainment* for 'harmony.' Neuroimaging revealed that the 'harmonizing stimulation' is such that not only does the listener's neocortex *mirror* processes in the speaker's brain with a slight time delay, it also *anticipates* some brain activities ahead of the speaker (Stephens, Silbert, & Hasson 2010).

Rewards of Entrainment

Modern parents want their children to experience reading as self-rewarding. Toward that end, they enrich early interactive reading sessions for maximum entrainment, including placing the child on their lap, jointly facing and manipulating the book (which allows sufficient physical contact to transfer the adult's vocal vibrations to the child). Together, adult and child experience physically the book's rhythms, rhymes, repetitions, and musicality. Such physical entrainment creates not only a feeling of satisfaction through the release of beta endorphin, serotonin, and melatonin (Siever 2006:9; cf. p. 167), but also a feeling of attachment through a mutual buildup of oxytocin. Not only is such a hertz-to-hertz experienced as rewarding in the moment and forms a positive association with book reading in general, it also eventually makes future social bonding easier by stimulating the growth of oxytocin receptors in the infant brain's reward center (Kuchinskas 2009:21; Olff et al. 2013:1884).

Oxytocin is a marker of synchrony—the entrainment of brain processes between adult and child (Olff et al. 2013). Entrainment requires *direct* interaction between child and adult. It does not occur otherwise—not even between a child and a life-like robot who looks at objects and speaks with a recorded human voice (Baldwin 1993). The cells in the left auditory cortex have significantly more oxytocin receptors than

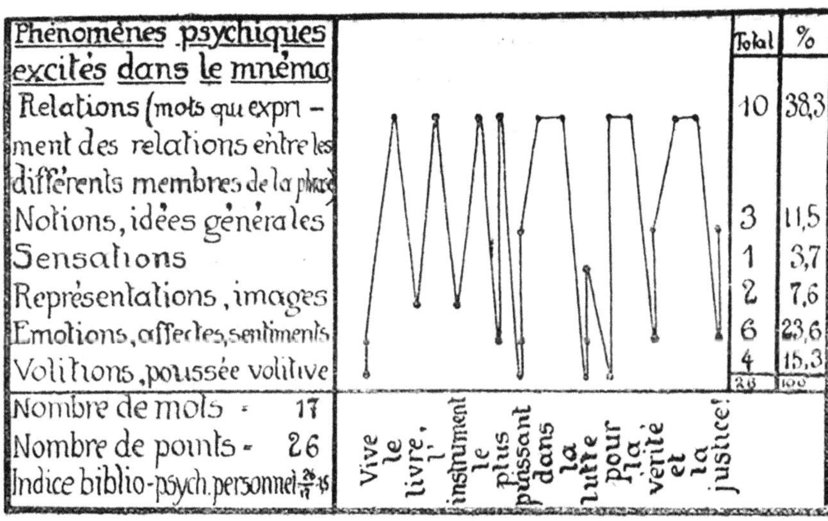

Figure 7.1 Literary Excitations (Rubakin 1922.2:350)

those in the right (Marlin et al. 2015), making mothers more sensitive and reactive to infant vocalizations and stimulating infants' speech processing circuits. Patricia Kuhl's earlier experiments confirm that infants process speech signals as linguistic information *only* in direct and trusting interaction: When speech was directed to the infant from a television screen, their brains did not show any evidence of phonetic acquisition (p. 40). Dimitri Christakis (2009) documented significant and substantial correlations between infants' TV time, language delay, and attention deficit.

Further confirming evidence comes from the study of how young children generally react to television watching. Television watching is not an interactive bonding experience, hence is not experienced as rewarding but as isolating. We see this when we compare how a reading session ends vs. how a session of television watching terminates. When the TV is eventually turned off, young children exhibit some kind of 'reentry syndrome' (Winn 2002:21) in which their behavior deteriorates (ibid.) and they exhibit 'a rapid rise in their ability to control themselves. They whine, they fuss, they absolutely regress' (22), a condition comparable to 'post-sleep crankiness' (24). The child's irritability signals 'I'm not ready to deal with you as my usual self.' In contrast, completing a reading session is accompanied by all the signs of feeling rewarded (Nell 1988:33), as is generally the case after a 'sudden drop in arousal' (38). It is reasonable to assume that the heightened mental activity causing such arousal during reading is in large part due to interaction—with the characters and the author in compositional, ludic reading (as described in Chapter 6), and of course with the reading adult. The child drifts 'into a state of delightful relaxation' (24). That is why there are bedtime stories.[4]

Russian psychologist Nicolas Rubakin, an early pioneer in cognitive science before the field even existed, attempted to quantify such arousals. Inspired by von Humboldt's notion of understanding a *message* as 'harmonizing stimulation,' he devised a scoring system for 'excitations' in the brain of a person experiencing a literary text, as the basis for a cognitive psychology of literature (Figure 7.1). To demonstrate, he scored the motto for his remarkable two-volume opus: 'Long live the book, the most powerful instrument in the battle for truth and justice!' From the bottom up, Rubakin's chart assigns points for intentions, emotions, representations, sensations, general ideas, and grammatical relations (essentially, function words). His sample sentence scores a total of 26 points for excitations, divided by 17 words, for a bibliopsychological index of 1.53. The chart also allows tracking how a single sentence distributes the reader's cognitive load in percentages; in Figure 7.1, the main emphases are on grammar and emotion.

Entrainment in Children's Literature: Rhythm

Literature for young children relies heavily on rhythmic speech, employing meter and rhyme. Just as authors playfully surprise children with unusual sound combinations, morphology, words, or syntax, they also establish a steady poetic meter and delight with deviations, half time, and double-time lines. The following poem has a steady, chatty pattern of iambic tetra- (4 feet) and trimeter (3 feet).[5]

WHO WAS SHE?

As I was going down the walk
    So pleasant, cool and shady,

Right in the middle of the path
  I met a little lady.

I made to her my sweetest bow;
  She only walked on faster;
I smiled, and said "Good-morning ma'am,"
  The moment that I passed her.

She never noticed me at all;
  I really felt quite slighted;
I thought, "I'll follow you, I will,
  Altho' I'm not invited."

Perhaps you think me very rude;
  But then, she looked so funny—
From head to feet all dressed in fur
  This summer day so sunny.

She didn't mind the heat at all,
  But wrapped the fur around her,
And hurried on, as if to say,
  "I'll tend to my own gown, sir!"

I followed her the whole way home;
  Her home was in *my* garden,
Beneath my choicest vines—and yet
  She never asked my pardon.

I never heard *her* speak a word;
  But once I heard the miller,
Coming down the sidewalk, say,
  "There goes Miss Caterpillar!"

The poem has the consistent meter of a ballad, but it is not without surprises. There are some 'mosaic' rhymes that involve two words (*faster/passed her*, *around her/gown, sir*); the second-to-last line breaks the metric pattern slightly by beginning with a stressed syllable (*cóming dówn the sídewalk* . . .); and then of course there is also the delightful solution to the riddle in the last line. The poem teases the child by supplying information about the 'lady' piecemeal (she is little, does not return a greeting, wears fur in summer, and lives in a garden), which turns the poem into play. The steady rhythms of the poem, however, feel predictable and inviting after the first stanza.

One Fish, Two Fish, Red Fish, Blue Fish masterfully establishes a groove (e.g. an iambic dimeter as in 'The móon was óut') and changes it up with a triple spondee (three adjacent primary stresses), '/ and we sáw sóme shéep.' The verse of *One Fish, Two Fish* also have a delightful time signature. I would read the following lines from Dr. Seuss to a young child (I timed myself) at a pace of about 100 beats per minute on a metronome, which translates to around 1.6 Hz. At that sustained frequency, I would tune into a child's delta band (.5–3 Hz), which is associated with deep sleep and meditation. The final five lines are double time, 200 beats per minute (3.3 Hz), and thus in the theta range (3–8 Hz), which is still associated with sleep and meditation, but also with creativity and intuition. Geisel keeps this pattern up for 63 pages, alternating 1.6 Hz and double time:

> 1.6 Hz The moon was out
> 3.3 Hz and we saw some sheep.
> 1.6 Hz We saw some sheep
> 3.3 Hz take a walk in their sleep.
> 3.3 Hz By the light of the moon,
> 3.3 Hz by the light of a star,
> 1.6 Hz they walked all night
> 1.6 Hz from near to far.
> 3.3 Hz I would never walk.
> 3.3 Hz I would take a car.

Theodor Geisel's rhythms correspond to natural biorhythms associated with rest and creativity. A frequency of 100 beats per minute corresponds to the average heart rate of an adult at rest. It is a frequency especially soothing for babies. That is why devices can be purchased playing the sound of an adult heartbeat in the crib. The double time shares the frequency with which adults pat an infant or child on the back for solace and comfort (e.g. Hyman et al. 2006:1523).

The theta-band range of oscillations may contain the frequencies in which entrainment via language occurs most readily. A particular theta-band oscillation signature in the dorso-frontal language network has recently been domain-specifically linked to language processing (Beese, Meyer, Vassileiou, and Friederici 2017). Children's verse appears to establish such a theta-band beat as the baseline and introduce variations that the infant finds entertaining, very much like a funny word. Taking an infant by the hands and performing *Pat-a-Cake* (p. 43) is a perfect illustration. The first one and a half lines establish the base rhythm; then, typically, a parent would switch to double time ('just as fast as you can') and then dramatically drop into half time ('prick it, and pat it' or, with verbs enacting slower movements, 'roll it, and pull it').

Rhythmic entrainment can turn into entrancement when a poem changes from theta range to delta range (half time) entirely. The children's book most credited with such an effect is Margaret Wise Brown's *Goodnight Moon*. From the beginning, reviewers made a point of the poem's 'lulling' (*Publisher's Weekly* 1947:115), 'hypnotic' (Benét 1947:132, qtd. in Marcus 1992:216) effect. A typical observation is the following by Lisa (2012) on the literary web site 'Vulpes Libris':

> . . . the book has a strange hypnotic effect on the *reader*, and the very act of reading it feels like winding down for sleep. The diction and syntax do

> something to the brain which in turn has an effect on the body, with the reader's breathing becoming a little slower and deeper, and tension in the body seeming to drain away. Even more odd is the effect the text has on the voice. The first page starts off quite jauntily and I launch into the story with a sort of plummy boom to my voice but gradually my voice becomes lower and quieter until the final page is recited in a whisper. Having conferred with other parents, I'm not alone in experiencing this bizarre voice-altering effect.

To fully appreciate what 'Lisa' experienced, one should, as does Barrie Hardymon (2017), divide the poem, into two parts—the 'invocation' and the 'benediction' sections. The rhythms in each section are different, a more alert pace improvising from a lively anapestic base to plodding spondees over an iambic pattern. Spondees slow down the tempo like poetic speedbumps. Visually, time is also slowed down by the advancement of the hands on the clock in the green room (over the space of the book, we see the time gradually advance from 7:00 to 8:10) and by the changes in light. The slow tempo and the repetitions of rhymes and words give the 'benediction' part of the poem the feel of a meditation, a biorhythm experienced as deeply relaxing by child and (apparently) reading adult alike.

Children's books can also invite adults and children to stay in more upbeat rhythms, of course. Jonathan London's *Hip Cat* captures the swing of jazz:

He was a hip cat
a hep cat
a cool cat

living all alone in a riverside shack:
Oobie-do John the Sax Man Scat Man,
the cool cat man.
One day he said to himself,
"All I want to do is to make jazzzzzy music."
So he picked up his sax—
what his friends called his "ax"—
and tipped his beret and said,
"Scat, cat. Go, cat, go!
Hip Cat daddy-o's got a horn to blow!"
And
that
cat
scat.

The book is dedicated to beat poet Herschel Silverman and jazz greats Bobby McFerrin, Miles Davis, and John Coltrane. The author himself performed it with a jazz quartet in the mid-nineties in Palm Springs.[6] Its musical quality, reinforced by the swinging type-set and by Woodleigh Marx Hubbard's illustrations, becomes fully apparent in the rendition by singer/actress and composer Ann Duquesnay for

Reading Rainbow, complete with a saxophone background by Joshua Redman. Adults and children can get in such equal measure into the groove of a rhythm that a book like this can cross from children's book to jazz performance and back to the children watching *Reading Rainbow*.

Another book whose rhythm has imprinted itself on children and adults alike and which has similarly traveled back and forth between both worlds is Anna Dewdney's *Llama Llama Red Pajama*. On the surface, the book is about the anxiety of a child being left alone in his bedroom to go to sleep. The main attraction of the book, however, is its rhythm:

> Llama llama
> red pajama
> reads a story
> with his mama.
>
> Mama kisses
> baby's hair.
> Mama Llama
> goes downstairs.
>
> Llama llama
> red pajama
> feels **alone**
> without his mama.
>
> Baby llama
> wants a drink.
> Mama's at the
> kitchen sink.

Throughout the book, the author never once fumbles her two-footed lines, which is a feat in itself. The result sounds like a jump rope- or counting-out rhyme—and also like rap. When Roger Sutton called llama creator Anna Dewdney a 'rock star to preschoolers' (2013), he uttered prophetic words. J Cruz, host of The Cruz Show at Los Angeles radio station Power 106, spotted the book at Barnes & Noble and bought it (in preparation of his son's birth). He started to read the book 'as if I was rapping' (Ready 2017). Cruz found that Dewdney's beat perfectly lent itself to rap, and started inviting famous rappers onto his show to free-style the book to a sound track of their choosing. The results sound surprisingly natural. Ludacris (2017) in particular, in the words of the host, 'killed it' (Ready 2017), and his rendition has become popular in turn with children. The fifth-grade class of Arkansas teacher Brittney McGraw (2017) actually *recreated* Ludacris' performance and tweeted their video back to him.

The rhythms of 'Who Was She?', *One Fish, Two Fish*, *Goodnight Moon*, *Hip Cat*, and *Llama Llama* are appealing to children and adults. They 'feel' respectively familiar, playful, calming, and inviting (inviting the child into the adult's world and vice versa). An interactive book reading settles into the tempo of each work. 'Who Was She?' feels like a jaunting, pitter-pat excursion, but always safe and steady. *One Fish, Two Fish* with its tempo changes has comedic timing, but shares the caterpillar poem's reassuring baseline. Time slows down in 'Goodnight Moon'; the language swings in *Hip Cat*, and *Llama Llama's* bipedal rhythm is dreamy and calming like the sound of a human heartbeat. The 'reward' these books offer—and I think that this is a mark of their quality—is that child and adult maintain prolongued periods of identical rhythms.

Future studies of rhythmic entrainment in interactive book readings will certainly also bring into focus sociological implications. In the discussion of how much speech a child is exposed to at home, I invoked the "Matthew Effect" in word learning (p. 69): Early gains in vocabulary lead exponentially to more gains—and early deficits correspondingly lead to increasing disparity. When an adult reads works like *Hip Cat* to a child, the book calls for a performance. A reader who is not literate enough to be fluent cannot sustain the syncopations of Jonathan London, nor likely the tempo changes of Theodor Geisel. A struggling reader, in other words, is less likely to sustain entrainment with the child in the frequencies required for the book's full effect. Here, then, we have a Matthew Effect for literary entrainment: Children of literate parents will reap the dividends of entrainment—among them improved phonemic awareness (Verney 2013) and mature receptors for oxytocin (Kuchinskas 2009:21). Experiencing interactive reading as bonding and rewarding carries forward a love of reading. Children who do not benefit from the same amount of entrainment over books (or a rich oral tradition of songs, rhymes, fingerplays, etc.) will be at a disadvantage both in terms of literacy and in terms of social bonding.

If low-level adult readers compensate by presenting the book to the child on an electronic device, they will but compound the problem. Electronic devices cannot achieve entrainment, because they are not interactive. When Anna Dewdney was queried about a Llama Llama game on her own web site, she made one thing perfectly clear: 'iPhones, iPads, Nooks, Droids, and all those gizmos are simply toys.' And she added the following observation (Sutton 2013):

> . . . if the toy is constantly being used as a substitute for the important stuff (creative play, interpersonal relationships, reading, and a sense of living on the real planet with living, breathing creatures), then I think it is no longer a toy for a child—it is a crutch for a parent, much like driving through McDonald's instead of cooking real food. I like a Big Mac as much as the next person, but I know it isn't giving me real nourishment.

Electronic devices are not associated with language acquisition and literacy. "Computer literacy," Librarian of Congress Daniel Boorstin famously warned, is a 'mirage' (Boorstin 1984:25), an oxymoron yoking together unrelated terms.

Entrainment research is charting new territory, and its possible benefit to the study of children's literature is here explored in a speculative manner. It should certainly be a rewarding research agenda, however, especially as neural imaging techniques allow less-intrusive observations. Research in adult-child entrainment over children's books in interactive reading sessions could benefit from a large body of existing pediatric research, particularly on how mothers and infants synchronize their biorhythms ('mother-infant synchrony'). A study in the linguistics of children's literature would be well advised not to study interactive play, entrainment, and cooperation in shared book reading as a sideline—but to put them front and center.

Notes

1. L'enfant, pour l'ordinaire, lit beaucoup mieux dans l'esprit du maître que le maître dans le cœur de l'enfant (Rousseau).
2. . . . motus pendula utriusque it ictibus adversis inter se consensere, ut nunquam inde vel minimum recederent, sed utriusque sonus una semper exaudiretur: imo si data opera perturbaretur concordia illa, semet-ipsam brevi tempore reduceret. (Huygens 1673:18–19).

   > "The motion of the pendulums synchronizes thus in opposing swings, such that the two clocks never deviate in the least, but their combined sound can be heard as one always: if the workings are disturbed in their agreement, it will be restored on its own in a short time."
   >
   > (translation mine)

Figure 7.2 Christiaan Huygens' Entrainment Experiment, 1665

   A picture of the recreated setup is reproduced in Bennet et al. (2002:566). Huygens had earlier described his discovery in two letters in French: one to Robert Moray (27 Feburary 1665), who read it to the Royal Society on March 1 (Bennett et al. 2002:563), and one to his father Constantijn Huygens (26 February 1665). The latter included a sketch of how the experiment can be setup with the use of two chairs (reproduced in Nijhoff 1967):
3. Mehler has been a long-time proponent of the theory that rhythms and contours of adult speech are processed and recognized prior to birth. A recent finding that the cries of newborns reflect whether their mother speaks a tonal language (like Cameroonian Nso) or a non-tonal language (German) adds confirmation (Wermke et al. 2016).

4. There is another advantage to bedtime stories: Peaceful sleep gives children's brains time to consolidate learned vocabulary (Henderson et al. 2012).
5. The author's name remains unknown. The earliest appearance of this poem in print is in a little children's book entitled *Dolls and Pets* (Boston: D. Lothrop & Co., c. 1885). In a book by the same publisher, *Doll's Tea Party* (1895), the poem is credited to 'J. S.' (Juniata Stafford, perchance?).
6. Jonathan London, personal communication, 20 July 2017.

References

Ariel, Mira. 2008. *Pragmatics and grammar* (Cambridge textbooks in linguistics). Cambridge, New York: Cambridge University Press.

Bahraminasab, Alireza. 2007. Synchronisation, 18 December. youtu.be/W1TMZASCR-I.

Baldwin, Dare A. 1993. Infants' ability to consult the speaker for clues to word reference. *Journal of Child Language* 20(2).395–418.

Beese, Caroline; Lars Meyer; Benedict Vassileiou; and Angela D. Friederici. 2017. Temporally and spatially distinct theta oscillations dissociate a language-specific from a domaingeneral processing mechanism across the age trajectory. *Nature Scientific Reports* 7(11202) (11 September). doi:10.1038/s41598–017–11632-z.

Benét, Rosemary C. 1947. Review of *Goodnight Moon. The New Yorker* 23(42 issue 1190) (6 December).132.

Bennett, Matthew; Michael F. Schatz; Heidi Rockwood; and Kurt Wiesenfeld. 2002. Huygens's clocks. *Proceedings of the Royal Society of London A* 458.563–79.

Boorstin, Daniel J. 1984. Letter of transmittal. *Books in our future: A report from the Librarian of Congress to the Congress*, 6–57. Washington, DC: Joint Committee on the Library of Congress of the United States. Online: files.eric.ed.gov/fulltext/ED253243.pdf.

Buzsáki, György. 2006. *Rhythms of the brain*. Oxford, New York: Oxford University Press.

Callela, Fabiano de Oliveira; Fabio Rohe; and Marcelo Gordo. 2009. Hunting strategy of the Margay (*leopardus wiedii*) to attract the Wild Pied Tamarin (*saguinus bicolor*). *Neotropical Primates* 16(1).32–34.

Christakis, Dimitri A. 2009. The effects of infant media usage: What do we know and what should we learn? *Acta Pediatrica* 98.8–16.

Crago, Hugh. 2014. *Entranced by story: Brain, tale and teller, from infancy to old age*. New York: Routledge.

Drahota, Amy; Alan Costall; and Vasudevi Reddy. 2008. The vocal communication of different kinds of smile. *Speech Communication* 50(4).278–87.

Duquesnay, Ann. 1997. Hip cat. Rendition for Reading Rainbow, with Joshua Redman (saxophone). Online: youtu.be/6pxD7GBCOio.

Ellis, Ralph, and Madison Park. 2017. Assault charge filed after tweet sent to journalist with epilepsy. *CNN*, 20 March. Online: www.cnn.com/2017/03/17/us/twitter-journalist-strobe-epilepsy/index.html.

Fish, Stanley. 1982. *Is there a text in this class?: The authority of interpretive communities*. Cambridge, MA: Harvard University Press.

Franciosi, R. A. 1987. A hypothesis: Sudden infant death syndrome is a disorder of entrainment. *Medical Hypotheses* 22.443–46.

Gowin, Joshua. 2011. Why sharing stories brings people together. *Psychology Today* blog entry, 06 June. Online: www.psychologytoday.com/blog/you-illuminated/201106/why-sharing-stories-brings-people-together.

Green, Percy B. 1899. *A history of nursery rhymes*. London: Greening & Co. [rpt. Singing Tree Press, Detroit 1968].

Grice, H. Paul. 1989. *Studies in the way of words*. Cambridge, MA: Harvard University Press.

Hardymon, Barrie. 2017. 'Goodnight moon' Author Margaret Wise Brown was no old lady whispering hush. *NPR* 'Weekend Edition', 22 January. Online: www.npr.org/2017/01/22/510642518/goodnight-moon-author-margaret-wise-brown-was-no-old-lady-whispering-hush.

Harsdörffer, Georg Philipp. 1650. *Poetischer Trichter: Die Teutsche Dicht- und Reimkunst ohne Behuf der Lateinischen Sprache in VI Stunden einzugiessen*. Nuremberg: Wolffgang Endter. Online: archive.org/stream/bub_gb_27M6AAAAcAA.

Henderson, Lisa M.; Anna R. Weighall; Helen Brown; and M. Gareth Gaskell. 2012. Consolidation of vocabulary is associated with sleep in children. *Developmental Science* 15(5).674–87.

Heuer, Anna, Christian Wolf, Alexander C. Schütz, and Anna Schubö. 2017. "The necessity to choose cause reward-related anticipatory biasing: Parietal-occipital alpha-band oscillations reveal suppression of low-value targets." *Nature: Scientific Reports* 7.14318. doi:10.1038/s41598-017-14742-w.

Hjortkjær, Jens; Jonatan Märcher-Rørsted; Søren A. Fuglsang; and Torsten Dau. 2018. Cortical oscillations and entrainment in speech processing during working memory load. *European Journal of Neuroscience*, special issue on 'Active Auditory System' (forthcoming). doi:10.1111/ejn.13855.

Huang, Tina I. 2008. A comprehensive review of the psychological effects of brainwave entrainment. *Alternative Therapies* 14(5).38–50.

Hughes, John R. 2008. Gamma, fast, and ultrafast waves of the brain: Their relationships with epilepsy and behavior. *Epilepsy & Behavior* 13(1).25–31.

Humboldt, Wilhelm von. 1836. *Über die Verschiedenheit des menschlichen Sprachbaues und ihren Einfluss auf die geistige Entwickelung des Menschengeschlechts*. Berlin: Königliche Akademie der Wissenschaften, Dämmler.

Huygens, Christiaan. 1665. A la Haye ce 27 fevrier 1665. Letter to Robert Moray, 27 February, transcription. Online: ckcc.huygens.knaw.nl/epistolarium/.

Huygens, Christiaan. 1665. A Mon Pere. Letter to his father, 26 February, transcription. Online: ckcc.huygens.knaw.nl/epistolarium/.

Huygens, Christiaan. 1673. *Christiani Hugenii Horologium oscillatorium sive de motu pendulorum ad horologia aptato domonstrationes geometricæ*. Paris: Muguet. Online: www.e-rara.ch/zut/content/titleinfo/3347187.

Hyman, Paul E.; Peter J. Milla; Marc A. Benninga; Geoff P. Davidson; David F. Fleisher; and Jan Taminiau. 2006. Childhood functional gastrointestinal disorders: Neonate/toddler. *Gastroenterology* 130.1519–26.

Kösem, Anne, and Virginie van Wassenhove. 2016. Distinct contributions of lowand high-frequency neural oscillations to speech comprehension. *Language, Cognition, and Neuroscience* 32(5).536–44.

Kuchinskas, Susan. 2009. *The chemistry of connection*. Oakland, CA: New Harbinger.

Leong, Victoria, and Usha Goswami. 2017. "Difficulties in auditory organization as a cause of reading backwardness? An auditory neuroscience perspective." *Developmental Science* 20.e12457. doi:10.1111/desc.12457.

Levinson, Stephen C. 2000. *Presumptive meanings: The theory of generalized conversational implicature*. Cambridge, MA: MIT Press.

Lisa. 2012. Goodnight moon by Margaret Wise Brown. *Vulpes Libris*, 4 April. Online: vulpeslibris.wordpress.com/2012/04/04/goodnight-moon-by-margaret-wise-brown/.

Locke, John. 1693. *Some thoughts concerning education.* London: Churchill. Online: sourcebooks.fordham.edu/mod/1692locke-education.asp#Some Thoughts Concerning Education.

Ludacris. 2017. Llama Llama freestyle. 105.9 *Power 106* FM Los Angeles, 13 April. youtu.be/PFtHeo7oMSU.

Marcus, Leonard S. 1992. *Margaret Wise Brown: Awakened by the moon.* New York: Quill, William Morrow.

Marlin, Bianca J.; Mariela Mitre; James A. D'amour; Moses V. Chao; and Robert C. Froemke. 2015. Oxytocin enables maternal behaviour by balancing cortical inhibition. *Nature* 520(7548).499+. Gale document # GALE|A411013108.

McGraw, Brittney. 2017. Hey Luda! We finished your Llama Llama Rap!, 4 May. *Twitter.* Online: twitter.com/MrsBMcGraw5.

Mireault, Gina C. 2017. Laughing matters. *Scientific American Mind* 28(3) (May/June).44–49.

Nazzi, Thierry; Josiane Bertoncini; and Jacques Mehler. 1998. Language discrimination by newborns: Toward an understanding of the role of rhythm. *Journal of Experimental Psychology* 24(3).756–66.

Nell, Victor. 1988. The psychology of reading for pleasure: Needs and gratifications. *Reading Research Quarterly* 23(1) (November).6–50.

Nijhoff, Martinus. (ed.) 1967. *Œuvres complètes de Christian Huygens publies par la Société hollandaise des sciences*, vol. 17. L'Horloge a Pendule de 1651 à 1666 travaux divers de Physique, de Mécanique et de Technique de 1650 à 1666. Traité des Couronnes et des Parhélies (1662 ou 1663), 156–89. The Hague: Hollandsche Maatschappij der Wetenschappen; Amsterdam: Swets & Zeitlinger.

Olff, Miranda; Jessie L. Frijling; Laura D. Kubzansky; Bekh Bradley; Mark A. Ellenbogen; Christopher Cardoso; Jennifer A. Bartz; Yason R. Yee; and Mirjam van Zuiden. 2013. The role of oxytocin in social bonding, stress regulation and mental health: An update on the moderating effects of context and interindividual differences. *Psychneuroendocrinology* 38.1883–94.

Pantaleone, James. 2002. Synchronization of metronomes. *American Journal of Physics* 70(10).992–1000.

Piéron, Henri. 1982. Mélanges dedicated to Monsieur Pierre Janet. *Acta Psychiatrica Belgica* 1.7–112.

Power, Alan J.; Natasha Mead; Lisa Barnes; and Usha Goswami. 2013. Neural entrainment to rhythmic speech in children with developmental dyslexia. *Frontiers in Human Neuroscience* 7(777).1–19.

Power, Alan J.; Lincoln J. Colling; Natasha Mead; Lisa Barnes; and Usha Goswami. 2016. Neural encoding of the speech envelope by children with developmental dyslexia. *Brain and Language* 160 (September).1–10.

Publisher's Weekly. 1947. A sampling of Fall juveniles. 152(9.1).101–22.

Ramachandran, Vilayanur S. 2009. The neurons that shaped civilization. *TEDIndia*, November. Online: www.ted.com/talks/vs_ramachandran_the_neurons_that_shaped_civilization.

Read, Kirsten, Megan Macauley, and Erin Furay. 2014. The Seuss boost: Rhyme helps children retain words from shared storybook reading. *First Language* 34(4).354–71.

Ready, Lauren. 2017. Rappers freestyle kids' book 'Llama Llama,' parents can't get enough. *USA Today*, 18 May. Online: www.usatoday.com/story/news/humankind/2017/05/18/rappers-freestyle-kids-book-llama-llama-parents-cant-get-enough/101801892/.

Riecke, Lars; Elia Formisano; Bettina Sorger; Deniz Basxkent; and Etienne Gaudrain. 2018. Neural entrainment to speech modulates speech intelligibility. *Current Biology* 28 (January 22)161–69. doi:10.1016/j.cub.2017.11.033.

Rousseau, Jean Jacques. 1762. *Émile: Ou de l'éducation*. La Haye: Jean Néaulme. Online: archive.org/stream/amileoudeldu01rous.

Rubakin, Nicolas. 1922. *Introduction à la psychologie bibliologique*, vol. II. Paris: Povolozky.

Schramm, Wilbur. 1961. How communication works. *The process and effects of mass communication*, ed. by Wilbur Schramm, 5–6. Urbana: University of Illinois Press.

Shannon, Claude F. 1948. A mathematical theory of communication. *Bell System Technical Journal* 27 (July, October).379–423, 623–56. Online: cm.bell-labs.com/cm/ms/what/shannonday/shannon1948.pdf.

Siever, David. 2006. Audio-visual entrainment: History and physiological mechanisms. *Mind Alive*. Online: www.scribd.com/document/76875810/AVE-History-Physiology.

Stephens, Greg J.; Lauren J. Silbert; and Uri Hasson. 2010. Speaker-listener neural coupling underlies successful communication. *PNAS—Proceedings of the National Academy of Science of the United States* 107(32).14425–30.

Strogatz, Steven H.; Daniel M. Abrams; Allan McRobie; Bruno Eckhardt; and Edward Ott. 2005. Theoretical mechanics: Crowd synchrony on the Millennium Bridge. *Nature* 438 (3 November).43–44.

Sutton, Roger. 2013. Five questions for Anna Dewdney. 'Read Roger,' *The Horn Book*, 12 April. Online: www.hbook.com/2013/04/blogs/read-roger/five-questions-for-anna-dewdney.

Trafton, Anne. 2016. Unique visual stimulation may be new treatment for Alzheimer's. *MIT News*, 7 December. Online: news.mit.edu/2016/visual-stimulation-treatment-alzheimer-1207.

Tripp, Valerie. n.d. Biography. Online: valerietripp.org/about.html.

Vassileiou, Benedict; Lars Meyer; Caroline Beese; and Angela D. Friederici. 2018. Alignment of alpha-band desynchronization with syntactic structure predicts successful sentence comprehension. *NeuroImage* 175.286–96.

Verney, John Parker. 2013. *Rhythmic perception and entrainment in 5-year-old children*. Centre For Neuroscience and Education, University of Cambridge: Ph.D. dissertation.

Watts, Isaac. 1741. *The improvement of the mind: Or, a supplement to the art of logick: Containing a variety of remarks and rules for the attainment and communication of useful knowledge, in religion, in the sciences, and in common life*. London: Brackstone.

Wermke, Kathleen; Johanna Teiser; Eunice Yovsi; Paul Joscha Kohlenberg; Peter Wermke; Michael Robb; Heidi Keller; and Bettina Lamm. 2016. Fundamental frequency variation within neonatal crying: Does ambient language matter? *Speech, Language and Hearing* 19(4).211–17.

Wilkins, John. 1668. *An essay towards a real character, and a philosophical language*. London: Gellibrand, Royal Society.

Wilson, Deirdre, and Dan Sperber. 2004. Relevance theory. *The hand-book of pragmatics*, ed. by Laurence R. Horn and Gregory Ward, 607–32. Malden, MA: Blackwell. Online: www.phon.ucl.ac.uk/publications/WPL/02papers/wilson_sperber.pdf.

Winn, Marie. 2002. *The plug-in drug: Television, computers, and family life*. New York: Penguin.

8 The Language of Cooperation

Il n'y a point d'assujettissement si parfait que
celui qui garde l'apparence de la liberté.
There is no subjugation so perfect as the one
that preserves the semblance of liberty.
(Rousseau, *Émile* 1762.2:84)

Human languages have advanced far (very far) beyond communication systems where one signal always stands for one meaning. Instead, meaning is created through combining signals. With the increased amount of signals required to convey a single meaning in speech, informational entropy increased. The gain is in obfuscation: Our communications are extremely hard to understand or imitate for anyone unfamiliar with our sounds and the rules that operate on them. The apparent loss is in efficiency: We had to turn into mind readers to enhance the signals. But we have turned that apparent loss into another gain: Our species is capable of reconstructing complex (hierarchical, parallel) meanings from a simple (flat, serial) stream of sounds. Paradoxically, by using an informationally less rich communication system we have increased the amount of information we transmit/imply. The previous chapter looked at linguistic entrainment, the synchronization of two brains, for an explanation for this kind of "mind reading." This chapter looks at linguistic cooperation, because entrainment presumes trust.

Cooperation begins early, when adults tailor their speech to the needs of an infant. Infants tune in to certain rhythmic and musical qualities of human speech; to cater to their biases, adults automatically modify the way they talk. Jerome S. Bruner concluded that adults must have a drive to present infants with 'arranged input,' an instinctive 'Language Acquisition Support System' (1983:39–42). Infant- and child-directed speech (once known as 'motherese' and 'fatherese' or 'parentese') has characteristics quite unlike speech between adults. Adults cooperate with infants and young children at all linguistic levels (Table 8.1):

Table 8.1 Characteristics of Child-Directed Talk

pronunciation	presentational (carefully enunciated)
intonation	exaggerated, greater ranges of pitch, loudness/stress
tempo	slow, with longer pauses between constituents
lexicon	mostly common, high-frequency words
syntax	simple sentences or single words, well-formed
discourse	context embedded, paraphrasing, repetitions, questions, commands; fewer utterances per turn

(adjusted from Owens 2008:170)

Children's books incorporate those adjustments, but their 'arranged input' aims beyond them in ways outlined so far: poetic meter may speed language up or slow it down; there are exotic 'juicy' words; the author may playfully stretch or violate morphology or morphosyntax; the content may be projected into the realm of the fantastic; and there are fewer paraphrases, commands, questions in children's books. With children's books involved, the nature of cooperation must be different from what it is between child and caretaker. This chapter identifies such cooperation both at the micro- (sentence) and macrolinguistic (textual) levels.

Cooperative Information Management at the Sentence Level

Adult speakers instinctively distribute information within sentences to reflect their intuition of what the listener knows. They typically begin with known information and place information that is newly introduced to the conversation toward the left. If information is particularly obvious, it can be placed in a TOPIC position preceding the subject. If it is particularly salient, it can be placed in a FOCUS position at the end of the clause or sentence.

To arrange information across a sentence so that it proceeds from 'given' to 'new,' languages have 'templates,' which are idiomatic, i.e. stored in the lexicon (Thiede 2007). Templates provide a formulaic lattice to grow sentences on, leaving the job of ensuring their well-formedness to morphosyntax. A template can be very simple. INVERSION, for example, merely specifies that the verb element with tense precede the subject (e.g. 'have you any wool?'). TOPICALIZATION specifies that a constituent other than the tensed verb should precede the subject (e.g. 'Begun, the Clone War has,' *has* being the tensed verbal element). The *there*-CONSTRUCTION maps a subject into the predicate. The latter may sound like a contradiction in terms, but this template is handy if the subject (usually a place for 'given' information) refers to new information. The sentence 'A wocket is in my pocket,' after all, would send mixed messages: *wocket* is marked as 'new' to the discourse by the use of the indefinite article *a*, yet it appears in subject position, where typically 'given' information is expected. Right-displacing the subject avoids the contradiction: 'There's a wocket in my pocket.' The dummy *there* is a mere place holder, marking the subject position that was left empty by the remapped noun phrase.

Templates also can be mixed and matched, though doing so can result in somewhat exotic sentence structures that one would not look for in transcriptions of child-directed speech. Yet Margery Williams uses TOPICALIZATION plus *there*-CONSTRUCTION in a sentence describing what happens when a blossom opens on a flower that had risen from *The Velveteen Rabbit* 's forlorn tear: '. . . and out of it there stepped a fairy.' The clause would not have served the author's literary purposes in the canonic clause structure we usually find in child-directed speech ('a fairy stepped out of it'). The topicalized 'out of it' connects to *blossom* in the previous clause, but it also delays what is going to happen. The *there*-construction, remarkably, manages to place the subject of the clause at its very end, allowing the surprise to buildup. Margery Williams thus achieves an increase of salience from given to new (with *fairy* in clause-final FOCUS) that a child can follow, but with a sentence structure highly exceptional for child-directed speech.

English has many templates. Speakers may not use every single one of them; a 2010 study by James Street and Ewa Dąbrowska (2010), for example, identified British high school students who never used the passive construction. Thus, it is remarkable to find several of these templates in just a single children's book, Virginia Lee Burton's *Mike Mulligan and his Steam Shovel* (1939). Among the templates in Table 8.2 are the following:

- MOVE DATIVE, which demotes the indirect object (Henry B. Swap gave [Mike Mulligan and Mary Anne] the job of digging the cellar of the new town hall) into a prepositional phrase ('Henry B. Swap . . . gave — the job of digging the cellar of the new town hall to [Mike Mulligan and Mary Anne]').
- EXTRAPOSITION moves a constituent into FOCUS position because it is particularly salient. The constituent could also just be very large, as when an infinitive or a clause functions as subject (as in '[To dig the cellar for our new town hall] would take a hundred men at least a week'). The vacated subject position in such case is marked by the dummy place holder *it* ('*It* would take a hundred men at least a week [to dig the cellar for our new town hall]').
- CLEFTING also fills the subject position with *it*. It is a somewhat rare sentence structure to encounter in adult speech, let alone in child-directed speech. Burton uses it repeatedly, almost like a mantra. Clefting creates two clauses ('[It was Mike Mulligan and Mary Anne and some others] [who dug the great canals for the big boats to sail from]') from a single one ('[Mike Mulligan and Mary Ann and some others dug the great canals for the big boats to sail through]'). Two clauses create two opportunities to allow a salient constituent in clause-final focus position (here, who did the digging and the resulting benefit that big boats can sail through). Finally, the book uses
- INVERSION, placing the tensed verb before the subject position ('Then along *came* the new gasoline shovels . . .').

Using templates to distribute material by salience *within* sentences is one form of sentential information management. Another is to distribute information *across* adjacent sentences. A *given-new chain* links the given information at the

Table 8.2 Syntactic Templates in *Mike Mulligan*

	given > > > > > >	*new* > >
canonic	Mike Mulligan and Mary Anne	were VERY SAD.
passive	All the other steam shovels	were being sold for junk . . .
"move dative"	. . . he . . . gave the job of digging the cellar of the new town hall	to Mike Mulligan and Mary Anne.
extraposition	It would take a hundred men at least a week	to dig the cellar for our new town hall.
it-cleft	It was Mike Mulligan and Mary Anne and some others	who dug the great canals for the big boats to sail through.
inversion	Never had they	dug so fast and so well.

left periphery to the new information of the previous sentence's right periphery. Such organization achieves cohesion and drives the narrative, as does the following passage from Roald Dahl's *Charlie and the Chocolate Factory* (1998:21). The sentence-final constituents and their reprises in the following sentence are underlined to show the given-new chaining:

> THE VERY NEXT DAY, the first Golden Ticket was found. The finder was a boy called Augustus Gloop, and Mr. Bucket's evening newspaper carried a picture of him on the front page. The picture showed a nine-year-old boy who was so enormously fat he looked as though he had been blown up with a powerful pump. Great flabby folds of fat bulged out from every part of his body, and his face was like a monstrous ball of dough with two small greedy curranty eyes peering out upon the world. The town in which Augustus Gloop lived, the newspaper said, had gone wild with excitement over their hero. Flags were flying from all the windows, children had been given a holiday from school, and a parade was being organized in honor of the famous youth.

A *topic chain*, in contrast, repeatedly refers to given information in the sentence-initial position. In the following passage from Bernard Wiseman's *Morris Goes to School* (1970:29–30), the underlined subjects all have the same reference (school children) until the final contrast with *Morris*. Interesting in this passage is that Wiseman not only chains the 'given' topic, but additionally also chains the 'new' information in the object positions (not that there is a term for that, but we could call it a *focus chain*). The formulaic parallelism insists on how uniformly well-prepared the school children are and then uses the same structure in the final punch line to single out Morris the unready moose:

> The children opened their *lunch boxes*.
> Some of them had *cheese sandwiches*.
> Some had *cream cheese and jelly sandwiches*.
> Some had *hamburgers*.
> Each of them had a *piece of fruit*.
> But Morris had *nothing* !

Topic chains can be used to build evidence, make a case, and slow down the plot for details.

Information management through templates, given-new chains, or topic chains is linguistic cooperation when it adjusts the speaker's/writer's syntax to the assumed needs of the listener/reader. The desired effect is, to borrow a metaphor from Ludics, to facilitate advancement through the text, co-creating sense step by step (Taylor 1979:28). Author and reader each assume their share of the effort, even if their respective amounts of effort may vary. Children's books tend to assign the burden of linguistic cooperation disproportionately to the author, but that does not entail that the authors cannot be as demanding as Margery Williams and Virginia Lee Burton. The investment of effort also varies proportionately among adults, even by culture. John Hinds found that Americans place the responsibility for clarity squarely on the side of the *author*, whereas in Japanese and classical Chinese literature a greater investment of interpretive effort is assigned to the *audience* (1987:143, so also Snively 1999). Given the double burden of cooperative responsibility for American authors and for children's book authors, it is no wonder that American children's authors can spend years on fine-tuning a single, "simple"-looking book (see p. 1)!

Cooperative Information Management at the Discourse Level

At the level of text, linguistic cooperation extends beyond the sentence-by-sentence level: The content of each sentence is additionally managed to align with the reader's presumed (or wishfully projected) *discourse* needs. One such cooperative information management technique for an entire text is framing.

A frame biases a text; the author selects only information that fits particular cognitive schemas or domains, such as good vs. bad outcomes, win vs. loss, natural vs. social, etc. (Goffman 1974). Frames have been studied in subliminal advertising (10% fat content vs. 90% lean meat, for example) and political spin ('estate tax' vs. 'death tax'). Children recognize *and use* frames once they are able to reflect upon language. A consistent frame appears in the following passage, the earliest known writing by Charlotte Brontë at age 10 (Alexander 1987:3):

> There was once a little girl and her name was Anne. She was born at a little village named Thornton and by and by she grew a good girl. Her father and mother were both very rich. Mr and Mrs Wood were their names and she was their only child, but she was not too much indulged.
>
> Once little Anne and her mother went to see a fine castle near London, about ten miles from it. Anne was very much pleased with it.
>
> Once Anne and her papa and her Mama went to sea in a ship and they had very fine weather all the way, but Anne's Mama was very sick and Anne attended her with so much care. She gave her medicine.

The budding author names her frame: being 'a good girl' deserving of approval. She states that she was 'not too much indulged' (John Newbery would certainly have approved of that), that she was 'very much pleased' with a family outing, and that she took 'so much care' to tend to her sick mother. The protagonist is projected into three narrative pasts (each introduced with 'once') and displaced as the character 'Anne,' though since this is not an introduction to a story but the entire story, and since we know that Charlotte Brontë herself hailed from Thornton, West Yorkshire, we can assume that the text is autobiographic and the frame is self-promotional, seeking the kind of narrative validation discussed above (p. 158).

A frame affects the audience's attitude toward the information presented. To demonstrate just how much the frame colors the information, let us look at a single poem placed into two different contexts, Robert Louis Stevenson's 'The Whole Duty of Children':

> A child should always say what's true
> And speak when he is spoken to,
> And behave mannerly at table:
> At least as far as he is able.

The poem appears originally in Stevenson's lavishly produced *A Child's Garden of Verses* (1895). The book's binding, illustrations, quality materials, and artful poetry are clearly aimed at a white, affluent clientele. The book was published at a time when authors began reaching out to children as who they are (my 'stage 3'). Within the framework of this book, the gesture of the poem is to make allowance for childhood and give the child a little license here and there to buck against the rigid behavioral codex and table manners of Newbery's *Little Pretty Pocket-Book* (q.v. p. 157). Yes, children should still follow middle- and upper-class etiquette—refrain from lying, from interrupting adult conversation, or from instant gratification. But children are children, and you have to expect the occasional lapse, and as long as the child generally does act in a 'mannerly' fashion, those little lapses are forgivable, if not lovable.

The same lines surely had a different ring to them when they were included in W. E. B. DuBois's *The Brownies Book* 1.1 (1920:10) and attributed to Robert Louis Stevenson. The cover of that serial proclaimed that the publication was 'Designed for all children, but especially for *ours*,' and the inaugural issue featured a photograph of 'her Royal Highness, Zaouditou, Queen of the Kings of Abyssinia, Empress of Ethiopia' (2) and a defiant poem by Annie Virginia Culbertson, 'The Origin of White Folks.' [1] To speak only when spoken to means something different within this framework, reflecting an expectation imposed even on adults. What is considered 'mannerly' in the world represented by the poem takes its definition from the elite, and the "ability" to show compliance with those manners meets its limits when the very pride is offended that W. E. B. DuBois tried to restore to his readers. Depending on the framework, the meaning of *able* flips between 'capable' and 'allowed.'

A more recent picturebook demonstrates to children how such frames define identity without direct reference to human ethnic affiliations. In Janell Cannon's *Stellaluna*, a little bat falls into a birds' nest when her mother is attacked by an owl. Stellaluna tries to be like the birds who raise her, then returns to the ways of bats when she is reunited with her family, albeit now with a better understanding of birds. Each setting spells out how things should and should not be done: sleeping upright or upside down/during daytime or at night, eating bugs or fruit, and generally behaving like a bat or 'as a good bird should.' Stellaluna is a different persona in each world. In the end, she and her feathered friends decide to enjoy their similarities and accept their differences, and to remain friends.

At the point when children begin to frame a story *and to interrogate* a frame, when they have learned to reconcile the requirements of the story with the needs of the self, and when they have understood the ludic logic of Story, they have entered the distributed cognition of the adult mind. The question is whether children should then interrogate the adult mind. Some children's books clearly advocate that they do so.

Children's literature, as evidenced in the previous chapter, can simultaneously occupy the worlds of adults and children, or else it shuttles back and forth between them. Some understand the implied beneficent presence of the adult in children's literature as its *raison d'être*. Others fear that it is. Is the purpose of children's literature, as Jacqueline Rose saw it (1984:2), to 'colonize' the child? Does children's literature 'seduce' children into aspiring to the image of childhood projected into the book? And if so, is "children's literature" (now with scare quotes) the genre where adult fantasies about childhood are translated into what the author thinks *should* be the language of childhood? Such a characterization would not be incompatible with my working definition of the genre (p. 10), which explicitly presumes a 'benefit' to the child. The understanding of what a 'benefit' is, of course, follows from the understanding of who the beneficiary is, the 'child.' Two notions conflict here: whether childhood is defined against the yet unattained portion of adulthood or as a separate state altogether. Between those two extremes, children's books reflect a range of concepts about what a child is:

- **Deficient adult: If** a child is a deficient adult, **then** a community of mature adults is called upon to provide remedial materials to bring the child up to par, **so** children's books introduce the young learners to classical literature, adult society, technology, matters of faith, the three R's (reading, writing, 'rithmetic), expected gender roles, nationalism.
- **Natural learner: If** a child is to be protected from the demands (and evils) of adult society, **then** children should ideally grow up like Rousseau's Émile, as "pastoral children" with their own keen senses interested in figuring out the world on their "own" terms (albeit subtly manipulated by a tutoring adult who arranges their learning environment). Or they may be left altogether 'fallow,' as Arthur Helps recommended (p. 5). After the protected period of natural learning, however, the child still needs to acculturate. **So** 'book learning' is thus merely deferred, and socialization may revert to the 'deficient adult' model eventually.

- **Different from adults: If** children can be engaged intellectually on their *developmental* terms, **then** the two preceding models can be fused **so** children's innocence can be shielded, in the words of Astrid Lindgren, 'from the somber trumpets of judgment day' (2017:190). At the same time, children learn and acculturate through playful, creative, and intelligent literature supplied by authors who can 'consult the child within themselves' (191).
- **Precocious adult: If** children are, in the words of Mo Willems, just shorter than adults, not stupider (see p. 2), **then** adults and children inhabit cultural space and distributed cognition jointly and right away, **so** children's literature is conceived as a literary art form that is inclusive, maybe age-less (i.e. the language may not have be adjusted for 'age-appropriateness'), and above all, partnering.
- **Sequentially unlocked adult: If** we understand the child's maturational stages and the requirements for linguistic and cognitive development at each stage, **then** adults can approach them playfully and with a sequence of age-tailored agendas, **so** children's literature brings sophisticated developmental expertise into the home. The book becomes the natural environment in which the child joyfully explores and hones linguistic, social, and cognitive skills at an optimized pace. Étienne Delessert, for instance, cooperated with developmental psychologist Jean Piaget in writing *How the Mouse Was Hit by a Stone and So Discovered the World* (1971; see Kümmerling-Meibauer 2015:261–62). The author becomes the trainer, the reading adult acts as coach, together optimizing the child's performance. The child is motivated intrinsically, thriving on playful exploration and on the rewards of bonding.

Implied in the language of each of these philosophies about childhood is a shared key feature: Children's literature is cooperative. The following examples concentrate on cooperative relations implicit in the texts that make children's literature a genre distinct from literary works for adults.

Cooperation through children's literature builds on linguistic entrainment. Consistent rewards from shared reading sessions build a relationship of trust between adult and child, which extends to the literature. Children bond with book characters as part of their in-group (cf. p. 155). 'Babes in arms,' writes Shirley Brice Heath, 'learn that it is appropriate for their cribs and walls to be decorated with characters which have no explanation outside a literary reference' (1983:255). They develop life-long (Wolf 2016:61) loyalties: to Mo Willems' characters Pigeon, Knuffel Bunny, Elephant & Piggie; Jonathan London's Froggie; H. A. Ray's Curious George; Joanna Cole and Bruce Degen's Ms. Frizzle and her Magic School Bus. Authors, too, inspire loyalty, such as "Dr. Seuss" and Janosch, their books added to the collection simply because the author wrote them. These loyalties develop beyond a dyadic space between caretaker and child. Thus, while spoken discourse prefers the dyad—even when a married couple interacts with a third party (Leisi 1978:137)—adult conversations are the wrong model for analyzing how loyalties develop in children's literature. If, for example, in *Emil und die Detektive* (1929) author Erich Kästner writes himself into a children's book to assist a child character (giving the protagonist Emil money and later interviewing him for the newspaper), and if we assume that young readers read to identify with a book's protagonist, then we have a three-way cooperation. Applying only a standard dyadic model of cooperation led Tao Zhang to conclude that such a blending of real person and literary character is puzzling and creates a distance-inducing "alienation effect" (2016:185). Instead, I will highlight a few of the many possible triads of cooperation below. They can be altruistic and inclusive as in *Émil*, but two parties can also collude against a third. I will include examples of both kinds of triadic cooperation/collusion.

Δ Child/Character/Character

Children's literature is traditionally rich with characters who cooperate, or feud, with each other. That a book's character should 'cooperate' or 'feud' with the child reader, however, is a new twist. In several recent books, characters acknowledge the child's presence, and they appear to talk to their young readers from the page and ask them to intervene in the story on their behalf. This is a particularly effective device for preliterate children in interactive book reading sessions, because the adult performing those characters delivers their requests 'live.' Those characters ask the child for cooperation by piggybacking on the dyadic cooperation between reading adult and child, which makes their words come alive (keeping in mind Samuel Taylor Coleridge's insight of how eager a reader can be to 'suspend disbelief' for the sake of literary experience).

The novelty here is not that a children's book should *address* the child. There are pretend letters from Santa Claus to children, there are morals and exhortations affixed to stories, etc. in which the text addresses the child as 'you' or even by name. What is different here is that a book's *character* professes *awareness* of the child's presence within the reading session. One of David Wiesner's *Three Pigs* (2001), for example, exploring the newly discovered free range of "three-dimensional" space (see p. 149), glances in the direction of the reader with surprise (eyes wide open, ears perked) and says: 'Wait—what's that?' The next page turn reveals an eye-popping closeup of the pig staring at the viewer: 'I think . . . someone's out there.' Ingeniously, the author avoids a direct discourse between pig and child. The pig (whose eyes were wide open in surprise a moment ago) now squints as if short sighted (i.e. is able to make out 'someone,' but unable to see the individual child), and another pig immediately diverts his attention ('Come help us with this').

Mo Willems, on the other hand, does not shy away from the challenge of setting up a direct cooperation between child and character in *Don't Let the Pigeon Drive the Bus* (2003). A bus driver greets the child with 'Hi!' and prefaces a request with 'Listen': He asks the child to watch his bus while he steps out. Specifically, he requests the child's cooperation in preventing 'the pigeon' from driving it. On the next page, the pigeon sticks its head into the picture on one margin even as the bus driver 'steps out' through the other margin. (The page is like a camera angle, and the book's plot may extend unseen to the left and right beyond the frame).

The ensuing 'discourse' consists of the pigeon trying to convince the child to let it drive the bus. The expected answer each time is the child's 'no,' to which the pigeon reacts with visible disappointment. The pigeon lies claiming to have a cousin who drives the bus—'True story.'), tries to bribe the child with friendship (alternatively, with 'five bucks'), attempts emotional blackmail ('I have dreams, you know'), throws a tantrum. At one point, the pigeon attempts to 'leave' the page to 'play drive the bus' and needs to be 'called back' on(to) the next page and into the child's frame of 'control.' When the bus driver returns, the child can truthfully 'reassure' him that the pigeon never got to drive his bus. (The pigeon does size up an opportunity to make off with a truck, though). Effectively, the book casts the child in the role of a supervising adult, cooperating with another adult (the bus driver) to deny a childish and irresponsible request acted out with strategies typically attributed to children. From the start ('Listen'), Willems counts on the book's being performed, with an adult proxy giving voice to the pigeon. That allows the child to talk to the pigeon, out loud, and the role playing surely is much more fun than imagining one's answers in a silent reading session.

A book entitled *Do Not Open This Book* (2017), by Andy Lee, reverses those roles: It puts the pleading character into the role of the *reasonable* petitioner and casts the child as disobedient and uncooperative to the end. Like the pigeon, the character tries every strategy in the book to prevent the book's pages from being turned (cajoling, threatening, pleading, reverse psychology, even a 'silent treatment' that stretches across several pages). Eventually, the reader's refusal to cooperate (i.e. the reader's refusal to cease being a reader) impacts the character directly. There is one final entreaty *not* to turn the last page because a witch has cast a spell that would turn the character into a frog if anyone ever 'made it to the end of this book.' The frog's final words: 'Thanks a lot.'[2]

Δ Child/Character/Book

Children's books can be innovative and creative when it comes to the characters' contribution to, and the book's role in, the reading session. The child may be asked to cooperate with a character against the book itself, or the character can attempt to protect the book from the reader. Either way, the child would have to agree that the character has a 'life' inside the book, and that the book itself can be a character.

Mo Willems appears to riff on David Wiesner's moment of discovery in which one of the three pigs notices the presence of a reader, in his *We Are in a Book!* (2010). Gerald the elephant feels being watched and whispers to Piggie: 'I think someone is looking at us.' An indignant Piggie advances toward the reader to investigate, and discovers the reader. Piggie explains to Gerald that, after all, they are in a book, being read (which makes them both very proud). Piggie then turns the table: 'I can make the reader say a word!' The word is 'banana,' and 'hearing' it said by the reader occasions one of children's literature's most memorable ROFL moments (Figure 8.1), prolonged when the characters 'hear' the reader say it again (because it was just read the page before, when the adult reader gave voice to Gerald saying 'The reader said "Banana!"'). The realization that they are in a book, however, also triggers an anxiety attack, because books do end (Piggie lifts up the lower right page corners to discover that this will occur on page 57). They ask the reader to read them again.

Figure 8.1 Book Characters 'Aware' of Reader (Mo Willems)

The book can be even more actively involved than impressing its imminent end upon the characters. It can become one of the characters. Richard Byrne's *This Book Just Ate My Dog!* (2015) opens with Bella walking her dog across the first two open sheets. As she proceeds, the dog on the leash behind her does not make it to the next page. Instead, he begins to disappear into the binding between the pages such that Bella is left tugging just a leash and the left-hand page shows nothing but blurred urban scenery. When her friend Ben arrives, Bella tells him that the book just 'ate' her dog. Ben decides to investigate, and he, too, disappears into the crease between the pages. So do a dog-rescue ambulance, a police car, and a fire truck. The book lets loose with an all-caps BURP! when Bella herself disappears. Just when it looks as if the book might move on to the reader's digestion, an envelope is tossed onto the page from inside the crease. It contains a note politely asking the reader to help by rotating the book and shaking it. There is an Ikea-like drawing to serve as instruction of how this is to be performed. The child has to rotate the book and shake it, with encouragement from the left (now upper) page. Things tumble out of the central crease of the book onto the right (now lower) page as the book regurgitates everything it has swallowed. Byrne's setup is ingenious: Bella asks the child for an alliance against the book in order to rescue her and her friends. Indeed, the back cover of the book advertises for a nice reader to show this book who is boss.

Byrne's follow-up *This Book Is Out of Control* (2016) has a door drawn *into* the gutter through which Bella, her dog, and Ben can safely traverse the pages. Ben means to demonstrate his remote-controlled toy fire truck to Bella, except that everything he instructs the truck to do (rise, spin, etc.) happens to the dog on the other side of the door. The malfunction gets worse with every attempt to remedy the situation as the remote makes increasingly impossible things happen, until everyone ends up stuck on the ceiling and the remote control falls to the floor and out of reach of the characters. The characters ask the reader for help, which, surprisingly, makes things even worse. They then ask for the child to reset the remote by holding down the Power button while counting down from ten to zero. The result is a 'power surge' that creates a *tohu va vohu*, out of which miraculously arises order. As in his previous book where the child became the book's mover and shaker, so here child assumes the role of the book's redeemer. But now the *dog* has, and operates, the remote, and it makes the fire truck work correctly on the other side of the door. The final page shows the remote and a hand-written note asking the child to press the single button that has not been pushed in the story (it is the 'repeat' button).

The alliances are reversed in Michaela Muntean's *Do Not Open This Book!* (2006). The character tries to protect the book against the reader. On page one, the reader is scolded for having *disobeyed* the book's very simple instruction on the title page, no different from a do-not-enter sign on a door. Of course you don't.' Another page turn reveals why: The book 'is not yet written.' The words on the right are not yet fixed and still a jumble. Another turn of the page reveals that the character doing the scolding—a little pig—is also the 'author' of the book and still in the process of creating it. The 'intrusion' of the reader becomes an increasing source of annoyance and hindrance to the creative progress of the 'author,' who wishes for the reader to go to sleep already. As a compromise, the little pig 'allows' the reader to stay in the book a while longer on condition that no more pages be turned because doing so might disturb the unsettled words. Which is of course exactly what happens. The pig then resorts to using construction equipment to push very heavy-looking words (spelling 'very heavy rock') up against the right margin to weigh it down and prevent any further page turning. The reader who at this point still disobeys the character's instructions 'causes' the heavy-rock words to crash upon the pages on the next turn, after which the pig feigns to give up. The 'reward' for the prying reader's pesky persistence will be that the pig will write the reader into a story. The character asks the reader's name, professes not to be able to spell it, and explains that he will simply leave a blank in the story where the reader's name should be.

What follows now is child-literature's truncated version of Austrian playwright Peter Handke's *Offending the Audience* ('Publikumsbeschimpfung'): In an invective little 'story,' the pig assigns to the reader the role of a giant pest that would not go away. The story ends with a call to the Giant Pest Control Company to exterminate the reader. The fiction fails; the reader is 'still here' on the next page, to the dismay of the pig, who had hoped that the reader would be insulted enough to leave by now. But the intrusion upon the book character's privacy continues. The pig's suggestion to the reader at this point is to do *anything else*, such as watching one's toenails grow. There is a helpful arrow pointing down to where the reader's toenails presumably are located. The book resolves itself by being completed: The little pig realizes that over all the antagonism, pages have accumulated. The pig goes to bed and dreams about receiving a book award medal, but not before shouting in all-caps: 'NOW GO AWAY!' The reader's role changed from unbidden eavesdropper to unintentional collaborator. In an interactive reading session, adult and child become accomplices in disobeying the book's instructions, while at the same time the adult also performs the voice of the petulant pig. The adult is both instigator and licenser, which confers upon the reading session the safety of play.

Δ Adult/Author/Child

The implied presence of the adult in children's books, as we have seen, has been blamed for an inherent asymmetry in how adults and children interact through children's literature (cf. Emer O'Sullivan, p. 1, and Jacqueline Rose, above). Often enough, there is indeed asymmetry, but past analyses are based on dyadic models of cooperation. In triads, the dynamics can shift:

- Authors can cooperate with adults for the child's benefit, e.g. when they both believe that children are the future agents of cultural transformation (Steiner 2015:200) and become aware that children's literature needs to change, e.g. to reflect diversity (weneeddiversebooks.org). Through books, authors cooperate with adults by means of prefaces, supporting expert testimony, instructions, implied messages, or the roles they ask them to play.
- Authors can conspire with the child directly—for the child's benefit and to influence the adults. Anti-authoritarian authors, for example, intended to 'invite parents to take children seriously and to treat them as equal conversation partners' (Kümmerling-Meibauer 2015:250).
- Authors can also conspire with the child at the expense of the adult. Dr. Seuss' *Oh Say Can You Say?* (1979) sets up the adult who tries to read the book fluently (see p. 46), as does *Fox in Sox* (1965). The author plays a 'prank' on the experienced reader—a beginning reader would simply not be able to read fast enough to get tripped up (Nel 2015:274).
- Adult and child can side against the author, as I imagine could happen during a reading of Shel Silverstein's *The Giving Tree* (1964). The book sets up a child-mother relationship between the little boy and an apple tree, who offers all of herself (her fruit, her branches, eventually her very trunk) until only a stump is left. Parent and child may reassure each other against the author's apparent message that children are naturally so selfish that parents have reason to expect their ultimate annihilation (cf. Margalit 2014)—or, as Bruce Handy read it, 'if you leave home it will kill your mother' (2017:33).
- Authors can even write books for adults that seem to *abuse* the genre of children's literature and exclude children, but with the ultimate goal of enhancing the adult's appreciation of children. Mo Willems, for example, invented the character of Beligerent Bunny [sic.], who is wasted on alcohol and slurs his words. *"Olive Hue Show Mutts": An intoxicatingly HARD READER* forces adult readers to rehearse the words in their minds until they make (mostly politically incorrect) sense ("I love you so much")—an attempt, in the words of

the author, 'at recreating for adults the decoding process that children must go through when they first learn to read' (quoted in Nel 2015:274).

The clandestine presence of adults often broadcasts in coded messages over the child's head—innuendos, dog whistles, cultural or historical allusions. There is the occasional linguistic nudge-nudge, wink-wink, as in George MacDonald's 'The Light Princess' (1864). The prince catches his first sight of the princess when she takes a reprieve from her zero-gravity affliction in the lake's water by moonlight, and the author mentions that the moonlight was just enough 'to show that she was a lady.' He 'rescues' her but is commanded to return her to the water at once. He does so by holding her in his arms and jumping in from a high ledge, a novel sensation of gravity for the weightless princess. The language of the ensuing exchange has more than a face-value meaning (Johnson 1962:213):

> "How do you like falling in?" said the Prince.
> After some effort the Princess panted out,
> "Is that what you call *falling in*?"
> "Yes," answered the Prince, "I should think it a very tolerable specimen."
> "It seemed to me like going up," rejoined she.
> "My feeling was certainly one of elevation, too," the Prince conceded.

Roald Dahl's adult messages broadcast at wavelengths much closer to the range of children's antennas. His retelling of Snow-White (*Revolting Rhymes*) implies the adult without plausible deniability. When thousands of girls apply to the Queen mother's advertisement that her son is looking for a queen, the prince's father wishes he could exercise his *droit du seigneur* on all of them.

Adult-adult collusion can be so patently *un*-beneficial for children that it would seem to intentionally exclude the child; one may ask whether in such cases the work can still be considered children's literature or whether the genre is being persiflaged *at the expense* of young ones. Joachim Ringelnatz's *Kinder-verwirr-buch* ('Children's Confusion Book,' 1931), for example, invites children to reflect on what transpires when mommy and daddy lock their bedroom door. The cover of Beryl Evans' dark and twisted *Charlie the Choo-choo* (2016) features an "endorsement": 'If I were ever to write a children's book, it would be just like this—Steven King.' ('Beryl Evans' is Steven King's pseudonym). The book is no more at home in children's hands than *IT* (1986). And there is a slew of recent titles written and illustrated as children's books but clearly marketed to adults, such as Adam Mansbach's exasperated *Go the Fuck to Sleep* (2011).

Roald Dahl's retelling of the Cinderella story in *Revolting Rhymes* derides the children's version as 'all soft and sappy,/just to make the children happy.' In his rendition, Cinderella gives the Prince the slip not just sans slipper. The Prince disrobes her by forcefully holding on to her dress.

Children may sense that they are not the intended audience—not only by sexual, violent, sexually violent, or morbid content, but especially by the use of language they themselves would in any other circumstance not have permission to repeat, such as describing a female character as a *slut* or *whore*. The following rhyme (presumably unfit to be repeated by children even in 18th century) appears in an early version of 'Mother Goose' rhymes reproduced by Colonel William Francis Prideaux (1904:64) and traced back by Prideaux to a 1765 (?) edition, now lost, by John Newbery:

> The sow came in with a saddle,
> The little pig rock'd the cradle,
> The dish jump'd a top of the table,
> To see the pot wash the ladle;
> The spit that stood behind the door
> Call'd the dishclout dirty whore;
> Ods-plut, says the gridiron,
>   Can't ye agree,
> I'm the head constable,
>   Bring 'em to me.

The notes (notes p. 8) reference a variant: 'The boom behind the butt/Call'd the dish-clout a nasty slut' (Halliwell 1844:162). Halliwell (103) also included a 'game' rhym that Lucy Rollin (1992:53) takes to be a reference to a prostitute:

> SEE, Saw, Margery Daw,
> Sold her bed and lay upon straw;
> Was not she a dirty slut,
> To sell her bed and lie in the dirt!

Roald Dahl calls his 'Cindy' the same thing. The prince of his 'Cinderella' beheads her sisters when they parade with Cinderella's slipper, not so much for their deception but because they are ugly. Cinderella hears the commotion and appears (now no longer decked in finery) at the scene of the crime. The Prince does not recognize her and reacts with violent language (1982:12), causing Cinderella to reconsider her pursuit of this brute when he orders 'this dirty slut' to be beheaded.

The adult presence in these works is nasty (Crago 2014:166). Often, adults in Roald Dahl's children's books are mean and selfish. Or conspicuously absent. In a 1980s interview with children's literature professor Mark West, he explained: 'Mark, the first thing you have to do when you're writing a kids' book is kill off the parents' (Thornton 2012; cf. Schneeberg 2016:115). One might speculate whether it is to the benefit of the child that the text not contain parental figures, or whether their absence makes it easier for *adults* to merge to the story and live a romanticized idea of innocence free of adult oppression.

Still, when Roald Dahl crosses the line of what is commonly considered child-appropriate language or content, children generally do seem to be his intended audience. In *Matilda*, children who cross Miss Trunchbull are punished by having to stand in the 'chokey,' a cupboard ten inches square, studded on the inside with nails and glass shards; the slightest movement by the child results in a cut or a puncture. Dahl restores here the violence that characterized (and was successively edited out of) the original Grimm's fairy tales. In the "happy ending" of the savage (there is really no other word for it) 'The Three Little Men in the Woods' ('Die drei Männlein im Walde'), the murderous stepmother and her selfish daughter die by being locked into a barrel that has long nails protruding into the inside and being rolled down the hill into a river. Author Adam Gidwitz shared in a PRI interview with Patrick Cox his experience of reading such a gory fairy tale ('Faithful Johannes' / 'Der treue Johannes,' Grimm) to second graders:

> Every kid looked traumatized—I think that *traumatized* is the word. So I dismissed the children; some of them were crying, I think one of the boys peed his pants, but a few of them came up to me afterwards. And they were shaking. But one of them pointed a finger in my face, and she said: 'That was good!' And I said, 'what?' She said: 'You should make that into a book.'

Possibly, a children's author may be aware that traumatic imagery can have something of a cathartic effect on children. What would compel such an author to provide it is beyond this author's capacity for empathy.

Author-adult collusion in children's literature can of course also be protective of the child's sensibilities. Theodor Geisel's children's books can deal with very adult problems, such as environmental devastation for the sake of profit (*The Lorax*). Geisel wrote some of his books under the impression of war and persecution. In *Yertle the Turtle* (1958), the child sees a story of a megalomaniac turtle bullying other turtles; the adult sees Adolf Hitler. The allusion was so obvious, in fact, that Geisel's final edit before the book went to print was to remove the mustache from Yertle (Morgan & Morgan 1996:319). In *Horton Hears a Who!* (1954), the fiercely loyal elephant talks to the Mayor of Who-ville—a city built on a single clover. The city is too small for the elephant to see and amounts to no more than a 'speck'—a word we also use to refer to a dot marking an entire city on a globe or on a map. The town and its kind-hearted guardian are separated by nasty animals, and the clover is carried away by a 'black-bottomed' eagle with the name 'Vlad Vlad-i-koff,' who eventually drops it into an entire field of clover from the air. When Horton finally locates the clover that has Who-ville on it, he hears the Mayor's account of the air drop:

> We've *really* had trouble! Much more than our share.
> When that black-bottomed birdie let go and we dropped,
> We landed so hard that our clocks have all stopped.
> Our tea-pots are broken. Our rocking-chairs smashed.
> And our bicycle tires all blew up when we crashed.

The illustration shows the tiny inhabitants of Who-ville surveying and repairing the damage. To the adult of 1954, when *Horton* was published, these five lines surely brought up freshly un-censored images in the wake of the famous 1952 exposé in *Life* magazine ("When Atom Bomb Struck: Uncensored")—a nuclear bomb dropped from a 'flying fortress,' charred tricycles, clocks and watches all stopped at 8:15, the moment of impact in Hiroshima. After the detonation of the first Russian nuclear bomb in 1949 and in the face of a rapidly escalating Cold War, those pictures, once withheld from the public, now served as a warning against a nuclear war (Moeller 2003:83)—hence the bird's Russian-sounding name.

Adults and authors can conceive of themselves as a team, caretakers joined in the welfare of the child. In his acceptance speech for the 2014 Geisel Award for his book *The Watermelon Seed*, author Gregg Pizzoli shared the story of six-year-old Hayley, on whose behalf he received the following email:

> Obviously typed up by a parent, but in Hayley's words. If you'll bear with me, I want to read this one email. It's short.
>
> *Dear Mr. Pizzoli,*
> The Watermelon Seed *is the funniest book I ever heard. It is the best.*
> *From Hayley*
> *Six years old*
>
> This email meant a lot to me. It struck a chord, partly because I think Hayley is funny. She borrowed some of my phrasing ("It is the best") but also, saying it's "the funniest book she ever HEARD"—ya know, cause she can't read. Her mom read it to her. I wrote back to Hayley, thanking her, and just joking around. Her mom wrote me back the next day and said that Hayley was thrilled to hear from me, and that at six, she was really struggling to learn to read. She had felt defeated and discouraged and ready to give up on books. She got *The Watermelon Seed* as a gift and read it with her mom ten times in one night.

Mo Willems builds this kind of cooperation with reading adults into the design of books such as *Don't Let the Pigeon Drive the Bus!* In exchange for 'an opportunity to be silly and have fun' (Willems 2015), the adult serves as the author's 'orchestra' (Cardi 2012) because Willems writes for 'illiterates' (young children):

> So what that means is I am dependent on my orchestra. And my orchestra can be a parent, it can be a teacher, it can be a librarian. But I have to make sure that my orchestra is engaged. That they are, you know, maybe being sillier than they normally are; that they are yelling and jumping around, so that that's what's going to make the book work better. It's very, very important. Also, because it's a time to be together. You know, I want parents to be engaged and I want them to laugh, because then it's cool. I think that sometimes parents forget that they are the coolest people in the world to kids. They're just awesome. So if they're enjoying reading books, suddenly the kid is going to say, wow, reading books is awesome.

The triad child/author/adult provides opportunities for inclusive and collusive cooperation, and these constellations are in great measure responsible for making children's literature a separate genre from adult literature. Like entrainment, cooperation merits future research in children's literature. It provides a framework within which to ascertain the significance of certain developments in children's literature. Among them, for example, is the 'groundbreaking decision' (Gubar 2009:7) for children characters to appear as narrators and protagonists in children's books. The ground being broken was inclusion.

Δ Adult/Author/Book

Adults have various incentives to cooperate in providing or restricting children's access to children's literature. They can mean to protect children from particular works they deem 'inappropriate,' or to protect them from the adult world altogether. They can also do the exact opposite: use children's books to ask for the child's collusion in excluding other adults (e.g. in using children's books as a vessel of propaganda and defamation).

Adults cooperate with each other to ensure that children's books benefit their target audience (and to intervene when books 'cross the line'). Censorship is a hot-button topic in the field of Children's Literature Studies. Adults who restrict children's access to certain books cooperate in order to exclude: They mean to cut off the *author's access to the child.* They understand themselves to be practicing benign intolerance for the sake of 'protecting innocent children and working for the benefit of society' (West 1996:507). Their efforts to exclude are often communal and also involve pressures by the editor on the author and additional adjustments if the book is to be marketed through schools (498).[3] One of the top concerns is age-appropriate language. 'Inappropriate language' has flagged (and kept out of school libraries) works like Roald Dahl's 1961 *James and the Giant Peach* (which includes the word *ass*), Mark Haddon's *The Curious Incident of the Dog in the Night-time* (2003), and pretty much anything written by Dav Pilkey (especially *Captain Underpants* 1997ff.). Next to (and including) sexual content, 'offensive' language triggers the most frequent challenges, brought especially by parents (American Library Association).

Jacqueline Rose's book *The Case of Peter Pan, or The Impossibility of Children's Fiction* includes an account of how adults cooperated to make James M. Barrie's creation into a vehicle of linguistic control for the 'benefit' of children. The character of Peter Pan first appears in a novel for adults (*The Little White Bird*, 1902) and was then written into a play (*Peter Pan, or The Boy Who Wouldn't Grow Up*, 1904) that was then recast as a book (*Peter and Wendy*, 1911). When *Peter Pan and Wendy* (1915) was subsequently adapted for use in public schools, English government and school officials edited its language. Textual devices that were deemed 'too literary' were removed, Latinate phrases and complex syntax altered. Middle-class children were still expected to read the original; the simplified school version reflected the adults' assessment of *lower-class* children's linguistic needs in the early 20th century. These classist adaptations of the language of *Peter Pan* are, for Rose, a prime example of how the teaching of language and literacy constitutes the 'machinery' of elitist repression (Rose 1996:118).

Based on that premise, Rose understands the shared narrative of adults-do-what-they-do-to-protect-the-innocence-of-children as a self-serving placebo. Innocence, upon closer analysis, is not really treated 'as a property of childhood but as a portion of adult desire' (Rose 1996:xii). Nostalgia for a sense of being 'unmonopolized' prior to being 'corrupted' may be 'the most fertile' sentiment for the adult (Breton 1924)[4], but writing children's books from that sentiment also makes adults accomplished manipulators of children. Today's books may no longer be known for heavy-handed didacticism, but the adult intentions are still there. They have merely been 'rendered invisible' (Rose 1996:60). Intrinsic motivation engendered by playful reading has replaced extrinsic motivation exacted through moralizing and lecturing. Rose sees children's literature entrenched in adult culture, camouflaged and licensed as a separate genre only by that romantic/nostalgic notion of children's innocence. She includes an example that she found particularly eye opening, having attended a performance of Bryony Lavery's *Peter Pan* by Dramatrix at London's Drill Hall Theatre in 1991 (cf. Stanton & Banham 1996:213). The performance was part of a series of 'lesbian theatre' pieces, which puts Peter's resistance to Wendy's advances in an entirely adult context. The author adds: 'Why not take that life-and-death moment of audience participation—'clap your hands if you believe in fairies'—at its word? (Once you see it performed like this it will never be the same again)' (Rose 1996:xiii).

It is most certainly the case that adults bring their own readings to the author's creation; in fact, as pointed out above, authors count on it and plan for a dual audience. However, the history that an adult brings to a book may affect the reading experience differently from what was intended by the author. At times, an adult's reaction to a book they enjoyed as a child may be diminished. Bruce Handy wondered what ever he saw in Madeleine L'Engle's *A Wrinkle in Time* (1962) as a child—as an adult, the book strikes him as 'Ayn Rand for kids' (2017:xvii). At other times, the adult may no longer affiliate with the author's culture. Linguist Arnold Zwicky's blog entry for 25 May 2010 saw 'a possible gay subtext in what is usually presented as a children's song,' 'Dancing with Bears.' In the song, Uncle Walter sneaks out at night and returns covered with hair and with tears in his clothes, and his family suspects he is out dancing with bears. Entreaties to be good do nothing to dissuade him, and the bears finally come to abduct Uncle Walter altogether. Zwicky's take:

> What attracts children to the song? Assuming that the child identifies with Uncle Walter: the pleasures of transgression, of disobedience; having secrets from the family (despite the give-away hair on Walter's clothes); negotiating dangers (going Where the Wild Things Are), as evidenced by the tears in Walter's clothes, but still Walter comes home safely after his night-time adventures; the attractive but also frightening prospect that Walter will some day leave home and live on his own, with his new, chosen, family. Probably more—this is just off the top of my head.

> Gay men and lesbians hearing the song hear the same things, but applied now to their own situation: the secret life, especially at night, hidden from their families of birth, moving them away from these families to potential new ones, but with the dangers of walking on the wild side. (And then there's the "funny uncle" theme.)

Alternate adult readings, to be sure, are insufficient evidence for an 'impossibility' (Rose) of children's literature. Zwicky makes allowance for a *dual* audience (even if unintended), assigning a legitimate space to each. Even Rose herself acknowledges a state prior to appropriation when she says that hearing the worlds 'clap your hands if you believe in fairies' in a lesbian production causes them never to be 'the same' again. There is still something not to be 'the same' as: the literary host body on which the parasitic performance fed. An adult appropriation that explicitly excludes children, such as Bill Osco's movie *Alice in Wonderland* (both adult and explicit), exists because it cashes in on Alice's iconic name recognition, not because pay-per-view is out to kill paper view (or could if it wanted to). Similarly, an adult parody of a children's book, such as Nathan J. Robinson's *Don't Let The Pigeon Question The Rules!* (2014) in response to Mo Willem's 'totalitarian classic' (back cover) *Don't Let the Pigeon Drive the Bus!*, only affirms the genre in its appropriation.

Adults may assert and insert their adultness in(to) children's literature, but they also rely on networks of trust between child, adult, and author. A current example of such cooperative networking is the booming Chinese children's book market. Middle-class parents in China, increasingly affluent and well educated, demand high-quality children's literature in order to enable their children to grow up as citizens of the world. Literary agent Andrew Nurnberg described what drives this fast-growing market after a visit to the 2016 China Shanghai International Children's Book Fair (Tan 2016):

> Chinese parents want to provide their children with the very best, and this includes buying the best books they can possibly get. Increasingly, they want to offer to their kids a global perspective with works by overseas authors and from different cultures. Diversity is the key word.

To help them decide what constitutes trusted quality in children's books, parents and publishers turn to the judgment of other adults, favoring authors who received awards—Caldecott, Hans Christian Andersen, Bologna Ragazzi (ibid.).

Finally, there are instances where the implied adult in children's literature colludes with the child in excluding other adults: Children's books as vehicles of propaganda. Julius Streicher, editor of the propaganda magazine *Der Stürmer* and executed in 1946 on the verdict that his incitements constituted a crime against humanity, published a children's book by Ernst Hiemer entitled *Der Giftpilz* (1938), 'The Poisonous Mushroom.' The book opens with a call for vigilance: 'Just as poisonous mushrooms are sometimes difficult to tell apart from the good ones, so it is often very difficult to recognize the Jews for the crooks and criminals they are.'[5] The book, which was used in schoolrooms, asks children to accept as natural the dehumanization of Jewish adults by other adults. An existing network of trust was here infiltrated and repurposed. One author, Philipp Bouhler, who published a 'reader for German youth' entitled *Kampf um Deutschland* ('Battle for Germany,' 1938) was later empowered, via a letter signed by Adolf Hitler (dated 1 September 1939), to authorize doctors in German hospitals to euthanize 'incurable' patients (Feldman 2018). It would be an interesting project to study how children's literature rehabilitated itself as a trustworthy genre in post-War West Germany, both during and after 'de-nazification.'

Authors can of course also write children's books to offer adults pointed alternatives to children's books they consider propagandistic. A picture book about the popular bunny of Vice President Mike Pence, *Marlon Bundo's Day in the Life of the Vice President* (Charlotte Pence, 2018) was co-opted by *A Day in the Life of Marlon Bundo* (Jill Twiss, 2018). Promoted on television by TV celebrity John Oliver, the book promotes the acceptance of LGBTQ values instead: Marlon the BOTUS meets handsome Wesley, and they fall in love.

Children Initiated Into the Community of Art

Part I of the book argued that children's books provide linguistic input *beyond* child-directed talk and even beyond adult-adult conversational English in order to lead them *toward* adult language. And here we are. A child engages with a children's book narrative as an individual, and the book is situated in adult cultural space. There are other books like it, sequels and prequels by the same author; they embody a community's taste or offend it, promote or flout values. Books even for very young children, as we saw in Chapter 2, can contain decidedly grown-up words. A child's storytelling, as seen above, will gradually emulate adult narrative grammar. When children's book authors play with sounds, words, and morphology, they do not do so childishly, they do it expertly. Book by book, children who co-create narratives grow themselves into a cultural landscape of distributed cognition (Brown et al. 1989; Salomon 1993). They grow into art.

Something changes for children once they 'get' the macrolinguistic dimensions of a text—its frame, its gesture, its genre: They can appreciate its craft (the how), not just its make-believe (the what). Something also changes in the attitude of the writer toward such a child: The child is treated as an equal (Kümmerling-Meibauer 2015:246). Author and child can, for instance, conspiratorially poke fun at the adult world. The text can still be playful, like the description of a particle detector in Tom Weller's *Science Made Stupid* (1985:26):

> At the target, the beam collides with an atom, causing its constituent particles to fly apart. The particles themselves are invisible; but their "tracks" can be detected using devices such as the cloud chamber, the bubble chamber, or the **cheese chamber**.
>
> The cheese chamber holds a solution of milk curd under precisely controlled pre-cheese conditions. The particle passing through the solution causes

> it to coagulate, leaving a track of cheese. The types of particles released can be determined from the types of cheese produced.

Besides being playful (and by virtue of it), the text is also cooperative, based on mutual trust. The child is let in on a secret: The adult world, too, can be a playground. Weller entrusts the child with sufficient sophistication to tell the difference between science (detecting particles in a cloud chamber) and silliness (particles deciding whether to brie or not to brie). The child trusts the author not to have any sinister intentions, i.e. the playfulness is not a facade for a propagandistic agenda. In adult play space, Grendel's devastation of Hrothgar's mead hall and his dispatch by Beowulf is replayed as a male mountain troll's trashing the girls' bathroom at Hogwarts with Harry Potter's magic wand stuck up his nose (J. K. Rowling, *Harry Potter and the Philosopher's Stone*), and the London Millennium Bridge (q.v. p. 166) is brought down not by synchronized steps, but by the wake turbulence of death eaters (*Harry Potter and the Half-blood Prince*).

Minds merge. Authors write (and read) to her or his 'inner child,' as Jonathan London readily admits (personal communication, 21 July 2017):

> As to reading my stories to kids before publishing (as did Margaret Wise Brown), I actually read aloud, over and over, to my inner kid, who is always near by, right near the surface—in fact, much of the time, I *am* a kid! flop flop bop!

The child, in turn, gets to play in adult space, to think (by reading) with someone else's head (Schopenhauer 1874:529), not realizing (Jacqueline Rose) or seeing right through (Jean-Jacques Rousseau) the adult agenda. The child rises to art.

Children's literature is art made by adults. This is visually apparent in the drawings, for example, of Ed Young's *Moon Mother* (1993, see p. 145), which has no trace of 'infantile esthetics' (Weld 2014, quoted in Reynolds 2015:97) but presents as timeless and age-less. Publishers like Quist produced children's books 'acclaimed for their elegant design and exceptional craftsmanship' (Kümmerling-Meibauer 2015:245). Illustrious painters have illustrated children's books: Marc Chagall (Der Nister, *A Mayse mit a Hon. Dos Tsigele*, 1917), Salvador Dalí (*Alice's Adventures in Wonderland*, 1969), David Hockney (*Six Fairy Tales from the Brothers Grimm*, 1970), and Andy Warhol (*The Little Red Hen*, 1958), to name just a few. The idea of enculturating children to/with art has attracted mainstream authors (cf. Table 8.3). Margaret Wise Brown recognized the artistic scope of children's literature when she was a children's books editor. She suggested inviting authors whose work she understood as playfully artistic and vivid to write a children's book to publish with William R. Scott: Ronald Firbank, Virginia Woolf, Gertrude Stein. Gertrude Stein, to the amazement of the publisher, accepted, and eventually did submit a manuscript, *The World is Round* (1939), which Margaret Wise Brown immediately tested on the children of the Bank Street nursery students (Marcus 1992:99–101). Given Lucy Sprague Mitchell's insistence that children be exposed only to *real*-world experiences, it was an utterly subversive thing

Table 8.3 Children's Books Written By Authors of Adult Literature

Angelou, Maya. 1977. *Life Doesn't Frighten Me*, illustrated by Jean-Michel Basquiat.
Attwood, Margaret. 1978. *Up in the Tree.*
Baldwin, James, and Yoran Cazac. 1976. *Little Man, Little Man.*
Bontemps, Arna, and Langston Hughes. 1932. *Popo and Fifina: Children of Haiti*, illustrated by Robert Bruce.
cummings, e. e. 1950. *Fairy Tales*, illustrated by Meilo So.
Eco, Umberto. 1989. *The Bomb and the General*, illustrated by Eugenio Carmi.
—. 1989. *The Three Astronauts*, illustrated by Eugenio Carmi.
—. 1992. *The Gnomes of Gnu*, illustrated by Eugenio Carmi.
Eliot, T[homas] S[tearns]. 1939. *Old Possum's Book of Practical Cats.*
—. [rpt. 2016] *Mr. Mistoffelees: The Conjuring Cat*, illustrated by Arthur Robins.
—. [rpt. 1991]. *Mr. Mistoffelees With Mungojerrie and Rumpelteazer*, illustrated by Errol Le Cain.
—. [rpt. 2016]. *Macavity: The Mystery Cat*, illustrated by Arthur Robins.
—. [rpt. 2016]. *Skimbleshanks: The Railway Cat*, illustrated by Arthur Robins.
Faulkner, William. 1927. *The Wishing Tree*, illustrated by Don Bolognese.
Fleming, Ian. 1964. *Chitty Chitty Bang Bang.*
Highsmith, Patricia, and Doris Sanders. 1958. *Miranda the Panda is on the Veranda*, illustrated by Patricia Highsmith.
Hughes, Langston. 1952. *The First Book of Negroes*, illustrated by Ursula Koering.
—. 1954. *The First Book of Rhythms*, illustrated by Robin King.
—. 1955. *The First Book of Jazz*, illustrated by Cliff Roberts.
—. 1956. *The First Book of the West Indies.*
—. 1960. *The First Book of Africa.*
Huxley, Aldous. 1967. *The Crows of Pear Blossom*, illustrated by Barbara Cooney.
Joyce, James. 1936. *The Cats of Copenhagen*, illustrated by Casey Sorrow.
—. 1936. *The Cat and the Devil*, illustrated by Roger Blachon.
Koontz, Dean. *Oddkins: A Fable for All Ages*, illustrated by Phil Parks.
Morrison, Toni. 1980. *The Big Box.*
—. 2002. *The Book of Mean People*, illustrated by Pascal Lemaître.
—, and Slade Morrison. 2003. *Who's Got Game: The Ant or the Grasshopper?*, illustrated by Pascal Lemaître.
—. 2003. *Who's Got Game: The Lion or the Mouse?*, illustrated by Pascal Lemaître.
—. 2004. *Who's Got Game: Poppy or Snake?*, illustrated by Pascal Lemaître.
—. 2004. *Who's Got Game: The Tortoise or the Hare?*, illustrated by Joe Cepeda.
Oates, Joyce Carol. 2002. *Big Mouth & Ugly Girl.*
—. 2003. *Freaky Green Eyes.*
—. 2003. *Small Avalanches and Other Stories.*
Plath, Sylvia. 1976. *The Bed Book*, illustrated by Emily Arnold McCully.
—. [rpt. 2014]. *The It-does-not-matter Suit and other Stories*, illustrated by David Roberts.
Rushdie, Salmon. 1990. *Haroun and the Sea of Stories.*
Sand, George. 2014. *What Flowers Say: And Other Stories*, illustrated by Mollie Crabapple.
Sandburg, Carl. 1922. *Rootabaga Stories*, illustrated by Miska Pertersham and Maud Fuller Petersham.
Shelly, Mary. 1820. *Maurice, or the Fisher's Cot.*
Sinclair, Upton. 1936. *The Gnomobile: A Gnice Gnew Gnarrative with Gnonsense, but Gnothing Gnaughty*, illustrated by John O'Hara Cosgrave II.
Stein, Gertrude. 1939. *The World is Round*, illustrated by Clement Hurd.
—. 1940. *To Do: A Book of Alphabets and Birthdays*, illustrated by Giselle Potter.

(*Continued*)

Table 8.3 (Continued)

Stevenson, Robert Louis. 1895. *A Child's Garden of Verses*, illustrated by Charles Robinson.
Thomas, Dylan. 1978. *A Child's Christmas in Wales*, illustrated by Edward Ardizzone.
Thurber, James. 1943. *Many Moons/The Princess Who Wanted the Moon.*
—. 1944. *The Great Quillow.*
—. 1945. *The White Deer.*
—. 1950. *The Thirteen Clocks*, illustrated by Marc Simont.
—. 1957. *The Wonderful O*, illustrated by Marc Simont.
Tolkien, J.R.R. (edited by Baillie Tolkien). 1976. *The Father Christmas Letters.*
Updike, John. 1965. *A Child's Calendar*, illustrated by Nancy Eckholm Burkett.
—. 1995. *A Helpful Alphabet of Friendly Objects.*
Vonnegut, Kurt. *Sun Moon Star*, illustrated by Ivan Chermayeff.
Welty, Eudora. 1964. *The Shoe Bird*, illustrated by Beth Krush.
Wilde, Oscar. 1888. *The Happy Prince and Other Tales*, illustrated by Laura Stutzman.
Woolf, Virginia. 1923. *The Widow and the Parrot*, illustrated by Julian Bell.

for her to do right under Sprague Mitchell's nose at Bank Street, of all places. But it shows that Margaret Wise Brown had learned something she was not supposed to at that nursery.

Margaret Wise Brown had witnessed children's absorbing fascination with the sounds and rhythms of adult language. She had experienced American three-year-olds loving every syllable even of a book read to them in French (p. 41). She understood the thrill of peeking into the trove of adult vocabulary, with mysterious words like *sanctimonious, ruminating*, and *rapscallion* (p. 68). And now here was Gertrude Stein's book with blue print on pink pages and Clement Hurd's drawings that were inspired by French modernism (Steiner 2015:202). Its rhythms were as accessible as they were adult (Stein 1939:6):

> Just then Willie began to sing
> *Drowning*
> *Forgetting*
> *Remembering*
> *I am thinking*
> And the chuette owl interrupted him.
> *Is it*
> *His it*
> *Any eye of any owl is round.*

Can a young child appreciate the artistry? Absolutely. I conclude with a poem in the style of Margaret Wise Brown dictated by Mollie, two years old (Sprague Mitchell 1937:3; also quoted in Bliven Jr. 1946:61):

> Remember the goldfish?
>   Remember?
> Remember the goldfish?

Goes round and round!
  Umn!
Swims?
  Umn!
Sleeps!
  Umn!

Remember the goldfish?
  Has no hands.
  No.
  Has no feet.
  No.

Remember the goldfish?
  Has no hands!
Remember the goldfish?
  Has no hands.

Notes

1. The Origin of White Folks

ANNIE VIRGINIA CULBERTSON

DE white folks nee-nter putt on airs
About them wash'out faces,
De culled folks wuz made de fust,
De oldes' uv de races.
Dey's kneaded out mud an' truck,
An' den stood up in places
Along the fence to bake 'em dry,
An' dat's de on'liest reason why
Dey's got dem sunburnt faces.

Dey had a scumpshous time ontwel
Olc Nick got on deir traces,
An' den dey et dat apple up,
An' fell in deep disgraces;
An' when dey hearn deir names called out,
Dey run fer hidin' places,
An' turnt so pale dey stayed dat way,
An' dat's the reason why, folks say,
Dey's go dem wash'ed out faces.
The Brownies' Book 1.1 (1920:7)

2. The implication is that the rewards of cooperation (between reading adult and child) outweigh the 'harm done' to the book character. The same eagerness to cooperate has been observed in a reanalysis of Stanley Milgram's 1963 'obedience' experiments, in which participants were made to believe they were administering increasingly potent (and eventually lethal) electric shocks to a 'learner' to improve his memory performance. A telling note written by Milgram, quoted in Haslam et al. (2014:57), reads: 'Cooperation implies a certain willingness to perform the action or help out, a certain internal desire to assist, while obedience implies an action that is totally in response to a command, with no motivational support from inner sources (Milgram, Box 46, Yale archive).'

3. Even so, a dissertation at Liberty University found Newbery Award winning books wanting in biblical values (Fleming 2011:iii, 4–9, 46, 110).
4. From André Breton's first *Surrealist Manifesto* (1924:n.p.): 'Des souvenirs d'enfance et de quelques autres se dégage un sentiment d'inaccaparé et par la suite de dévoyé, que je tiens pour le plus fécond qui existe'—'Memories of childhood (and a few others) bring forth a feeling of being unmonopolized and subsequently perverted, which I think is the most fertile in existence' (translation mine).
5. 'Wie die Giftpilze oft schwer von den guten Pilzen zu unterscheiden sind, so ist es oft sehr schwer, die Juden als Gauner und Verbrecher zu erkennen . . .' (translation mine). Given the existence of such work, it is hard to fathom why Roald Dahl thought it funny to include a similar line in *The Witches* about how hard it is to tell whether a woman is a witch, making it impossible to just line them up and feed them into the meat-grinder.

References

Alexander, Christine. 1987. *An edition of the early writings of Charlotte Brontë*, vol. 1. Oxford: Basil Blackwell.

American Library Association. n.d. Number of challenges by reasons, initiator, & institution, 2000–09. Online: www.ala.org/advocacy/bbooks/frequentlychallengedbooks/statistics/2000-09#reasons2000.

Bliven, Bruce, Jr. 1946. Child's best seller. *LIFE* 21(23) (2 December).59–66.

Breton, André. 1924. Manifeste du surréalisme. Online: inventin.lautre.net/livres/Manifeste-du-surrealisme-1924.pdf.

Brown, John Seely; Allan Collins; and Paul Duguid. 1989. Situated cognition and the culture of learning. *Educational Researcher* 18(1) (January–February).32–42.

Brown, Roger. 1973. *A first language: The early stages*. Cambridge, MA: Harvard University Press.

Bruner, Jerome S. 1983. *Child's talk: Learning to use language*. New York: W.W. Norton.

Cardi, Annie. 2012. Doing the voices: Reader as orchestra, 27 April. Online: Anniecardi.com/2012/04/27/doing-the-voices-as-orchestra/.

Crago, Hugh. 2014. *Entranced by story: Brain, tale and teller, from infancy to old age*. New York: Routledge.

Ely, Richard. 2005. Language and literacy in the school years. *The development of language*, ed. by Jean Berko Gleason, 6th ed., 395–443. Boston: Pearson.

Feldman, Daniel. 2018. The science of persecution: Racial theories and children's Holocaust literature, at *Growing Scientists!: Children's literature and the sciences*, symposium at the University of Antwerp, Belgium, 7 March.

Fleming, Kimberly. 2011. *An examination of Newberry medal books from the 1920's through the 2000's: Biblical perspective*. Liberty University doctoral dissertation, School of Education.

Gidwitz, Adam. 2014. We love fairy tales—Maybe we'd love them more if they were translated right. 'The World in Words.' *PRI,* 15 September. Online: www.pri.org/stories/2014-09-15/we-love-fairy-tales-and-we-might-love-them-even-more-if-theyd-been-accurately.

Goffman, Erving. 1974. *Frame analysis: An essay on the organization of experience*. Boston: Northeastern University Press.

Gubar, Marah. 2009. *Artful Dodgers: Reconceiving the Golden Age of children's literature*. Oxford, New York: Oxford University Press.

Halliwell, James Orchard. 1844. *The nursery rhymes of England, collected chiefly from oral tradition*, 4th ed. London: John Russell Smith.

Handy, Bruce. 2017. *Wild things: The joy of reading children's literature as an adult*. New York: Simon & Schuster.

Haslam, S. Alexander; Stephen D. Reicher; Kathryn Millard; and Rachel McDonald. 2014. 'Happy to have been of service': The Yale archive as a window into the engaged followership of participants in Milgram's 'obedience' experiments. *The British Journal of Social Psychology* 54.55–83.

Hinds, John. 1987. Reader vs. writer responsibility: A new typology. *Writing across languages: Analysis of L2 text*, ed. by Ulla Connor and Robert B. Kaplan, 141–52. Reading, A: Addison-Wesley.

Kümmerling-Meibauer, Bettina. 2015. Just what is it that makes Pop Art picturebooks so different, so appealing? *Children's literature and the Avant-Garde*, ed. by Elina Drucker and Bettina Kümmerling-Meibauer, 241–65. Amsterdam, Philadelphia: John Benjamins.

Leisi, Ernst. 1978. *Paar und Sprache: Linguistische Aspekte der Zweierbeziehung*. Uni-Taschenbücher 824. Heidelberg: Quelle & Meyer.

Marcus, Leonard S. 1992 *Margaret Wise Brown: Awakened by the moon*. New York: Quill, William Morrow.

Margalit, Ruth. 2014. The giving tree at fifty: Sadder than I remembered. 'Page-turner', 5 November. *The New Yorker*. Online: www.newyorker.com/books/page-turner/giving-tree-50-sadder-remembered.

Moeller, Susan D. 2003. Pictures of the enemy: Fifty years of images of Japan in the American Press, 1941–1992. *The American experience in World War II*, vol. 11: "Remembering and Representing the Second World War," ed. by Walter L. Hixson, 79–92. New York, London: Routledge.

Morgan, Judith, and Neil Morgan. 1996. *Dr. Seuss & Mr. Geisel: A biography*. New York: Da Capo Press, Perseus.

Nel, Philip. 2015. Surrealism for children: Paradoxes and possibilities. *Children's literature and the Avant-Garde*, ed. by Elina Drucker and Bettina Kümmerling-Meibauer, 268–83. Amsterdam, Philadelphia: John Benjamins.

Osco, Bill [William]. 1976. *Alice in Wonderland: An X-rated musical fantasy*. Essex Pictures Company, Cruiser Productions. Online: www.imdb.com/title/tt0074113/.

Owens, Robert E., Jr. 2008. *Language development: An introduction*, 7th ed. Boston: Pearson.

Prideaux, W[illiam] F[rancis]. 1904. *Mother Goose's melody: A facsimile reproduction of the earliest known edition*. London: A. H. Bullen.

Reynolds, Kimberley. 2015. The forgotten history of avant-garde publishing for children in early twentieth-century Britain. *Children's literature and the Avant-Garde*, ed. by Elina Drucker and Bettina Kümmerling-Meibauer, 89–109. Amsterdam, Philadelphia: John Benjamins.

Robinson, Nathan J. 2014. *Don't let the pigeon question the rules: A parody*. New Haven, CT: Demilune Press.

Rollin, Lucy. 1992. *Cradle and all: A cultural and psychoanalytic reading of nursery rhymes*. Jackson, MS, London: University Press of Mississippi.

Rose, Jacqueline. 1996. *The case of Peter Pan, or the impossibility of children's fiction*. Philadelphia: University of Pennsylvania Press.

Salomon, Gavriel. 1993. No distribution without individuals' cognition: A dynamic interactional view. *Distributed cognitions: Psychological and educational considerations*, ed. by Gavriel Salomon, 111–14, 128–35. Cambridge: Cambridge University Press.

Schneeberg, Ulrike. 2016. *Making boys and girls in picturebooks with monsters*. Hamburg: Marta Press.

Schopenhauer, Arthur. 1874. *Parerga und Paralipomena II*. Leipzig: Brockhaus. Online: ia802606.us.archive.org/15/items/parergaundparal01fraugoog/parergaundparal01fraugoog.pdf

Snively, Helen. 1999. *Coming to terms with cultural differences: Chinese graduate students writing academic English*. Harvard Graduate School of Education: Doctoral dissertation.

Stanton, Sarah, and Martin Banham. 1996. *Cambridge paperback guide to theatre*. Cambridge: Cambridge University Press.

Steiner, Evgeny. 2015. Mirror images: On Soviet-Western reflections in children's books of the 1920s and 1930s. *Children's literature and the Avant-Garde,* ed. by Elina Druker and Bettina Kümmerling-Meibauer, 189–213. Amsterdam, Philadelphia: John Benjamins.

Stevenson, Robert Louis. 1895. Whole duty of children. *A child's garden of verses*, n.p.

Street, James A., and Ewa Dąbrowska. 2010. More individual differences in language attainment: How much do adult native speakers of English know about passives and quantifiers? *Lingua* 120.2080–94.

Tan, Teri. 2016. The booming rights scene for children's books in China. *Publishers Weekly*, 29 November. Online: www.publishersweekly.com/pw/by-topic/childrens/childrens-industry-news/article/72153-the-booming-rights-scene-for-children-s-books-in-china.html.

Taylor, Charles. 1979. *Sources of the self.* Cambridge: Cambridge University Press.

Thiede, Ralf. 2007. MERGE and information management. *Human Sciences* 55.57–70. Online: www.sid.ir/fa/VEWSSID/J_pdf/64413865510.pdf.

Thornton, Lisa. 2012. Parents a liability? In children's books, yes. *The Charlotte Observer*, 19 February. Online: www.charlotteobserver.com/news/local/community/university-city/article9077114.html.

Weld, Sara Pankenier. 2014. *Voiceless vanguard: The infantilist aesthetic of the Russian Avant-garde*. Evanston IL: Northwestern University Press.

West, Mark I. 1996. Censorship. *International companion encyclopedia of children's literature*, ed. by Peter Hunt, 498–507. London, New York: Routledge.

When atom bomb struck: Uncensored. 1952. *Life* 33(13) (29 September).19–25. Online: books.google.com/books?id=VVYEAAAAMBAJ&pg=PA19false.

Willems, Mo. 2015. I want my books to be played. *Transcript of 'Ask Me Another'*, 12 February. NPR. Online: www.npr.org/2015/02/12/385546965/mo-willems-i-want-my-books-to-be-played.

Wolf, Maryanne, with Stephanie Gottwald. 2016. *Tales of literacy for the 21st century*. Oxford: Oxford University Press.

Zauche, Lauren Head; Ashley E. Darcy Mahoney; Taylor A. Thul; Michael S. Zauche; Arianne B. Weldon; and Jennifer L. Stapel-Wax. 2017. The power of language nutrition for children's brain development, health, and future academic achievement. *Journal of Pediatric Health Care* 31(4) (July/August).493–503.

Zhang, Tao. 2016. *Vom Premake zum Remake: Gender-Diskurse und intermediale Bezüge in den deutschen Verfilmungen der Kinderromane Erich Kästners*. Heidelberg: Universitätsverlag Winter.

Zwicky, Arnold. 2010. Waltzing with bears. *Arnold Zwicky's Blog: A Blog Mostly About Language*, 25 May. Online: arnoldzwicky.org/2010/05/25/waltzing-with-bears/#more-2378.

Conclusion

Giving Children an Advantage Through Interactive Book Reading

We have learned not to underestimate babies. Their mental accomplishments may be less obvious than their first steps, but they are just as impressive. A two-month-old baby can already detect pattern deviations in 'cats jump wood benches' vs. 'cats would jump benches,' even when the sentences are presented two minutes apart (Mandel, Kemler Nelson, & Jusczyck 1996). A six-month-old's eyes already look at the animal named and revealed when his mother reads Martin and Carle's *Brown Bear, Brown Bear, What Do You See?* (Bergelson & Aslin 2017). Attention to the sounds, rhythms, patterns, and rules of language is as much in our genetic makeup as imprinting and greeting are part of the gosling's. From birth, a kitten's visual cortex awaits specific input from the eyes: vertical lines, horizontal lines, angles. From birth, a baby's brain surely awaits specific input from caregivers: speech sounds, word categories, events, qualities, states, actions, relations, schemas, scripts, and stories. We know what happens if the kitten is deprived of visual input. What happens if a baby grows up linguistically impoverished?

A child could grow up *around* language and still be linguistically starved: Input must come through meaningful interaction (Brice Heath 1983). Post-Gutenberg, that includes shared book reading. Technological societies emerged when humans left the mountains to build their own—monumental sites such as Göbekli Tepe in Turkey that required logistically organized division of labor and agriculture (and beer). Within those 14,000 years of metropolitan life, did humans adapt for wheat, dairy, olive oil, alcohol, and literacy? Is the Matthew Effect for literacy the medical presentation of a linguistically starved brain? If so, then linguistic input for infants and children amounts to 'language nutrition' (Zauche et al. 2017), and many children can be diagnosed as linguistically malnourished.

As the size of the neocortex increased in human evolution, so did our ability to live in larger groups and participate in their distributed cognition (Dunbar 1992). Children's socialization follows the same trajectory. Thinking of language as brain food now, we can expect linguistic nourishment and socialization to be mutually reinforcing. As caregivers provide linguistic input both in sufficient quantity and quality, the child's social capacity expands—providing more and (and more diverse) linguistic input in return. Linguistic malnutrition should be equally reinforcing: Minimal linguistic input can be expected to retard socialization, leading to additional deficits in linguistic input from beyond the family. As Shirley Brice

Heath's study documented, children who grew up in such a language desert are less able to author or interrogate narratives: In school, they continue to be *around* language with minimal skills to engage, to participate, and to assimilate.

If children are to benefit from linguistic cooperation, they must grow up with linguistic cooperation. Modern children's books are safe zones in which children can explore and rise to the language and cognition of adults on their own time and on their own terms. No longer the place for lecture and admonition, children's books are the place of guided play—interactive 'organized language stimulation' (Ervin-Tripp 1991:85) with 'arranged input' (Bruner 1983:39–42, cf. p. 183). Playful interaction both adds the needed quantity of verbal engagement and constitutes 'quality time.' It has two anticipated outcomes:

1. In the moment, interactive reading supports and enhances bonding between adult and child through entrainment and joint attention, and
2. for the future, it promises dividends in cognitive development, early literacy, and social development.

Both outcomes are realistic.

Children's books offer linguistic input beyond what is ordinarily offered by adults. For the youngest, noisy books provide offbeat sounds and funny words, outliers that infants and babies find funny and enjoyable. Those exceptions and downright violations confirm the rules—important as the infant progresses from stochastic sampling and pattern extracting ('baby taking statistics') to imposing perceptive control ('apperception'). The medium of the book is a crucial part of the message: Only language presented in *interaction* (here: joint book reading) is processed linguistically by infants and babies and contributes to language development. Educated parents appear to have come to appreciate the central role of linguistic interaction and are adding quality time. The steadily increasing demand and supply of high-quality children's books indicates how much parents rely on children's books to ensure that their children will not languish in the '30-million-word gap.'

Playful linguistic outliers as well as clever violations of phonotactic, morphological, lexico-semantic, and syntactic rules trigger the child's exploration instincts. However, without negotiated joint attention with an adult a child cannot identify her 'zone of proximal development.' Inferential talk during joint book reading focuses anticipation and suspense, narrative logic and event modeling (plots, inventories), and the adult's performance of the book creates entrainment. By performing and commenting, the adult thus stimulates the child's cognitive arousal both in actively experiencing and in interrogating (cognitive appraisal and control).

The subject matter of children's books alone necessitates a vocabulary that is different from everyday shop talk, but authors also make it a point to include 'juicy words.' The additional vocabulary populates archetypal lexical fields, firming up their structural support. New words from children's books become the glial cells, so to speak, in the child's semantic networks.

Children's books establish the association between spoken and written word like no other medium. They use icons for words, shape words into icons, or combine the two in rebus constructions. Illustrations make words visible. Book characters can make reference to being in a book, and the book itself can become a book character: Written and spoken wor(l)d begin to occupy the same space for the child, and cooperation extends into the book and through the book to the author. As cooperation extends from dyad to triad, distributed cognition adds efficacy to various adult agendas for the child, such as:

- preserving heritage cultures and languages;
- adding to the child's expertise in syntactic information management with templates that distribute given and new information in anticipation of the audience's needs;
- empowering the child's cognitive self-control through inner narrative (both autobiographical and for validation);
- promoting the child's skills in storytelling—completing a story, balancing the story's requirements for plot, suspense, and coherence in alignment with the imputed needs of the audience;
- optimizing the child's interfacing of language, logic, predetermination, and event modeling;
- leading the child to early literacy and experiencing reading as a reward in itself; and
- socializing the child into adult distributed cognition and esthetic culture.

The book has become part of the child's neural, intellectual, individual, and social growth. Like food and water, it has become a sustenance, hence a human right.

But not so fast. Cooperation is not always inclusive.

Food and water can be used for cultivation, and they can just as easily be withheld or provided in inferior quality (or even contaminated). Rivers can be (and are being) diverted, lead-contaminated water can be knowingly piped to households, humanitarian aid can be intercepted, and plant seeds can be genetically modified to prevent future reproduction even in neighboring fields. Underprivileged children and children living in poverty are not the recipients of care packages that contain books, and even if they were they may not necessarily have an adult to perform and interrogate them for entrainment and inspiration. Just like there are 'food deserts'—a concept more aptly captured by Karen Washington's term 'food apartheid' (Brones 2018)—where junk food covers the spectrum of options and leads to obesity, so there are 'brain food deserts' where selections are on the shelves of department and drug stores and lead to illiteracy (the inability to read) and aliteracy (the lack of desire to read). Obesity, like starvation, impairs physical health; not-reading impairs citizenship, as the Librarian of Congress made explicit in 1984, echoing Nicolas Rubakin (p. 171):

> We must face and defeat the twin menaces of illiteracy and aliteracy—the inability to read and lack of the will to read—if our citizens are to remain free and qualified to govern themselves.
>
> (Boorstin 1984:18)

Children's books have the potential to empower, and they equally have the potential to be a gatekeeper separating those who have in abundance and to whom will be given from those who have little and from whom will be taken away.

Why Children's Literature? An Answer (Finally) to Isaac Bashevis Singer

In his December 10, 1978 Nobel Banquet speech, Isaac Bashevis Singer famously made ten observations about children's literary needs and expectations. As frequently cited and endorsed as they are even by famous writers such as Astrid Lindgren (2017), there is much to correct and qualify about them from the perspective of this book. As a way of taking stock, I repeat his ten claims here with a device that has of late sustained public discourse, a 'fact checker':

- *Children read books, not reviews. They don't give a hoot about critics.* **True, but irrelevant**. Their books and access to them are tightly controlled by adults (p. 200) who read, at the very least, the endorsements on the flap and pay attention to award medals embossed on the cover.
- *Children don't read to find their identity.* **False**. Children try out identities as they merge to a story's protagonist. Books are a socialization tool (Chapter 8) and offer role models with whom the young readers identify. They also validate a child's inner narrative of self, especially important when their story is not mainstream (e.g. children of immigrants, with same-gender parents, from ethnic or religious minorities).
- *They don't read to free themselves of guilt, to quench their thirst for rebellion, or to get rid of alienation.* **Increasingly false with age**. Those can be the very objectives of bibliotherapy for children, and there are books that specifically address guilt (John Grandits, *Technically, It's not My Fault*), rebellion (Pippi Longstocking was called a 'revolutionary in the nursery'), and overcoming alienation (*Stellaluna*).
- *They have no use for psychology.* **Equivocation**. They have limited use for psychological *terminology*. However, children have an acute Theory of Mind and make active predictions based on their profiling of characters and authors. Infants will not learn new words from an adult who has previously mislabeled familiar objects.
- *They detest sociology.* **False**. Early on, they adopt stereotypes (p. 155) and align with in-groups (p. 155) based on socially validated generalizations.
- *They don't try to understand Kafka or* Finnegans Wake. **True**. But maybe that is for lack of exposure. 'Perhaps,' writes Kelsey Osgood, 'Kafka's works can be best confronted by children, who have that empyrean way of digesting the surreal and decoding symbols, who are braver, in their innocent beliefs, than we can ever be.'
- *They still believe in God, the family, angels, devils, witches, goblins, logic, clarity, punctuation, and other such obsolete stuff.* **A clear example of what authors project into childhood**. Gertrude Stein did not need punctuation;

story logic has nothing to do with truth values; and witches populate children's literature *because* children know they are not real, not because they could actually be rounded up and fed to the meat-grinder (see p. 208 n. 5).

- *They love interesting stories, not commentary, guides, or footnotes.* **Mostly True**. Those scientific accoutrements do not typically feature in ludic reading. However, a children's book can playfully *imitate* the adult use of commentary, footnotes, and scientific language, such as Robert Sullivan's *Flight of the Reindeer*, just as the scientific trappings are part of the success of NORAD's annual presentation of geostationary satellite feeds tracking Santa.
- *When a book is boring, they yawn openly, without any shame or fear of authority.* **True**. That is why Bruce Bliven called them a 'merciless audience' (1946:60). Things have changed since the time of John Newbery.
- *They don't expect their beloved writer to redeem humanity.* **False**. That is why there are happy endings; why my son refused, as a child, to read the final installment of C. S. Lewis' *Narnia* books; and why there are children's books about war and holocaust such as *What is War? What is Peace?* by Richard Rabinowitz. Children base their cooperation on trust, and a trusted author can become a beacon for them.

The central premise from which all of Bashevis Singer's ten points arise, however, is also the central premise of this book: Children are a natural audience for books; they can love books and, if they do, profit from them in very specific ways.

Children naturally *acquire* their first languages as their brains mature, and books can enrich their linguistic environment with new sounds, with entraining rhythms, with words to populate their prototypical categories, with salient morphemes and word orders. Children also *learn* their first languages as they explore them, and books can stimulate language play and discovery with rare words, unusual syntactic templates, and masterful linguistic outliers and violations. While it is true that language acquisition and language learning will occur when children interact with a community, children's books aim to invite them beyond everyday speech. The profit that children take from books appears to increase especially when the linguistic profile of those books is atypical, different from child-directed speech in virtually every respect. Modern authors 'get it': More effective than lecturing, more effective than drill and repetition, more effective than concentrating on the familiar are surprise and exploration, play and cooperation, entrainment and reward. In providing high-quality language nutrition, these authors offer brain food *beyond and toward* what is needed for linguistic maturation, cognitive development, and early literacy. The sophistication of their work has changed our culture.

Why children's literature? Because sophistication is in our DNA. Humans need quantity *and* quality input to mature to their full potential. They can receive it in tight-knit communities with a rich oral culture that values storytelling and memorization. Absent that, the sophisticated input that delights and surprises beyond domestic shop talk comes from the performance and interrogation of books with adults. Absent both, children are left in charge of identifying and exploring their own zones of proximal development unprompted. That is dysfunctional. Healthy mental development requires care, trust, and cooperation.

We are designed for a rich banquet, but we come to the table wide eyed. Humans are not like little sea turtles who can take care of themselves once they hatch. We are born fantastically talented, but premature and dependent. A classic Jewish tale (Feinstein 2008) imagines us with arms without elbows, able to grasp at the delicacies of the banquet prepared for us but unable to put them into our own mouths. The secret to opulence is: feeding one another.

References

Bergelson, Elika, and Richard N. Aslin. 2017. Nature and origins of the lexicon in 6-mo-olds. *PNAS—Publications of the National Academy of Sciences* (early edition, September). www.pnas.org/cgi/doi/10.1073/pnas.1712966114.

Boorstin, Daniel J. 1984. Letter of transmittal. *Books in our future: A report from the Librarian of Congress to the Congress*, 6–57. Washington, DC: Joint Committee on the Library of Congress of the United States. Online: files.eric.ed.gov/fulltext/ED253243.pdf.

Brones, Anna. 2018. Food apartheid: The root of the problem with America's groceries. *The Guardian,* 15 May. www.theguardian.com/society/2018/may/15/food-apartheid-food-desertsracism-inequality-america-karen-washington-interview.

Bruner, Jerome S. 1983. *Child's talk: Learning to use language*. New York: W.W. Norton.

Dunbar, Robin I. M. 1992. Neocortex size as a constraint on group size in primates. *Journal of Human Evolution* 22(6).469–93.

Ervin-Tripp, Susan M. 1991. Play in language development. *Play and the social context of development in early care and education*, ed. by Barbara Scales, Millie (Ed) Almy, Ageliki Nicolopoulou, and Susan M. Ervin-Tripp, 84–97. New York: Teachers College, Columbia University.

Feinstein, Edward M. 2008. Heaven and hell. *Capturing the moon: Classic and modern Jewish tales*, retold by Rabbi Edward M. Feinstein, 47–49. Springfield, NJ: Behrman House.

Lindgren, Astrid. 2017. Why do we write children's books?, translated by Elizabeth Sofia Powell. *Children's Literature: Annual of the Children's Literature Association and the Modern Language Association division on children's literature* 45.188–95. Baltimore: Johns Hopkins University Press.

Mandel, Denise R.; Deborah G. Kemler Nelson; and Peter W. Jusczyck. 1996. Infants remember the order of words in a spoken sentence. *Cognitive Development* 11.181–96.

Osgood, Kelsey. 2013. Kafka for kids. 'Page Turner,' *The New Yorker*, 19 June. Online: www.newyorker.com/books/page-turner/kafka-for-kids.

Singer, Isaac Bashevis. 1978. Speech at the Nobel Banquet, 10 December 1978. Online: www.nobelprize.org/nobel_prizes/literature/laureates/1978/singer-speech.html.

Zauche, Lauren Head; Ashley E. Darcy Mahoney; Taylor A. Thul; Michael S. Zauche; Arianne B. Weldon; and Jennifer L. Stapel-Wax. 2017. The power of language nutrition for children's brain development, health, and future academic achievement. *Journal of Pediatric Health Care* 31(4) (July/August).493–503.

Children's Books Cited (by Author)

[brackets indicate year of first edition]

Abbott, Edwin A. 1992 [1884]. *Flatland: A romance of many dimensions*, Dover Thrift editions. New York: Dover.

Andreae, Giles. 2003. *Pants*, illustrated by Nick Sharratt, ed. by Alice Corrie. London: Corgi Childrens', Random House Children's Publishers.

Anonymous. 1805. *The puzzling-cap: A choice collection of riddles, in familiar verse, with a curious cat to each*. Philadelphia: John Adams.

Anonymous. 1820. *Infant's cabinet of birds & beasts*. London: Harvey & Danton. Online: archive.org/details/infantscabinetof00londiala.

Anonymous. ca. 1820. *The world turned upside down: or, no news, and strange news*. New York: J. Kendrew. Online: archive.org/details/historyoflittlek00bewiiala.

Anonymous. 1875 to 1887 (n.d.). How baby cleaned the watch. *Dolls and pets*, 14–18. Boston: D. Lothrop and Company.

Anonymous. 1880s (n.d.). *The children's object book*. London, New York: Frederick Warne.

Anonymous. Early 1900s (n.d.). *My very first German book*. New York, London: Hodder & Stoughton.

Appleton, George S. 1849. *Mother Goose in hieroglyphs*. New York: Sherman.

Banks, Kate. 2006. *Max's words*, illustrated by Boris Kulikov. New York: Farrar, Straus and Giroux.

Barrie, J[ames] M[atthew], Sir. 1911. *Peter Pan and Wendy*, illustrated by F. D. Bedford. London: Hodder & Stoughton.

Bell, Cece. 2014. *El Deafo*, colored by David Lasky. New York: Abrams.

Berger, Carin. 2009. *Ok go*. New York: Greenwillow, HarperCollins.

Bewick, Thomas. 1810(?). *The history of Little King Pippin: With an account of the melancholy death of four naughty boys who were devoured by wild beasts*. Wellington: Houlston and Son. Online: archive.org/details/historyoflittlek00bewiiala.

Bisbee, Susie A. 1883. *The Daisy Green stories*. Boston: D. Lothrop and Company.

Bouhler, Philipp. 1938. *Kampf um Deutschland: Ein Lesebuch für die deutsche Jugend*. Munich: Zentralverlag der NSDAP. archive.org/details/Bouhler-Philipp-Kampf-um-Deutschland

Boynton, Sandra. 1982. *Moo baa la la la*. New York: Little Simon, Simon & Schuster.

Brown, Margaret Wise. 1972 [1942]. *The runaway bunny*. New York: Harper & Row.

Brown, Margaret Wise. 1982 [1947]. *Goodnight moon*, illustrated by Clement Hurd. New York: HarperFestival, HarperCollins.

Brown, Margaret Wise. 1993. *Under the sun and the moon and other poems*, compiled by Roberta Brown Rauch, illustrated by Tom Leonard. New York: Hyperion Books for Children.

Brown, Rick. 1994. *What rhymes with snake? A word and picture flap book*. London: Tambourine, HarperCollins.

Burton, Virginia Lee. 1939. *Mike Mulligan and his steam shovel*. Boston: Houghton Mifflin.

Byrne, Richard. 2015. *This book just ate my dog!* New York: Scholastic.

Byrne, Richard. 2016. *This book is out of control!* New York: Henry Holt, Macmillan.

Cannon, Janell. 1993. *Stellaluna*. New York: Scholastic.

Carle, Eric. 1994. *The very hungry caterpillar*. New York: Philomel, Penguin.

Carle, Eric. 1997. *From head to toe*. New York: HarperFestival, HarperCollins.

Carle, Eric. 2007. *My very first book of animal sounds*. New York: Philomel, Penguin.

Carroll, Lewis. 1865. *Alice's adventures in Wonderland*, illustrated by John Tenniel. *The annotated Alice*, ed. by Martin Gardner, 17–164. New York: Bramhall House, 1960.

Carroll, Lewis. 1871. *Through the looking-glass and what Alice found there*, illustrated by John Tenniel. *The annotated Alice*, ed. by Martin Gardner, 167–345. New York: Bramhall House, 1960.

Carroll, Lewis. 2015 [1969]. *Alice's adventures in Wonderland*, illustrated by Salvador Dalí, ed. by Mark Burstein. New York: National Museum of Mathematics; Princeton, Oxford: Princeton University Press.

Cleary, Brian P. 1964 [rpt. 2008]. *The frail snail on the trail: A long vowel sounds book with consonant blends*, illustrated by Jason Miskimins. Minneapolis: Millbrook Press, Lerner.

Clemens, Samuel. see Twain, Mark.

Cole, Joanna. 1997. *The magic school bus shows and tells: A book about archaeology*. New York: Scholastic.

Commenius [Komensky], Johannes Amos. 1705. *Joh. Amos Commenius's visible world: Or, a* nomenclature, *and* pictures *of all the chief things that are in the world, and of mens employment therein. Written by the author in Latin and High-Dutch being one of his last essays, and the most suitable to childrens capacities of any that he hath hitherto made*, translated by Charles Hoole. London: John Bryant. Online: archive.org/details/johamoscommeniio00come.

Cullison, Irene Margaret. 1915. *Mother Goose finger plays*. Philadelphia: George W. Jacobs.

Dahl, Roald. 1982. *The BFG*, illustrated by Quentin Blake. New York: Farrar Straus Giroux, Macmillan.

Dahl, Roald. 1982. *Revolting rhymes*, illustrated by Quentin Blake. New York: Puffin, Penguin.

Dahl, Roald. 1983. *The witches*, illustrated by Quentin Blake. New York: Puffin, Penguin.

Dahl, Roald. 1988. *Matilda*, illustrated by Quentin Blake. New York: Viking, Penguin.

Dahl, Roald. 1998 [1964]. *Charlie and the chocolate factory*, illustrated by Quentin Blake. New York: Puffin, Penguin.

Dahl, Roald. 2002 [1961]. *James and the giant peach*, illustrated by Quentin Blake. New York: Knopf Books.

Daste, Larry. 2001. *Hidden pictures* (Dover children's activity books). Minneola: Dover.

Defoe, Daniel. 2003 [1719]. *Robinson Crusoe* (Penguin Classics). New York: Aladdin, Simon & Schuster.

Delafosse, Claude, and Philippe Biard. 1995. *Pyramids*, illustrated by Philippe Biard. New York: Scholastic.

Dewdney, Anna. 2005. *Llama Llama red pajama*. New York: Viking, Penguin.

Dickens, Charles. 1940 [1859]. *David Copperfield*, illustrated by Hablot Knight Browne, Classic editions, 2 vols. New York: Walter J. Black.

Drescher, Henrik. 1993. *Pat the beastie*, illustrated by Henrik Drescher, paperwork engineering by Dennis K. Meyer. New York: Hyperion Books for Children.

DuBois, W[illiam] E[dward] B[urghardt]. 1920–21. *The Brownies' Book: A monthly magazine for the children of the sun. Designed for all children but especially for ours*. New York.

Eastman, P[hilip] D[ey]. 1960. *Are you my mother?* New York: Random House.

Eastman, P[hilip] D[ey]. 1961. *Go, dog. Go!*, ed. by Dr. Seuss [Theodor Geisel]. New York: Random House.

Eckert, Horst. see Janosch.

Eichten, Philip I. 2000. *Two words together: A picture book of line drawings for two-word phrases*, illustrated by Andrew Thornton. Glen Allen, VA: PI Communication Materials.

Ende, Michael. 1997. *The neverending story*, translated by Ralph Manheim. New York: Puffin, Penguin.

Evans, Beryl. 2016. *Charlie the Choo-Choo: From the world of the dark tower*, illustrated by Ned Dameron. New York: Simon & Schuster.

Evic, Vera. 2013. ᑕᖅᑭᓕᐊᖅᑐᑦ *Trip to the moon*, ed. by Ryan Oliver and Mark Oliver, translated by Sheena Machmer, illustrated by Elisapee Ishulutaq, Andrew Quappik, Jolly Atagoyuk, Peona Keyuakjuk, and Jessica Akpalialuk. Iqaluit, Nunavut: Inhabit Media. inhabitmedia.com/2012/11/03/trip-to-the-moon/.

Falwell, Cathryn. 1998. *Word wizard*. HMH Books for Young Readers. New York: Clarion.

Fitzgerald, S. J. Adair. 1896. *The Zankiwank & the Bletherwitch*. London: Dent.

Flanagan, Alice K. 1999. *Play Day: The sound of long a* (Wonder books phonics readers). Mankato, MN: The Child's World.

Fleming, Denise. 2007. *Beetle Bop*. Orlando: Harcourt.

Florian, Douglas. 2000. *mammalabilia*. San Diego: Harcourt.

Foglesong Guy, Ginger. 2006. *¡Perros! ¡Perros! Dogs! Dogs!: A story in English and Spanish*, illustrated by Sharon Glick. New York: Greenwillow, HarperCollins.

Foster, Elizabeth Frances. 1899. Jimmy Crow. *Little folks: An illustrated monthly for youngest readers* (December), 62–63. Salem, MA: S. E. Cassino. Online: www.pem.org/library/blog/?p=2990.

Foster, Elizabeth Frances. 1899. *Jimmy Crow*. Salem, MA: S. E. Cassino. Rpt. Boston: Dana Estes, 1902.

Foster, Elizabeth Frances. 1903. *Mary's little lamb: A picture guessing story for little children—With 500 pictures by the author*. Salem, MA: S. E. Cassino.

Funn, A. J. [Dale Vandenborre]. 2013. *Penelope's imagination runs wild: A Glyffix original*. Bloomington, IN: AuthorHouse.

Funn, A. J. [Dale Vandenborre]. 2015. *Freeda Firefly's fantastic flight: A Glyffix original*. Bloomington, IN: AuthorHouse.

Geisel, Theodor. see Seuss, Dr.

Gibson, Eva Katharine. see Eva Klapp.

Gibson, Ginger Foglesong. see Foglesong Guy, Ginger.

Gilman, Phoebe. 1992. *Something from nothing*. New York: Scholastic.

Goodhart, Pippa. 2007. *Three little ghosties*, illustrated by AnnaLaura Cantone. New York: Bloomsbury Children's Books.

Grandits, John. 2004. *Technically, it's not my fault*. New York: Clarion Books.

Gravett, Emily. 2006. *Orange pear apple bear*. New York: Simon & Schuster Books for Young Readers.

Grimm, Jacob and Wilhelm Grimm. 2014. *The original 1812 Grimm fairy tales: A new translation of the 1812 first edition—Kinder- und Hausmärchen*, translated by Oliver Loo. Oliver Loo: Lulu.com.

Gurney, Nancy. 1965. *The king, the mice, and the cheese*, illustrated by Eric Gurney. New York: Random House.

Guy, Ginger Foglesong. see Foglesong Guy, Ginger.

Gwynne, Fred. 1970. *The king who rained*. New York: Prentice Hall, Simon & Schuster.

Gwynne, Fred. 1988. *A little pigeon toad*. New York: Simon and Schuster Books for Young Readers.

Haddon, Mark. 2003. *The curious incident of the dog in the night-time*. New York: Doubleday, Random House.

Halliwell, James Orchard. 1844. *The nursery rhymes of England, collected chiefly from oral tradition*, 4th ed. London: John Russell Smith.

Hastings, Rosetta B. 1883. The pretty fire. *Rosebud's letter and other stories*, 7. Boston: D. Lothrop and Company.

Herr, Judy, and Terri Jo Swim. 2002. *Making sounds, making music, & many other activities for infants: 7 to 12 months* (Creative resources infant and toddler). Andover: Cengage Learning.

Hiemer, Ernst. 1938. *Der Giftpilz*. Nuremberg: Stürmerverlag. Online: research.calvin.edu/german-propaganda-archive/thumb.htm.

Hills, Tad. 2000. *Knock knock who's there: My first book of knock knock jokes*. New York: Little Simon, Simon & Schuster.

Hoffman, Heinrich. 1945. *Der Struwwelpeter*. Frankfurt: Literarische Anstalt. Online: www.gutenberg.org/files/24571/24571-h/24571-h.htm.

Hubbell, Patricia. 1998. *Pots and pans*, illustrated by Diane de Groat. New York: HarperFestival, HarperCollins.

Hurd, Thacher. 1996. *Art dog*. New York: HarperCollins.

Hutchins, Pat. 1978. *The best train set ever* [also *Peter's train set*]. New York: Greenwillow.

Janeway, James. 1671 [rpt. 1771]. *A token for children, being an exact account of the conversion, holy and exemplary lives and joyful deaths of several young children. To which is added, a token for the children of New-England, or, some examples of children, in whom the fear of god was remarkably budding before they died; in several parts of New-England*. Boston: Z. Fowle.

Janosch [Horst Eckert]. 1980. *Schuddelbuddel baut ein Haus* (dtv junior Lesebär). Munich: Deutscher Taschenbuch Verlag.

Janosch. 1980. Wandertag nach Paderborn. *Schnuddelbuddel baut ein Haus* (dtv junior Lesebär), 39–62. Munich: Deutscher Taschenbuch Verlag.

Janosch. 1987. *Kasper Mütze holt einen Hasen*. Hamburg: Cecilie Dressler Verlag; Zurich: Atrium Verlag.

Janosch. 1987. *The trip to Panama*, translated by Anthea Bell. New York: Macmillan Children's Books, Macmillan.

Johnson, Sally Patrick (ed.) 1962. *The Princesses*, illustrated by Beni Montresor. New York: Harper & Row.

Kästner, Erich. 2017 [1929]. *Emil und die Detektive*. Hamburg: Dressler.

Kelman, Marcy. 2007. *Opposites* (Baby Einstein playful discoveries). New York: Scholastic.

King, Steven. see Evans, Beryl.

Klapp [Gibson], Eva, and John A. Stevens. 1901. *Zauberlinda, the wise witch*, illustrated by Mabel Tibbitts. Chicago, Lansing: Robert Smith.

Klein, Norma. 1974. *A train for Jane*, illustrated by Miriam Schottland. New York: The Feminist Press.

Kraus, Robert. 1980. *Another mouse to feed*, illustrated by Jose Aruego and Ariane Dewey. New York: Simon & Schuster.

Kunhardt, Dorothy. 1940 [rpt. 2001]. *Pat the bunny* (Touch and feel book). New York: Golden Books, Penguin, Random House.

Leaf, Munroe. 1936 [rpt. 2011]. *The story of Ferdinand*, illustrated by Robert Lawson. New York: Grosset & Dunlap, Penguin.

Lear, Edward. 1846 [rpt. 1992]. *A book of nonsense* (Everyman's library—Children's classics). New York: Alfred A. Knopf.

Lear, Edward. 1871. *Nonsense songs, stories, botany, and alphabets*. London: R. J. Bush.

Lee, Andy. 2017. *Do not open this book: A ridiculously funny story for kids, big and small . . . do you dare open this book?!* (Studio stories), illustrated by Heath McKenzie. Dorking, Surrey: Templar Publishing, Bonnier.

Leedy, Loreen, and Pat Street. 2003. *There's a frog in my throat!: 440 animal sayings a little bird told me*, illustrated by Loreen Leedy. New York: Holiday House.

L'Engle, Madeleine. 1962. *A wrinkle in time*. New York: Macmillan.

Lenski, Lois. 1970. *Debbie and her dolls*. New York: Henry Z. Walck.

Lester, Helen. 1999. *Hooway for Wodney Wat*, illustrated by Lynn Munsinger. New York: Houghton Mifflin.

Lindgren, Astrid. 1997 [1950]. *Pippi Longstocking*. New York: Puffin Books, Penguin.

London, Jonathan. 1996. *Hip cat*, illustrated by Woodleigh Marx Hubbart. San Francisco: Chronicle Books.

London, Jonathan. 2000. *Who bop?* Illustrated by Henry Cole. New York: HarperCollins.

Low, Joseph, and Ruth Low. 1953. *Mother Goose riddle rhymes*. New York: Harcourt, Brace.

MacDonald, George. 1864. The light princess. *The princesses: Sixteen stories about princesses*, selected by Sally Patrick Johnson, 190–233. New York, Evanston: Harper & Row.

Mansbach, Adam. 2011. *Go the fuck to sleep*, illustrated by Ricardo Cortés. Brooklyn, NY: Akashic Books.

Martin, Sarah Catherine. 1819 [1805]. *The comic adventures of Old Mother Hubbard and her dog*. London: Harris & Sons. Online: publicdomainreview.org/collections/the-comic-adventures-of-old-mother-hubbard-and-her-dog-1819/.

Martin Jr., Bill. 2007 [1967]. *Brown bear, brown bear, what do you see?*, illustrated by Eric Carle. New York: Henry Holt.

Martin Jr., Bill, and John Archambault. 2012. *Chicka chicka boom boom*, illustrated by Loise Ehlert. New York: Beach Lane Books.

McCullough, Ethel. 1938. *Cottontails: A tactile book*, illustrated by Sister Mary Veronica. New York: William R. Scott. Manufactured by The Catamount Press (Bennington, Vermont). Online: bennington.pastperfectonline.com/library/DA0F867B-7EE7-4742-A383-329455536217.

McErlean, Victoria C. see Shannon, Anita.

Milne, A. A. 1961. *The house at Pooh Corner*, illustrated by Ernest H. Shepard, redesigned by Warren Chappell. New York: E. P. Dutton.

Milne, A[lan] A[lexander]. 1961. *We are six*, illustrated by Ernest H. Shepard. New York: E. P. Dutton.

Milne, A. A. 1963. *Winnie-the-Pooh*, illustrated by Ernest H. Shepard, redesigned by Warren Chappell. New York: E. P. Dutton.

Mitchell, Lucy Sprague. 1921. *Here and now story book*, illustrated by Hendrik Willem van Loon and Christine Price. New York: Parents' Institute, E. P. Dutton. Reprinted 1948, Mineola, NY: Dover.

Mitchell, Lucy Sprague, et al. 1937. *Another here and now story book*, illustrated by Rosalie Slocum. New York: E. P. Dutton.

Moers, Walter. 1993. Ein echtes Goldschiff. *Käpt'n Blaubärs Seebär-Geschichten*, 61–66. Ravensburg: Otto Maier.

Moers, Walter. 2001. *The 13½ lives of Captain Bluebear: Being the demibiography of a seagoing bear, with numerous illustrations and excerpts from the 'Encyclopedia of the marvels, life forms and other phenomena of Zamonia and its environs' by Professor Abdullah Nightingale*, translated by John Brownjohn. London: Vintage Books.

Munk, Arnold. see Piper, Watty.

Muntean, Michaela. 2006. *Do not open this book!*, illustrated by Pascal Lemaitre. New York: Scholastic.

Nesbitt, M[ilton] L[ee]. 1878. *Grammar-land: Or, grammar in fun for the children of Schoolroom-shire*. New York: Henry Holt & Co.

Newbery, John. 1787. *A little pretty pocket-book: Intended for the instruction and amusement of little Master Tommy, and Pretty Miss Polly*. Worcester, MA: Isaiah Thomas. Online: lcweb2.loc.gov/cgi-bin/ampage?collId=rbc3&fileName=rbc0001_2003juv05880page.db.

Newell, Peter. 1893. *Topsies & turveys*. New York: The Century Co.

Newell, Peter. 1910. *The slant book*. New York: Harper & Brothers.

Newell, Peter. 1912. *The rocket book*. New York: Harper & Brothers.

Niemann, Christoph. 2016. *Words*. New York: Greenwillow.

Nister, Der [Pinkhas Kahanovitsh]. 1917. *A May-seh mit a Hon. Dos Tsigele*, illustrated by Mark Zaharovich Chagall. Petrograd: Vilner Verlag.

Numeroff, Laufe Joffe. 1991. *If you give a moose a muffin*, illustrated by Felicia Bond. New York: Laura Geringer, HarperCollins.

Obligado, Lilian. 1986. *Faint frogs feeling feverish: & Other terrifically tantalizing tongue twisters*. New York: Puffin, Penguin.

Oxenbury, Helen. 1987. *Clap hands*. New York: Little Simon, Simon & Schuster.

Parish, Peggy. 1963. *Amelia Bedelia*, illustrated by Fritz Seibel. New York: Holt, Rinehart and Winston.

Park, Barbara. 1992. *Junie B. Jones and the stupid smelly bus*, illustrated by Denise Brunkus. New York: Random House.

Park, Barbara. 1997. *Junie B. Jones has a monster under her bed*, illustrated by Denise Brunkus. New York: Random House.

Patricelli, Leslie. 2014. *Toot* (Leslie Patricelli board books). Somerville, MA: Candlewick.

Pence, Charlotte. 2018. *Marlon Bundo's day in the life of the Vice President*, illustrated by Karen Pence. Washington, DC: Regnery Kids.

Pilkey, Dav. 1997. *The adventures of Captain Underpants*. New York: The Blue Sky Press.

Piper, Watty [Arnold Munk]. 1976. *The little engine that could*, illustrated by Ruth Sanderson. New York: Platt & Munk.

Pizzoli, Greg. 2013. *The watermelon seed*. New York: Disney-Hyperion.

Porter, Sue. 1994. *Moose music* (Golden books). Racine, WI: Western Publishing Company, HarperCollins.

Potter, Beatrix. 2002 [1909]. *The tale of the flopsy bunnies*. London: Frederick Warne & Co., Penguin.

Pratt, Pierre. 2001. *The very busy life of Olaf and Venus: Home*. Somerville, MA: Candlewick.

Prelutsky, Jack. 1986. *Ride a purple pelican*, illustrated by Garth Williams. New York: Greenwillow.

Prelutsky, Jack. 1995. *The dragons are singing tonight*, illustrated by Peter Sis. New York: Scholastic.

Prelutsky, Jack. 2004. *If not for the cat*, illustrated by Ted Rand. New York: Greenwillow, HarperCollins.

Priddy, Roger. 2004. *First words (Bright Baby)* (Priddy books: Big ideas for little people). New York: St. Martin's Press, Macmillan.

Prideaux, W[illiam] F[rancis]. 1904. *Mother Goose's melody: A facsimile reproduction of the earliest known edition*. London: A. H. Bullen.

Rabinowitz, Richard. 1991. *What is war? What is peace?: 50 questions and answers for kids*. New York: Byron Preiss, Avon Camelot.

Raffi. 1985. Apples and bananas. Track 2 of *One light one sun*. Vancouver: Homeland Publishing Socan, Troubadour Records.

Ringelnatz, Joachim. 1931. *Kinder-Verwirr-Buch*. Berlin: Rowohlt.

Robinson, Nathan J. 2014. *Don't let the pigeon question the rules!: An antifascist children's story*. New Haven, CT: Demilune Press.

Rowling, J[oanne] K[athleen]. 1998. *Harry Potter and the philosopher's stone*. New York: Scholastic.

Rowling, J. K. 2005. *Harry Potter and the half-blood prince*. New York: Scholastic.

Seuss, Dr. [Theodor Geisel]. 1950. *If I ran the zoo*. New York: Random House.

Seuss, Dr. 1953. *Scrambled eggs super!* New York: Random House.

Seuss, Dr. 1954. *Horton hears a Who!* New York: Random House.

Seuss, Dr. 1955. *On beyond zebra*. New York: Random House.

Seuss, Dr. 1957. *The cat in the hat* (Beginner books). Boston: Houghton Mifflin.

Seuss, Dr. 1958. *The cat in the hat comes back* (Beginner books). New York: Random House.

Seuss, Dr. 1958. *If I ran the circus*. New York: Random House.

Seuss, Dr. 1958. *Yertle the Turtle and other stories*. New York: Random House.

Seuss, Dr. 1959. *Happy birthday to you!* New York: Random House.

Seuss, Dr. 1960. *Green eggs and ham* (Beginner books). New York: Random House.

Seuss, Dr. 1960. *One fish two fish red fish blue fish* (Beginner books). New York: Random House.

Seuss, Dr. 1963. *Dr. Seuss's ABC* (Beginner books). New York: Random House.

Seuss, Dr. 1963. *Hop on pop* (Beginner books). New York: Random House.

Seuss, Dr. 1965. *Fox in socks*. New York: Random House.

Seuss, Dr. 1968. *The foot book* (Bright and early books). New York: Random House.

Seuss, Dr. 1968 [1940]. *Horton hatches the egg*. New York: Random House.

Seuss, Dr. 1970. *Mr. Brown can moo! Can you?* New York: Random House.

Seuss, Dr. 1971. *The Lorax*. New York: Random House.

Seuss, Dr. 1974. *Great day for up* (Bright and early books), illustrated by Quentin Blake. New York: Random House.

Seuss, Dr. 1974. *There's a Wocket in my pocket* (Bright and early books). New York: Random House.

Seuss, Dr. 1975. *Oh, the thinks you can think!* (Beginner books). New York: Random House.

Seuss, Dr. 1979. *Oh say can you say?* (Beginner books). New York: Random House.

Seuss, Dr. 1984. *The butter battle book.* New York: Random House, Penguin.

Shannon, Anita [Victoria C. McErlean]. 2012. *Stomp like an elephant*, illustrated by Abigail Bythell. Manahawkin, NJ: V. C. McErlean.

Shannon, Anita. 2013. *Consonant-vowel words* (Toddler talk). CreateSpace Independent Publishing Platform.

Shrek. 2001, directed by Andrew Adamson and Vicky Jenson. Redwood City, CA: Pacific Data Images, DreamWorks Animation (NBCUniversal).

Silverstein, Shel. 1964. *The giving tree.* New York: Harper & Row.

Sirett, Dawn. 2011. *Baby peekaboo!* (Baby Chunky board books). New York: DK Publishing.

Sprague Mitchell, Lucy. see Mitchell, Lucy Sprague.

Steichen, Edward. 1991 [1930]. *The first picture book.* Portfolio, Penguin.

Stein, Gertrude. 2013 [1939]. *The world is round*, illustrated by Clement Hurd. New York: Harper Design, HarperCollins.

Steiner, Violette G., and Roberta Evatt Pond. 1970. *Finger play fun.* Columbus, OH: Charles E. Merrill, Bell & Howell.

Stevenson, Robert Louis. 1895. *A child's garden of verses.* New York: Charles Scribner's Sons.

Stickland, Paul. 2004 [1986]. *Trucks.* Columbus, OHs: Waterbird Books.

Stileman, Kali. 2013. *Snack time for Confetti.* Wilton, CT: Tiger Tales.

Stowe, Harriett Beecher. 2007. *The annotated uncle Tom's cabin*, ed. by Henry Louis Gates, Jr. and Hollis Robbins. New York: W.W. Norton.

Streicher, Julius. 1938. *Der Giftpilz.* Nuremberg: Stürmerverlag. Online: research.calvin.edu/german-propaganda-archive/thumb.htm.

Sullivan, Robert. 1996. *Flight of the reindeer: The true story of Santa Claus and his Christmas mission*, illustrated by Glenn Wolff. New York: Simon & Schuster, Macmillan.

Swift, Jonathan. 1980 [1726]. *Gulliver's travels*, ed. by Christopher Fox. Boston: Bedford, St. Martin's.

Tripp, Valerie. 2000. *Again, Josephina!* (The American girls collection), illustrated by Jean-Paul Tibbles. Middleton, WI: Pleasant Company Publications.

Tullet, Herve. 2011. *Press here.* San Francisco: Ina, Chronicle Books.

Twain, Mark [Samuel Clemens]. 1864. Those blasted children. Reprinted in *Mark Twain's San Francisco*, ed. by Bernard Taper, 32. New York: McGraw-Hill.

Twain, Mark. 1935 [1891]. *Slovenly Peter (Der Struwwelpeter): Freelyt translated into English jingles by Mark Twain.* New York: Harper & Bros.

Twain, Mark. 1958 [1885]. *Adventures of Huckleberry Finn*, ed. by Henry Nash Smith. Boston: Houghton Mifflin.

Twain, Mark. 2013 [1867]. *Advice to little girls*, illustrated by Vladimir Radunsky. Brooklyn, NY: Enchanted Lion Books.

Twiss, Jill. 2018. *Last Week Tonight with John Oliver presents A Day in the Life of Marlon Bundo*, illustrated by EG Keller. San Francisco: Chronicle Books.

Van Allsburg, Chris. 1985. *The polar express.* New York: Houghton Mifflin.

Vandenborre, Dale. see Funn, A. J.

Vanden-Heuvel, Sr., and John C. 2011. *HTML for babies: Volume 1 of web design for babies.* New York: Code Babies Media.

Watts, Isaac. 1715 [rpt. 1st. stanza 1870's?]. Cradle hymn. *Lullabies and Ditties*, 5. Boston: D. Lothrop & Co.

Weller, Tom. 1985. *Science made stupid: How to discomprehend the world around us*. Boston: Houghton Mifflin.

Wiesner, David. 1991. *Tuesday*. New York: Clarion, Houghton Mifflin Harcourt.

Wiesner, David. 2001. *The three pigs*. New York: Clarion Books, Houghton Mifflin.

Wildish, Lee. 2009. *Noisy zoo*. Sounds: Barry Gibson (Busy sounds board book). London: Usborne.

Wilkin, Esther. 2012 [1960]. *Baby listens*. New York: Random House.

Willems, Mo. 2003. *Don't let the pigeon drive the bus*. New York: Hyperion.

Willems, Mo. 2010. *We are in a book!* (An Elephant and Piggie book). New York: Hyperion, Disney.

Willems, Mo. 2014. *Who says that, Cat the cat?* New York: HarperCollins.

Williams, Margery. 1991 [1922]. *The velveteen rabbit*, illustrated by Lynn Binder. New York: Barnes & Noble.

Wiseman, B[ernard]. 1970. *Morris goes to school*. New York: Harper & Row.

Woodcock, Richard W. 1965. *The rebus reading series*. George Peabody College, Nashville: Institute on Mental Retardation and Intellectual Development.

Young (ed.). 1993. *Moon mother: A Native American creation tale*. Providence, RI: Willa Perlman Books, HarperCollins.

Zolotow, Charlotte. 1972 [rpt. 1985]. *William's doll*, illustrated by William Pene du Bois. New York: HarperTrophy, Harper & Row.

Indices

Subject Index

Secondary Authors Index

Writers and Illuminators Index

Children's Books by Title

For Product Safety Concerns and Information please contact our EU representative GPSR@taylorandfrancis.com
Taylor & Francis Verlag GmbH, Kaufingerstraße 24, 80331 München, Germany

www.ingramcontent.com/pod-product-compliance
Ingram Content Group UK Ltd.
Pitfield, Milton Keynes, MK11 3LW, UK
UKHW022001180926
475701UK00003B/131
9780367583323